SOCIETY FOR NEW TESTAMENT STUDIES

MONOGRAPH SERIES

GENERAL EDITOR

MATTHEW BLACK, D.D., F.B.A.

2

THE TEMPTATION AND THE PASSION: THE MARKAN SOTERIOLOGY

THE TEMPTATION AND THE PASSION:

THE MARKAN SOTERIOLOGY

BY

ERNEST BEST

Lecturer in Biblical Literature and Theology
St Mary's College, St Andrews

CAMBRIDGE

AT THE UNIVERSITY PRESS

1965

PUBLISHED BY
THE SYNDICS OF THE CAMBRIDGE UNIVERSITY PRESS

Bentley House, 200 Euston Road, London, N.W. 1
American Branch: 32 East 57th Street, New York, N.Y. 10022
Nigerian Office: P.O. Box 33, Ibadan, Nigeria

©

CAMBRIDGE UNIVERSITY PRESS

1965

Printed in Great Britain at the University Printing House, Cambridge
(Brooke Crutchley, University Printer)

LIBRARY OF CONGRESS CATALOGUE
CARD NUMBERS: 65-15312

To the memory of
THE VERY REVEREND J. ERNEST DAVEY, D.D.

*Professor and then Principal of
The Presbyterian College, Belfast*

1917–1960

CONTENTS

PREFACE

Our primary concern in the following essay is with the soteriology of Mark: What does Mark hold to have been achieved by the life, death and resurrection of Jesus the Christ? Since it is often held that the death and resurrection of Jesus signalled his defeat of Satan, it is necessary to begin with a study of the Markan Temptation narrative; this is followed by an examination of the general place in the Gospel of demonic forces and of Satan. Thereafter we turn to a more direct consideration of our main aim.

Because we are not interested in what Jesus himself thought of the meaning and purpose of his life and death but only with the view that Mark adopts we have to proceed with caution. It is necessary to distinguish in relation to the pericopae of the Markan account the form in which the tradition reached him and the modifications he gave to it. Thus in any particular incident we may have to separate Mark's view of the incident from its original place in the life of Jesus and also from the varying modifications which thereafter it may have received in the early Church. To single out the Markan contribution we need to look at the phrases by which Mark has joined together the incidents he uses; these appear at the beginnings and ends of pericopae: the Markan seams. We also examine the explanatory additions Mark may have made within incidents in order to align them with his main purpose. This by no means exhausts the Markan editing. Since we have no reason to assume that Mark had only at his disposal the incidents he records we must examine his selection of material. Following on that we must consider the order in which he has put together the incidents he chooses, for the relationship of one incident to those which precede and follow it may express Mark's purpose. But since Mark cannot be regarded as being out of touch with the material he uses we must assume that in large part he agrees with it, and where there are within it statements of the function and activity of Jesus we must assume that he accepts these as true statements with which he agrees (we may note how Luke omits Mark x. 45); this is only to say that Mark must have taken a positive and not a negative attitude to what he records; it is incumbent on any alternative view to show actual discrepancy between the material and the editorial work. From that we go on to discuss the titles and names which Mark uses to describe Jesus; all writers and speakers have favourite titles to use of Jesus and in their choice they disclose something of their theology. Finally we look briefly at the Christian community which Mark supposes to have come into existence through the preaching of the Gospel; in what way is that which Jesus has achieved for it reflected in its life?[1]

We may state our problem somewhat differently by saying that we are seeking to determine the Markan kerugma. Within the early Church there would appear to have been a number of different forms of the kerugma.[2] Paul preserves two in I Cor. xv. 3 f. and Phil. ii. 5–11; the first of these would appear to be primarily concerned with human sin, the second with triumph over cosmic forces of evil. In what form did Mark present the kerugma? We are not concerned with the whole of the kerugma, which in some of its forms contained a reference to the eventual return of Jesus. Rather we are setting out to see what the Markan kerugma says about what Jesus has already accomplished. To use a traditional phrase, we are seeking what Mark holds to be 'the benefits of Christ's Passion'. This is not an inaccurate phrase because Mark's Gospel is really a Passion story with a preliminary introduction leading up to the Passion.[3]

We do not view Mark as the last of a series of editors who have worked over the material, introducing new material and modifying what the previous author had put together, nor have we any confidence in elaborate theories of an Ur-Markus. We regard Mark as himself the first to put together the material he uses to make a Gospel, and we assume that he did this in Rome.

[1] It will be seen that our methodology differs from that of Schreiber (pp. 154 f.). Justification for any methodology can only lie in the results achieved. It may be noted that Schreiber does not abide by his own chosen course. He considers that where Matthew or Luke changes Mark this is significant for Markan theology. Yet in discussing the significance for Mark of the death of Christ he makes no use of Mark x. 45 which Luke omits!

[2] Cf. p. 128, n. 6.

[3] Cf. M. Kähler's dictum that the Gospels are 'Passionsgeschichten mit ausführlicher Einleitung'.

This is not to say that Mark could treat incidents in an entirely free way; obviously the Passion had to come at the end and the Baptism by John at the beginning, but the Temptation might have been retained until later in the story or spread out through the Gospel. Prior to Mark some of the material may have already existed in collections, for example, ii. 1–iii. 6, or the Passion story. In many ways Mark was thus bound by the tradition which came to him, but yet he remained a real author, not just a recorder of tradition. It was his purpose to proclaim the Gospel through the events which he believed, rightly or wrongly, to have happened in the life of Jesus. (We must assume that Mark believes that the incidents he uses actually happened.) His Gospel is itself kerugma. This, of course, does not mean that it was intended only for missionary use; it was intended for use within the community and by the community in its missionary outreach. The strict line which is sometimes drawn between kerugma and didache is not applicable here; every sermon will contain both, and both are contained in Mark. We use kerugma not then in the narrower sense of evangelistic preaching to the outsider but in the wider sense of the essential relevance of Jesus Christ to the world and the Christian community.

All this means that we treat Mark seriously as an author. He has his place in the canon, not because he gives certain historical facts about the life of Jesus, but because, in the same sense as Paul, he preaches Christ. If Paul is viewed as inspired, then in exactly the same way we must so view Mark—though Paul and Mark make their approach to the problem of presenting Christ in very different ways. This also means that if with any confidence we may take a text or passage of Paul as the inspired Word of God and preach it then we may do the same with Mark, not just seeking to determine the original nature of the incident or the *ipsissima verba* of Jesus, but preaching what we may term Mark's inspired comment.

On the other hand our interest in Mark as author and theologian should not be taken to imply that interest stops there. If we are in any way to seek the historical Jesus then the evidence which we have lies almost entirely in the Gospels. If we are to push back from the Gospels to Jesus then we need to disentangle, not only the influence of the early community on the material as it passed through its hands, but also the distinctive contributions of the evangelists to the material as they put together their Gospels. Any full study of a Gospel involves an examination of three factors: the evangelist's theology, the early Church's modification of the tradition, and the original event. None of these can be taken in isolation, nor can any be neglected, but at times emphasis will lie more on one than on another. If therefore we offer this as an essay in the understanding of the Markan theology we also hope that it will be useful in some small way in the quest of the historical Jesus.

Dr T. A. Burkill's *Mysterious Revelation* (Cornell, 1963) became available just as the MS was completed for the press. The leading themes of his thesis have already appeared in the numerous articles he has published and references to these will be found at relevant points. It has thus not been thought necessary to give page references to the book. The Pelican Gospel Commentary of Professor D. E. Nineham also appeared too late for me to make use of it.

My thanks are due to my wife for her careful typing of my manuscript, to Principal M. Black and Dr R. McL. Wilson, both of St Mary's College, for much useful advice and help in the preparation of the manuscript for the press; to the Rev. J. L. Bailey and the Rev. J. Roberts-Thomson for assistance in the reading of the proofs and the compilation of the indices; to the editors and printers of the Cambridge University Press for their exact work and to the congregations of Minterburn and Caledon who while I was their minister left me sufficient time to write the greater part of what is offered here.

E. B.

LIST OF ABBREVIATIONS

Branscomb = B. H. Branscomb, *The Gospel of Mark* (Moffatt Commentaries). London, 1937.

Bultmann = R. Bultmann, *The History of the Synoptic Tradition* (Eng. trans. J. Marsh). Oxford, 1963.

Bundy = W. E. Bundy, *Jesus and the First Three Gospels*. Cambridge, Mass., 1955.

Bussmann = W. Bussmann, *Synoptische Studien* I–III. Halle, 1925–31.

Conzelmann = H. Conzelmann, *The Theology of Saint Luke* (Eng. trans. G. Buswell). London, 1960.

Cranfield = C. E. B. Cranfield, *St Mark*. Cambridge, 1959.

Dehn = G. Dehn, *Der Gottessohn*[6]. Hamburg, 1953.

Dibelius = M. Dibelius, *From Tradition to Gospel* (Eng. trans. B. E. Woolf). London, 1934.

E.T. = *The Expository Times*.

Hauck = F. Hauck, *Das Evangelium des Markus* (Theologischer Handkommentar zum N.T.). Leipzig, 1931.

J.B.L. = *Journal of Biblical Literature*.

Johnson = S. E. Johnson, *The Gospel According to St Mark*. London, 1960.

J.T.S. = *Journal of Theological Studies*.

Klostermann = E. Klostermann, *Das Markusevangelium*[2]. Tübingen, 1926.

Knox = W. L. Knox, *The Sources of the Synoptic Gospels*, vol. I. Cambridge, 1953.

Lagrange = M.-J. Lagrange, *Évangile selon Saint Marc*. Paris, 1947.

Lightfoot, *Gospel* = R. H. Lightfoot, *The Gospel Message of Mark*. Oxford, 1950.

Lightfoot, *History* = R. H. Lightfoot, *History and Interpretation in the Gospels*. London, 1935.

Lightfoot, *Locality* = R. H. Lightfoot, *Locality and Doctrine in the Gospels*. London, 1938.

Lindars = B. Lindars, *New Testament Apologetic*. London, 1961.

Lohmeyer = E. Lohmeyer, *Das Evangelium des Markus*[11]. Göttingen, 1951.

Marxsen = W. Marxsen, *Der Evangelist Markus*[2]. Göttingen, 1959.

Mauser = U. W. Mauser, *Christ in the Wilderness* (Studies in Biblical Theology 39). London, 1963.

Menzies = A. Menzies, *The Earliest Gospel*. London, 1901.

Moore = G. F. Moore, *Judaism*, 3 vols. Cambridge, Mass., 1927–30.

N.T. = *Novum Testamentum*.

N.T.S. = *New Testament Studies*.

Rawlinson = A. E. J. Rawlinson, *The Gospel According to St Mark* (Westminster Commentaries). London, 1925.

Robinson = J. M. Robinson, *The Problem of History in Mark* (Studies in Biblical Theology 21). London, 1957.

Schmidt = K. L. Schmidt, *Die Rahmen der Geschichte Jesu*. Berlin, 1919.

Schniewind = J. Schniewind, *Das Evangelium nach Markus*[6]. Göttingen, 1952.

Schreiber = J. Schreiber, 'Die Christologie des Markusevangeliums', *Z.T.K.* LVIII (1961), 154–83.

S.J.Th. = *Scottish Journal of Theology*.

Strack–Billerbeck = H. L. Strack and P. Billerbeck, *Kommentar zum Neuen Testament aus Talmud und Midrasch*. 5 vols.

Swete = H. B. Swete, *The Gospel According to St Mark*. London, 1908.

Taylor = V. Taylor, *The Gospel According to St Mark*. London, 1952.

Turner = C. H. Turner, A series of articles in *J.T.S.* 1924–9.

T.W.N.T. = *Theologisches Wörterbuch zum Neuen Testament* (ed. G. Kittel and G. Friedrich), 1932– .

Weiss = J. Weiss, *Das Älteste Evangelium*, Göttingen, 1903.

Wellhausen = J. Wellhausen, *Das Evangelium Marci*. Berlin, 1903.

Wohlenberg = G. Wohlenberg, *Das Evangelium des Markus*. Leipzig, 1910.

Z.N.T.W. = *Zeitschrift für die neutestamentliche Wissenschaft*.

Z.T.K. = *Zeitschrift für Theologie und Kirche*.

PART I

THE TEMPTATION

CHAPTER I

THE TEMPTATION NARRATIVE

WE are concerned here neither with the origin of Mark i. 12 f. nor with an estimate of its historical reliability; rather it is our purpose to discuss its place in the Gospel and seek its meaning for Mark. In so doing we make the normal assumption that the Markan narrative at this point contains no knowledge of the tradition common to Matthew and Luke (Q). That is not merely to say that Mark did not know Matthew or Luke, nor that he did know Q, but also that he did not know the tradition of the content of the temptations of Jesus. If this assumption is incorrect and Mark did have some knowledge of the Q tradition,[1] even in a rudimentary form, it will be seen that our conclusions would be reinforced; for we would then be able to argue that Mark has deliberately omitted certain elements in the Q tradition and chosen to emphasise a few details, which thereby receive a new importance: for example, Mark is not interested in the nature of the temptations, only in the fact that a struggle took place. The assumption that Mark did not know Q means that we must banish from our minds our knowledge of Q in discussing Mark. Whereas when we come to read Matthew and Luke it is of great importance to know Mark so that we may see exactly how they have modified his narrative, our very knowledge of Matthew and Luke can form a hindrance to our understanding of Mark because we tend to see him through the eyes of Matthew and Luke. Neither he nor his first readers knew the other Gospels and they were not background material for him as they tend to be for us. With particular reference to the Temptation narrative, Luke (iv. 13; xxii. 28) is often taken to suggest that the three temptations were only the beginning of temptations which continued throughout the earthly life of Jesus with greater or less intensity.[2] It is not however correct to read this back into Mark and assume that he is giving us the

---

[1] So Bacon, *The Gospel of Mark* (New Haven, 1925), pp. 156 f.

[2] This is not necessarily the meaning of these verses in Luke; cf. Conzelmann, pp. 27 f.

I-2

beginning of temptations. Indeed we shall see that such a view is untrue to Mark's purpose.

The account of the Temptation in Mark is bare of details. Not only are we not told in what way Jesus was tempted but we are not even told the outcome of the Temptation. The nature of the Temptation must be read from the context; it follows the baptism and precedes the ministry. The result of the Temptation must likewise be gathered from the wider context, though it is possible that Mark intends to convey to us a hint of the issue from some of the details, but this is not certain; it is much more probable that the result must be learnt elsewhere in the Gospel. We shall see that Mark does make explicit elsewhere the outcome of the struggle.

We must now examine the somewhat scanty details of the account itself. The two verses i. 12 f. were not necessarily always united to the baptismal account. They are introduced by Mark's much-loved καὶ εὐθύς. Certain internal evidence suggests different strands of tradition.[1] But Mark, if not earlier tradition, has welded baptism and temptation together. Thus the initial statement of the Temptation narrative, the expulsion by the Spirit into the desert, has had its necessary preliminary in the coming to Jesus of the Spirit in baptism. To describe the action of the Spirit in initiating the Temptation Mark adopts the word ἐκβάλλειν. The element of violence cannot be excluded from the word since he uses it repeatedly in connection with the expulsion of demons (i. 34, 39, 43; iii. 15, 22; vi. 13; vii. 26; ix. 18, 28), and as we shall see there is a strong connection between this present passage and the demonic exorcisms. We must then take it that Mark views Jesus as 'driven out' by the Spirit into the desert. It is not however necessary to equate this with the concept of transportation by the Spirit (I Kings xviii. 12; II Kings ii. 16; Ezek. iii. 12, 14; viii. 3; Acts viii. 39).[2] Jesus is not violently taken up and carried to another place (indeed there is no other instance where the Spirit is said to transport towards evil), but compelled to go. The nature of the compulsion is not made clear, but there is nothing to suggest that Jesus was in an ecstatic condition. The compulsion may have been moral,[3] or it may have been deterministic as in

[1] Cf. Lohmeyer.
[2] Cf. Volz, *Der Geist Gottes* (Tübingen, 1910), pp. 17, 196.   [3] So Cranfield.

4

1QS iii. 13 ff. where the member of the Qumran community is under the control of the Spirit of Truth. In the Temptation narrative nothing more is said about the activity of the Spirit. He drives out Jesus to the place of temptation, the desert, but he is neither said to tempt Jesus (in the Old Testament God tests or tempts men to train them) nor is he said to help Jesus in his temptation by Satan.[1] This is surprising since it was the experience of the early Church to enjoy the Spirit's assistance in trial and temptation.[2]

It is to the desert that the Spirit leads Jesus. The 'desert' is emphasised. It is both said that Jesus is led to it and that he continues in it forty days. 'Desert' may signify either loneliness and remoteness or the abode of demons. In the former sense it is in Mark the place where Jesus withdraws from the crowds (i. 35, 45; vi. 31, 32, 35). But also according to Jewish demonology the desert is one among other places which demons are specially supposed to inhabit.[3] Probably both ideas are to some extent present in our passage.

In the desert he spent forty days. This is a traditional phrase in Judaism for a lengthy period of time. Some commentators see in this a link with the forty years spent by Israel in the desert after the Exodus,[4] and so picture Jesus here as himself embodying Israel. But Israel was forty years, not forty days, in the wilderness. Moreover they put God to the test rather than were tested by God; certainly they were not tested by Satan. The period of forty days occurs in the lives of both Moses and Elijah (Exod. xxiv. 18; xxxiv. 28; Deut. ix. 9; x. 10; I Kings xix. 8). It is associated in these instances with fasting. Are we so to associate it here? If we are certain that the forty

---

[1] In the Lukan account Jesus is said to be 'full of the Spirit' (iv. 1) and from this it may be inferred that he had the help of the Spirit in his Temptation.

[2] This may suggest that the Markan form of the tradition did not arise out of the experience of the early Church. That experience would not have shown the Spirit leading to Temptation but delivering from it.

[3] Cf. Strack–Billerbeck, IV, 515f. Marxsen (pp. 26–8) argues that ἔρημος is not here a geographical designation but represents the abode of Satan; it is thus to be understood theologically rather than spatially. On the desert as evil, cf. Mauser, pp. 36 ff. He emphasises the mythological connections in the Psalms and II Isaiah, pp. 42–4, 51 f.

[4] E.g. Hauck; Lightfoot, *History*, pp. 65 f.

days Jesus spent in the desert is deliberately modelled on the forty days in the lives of Moses and Elijah we must draw that conclusion; but there is nothing to suggest that what happened to Moses and Elijah in their forty days is in any way comparable to what happened to Jesus; for them it was a time with God, not with Satan. The forty days is rather a general period of time; the idea that he fasted during this period will then probably have grown up as a secondary tradition through reflection on the forty-day incidents in the life of Moses and Elijah and also through backward reference from the first temptation in Q. There is thus no need to find in Mark any implicit reference to fasting. In any case Mark has just told us that John the Baptist was able to exist on locusts and wild honey in the desert and therefore was not compelled to starve because he was in desert country; 'desert' does not therefore imply being without food. (Cf. vi. 31 which seems to imply the possibility of eating in the desert.) In Mark, unlike Q, there is no suggestion that the time of temptation fell at the end of the forty-day period. The Temptation rather took place within the period of the forty days and may indeed, so far as Mark is concerned, have lasted throughout that period.

Jesus is here said to be tempted by Satan. In the Old Testament and in Judaism the root πειράζειν and its Hebrew equivalent, the pi'el of נסה, is used religiously of the way in which man tempts God and in which God tests man in order to train him;[1] the great example for Judaism was that of Abraham (Gen. xxii). While the root is not used in the story of the Fall of Adam the conception of temptation is obviously present and in a form closer to our present narrative since in Gen. iii it is the serpent who tempts as it is Satan in Mark i. 12 f. This conception of the testing of man by the powers of evil in order to turn him aside from the ways of God is inevitably present where the powers of evil are given a personal form and a measure of dualism appears, as in the Qumran writings. Thus an element in the Markan form of the temptation narrative may be the Fall of Adam; as we know Christ was represented as the Second Adam in much early Christian literature. This is not to

[1] Cf. Seesemann, *T.W.N.T.* vi, 23–37; Strack–Billerbeck, I, 135 f.; M. H. Sykes, 'And do not bring us to the test', *E.T.* LXXIII (1961/2), 189 f.

be taken as suggesting that Mark i. 12 f. is in origin an explicit reversal of Gen. iii.[1]

There are three other occasions on which πειράζειν is used by Mark in reference to Jesus—namely viii. 11; x. 2; xii. 15. Each time it is the Pharisees (in xii. 15 in association with the Herodians) who attempt to test Jesus. Whereas x. 2 and xii. 15 may be regarded as attempts to test Jesus as to his opinion in regard to certain matters, in viii. 11 the Pharisees tempt him by asking for a sign, one of the ways in which according to the Q tradition the Devil tempted Jesus. Although the word πειράζειν is not used either in the account of Peter's confession at Caesarea Philippi (viii. 32 f.) or in the Gethsemane account (xiv. 32–42) with reference to Jesus, the conception of temptation is definitely present on these two occasions. We shall have occasion to return to this.[2]

Jesus is said to be tempted by Satan, which is obviously used here as a personal name. It is unnecessary to discuss the origin or meaning of this name since by the time of the Gospels its original sense as 'accuser', while not lost, had been swallowed up in the general belief in spiritual powers of evil.[3] The Devil, Mastema, Satan, etc., were names in use to describe the chief among these powers. This is obviously the meaning which Satan has for Mark or his tradition (cf. iii. 22–30). The temptation story is thus seen as a conflict between the Son of God, for so he has been described in the immediately preceding pericope, and the Prince of evil.

There were present with Jesus not only the Tempter, Satan, but also the wild beasts and the angels. Different interpretations have been given of the presence of the beasts. They have been thought to emphasise the loneliness of the desert,[4] but the suggestion of loneliness is immediately contradicted by the

[1] The relationship of Mark i. 12 f. to Gen. iii has been thoroughly examined by H.-G. Leder, 'Sündenfallerzählung und Versuchungsgeschichte: zur Interpretation von Mc i. 12 f.', *Z.N.T.W.* LIV (1963), 188–216, who finds against the interpretation of Christ as the Second Adam. Cf. J. Jeremias, 'Nachwort zum Artikel von H.-G. Leder', *Z.N.T.W.* LIV (1963), 278 f.

[2] Pp. 28 ff.

[3] Cf. Foerster and von Rad, *T.W.N.T.* II, 69–80; Foerster, *T.W.N.T.* II, 1–21; VII, 151 ff.; Strack–Billerbeck, I, 136–49.

[4] E.g. Cranfield.

reference to the presence of the angels who minister to him. Moreover it is unlikely that Mark would have wished to emphasise human loneliness at this stage of the story, and in his conflict with Satan the Son of God could hardly have expected to find assistance from men. The beasts have been taken as another trait indicating Christ as the Second Adam; as in the days before the Fall Adam lived peacefully with the beasts, so does Christ in the desert.[1] But the parallelism is not very exact in that Christ was in the desert whereas Adam was in the Garden of Eden; nor is great emphasis put in Jewish tradition on the presence of the wild beasts with Adam. A variant of this view sees in the presence of the wild beasts the sign of victory; as in the Messianic times harmony was expected to be recreated between man and the world of nature (Isa. xi. 6–9; lxv. 25, etc.), so this is seen to take place in the presence of the Messiah.[2] But we would expect this to be more clearly indicated; wild beasts normally suggest evil rather than good. That they signify evil is the more probable interpretation; the beasts are congruent with Satan and the desert, all of them suggesting the evil with which Jesus must contend.[3] The theme appears in the Old Testament, namely, Ps. xxii. 13–22; xci. 13;[4] Isa. xiii. 21 f.; Ezek. xxxiv. 5, 8, 25. Isa. xxxiv. 14 should be compared in its Hebrew and Greek forms (M.T. 'wild beasts', צִיִּים,[5] LXX δαιμόνια). The very fact that in the Messianic kingdom the beasts are at peace with man implies their normal fierceness and opposition, a fact which would have been much more obvious to those living in the Palestine of the first century than to citizens of the western world today. The Roman reader of Mark would also immediately think of their fierceness because of their association with the arena, where at any moment he might have to face their enmity.[6] When we trace this theme of the wild beasts further in Jewish thought we find that they are

---

[1] Cf. Jeremias, *T.W.N.T.* I, 141; Dehn; Taylor; W. A. Schulze, 'Der Heilige und die wilden Tiere', *Z.N.T.W.* XLVI (1955), 280–3.

[2] Cf. Schniewind.

[3] Cf. Lohmeyer *ad loc.*; Mauser, pp. 100 f.

[4] In ancient mythology the gods are sometimes depicted as conquerors of evil, standing in a triumphant pose over slain beasts; cf. H. J. Kraus, *Psalmen, ad loc.*

[5] Cf. Langton, *Essentials of Demonology*, p. 42.

[6] F. C. Grant, *The Earliest Gospel* (New York and Nashville, 1943), p. 77.

also associated with the demons and with the angels, though naturally they are not on the side of the angels. The beasts and angels are set in opposition in Ps. xci. 11–13. The beasts and the demons are associated in Test. Issach. vii. 7; Test. Benj. v. 2. Angels, beasts and demons are all associated in Test. Naph. viii. 4.[1]

This then brings us to the ministry of the angels. With Lohmeyer[2] we take it that they and the beasts stand over against one another. But what is their ministry? The obvious answer is that they feed Jesus. This accords with the Q tradition in which the first temptation concerns hunger, and Jesus is said to hunger, and it accords with the basic meaning of διακονεῖν.[3] While it must be agreed that this word retains its basic meaning in the New Testament, including Mark (i. 31), the word also underwent considerable development and was given an important theological overtone. Moreover if we did not have the Q tradition there is nothing in the Markan story other than this reference which would necessarily suggest hunger. Indeed even within the Q form of the tradition the angels are mentioned in another way: Satan tempts Jesus to throw himself from the pinnacle of the Temple saying that the angels will guard him (Matt. iv. 6 = Luke iv. 10, 11 = Ps. xci. 11 f.); now, though it is Satan who says this to Jesus, it surely represents the point of view of the time that in this way angels might minister to the Messiah. It is indeed well known that they minister to men in many different ways.[4] They act as their guardian angels, they intercede for them before God, they mediate visions to them. For our purpose it is important to note that in Heb. i. 14 the word διακονία is connected with their activity. The angels minister to the Son of Man in maintaining intercourse between himself and the Father (John i. 51). Angels are also associated with the Son of Man in Matt. xvi. 27, 28 par. In the War Scroll the angels form an army fighting on the side of God against the hosts of evil (i. 10 f.; xiii. 10; xii. 8, 9; xvii. 6; cf. 1QS iii. 24 f.; 1QH v. 21). In the light of this it is impossible

---

[1] Quoted below, p. 10.   [2] *Ad loc.*

[3] Cf. Lohmeyer; Klostermann. On διακονεῖν, see Beyer, *T.W.N.T.* II, 81–93.

[4] Cf. von Rad and Kittel, *T.W.N.T.* I, 75–87; Moore, I, 401–13; Bousset–Gressmann, *Die Religion des Judentums*[3], pp. 320–31.

to restrict the ministry of the angels in the Markan account to
the supply of food and drink. Rather they ministered to Jesus
in his contest with Satan. Most striking testimony is the connection of angels, wild beasts and the Devil in Test. Naph. viii. 4.

> If ye work that which is good, my children,
> Both men and angels shall bless you:
> And God shall be glorified among the Gentiles through you,
> And the devil shall flee from you,
> And the wild beasts shall fear you,
> And the Lord shall love you,
> (And the angels shall cleave to you).[1]

We have now examined the details of the account, but these
taken together do not reveal any overwhelmingly convincing
theme. We cannot regard Jesus as the new Israel in the desert.
Some evidence points to him as the Second Adam engaged in
a second duel with the Devil. The Spirit plays a surprising role:
it drives Jesus towards Satan but does not assist him in his
contest with Satan. Finally none of the evidence indicates in
any clear way the result of the Temptation. If we possessed the
Markan account only as an isolated pericope and did not know
the Q narrative we should be entirely ignorant of the outcome.
Information about this must be looked for elsewhere in Mark.
It is remarkable that commentators do not seem to mention
this surprising lack of conclusion to the account. Lohmeyer
alone draws attention to it, but states weakly that the result does
not need to be set down because for a divine being it is obvious
what it must be.[2] However, Mark does state the result quite
clearly in another passage and it is to this we must now turn.

Mark iii. 19b–35 is a section which hangs together under the
theme of the possession of Jesus by a spirit. His family, or

---

[1] Translation as Charles, *Apocrypha and Pseudepigrapha*, ii. Charles
brackets the last line as a Christian addition. If this is so then it confirms
our view that at an early period the ministry of the angels was not regarded
as restricted to the supply of food.

It may be noted that Test. Naph. is one of the oldest parts of Test. XII
Patriarchs; traces of it have been found among the Qumran material,
though not in its present form; cf. F. M. Cross, *The Ancient Library of
Qumran*, pp. 34, 149 n. 6; J. T. Milik, *Ten Years of Discovery in the Wilderness
of Judah*, pp. 34 f.

[2] *Ad loc.* Cf. Mauser, p. 100; Bundy, p. 61.

friends (οἱ παρ' αὐτοῦ), come to him saying that he is possessed; the scribes from Jerusalem name the devil, Beelzebul, by whom he is possessed; but he argues that what he does, he does by the Holy Spirit. It is not necessary for us to explore whether these separate pericopae represent one incident or the joining of a number of separate incidents under one theme; in certain cases, for example the unforgivable sin, the Q tradition shows significant variation. It is possible that these pericopae were already welded together before Mark received them,[1] but since they reflect one of his favourite editorial tricks in sandwiching incidents together, their conjunction may well be due to Mark.

For our particular purpose the important verse is 27. In the preceding verses Jesus, in a half-humorous argument, accepts the premise of the Scribes that he has an evil spirit and shows that this leads to the conclusion that the downfall of Satan is assured; the premise must therefore be incorrect. In *v.* 27 'The true account of the matter is now given: the positive conclusion to which Jesus himself has been led'.[2] The scribes begin by saying that Jesus is possessed by Beelzebul, a demon of whom little is known.[3] But Jesus at once changes the terminology by referring to Satan. Beelzebul may have been a named subordinate demon or he may have been Satan under another guise; the latter would appear to be the opinion of Mark who says 'by the ruler[4] of the devils he casts out devils'. Thus we have the picture of Satan as ruler of the devils, who are subordinate to him. This is a new feature in Jewish demonology; Satan has not previously appeared as the head of a host of demons.[5] But Satan would also appear to be used not merely as the name of the chief devil but also in a corporate way to denote the whole assemblage of devils: this seems to be the meaning of *vv.* 24, 26 where reference is made to Satan casting out Satan, and to Satan as divided. The personal aspect reappears in *v.* 27 where the strong man is undoubtedly Satan.

---

[1] Taylor, pp. 92 f.　　　　[2] Menzies, *ad loc.*

[3] Even the spelling of the word is uncertain. The most probable meaning appears to be 'Lord of the House'; cf. the commentaries and Langton, *Essentials of Demonology*, pp. 166 f.; Foerster, *T.W.N.T.* I, 605 f.

[4] ἄρχων equivalent to βεελ equivalent to בעל.

[5] So Foerster, *T.W.N.T.* VII, 159.

The stronger man who enters the house is also undoubtedly Jesus. It would seem wrong to connect this with i. 7 where Jesus is called 'the stronger'.[1] For at i. 7 ὁ ἰσχυρότερος is set in contrast to John the Baptist and not to Satan. Menzies[2] points out an apparent difficulty in the identification of Jesus with the one who enters the strong man's house in that in the only previous encounter between Jesus and Satan, the Temptation, Satan is the attacking power and not the attacked. But is this correct? One of the difficulties of the Temptation story is just the fact that the Spirit is said to drive Jesus out to be tempted, or tested. Jesus thus goes to the desert, the abode of demons, to encounter Satan. The implication of the Q narrative may be that Satan comes to tempt Jesus, but this is not true of the Markan account. Thus we find a link here between the Markan Temptation narrative and iii. 27, in that one of the difficulties of iii. 27 is explained by the reference to the Spirit as driving Jesus to the conflict, just as this peculiar reference in i. 12, contrary to all the experience of the early Christians who found the Spirit defending them from temptation, gives the backing to iii. 27. Thus it was in the Temptation that the strong man met the stronger.

But what happened to the strong man whose house was entered? He is bound and his goods are plundered. The conception of the binding of evil spirits is common in the apocalyptic writings. It presumably takes its Jewish origin[3] in Isa. xxiv. 21 f. and becomes more explicit in Tob. viii. 3; I Enoch x. 4 f., 11 f.; xviii. 12–xix. 2; xxi. 1–6; liv. 4 f.; Test. Levi xviii. 12; Jub. xlviii. 15. It reappears in the New Testament in Rev. xx. 2, where it is explicitly said that it is Satan who is bound. A consideration of these texts will reveal at once that to bind means to render powerless. Satan bound is not a Satan who can still carry on his activities, tempting and deceiving man within limits, but Satan out of the way. Charles notes that in respect of most of the references to the binding of evil spirits, their binding is only temporary and their final punishment comes

---

[1] Cf. Lohmeyer, Cranfield *ad* i. 7. On ὁ ἰσχυρός see Grundmann, *T.W.N.T.* III, 402–5.

[2] *Ad loc.*

[3] The idea existed also in Persian circles; cf. Charles, *Revelation* (I.C.C.), II, 142.

later and is distinct from their binding; for example, cf. I Enoch
x. 4 f. with x. 6, also x. 11 with x. 12 and Rev. xx. 2 with Rev.
xx. 3. Christ has already bound Satan according to Mark
iii. 27; δήσῃ, aorist subjunctive, would suggest one definite act,[1]
and this must be the trial of strength which he had with Satan
in the desert—the Temptation.[2] Test. Levi xviii. 12 is particularly interesting. Of the new priest whom God raises up it is
said 'And Beliar shall be bound by him, and he shall give
power to his children to tread upon the evil spirits'.[3] In Mark,
Satan is bound by Jesus and Jesus gives his disciples authority
over unclean spirits (vi. 7, cf. iii. 15). The argument in Test.
Levi and in Mark is precisely the same. Test. Levi xviii may
either be pre-Christian, in which case it may be the origin of
Mark's argument, or it may have been edited by a Christian
who has appreciated the argument of Mark, or some similar
explanation in the early Church. In either case it is confirmatory evidence for the view we take of Mark's theology of Satan
and his conquest.[4]

Having bound Satan, the Stronger has also plundered his
possessions—τὰ σκεύη. Are we to give a meaning to this, in
effect to allegorise the story, or are we to regard it as picturesque
detail without intended meaning?[5] Since Jesus is making reference to the defeat of underlings of Satan it is probably better to
take τὰ σκεύη as having some definite reference thereto. But
what are they? Men set free from the power of Satan[6] or lesser
devils pillaged and made the possession of Christ?[7] The former
seems the more probable in view of the biblical and non-

---

[1] Leivestad argues that it 'seems a natural assumption...that the
decisive victory must have taken place on a previous occasion' (*Christ the
Conqueror*, p. 46), yet he rejects this assumption as improbable; his rejection,
however, is based on a consideration of the Q form of the Temptation
narrative, which Mark does not use. Cf. Grundmann, *T.W.N.T.* III, 404.

[2] The objection of F. C. Grant (*Interpreter's Bible ad* iii. 27) that the
Scribes would not have known of the Temptation is hardly relevant; Jesus
is stating what has happened, and in any case, Mark's readers do know of
the Temptation, and it is they who are reading the Gospel.

[3] Translation as Charles, *Apocrypha and Pseudepigrapha*.

[4] Cf. pp. 187–9.

[5] Taylor *ad loc.*

[6] Grundmann, *T.W.N.T.* III, 404; Robinson, p. 31; Cranfield, Lagrange,
etc.

[7] Klostermann.

biblical parallels: for example, Isa. xlix. 25; Jub. x. 5–8; Luke xiii. 16.[1]

iii. 28, 29 in their reference to the sin against the Holy Spirit obviously imply that the activity of Jesus in the casting out of demons is also an activity of the Holy Spirit. References to the Holy Spirit in Mark (and Matthew) are surprisingly few when we consider the great prominence given to the Spirit in the early Church. Jesus once attributes an Old Testament saying to the Holy Spirit in accordance with the general Jewish view of the Spirit as the inspirer of prophecy (xii. 36). Three times the activity of the Spirit in the community is described: i. 8, baptism with the Spirit being a reference to the permanent endowment of the Church with the Spirit at Pentecost;[2] xiii. 11, the Spirit as inspiring the speech of the Christian when on trial; xiv. 38, the Spirit as giving courage in temptation.[3] There are four references to the activity of the Spirit in the life of Jesus: i. 8, he is able to baptise with the Spirit, it being at his disposal; i. 9–11, he is permanently endowed with the Spirit at his baptism; i. 12, the Spirit drives him to the contest with Satan; iii. 28, 29, by the power of the Spirit he casts out Satan's underlings. It is really only in the last two instances that we can say that we see the Spirit active in the ministry of Jesus and both refer to the same subject—his warfare with Satan. While in the early Church almost all the activities of Christians are ascribed to gifts of the Spirit, here Christ's warfare with Satan is alone so ascribed. Thus we find again that the temptation narrative and our present passage are closely linked.[4] Moreover what we found surprising in the Temptation story, namely, that it is never said that Jesus was helped by the Spirit in the defeat of Satan, is made clear at this point, since it is with the help of the Spirit that Satan's underlings are defeated, and so we may understand the same to have happened in the Temptation itself, the Spirit assisting Jesus against Satan.

[1] Cf. *Gospel of Truth*, xxv. 25 ff.; this appears, however, to depend on Rom. ix. 20–4 rather than on our present passage.

[2] Best, 'Spirit-Baptism', *N.T.* IV (1961), 236–43.

[3] Cf. below, p. 30. We take πνεῦμα in xiv. 38 to refer to the Divine Spirit rather than to the human; cf. E. Schweizer, *T.W.N.T.* VI, 394; F. Büchsel, *Der Geist Gottes im Neuen Testament*, pp. 180 ff.

[4] Cf. J. E. Yates, *The Spirit and the Kingdom* (London, 1963), pp. 29 ff.

Considering together these two passages, i. 12 f. and iii. 22–30, we see that they supplement one another. i. 12 f. has no conclusion; the conclusion is supplied by iii. 27. They are the only incidents in which the Spirit is seen as active in the ministry of Jesus and both concern his warfare with the spiritual powers. We are thus justified in taking them together and seeing in the Temptation in Mark not a psychological process but a contest between Jesus and Satan.[1] For Mark, Satan was thus defeated and rendered powerless at the very beginning of the ministry of Jesus and he proclaims his own victory in iii. 27: 'Man höre den Siegesklang, der durch diese Worte geht.'[2] The Temptation is not then a preliminary to the ministry of Jesus in which he settles for himself the broad outlines along which his ministry will run. The Temptation lies within the ministry as its decisive first act: Satan is overcome; the demonic exorcisms of the remainder of the ministry represent the making real of a victory already accomplished. The exorcisms are mopping-up operations of isolated units of Satan's hosts and are certain to be successful because the Captain of the hosts of evil is already bound and immobilised. The defeat of Satan is thus attached to the Temptation rather than to the Passion.

If this is the Markan interpretation of the Temptation certain questions at once raise themselves. (1) Does Jesus suffer temptation again after the initial encounter with Satan, and, if so, from what source does it come? (2) If Satan has been defeated at the beginning of the ministry what is the meaning of the Cross for Mark? (3) The early Christians undoubtedly found Satan very active; how could this be if he is already bound?

Before we turn to an examination of these questions we must look at the various incidents in which Jesus expels demons from men and see if these confirm our interpretation of iii. 27. Since Wrede the importance of these incidents in the thought structure of Mark has been increasingly emphasised. He drew attention to the knowledge that the demons had of the nature of Jesus and of Jesus' attempts to keep them silent so that that knowledge

---

[1] Leivestad (*Christ the Conqueror*, p. 53), who reaches the conclusion that the Temptation is a testing rather than a contest, bases his argument on the Q form of the Temptation story.

[2] Dehn, p. 87.

was not spread abroad.[1] We are not at present concerned with this latter aspect but rather with the status which the demons accorded to Jesus. In i. 24 the demon terms Jesus 'The Holy One of God', whereas in iii. 11 they call him 'The Son of God' and in v. 7 'Son of the Most High God'.[2] We may note that it was as Son of God that Jesus encountered Satan, for at the baptism immediately preceding the Temptation in the Markan narrative Jesus had been termed 'Son of God' by the heavenly voice. The demons thus recognise him under the same category, Son of God, as he defeated their master, the strong one. The title 'The Holy One of God' is much more difficult to explain. '... (it) does not appear to have been an accepted Messianic title. It describes a man set apart and consecrated to the service of God. In some early Christian communities it may have been used for a time as a Messianic name, but the New Testament examples are few and uncertain.'[3] In our present context it presumably refers to someone who stands in a particular relationship to God. The suggestion of Proksch[4] that ἅγιος refers here to the Holy Spirit, if it could be sustained, would be very interesting; as bearer of the Spirit in whose power he encountered Satan, Jesus now encounters Satan's underlings and is so recognised by them. Much more probably the explanation lies in the contrast between ἀκάθαρτος and ἅγιος. 'St Mark's special designation for a demon is "unclean spirit".'[5] Although he uses δαιμόνιον the term 'unclean spirit' crops up again and again as if explanatory of the other word. Matthew and Luke often omit it where Mark has it and only introduce it once each where it is not in Mark.[6] The usage of 'holy' in the cry of the demoniac once again emphasises the irreconcilable difference between Jesus and the demonic powers.

Passing from this to the meaning of the demonic acknowledgement, this can be taken as like recognising like: the demons

[1] Wrede, *Das Messiasgeheimnis in den Evangelien*[2], pp. 22–32.

[2] The stories in vii. 24–30 and ix. 14–29 are not told primarily to show Jesus in conflict with the demonic world, and do not contain demonic 'confessions'.

[3] Taylor, *The Names of Jesus*, p. 80.   [4] *T.W.N.T.* I, 102.

[5] Ling, *The Significance of Satan*, p. 14.

[6] The Markan phrase 'unclean spirit' in i. 26; v. 2, 13; vi. 7; vii. 25; ix. 25 is altered by either Matthew or Luke or both in their parallels. They introduce the phrase in Luke xi. 24 = Matt. xii. 43.

being supernatural know supernaturally the supernatural nature of the prophet of Nazareth.[1] That the demons should have
more than human insight is undoubtedly true, but this in itself
does not seem to exhaust the meaning of their recognition of
Jesus. In exorcism it was important for the exorcist to know the
name of the devil which he was attempting to expel; the
demons may then be using the true name of Jesus in an attempt
to obtain control over him. Bauernfeind[2] has shown that
parallels exist in the magical papyri to the words of the demons
in i. 24, iii. 11 and v. 7. While this may again be a factor it does
not provide a full explanation. A title is used as the acknowledgement of superiority, not as an attempt to gain control. For
Mark the title Son of God is obviously the highest title that can
be given; it is the title by which he would have his readers
recognise Jesus as their Lord; it is unlikely then that he would
have regarded its use by the demons as an attempt to overpower
him; rather as a recognition of his overlordship.[3] Equally their
description of him as ἅγιος signifies the gulf that lies between
them and himself and implies his vast superiority. It is obvious
from the stories that the demons wish to have nothing to do with
Jesus, τί ἡμῖν καὶ σοί (i. 24; cf. v. 7); whenever they see him
they prostrate themselves before him (iii. 11; cf. v. 6, though it
is not clear in this latter case whether it is the man or the demon
who worships Jesus); they are obviously thrown into confusion
at the presence of Jesus, convulsing their 'hosts' (i. 26; cf. ix. 20);
at the approach of Jesus the demon cries out (i. 23). The whole
implication of these accounts is then the recognition by the
demons that Jesus is their master.

Moreover, Jesus behaves throughout as their master. He
rebukes and commands them (i. 25; iii. 12; ix. 25). There are
no signs of a struggle between Jesus and the demons similar to
his struggle with Satan. From the beginning of the encounter
with each demon Jesus is in control of the situation.

---

[1] Cf. Lightfoot, *History*, p. 68; Wrede, *Das Messiasgeheimnis in den Evangelien*[2], pp. 28 ff.; Dibelius, pp. 54 f.

[2] *Die Worte der Dämonen im Markusevangelium.* Unfortunately I have not been able to obtain access to a copy of this book and depend on references to it in other writers.

[3] Cf. Ebeling, *Das Messiasgeheimnis und die Botschaft des Marcus-Evangelisten*, pp. 127 f.

The mastery assumed by Jesus over the demons is seen also in the strange phrase which Mark uses when Jesus gives his disciples their commission. He does not send them to exorcise but he gives them authority (ἐξουσία) over the demons (iii. 15; vi. 7). He could not give what he did not already himself possess. All this is so because Jesus has already defeated their master, Satan. With him took place the real contest. It ended victoriously for Jesus, and so when he meets one of Satan's underlings the latter recognises his overlordship from the beginning; at best all he can do is bargain for good terms for himself (v. 10); defeat is certain. Thus a study of the particular demonic exorcisms confirms the conclusion we drew from iii. 27. Satan has been decisively defeated and his kingdom is being reduced.

Since the point of view we have expressed in respect of the Temptation narrative and the demonic exorcisms is so entirely different from that of J. M. Robinson in his book *The Problem of History in Mark*, which itself represents a current trend in the discussion of Mark's Gospel in finding the key to its understanding in the demoniacal,[1] it is necessary that we examine his contentions and endeavour to show their inadequacy.

Robinson begins by noting that in Mark the Baptism and the Temptation are cosmic events. These events signify 'for Mark a decisive occurrence in the realization of the eschatological hope' (p. 27).[2] 'An essential part of the eschatological hope is the overthrow of the devil' (p. 28). The Temptation story and exorcism debate (iii. 22-30) are closely linked and indicate that the struggle between the Spirit and Satan which began in the Temptation continues in every exorcism, 'and the single event of the temptation becomes in the exorcisms an extended history of redemptive significance. . . . For once the saving action of Jesus over Satan is divided into a series of stories, it has lost its single-event character and is already on the way to becoming a history open to potential continuation within the Church' (p. 30). 'The exorcisms are interpreted in iii. 22-30 in terms of the cosmic struggle between the Spirit and Satan begun in the

[1] Cf. J. Kallas, *The Significance of the Synoptic Miracles*; G. Hebert, *The Christ of Faith and the Jesus of History*; H. Sawyerr, 'The Marcan Framework', *S.J.Th.* XIV (1961), 279-94.   [2] Page references refer to Robinson.

temptation' (p. 35). 'The exorcisms ... are the points in a historical narrative where the transcendent meaning of that history is most clearly evident' (p. 33). Robinson examines the various exorcism accounts and finds in them evidence of the continuing struggle between the Spirit and Satan (pp. 36–8). Though less evident the same struggle is present in the other miracle stories of the Gospel, and he finds traces of exorcism language in three Markan miracle stories (i. 43; iv. 39; vii. 35; cf. p. 40). Furthermore, following on the struggle in the exorcism there comes a period of peace, it being made 'evident that violence and death itself have been cast out' (p. 39). He points in particular to ix. 27 where Jesus is said to 'raise' the epileptic boy. Thus he is able to make the step from the exorcism narratives to the Passion and the Resurrection itself: 'The sudden reversal of the situation as the passion narrative is replaced by the Easter story is already anticipated in the exorcism stories, and here the shift is identified as due to the victory over the demon, i.e. Satan' (p. 39).

Robinson then seeks to show that the remainder of the historical narrative must be understood in terms of the cosmic struggle and he proceeds to discuss the debates between Jesus and his opponents.[1] 'For Mark, the nearest parallel to Jesus' debates is not the rabbinic debate, but rather the exorcism' (p. 44). Both debates and exorcism begin in hostility on the part of the opponents of Jesus, whether the opponents be demons or Pharisees: the word πειράζειν is used 'thus making their diabolic instigation clear' (p. 45). The disciples in their debates with Jesus about the Passion are equally instigated by Satan (viii. 33; cf. p. 52). In the debates there is a 'breakthrough to the truth of history and its eschatological basis' (p. 46). Thus Robinson can conclude,

The history which Mark selects to record is presented in its unity as the eschatological action of God, prepared by John the Baptist, inaugurated at the baptism and temptation, carried on through the struggles with various forms of evil, until in his death Jesus has experienced the ultimate of historical involvement and of diabolic antagonism. In the resurrection the force of evil is conclusively broken and the power of God's reign is established in history (p. 53).

[1] Cf. J. C. Fenton, 'Paul and Mark', Studies in the Gospels (ed. D. E. Nineham), pp. 89–112, at pp. 102 ff.

As we have done, Robinson connects the debate of iii. 22–30 with the Temptation, but because he fails to understand the metaphor of 'binding', Satan is still active for him in the exorcisms which are a continuation of the struggle of the Temptation. The Temptation has, in effect, been only the first round in the contest and apparently lacks a decisive conclusion. To us the exorcisms represent the plundering of the strong man's house, only possible because the strong man has been bound. We would further hold that in his actual discussion of the exorcism narratives Robinson lays too much stress on the element of struggle; we have sought alternatively to show that on each occasion Jesus is from beginning to end the master, though the demon may attempt to struggle, and he is master because he has defeated already the demon's own master, Satan. Now it is true that many of the other miracles resemble in varying ways the exorcism narratives and that among the Jews sickness was sometimes ascribed to demonic possession. In particular, as pointed out by Ling,[1] the uncleanness of leprosy may be related to the uncleanness of demons:[2] now while this demonic element is present in some of the Markan miracle stories it cannot be easily traced in all of them and it is a big step to take to argue that it must be so discerned. It is only natural that in the healing miracles the cure is emphasised and the period of 'peace' after the miracle stressed. To suggest that for this reason the miracles are to be understood in the same way as the exorcisms because in both the end of the story is 'peace' is surely to draw deep meaning out of a similarity that is inherent in the very nature of healing stories; it is impossible to relate them without mentioning the cured state and the difference between 'before' and 'after'. The attempt moreover to move from the exorcism stories to the resurrection is inadequately based. This movement is made to rest on two features: (a) The violence of the demoniac before cure suggests the violence of the Passion and the peace afterwards suggests the Resurrection; this is again too great a step to take unless there is some deliberate indication in the text that it is intended. (b) Robinson finds such a deliberate indication in the words to the cured epileptic boy when Jesus takes him by the hand and 'raises' him; but

[1] *The Significance of Satan*, pp. 14 ff.
[2] But it may also be related to sin; cf. pp. 106 f. below.

the word 'raise' here is perfectly natural; the demon has already thrown the boy to the ground! There is not in Mark any clear indication that Satan was active in the Passion; Luke by some additions to the Passion narrative does suggest the activity of Satan at the time (xxii. 3, Satan enters Judas; xxii. 31, Satan desires Simon), but such indications are wholly absent in Mark.[1]

Equally to be rejected is Robinson's attempt to find Satan present in the debates that Jesus has with his disciples and with his opponents. It is undoubtedly true, as he stresses, that the actions and the words of Jesus cannot be separated, but since he has failed to show that opposition to Satan governs all the actions of Jesus this in itself is not a reason for expecting to find opposition to the demoniac in the words of Jesus. In making the assumption that the nearest parallel to the debates is the exorcisms, Robinson ignores the fact that in the exorcisms there really are no debates; there are words of command by Jesus but no attempts to prove by argument or use of Scripture the inadequacy of the position of the demon; the demon acknowledges from the beginning the true position of Jesus as Son of God or as Holy One, the opponents in the debates do not; the demons behave utterly differently from the human opponents of Jesus; it is only necessary to quote Robinson himself on this:

We do not find calm conversations, but shouts and orders. The demons 'shout' at Jesus: i. 23; iii. 11; (v. 5); v. 7; ix. 26. In v. 7 the demon 'adjures' Jesus. Jesus 'orders' the demons (i. 27 (*sic*); ix. 25), or 'reproaches' them with an order (i. 25; iii. 12; ix. 25). The only passage approaching normal conversation is in v. 9–13, after the struggle is over and the authoritative word of exorcism had been uttered (*v.* 8) (p. 36).

Robinson points out also the similarity of the hostility of opponents and demons to Jesus; this does not seem exceptional; it is only in the nature of the case that opponents should be hostile; this does not imply they are demonically inspired.[2] Robinson would appear to have more of a point when he draws attention to instances where the opponents of Jesus are said to 'tempt' him (viii. 11; x. 2; xii. 15). We will examine this in our next chapter and see that these temptations come from men

---

[1] Cf. Leivestad, *Christ the Conqueror*, pp. 63 ff.
[2] Cf. also pp. 38 ff below.

and not Satan;[1] in the LXX there is no connection between the root πειράζειν and evil spiritual powers. Robinson also finds a connection with the Cross in Jesus' debate with the disciples about the Passion when Peter is called Satan (viii. 31 ff.); we will see also in our next chapter that this does not imply that Peter is a tool of Satan, rather that he behaves as Satan would behave, were Satan free so to behave.[2] Thus the debates cannot be regarded as extensions of the demonic exorcisms and consequently any argument from the debates as demonic to the Passion as Satanic cannot be made.

When we examine the certain instances of demonic influence in Mark we see that it is confined to the Temptation story itself plus the exorcisms and certain of the miracle stories. In the Temptation story temptation is definitely present, that is, Satan tempts to moral evil, though Mark stresses the conflict rather than the actual tempting. But when we consider the other events we see that in them it is impersonal forms of evil that are involved, for example, madness, leprosy, storm (cf. i. 25 and iv. 39 where Jesus in similar words commands the demon and the storm to be silent). Thus Satan being defeated Jesus encounters his underlings and has to deal with powers that disturb the life of men on the physical plane but do not drive them to moral evil. This is not to deny that there is a unity in evil, but it is to suggest that the demonic powers were not concerned with those aspects of evil which essentially separate a man from God and the removal of which, as we shall see, was at least one of the purposes of the Passion and Resurrection. In actual fact the demonic slowly fades out of Mark; highly concentrated at the beginning, it gradually disappears so that in the Passion story it escapes mention altogether. Robinson would take its high concentration at the commencement of the Gospel as indicating it as a main theme for the whole and signifying the true interpretation. It is *a priori* equally probable that it disappears because Mark does not consider it of supreme importance. We have sought to show negatively that Robinson's interpretation is not tenable. We have yet to show positively that an interpretation other than the demonic is what Mark would have us see. But indicative of that other interpretation is the disappearance of the demonic from the Gospel while moral

[1] Pp. 30 ff. [2] Pp. 28 ff.

evil still remains and comes at Jesus from his opponents, his disciples, and finally from within himself in Gethsemane.

Kallas[1] has enunciated views somewhat similar to Robinson concerning the significance of the demonic in the life of Jesus. While his main concern lies with the miracles of Jesus which he views as evidence of the activity of Jesus against Satan and the demonic powers which now rule the world, he also sees the death of Jesus as the final defeat of Satan.

It was in death that Satan's rule became vindicated and perpetuated. Death made his victory final. If Jesus came to fight the strong man, if Jesus intended to break the reign of Satan, then he would have to fight Satan in this, the place where Satan was strongest; in the valley of the shadow of death (pp. 98 f.).

Unlike Robinson, Kallas seeks to set out the significance of the Synoptic miracles, and therefore of the demonic element, for Jesus himself, and is not concerned with the theology of the evangelists, least of all of Mark. But this does not mean that Kallas has nothing to say relevant to our theme. He works throughout with an uncritical view of the Gospels. Whatever he finds in them he assumes to be true of Jesus. This is particularly true of his examination of the self-consciousness of Jesus (pp. 24 ff.), where he makes no attempt to estimate the genuineness of sayings of our Lord. On the basis of the Gospels as they are he quickly reaches the conclusion that Jesus regarded himself as divine (p. 31). This uncritical use of the Gospel also means that what he finds to be true of Jesus and of the demonic element in his life is necessarily also true of all three evangelists, and in particular of Mark, and it permits him to regard the evangelists as possessing a common mind in these matters.

We can go a considerable part of the way with Kallas when he argues that not only in the exorcisms is Jesus waging war against demonic forces but also in the healing miracles. Here he instances Luke xiii. 16; iv. 39 as evidence that this was Jesus' own understanding of what he was doing. The weakness of his method is apparent at this very point. In the latter of these Luke says that Jesus 'rebuked' the disease, just as he is said to rebuke demons (Mark i. 25; ix. 25). But Luke's use of ἐπιτιμᾶν is here an alteration of the Markan account. Moreover, Luke

[1] *The Significance of the Synoptic Miracles.*

xiii. 16 belongs to Luke's special material. It is thus impossible to argue from the Lukan view here either that Mark held the same view and that all his healing miracles should be interpreted in this way, or that Jesus himself held this view. Indeed the very fact that one of these cases is definitely editorial on Luke's part and the other comes from his special material would rather suggest that this view belongs either to Luke the editor, which is the more probable, or that it belongs to his special material. This in turn suggests that the entrance of the demonic interpretation into the material came during its transmission and was not original. Just as Luke has a special interest in the Holy Spirit and introduces many references to him, so he may equally have a special interest in the Evil Spirit; the two would go together. It is not our concern here to argue about the view of Jesus himself, but what we have said would suggest that the demonic-cosmic element may have played less part in his viewpoint than is sometimes held. In any case we cannot simply transfer the Lukan view to Mark. In order to find this in Mark, Kallas draws attention to Mark's use of μάστιξ when referring to disease (iii. 10; v. 29, 34). 'In other words, for Jesus and the gospel writers, these ordinary "diseases" were not ordinary at all. They were, instead, scourges, or whips; they were curses, sources of affliction by the evil one. Satan was persecuting these people' (p. 79). But μάστιξ was already used metaphorically of disease without reference to Satan;[1] and so it is not necessary to introduce him at this point. Kallas would have us also see the fight against the demons as continued in the nature miracles; it is easier to agree with him here, especially in the light of the rebuking of the storm (iv. 37–41).

Finally, Kallas considers the Resurrection, the final miracle, as the ultimate contest with Satan. He fails to provide here the necessary evidence from the Gospels themselves that Satan is the angel of death; he fails to show adequately the place of Satan in the Passion story; his attempt to show its cosmic dimension from Matt. xxvii. 51–3 is to make use of very secondary material; his claim to see in Passion and Resurrection the final contest with Satan in which the stronger one wins (cf. pp. 98 f.) ignores Mark's clear statement that at iii. 27 this contest is already over.

[1] Cf. C. Schneider, *T.W.N.T.* IV, 524; Liddell and Scott; Bauer, etc., on the word.

The extent to which the demonic background permeates Mark will appear as we proceed: we thus give no direct rebuttal of Kallas's view that it is present and dominant in the Passion and Resurrection.

The approach of Mauser is somewhat different though he arrives at a similar conclusion to Robinson and Kallas. He considers that Mark views the life and passion of Jesus as spent in the 'wilderness'. The 'wilderness' is not a place but a theological theme; in the Old Testament it is the place of evil, of the judgement of God, of repentance, renewal and deliverance. Mark depicts Jesus as continually going into the wilderness and so as constantly in contact with evil, demonic evil. The forty days of the Temptation in the wilderness are typical in this respect; they are not decisive moments in a conflict with Satan but at the beginning set out the whole tenor of the life of Jesus as one of incessant temptation.

But it is not the power of Jesus to overcome evil which is stressed by Mark in i. 13, otherwise a victory over Satan would certainly have been told. In the prologue, the Evangelist simply sets the stage— Jesus and Satan are going to be the main actors in the commencing drama and their encounter alone is the fact emphasised in i. 13. Now, at the end of the drama, the main characters are still engaged in battle, and temptation is still the name of their clash. But the word has assumed a decidedly sinister tone; it is clear that in this last encounter the devil's power is going to carry the day—the hour when the Son of Man is delivered into the hands of sinners is Satan's hour, because the sinners are his instruments.[1]

The final conflict with Satan is thus, as in Robinson and Kallas, the Cross.

We must admit at the outset that the 'wilderness' plays a large part in the Old Testament and that a great many ideas are connected with it. Mauser has shown in the first part of his study how important and widespread is this conception. But many of the ideas connected with the wilderness exist also without this connection. For David the place of evil and temptation was not the wilderness but a built-up area of Jerusalem where he espied Bathsheba; and in the same area he learnt and suffered the judgement of God, repented and was renewed. For Isaiah the temple was the place of revelation;

[1] Mauser, p. 130.

there he met God and responded to him. Mark speaks of the judgement of God borne by Christ, of temptation as coming to Christ, and of deliverance through Christ; the fact that these themes appear does not mean that they can be seen only against the background of the 'wilderness'. If Mark is to be viewed as dominated in them by the 'wilderness' theme then we would expect to see this much more clearly. But Mark's references to the 'wilderness' are not sufficiently clear and precise to enable us to draw the conclusions to which Mauser would lead us.

We may begin with the word 'wilderness'. On p. 78 Mauser tells us that 'the "wilderness" theme is repeatedly used by the Evangelist in editorial remarks' and refers us to pp. 104 f.; but at pp. 104 f. he only indicates three places (i. 35; i. 45; vi. 31–3) where it is used editorially. Not only is it used only occasionally editorially but the phrase so used is different from that which came to Mark in the tradition. In the editorial passages Mark used ἔρημος τόπος (or the plural), whereas the phrase in the tradition is ἡ ἔρημος (γῆ) (i. 3, 4, 12, 13); ἡ ἐρημία (viii. 4) also appears in the tradition.[1] The normal LXX phrase for the wilderness is ἡ ἔρημος (γῆ). Mark's editorial phrase ὁ ἔρημος τόπος is only found once (Dan. LXX iv. 25; Jer. xl. 12 is not a true parallel) in five columns of Hatch and Redpath's LXX concordance. Mauser fails to consider why in giving an Old Testament concept Mark fails to use the universal Old Testament word. The simplest solution is that Mark is not conscious of the Old Testament idea and is using ἔρημος in a different way. And when we examine i. 35, 45; vi. 31–3 we see that the translation 'lonely' (cf. R.S.V. at i. 35) fits the context. At i. 35; vi. 31[2] Jesus wants solitude for himself or his disciples; at i. 45 the phrase is in natural opposition to πόλις. On each occasion it would have been simple enough for Mark to use the normal phrase and so connect what he is saying to i. 4, 12, but he does not do so. Perhaps Mark's change indicates that for him the wilderness period ended with i. 13: thereafter he avoids the normal phrase for the wilderness! There is also too easy an identification of the 'mountain' and the 'sea' with the 'wilderness'. Mauser draws a strong parallel

[1] 'It is reasonable to suppose that in vi. 35 Mark also found ἔρημος or ἐρημία in his tradition...' (Mauser, p. 105).

[2] Note κατ' ἰδίαν at vi. 31, 32.

between the Transfiguration and the events of Exod. xxiv. There are difficulties in this parallel, but even supposing that we allow it holds, this of itself does not bring us to the wilderness theme. Admittedly the 'mountain' of Exod. xxiv is in the 'wilderness', but that does not mean that therefore the 'mountain' of Mark ix. 2–8 is part of the 'wilderness' theme, and that every other reference to mountains in Mark should be taken as a reference to the 'wilderness'. If the background of ix. 2–8 is Exod. xxiv, then Mark is only making a connection between the Transfiguration and the law-giving of Sinai, and not necessarily drawing in a whole background of ideas in relation to the wilderness. The 'sea' is certainly demonic in Mark (cf. iv. 35–41) and that associates it with the 'wilderness', but it does not mean that every reference to the sea, and there are many, is to be taken as suggesting the wilderness theme. We are thus unable to view the 'wilderness' as a dominant theme in Mark.

Turning more directly to i. 12 f. we are also unable to accept Mauser's contention[1] that the forty days were not a decisive period. The connection which we have attempted to make with iii. 22–30, if correct, obviously refutes such a view. Finally we are unable to view the Passion of Jesus as taking place in the 'wilderness'. As Mauser himself shows, the 'wilderness' theme tends to disappear after viii. 27.[2] Since Jerusalem was hardly the wilderness the recurrence of the theme at this point would need to have been made expressly clear. Mauser's proof seems to lie in the argument that in Gethsemane temptation recurs and therefore we are back in the wilderness; this depends on the assumptions: (a) that temptation must be due to the devil; this is doubtful in the case of Mark;[3] Mauser draws here on the work of Robinson, which we have been questioning, 'that Mark understands Jesus' whole mission as an encounter with Satanic forces';[4] (b) that the 'wilderness' is the only place where the Devil operates; this assumption rather begs the question. Even if Robinson's view is correct this second assumption is wrong because the conflict of Jesus with demonic forces takes place not in the wilderness but in crowds and in public places (i. 21–8; i. 33 f.; iii. 9–12). However, the wilderness theme and the views of Robinson do not necessarily go together; Robinson's ideas could still stand, though the former were untrue.

[1] Cf. pp. 97–100, 129 f.   [2] P. 128.   [3] Cf. ch. ii.   [4] Mauser, p. 130, n. 1.

CHAPTER II

THE ORIGIN OF TEMPTATION

It would appear that we have left little place for Satan in the remainder of the Gospel and so we must examine those places in which he appears and those in which Jesus is said to be tempted, to discover his role therein. This will lead us to a general discussion of evil and its origin in Mark, which will in turn lead to a similar discussion of the same question in the whole of the biblical and post-biblical material.

There are two passages other than i. 12 f. in which Satan is mentioned in the Gospel. He appears first in the interpretation of the Parable of the Sower at iv. 15. It might be thought that we could evade this occurrence by arguing that the interpretation is not original; we however are concerned with the Gospel as it stands, not with what we would put in it if we were writing a life of Jesus. We must point out though that the activity of Satan in the interpretation of the parable is an activity among men; he is not seen as active in the life of our Lord. The interpretation represents for Mark an attempt to place the parable in the life of the early Church, and therefore Satan is here viewed as active in the lives of men. We are at the moment dealing with Satan as active in the life of Jesus and therefore may leave this reference in iv. 15 until later.[1]

The one place where Satan explicitly reappears in the life of Jesus is viii. 33 where, following on Peter's confession of Jesus as Christ and Jesus' own prediction of his sufferings, Peter rebukes him and Jesus in reply says, 'Get thee behind me, Satan'. Cullmann links the phrase closely to Matt. iv. 10 where we have the similar phrase ὕπαγε, Σατανᾶ and continues, 'The devil is now making use of Jesus' own disciple, Peter; that is his greatest trick. . . . He who tries to force upon Jesus another Messianic task than the one he has received from God, he who thereby seeks to turn him from this task he has received from God, is a tool of Satan.'[2] In so describing Peter as the tool of Satan, the implication is that Satan is no longer

---

[1] Cf. p. 182. [2] *Peter: Disciple, Apostle, Martyr*, p. 174.

bound, or else Peter must be regarded as possessed by a demon. We must however note that Cullmann is interpreting the phrase as both it and the story appear in the Gospel of Matthew, and not as in Mark. For us it is illegitimate to introduce Matt. iv. 10 into our discussion since Mark, not knowing the story of the three temptations, cannot here be making a veiled allusion to them. Without this direct link the conclusion that Peter is a tool of Satan is not so obvious.

The phrase ὕπαγε ὀπίσω μου is difficult to interpret. From the time of Origen[1] attempts have been made to take the words in a light as favourable as possible to Peter. Thus some commentators have taken it as a plea to Peter to return behind Jesus again as his disciple.[2] ὀπίσω μου is definitely associated with discipleship in v. 34 (cf. i. 17, 20) but the verb used is ἐλθεῖν and not ὑπάγειν.[3] An Aramaic or Syriac idiom has been suspected behind the phrase, based on an original σου rather than μου, but this seems unlikely.[4] It is very probable that it must be given the general sense: 'Away from me so as to be out of my sight.'[5] Jesus dismisses Peter because of his Satanic suggestion. But does he mean by this that Peter has taken up the role of Satan or that Satan is making use of Peter as his tool? This is a real distinction. The normal English rendering, 'Get thee behind me, Satan', can be interpreted in either way, but Moffatt's translation, 'Get behind me, You Satan', definitely suggests the former alternative. When in the Matthean account Jesus calls Simon 'Peter', he means that he is to perform the role of a rock in steadying his fellows; when he calls the sons of Zebedee 'Boanerges', he means that they behaved in the tempestuous manner of a storm. Thus it seems better to see Peter behaving after the manner of Satan than as either indwelt by Satan or as his tool. This interpretation is confirmed by the immediately succeeding words where Peter is accused of thinking not the thoughts of God but those of men (cf. viii. 27: Peter is no further on than the crowd). What he puts before Jesus is a

[1] *Commentary on Matt. ad* xvi. 22 f.
[2] Schlatter, *Der Evangelist Matthäus, ad* xvi. 23.   [3] Cf. Swete *ad loc.*
[4] See M. Black, *An Aramaic Approach to the Gospels and Acts*[2], pp. 263 f.
[5] C. H. Turner, *J.T.S.* xxix (1928), 287 f., shows that in Mark the fundamental meaning of ὕπαγε is movement away from ('go' as distinct from 'come') the speaker.

pattern of all too human behaviour and not of divine.[1] In putting this temptation before Jesus he is playing the role of Satan, one of whose activities is to tempt men, but he is not Satan; nor may the temptation even be described as Satanic: it is human.

Consequently there is no reason to believe that Mark at this point sees Satan as set free from his binding and as coming again to tempt Jesus. Nor is there any need to accuse Mark of inconsistency at this point in relation to Satan. Satan has been bound, but temptation does not cease: it comes now from man, and from a man who stands in a close personal relationship to Jesus—for those reasons it is perhaps all the more deadly.

Jesus also undergoes temptation in the Garden of Gethsemane (xiv. 32–42). Here we are moving in the same circle of ideas, those of the Old Testament. Jesus sees opposed two wills, his own and God's. Satan is not even mentioned. The temptation now definitely comes from within Jesus himself. There is here no cosmic conflict (the strengthening angel of the Lukan account might imply such) but the simple struggle of human will against divine will. And we may note at this point that this is also the experience of the disciples, with a very different result. They entered into temptation and fell because though the Spirit was ready the flesh was weak (xiv. 38). The dualism of flesh and spirit here is not an inner dualism in man between his upper and his lower natures but the dualism of opposition between God and man; σάρξ is man's whole being in weakness and opposition to God; πνεῦμα is God's Spirit ready to help man.[2] Verse 38a may represent the experience of Jesus himself, out of which he gives his counsel to the disciples. It is however unlikely that Mark took it in that way; he does not attribute it to Jesus' own experience and he nowhere shows much interest in the inner consciousness of Jesus.

There are three passages in which the root πειράζειν appears, viii. 11; x. 2; xii. 15, and we must now look at these to see if in them it carries the meaning of 'tempt'.

[1] The thought is similar to Rom. viii. 5 ff., which if Mark wrote the Gospel in Rome he will have known. Men, not Satan, and God are also in opposition at x. 27; xi. 30–2; cf. vii. 7; ix. 31 for 'men' used in a bad sense.

[2] Cf. Schweizer, *T.W.N.T.* VI, 394 (= *The Spirit of God*, pp. 24 f.); Büchsel, *Der Geist Gottes im Neuen Testament*, pp. 180 ff.

We examine first viii. 11 in which the Pharisees seek a sign from Jesus. Their request comes directly after the feeding of the four thousand and immediately before the discussion of the leaven of the Pharisees and the Herodians, which is itself occasioned by the almost total absence of bread in the ship in which they were crossing the lake. Whether this is the original place of the tradition is unimportant for us; this is where Mark puts it. Whether also Jesus in his historical existence was conscious of himself as Messiah or not is again irrelevant for us; Mark undoubtedly took him to be. All that the Pharisees originally asked may have been a sign that he was a prophet come from heaven, and this may be all that Jesus may have refused them,[1] but Mark sees Jesus as refusing to confirm his Messianic office by a sign from Heaven. Heaven may be taken literally and the Pharisees considered as seeking a sign out of the heavens, as in xiii. 24, 25, that is, a sign of the consummation of the Messianic kingdom;[2] or it may be taken as a Jewish circumlocution for God, and the sign be another miraculous feeding:[3] as Moses fed the Israelites in the desert, so should the Messiah feed his people now (cf. John vi. 30 f.).[4] If the former interpretation is taken then there is a resemblance here to the second temptation in the Matthean form, and if the first interpretation, then a resemblance to the first temptation. This very resemblance suggests at once that πειράζειν cannot be taken here in the simple sense of 'test'.[5] The Pharisees would undoubtedly try out Jesus to see if he was divinely sent, but this very trial was a temptation for Jesus that he should seek to convince men of his Messiahship through a mighty work—something other than the healings and exorcisms which both he and others performed (Matt. xii. 27; Luke xi. 19). We must therefore take this to be a temptation of Jesus. This temptation comes to him from men; explicitly it originates with the Pharisees, but Jesus widens it out to include all men—'this generation seeks a sign'. 'This generation' is apparently used in a bad sense; it denotes men in their opposition to God (cf. viii. 38; ix. 19; xiii. 30).[6]

[1] Cf. Branscomb.　　　　　[2] Cf. Lohmeyer, Menzies, etc.
[3] Cf. Schniewind, etc.
[4] Cf. Bultmann, Hoskyns and Davey, etc., on John vi. 31.
[5] Seesemann, *T.W.N.T.* vi, 28, takes it in the secular sense of 'test'.
[6] Cf. Büchsel, *T.W.N.T.* i, 661.

There is thus here no trace of Satan.[1] The Pharisees and this generation think the thoughts of men and not of God (cf. viii. 33). An interesting sidelight would be thrown on this if we could take the reference to the spirit of Jesus in viii. 12 as a reference to the Holy Spirit:[2] then we would have the reappearance of the Spirit of God at a moment of temptation. It is however unlikely that πνεῦμα should be taken here of the Holy Spirit.

The two remaining passages do not need detailed discussion. At x. 2 Jesus is asked concerning divorce; there was already considerable divergence of opinion in Judaism, and probably also in early Christianity, on this matter; an attempt is made to trap him into coming down on one or other side. πειράζειν thus has probably the sense of testing someone as to his opinion, hostile intent being present.[3] At xii. 15 it is Jesus himself who uses the word, describing the Pharisees and Herodians who ask him the question about tribute money as 'testing' him. They are again seeking to find out his opinion in the hope that he will commit himself to a view whereby he will either lose the support of the people, if he advises to pay, or will run into conflict with the Roman authorities, and so destroy himself, if he advises to refuse to pay. We come much nearer the meaning of 'tempt' in this passage; a straightforward statement by Jesus that the tax should not be paid might be regarded as a raising of the Messianic standard of revolt; here was an opportunity to win the crowds to himself; there are thus resemblances between this and the third Matthean temptation in that Jesus is here involved in a temptation to obtain power by a political slogan. It should also be noted that on any occasion when Jesus is asked a question

[1] The Lukan parallel is xi. 16. If we accept the view of Conzelmann, pp. 27–9, that, for Luke, Satan left Jesus alone between iv. 13 and xxii. 3 then Luke also can use πειράζειν without any reference to Satan but only to men.

[2] So Schniewind. It may be pointed out that (ἀνα)στενάζειν and πνεῦμα are connected both here and in Rom. viii. 23.

[3] Hebert, *The Christ of Faith and the Jesus of History*, p. 89, considers that Mark has carefully placed this incident and that for him its reference is not to the marriage and divorce of individuals but to the marriage of the Messiah to Israel. 'The answer comes clear and strong, "What God has joined together, let not man separate". The union stands; he is one with his bride, and therefore he must bear her sins.' The Temptation is then a temptation to Jesus to forsake his mission towards Israel.

which involves him in a statement either about his ministry or concerning how men should behave there is the temptation not to speak the truth but to say what men would like to hear. We cannot thus exclude from either x. 2 or xii. 15 the meaning of 'tempt'. Temptations continue to come to Jesus, but they come, not from Satan, or demonic powers, but from men, who are not in any way regarded as satanically possessed.

Having seen that it is not necessary to introduce the figure of Satan into the passages in which Jesus is said to be tempted and that Peter is not regarded as motivated by Satan, we must go on to examine the role of Satan in temptation. In actual day-to-day sin, as distinct from the cosmic origin of sin and evil, what part does Satan play? We are accustomed to think of him as responsible for all temptation. Did Mark hold this view? Is it found in the biblical and post-biblical material? By an examination of his Gospel and of the other material we shall seek to show that neither Mark nor contemporary Judaism attributed the origin of all temptation to Satan.

According to the Markan story Jesus first encountered evil in his conflict with Satan (i. 12 f.). We are not told the content of the tempting or testing and it would be wrong for us to read into this short narrative the meaning given by Q, where the testing takes quite definitely the form of an attack on the purpose of his ministry. From Mark all we know is that he was divinely led to a clash with Satan in which he was victorious, and victorious to such a degree that he was afterwards able to spoil Satan's house and kingdom.

Closely linked to this encounter with evil in Satan is Jesus' encounter with evil in demon-possessed men, as iii. 27 makes clear. At no point does Mark attribute moral evil, that is sin, to demon possession. Much modern popular preaching, at a loss what to make of the exorcism stories, takes them as analogies of what Jesus can do in the casting out of a grave sin or evil habit; the person is cleansed. Such an approach would have been foreign to Mark. Nor would he have regarded the demoniac as in need of psychiatric treatment in a mental home. The demoniac is one in whom a spiritual power of evil has replaced either permanently or temporarily the normal rational, conative and emotional faculties of man; treatment will not cure him; only the presence of a greater spiritual power. In all this Mark is in line with the prevailing thought of his day.

But the demonic is also present for Mark both in the world of nature and in ordinary sickness (i. 43; iv. 39; vii. 35).[1] The presence of this evil in the world around is seen most clearly in the way in which Jesus stills the storm (iv. 37 ff.).[2] Here there can be no question of moral evil; the universe cannot be accused of sinning. Sickness may also be due to demon possession; this, as Ling has shown, may be true of leprosy.[3] However the analysis of Ling at this point is not sufficiently accurate. He is correct in emphasising that Mark calls the demons who possess men 'unclean spirits', that the leper is 'cleansed' (i. 40–5) and that there are examples in Mark of the two other classes denoted in Num. v. 2 ff. as unclean, namely the woman with the issue of blood and those in contact with the dead (v. 21–43).[4] In the exorcism it is not the man who is unclean, but the demon; in leprosy it is the man who is unclean because of his leprosy and who because he is unclean is put out of the camp; again in Mark i. 40 it is the leper who desires to be cleansed and he is made clean by Jesus; the woman with the issue of blood is healed and so made clean; the unclean corpse of Jairus' daughter is brought back to life and so to cleanness. Those who because of uncleanness would have been put outside the camp are accepted by Jesus and in every case are touched by him (i. 41; v. 30, 41); the uncleanness has disappeared altogether. In the case of the demoniacs the unclean spirits are driven out but remain unclean; they still exist; but the leprosy and the issue of blood disappear. The unclean spirit is driven out but the unclean person is made whole. Because leprosy and an issue of blood lead to exclusion from the worship of God they resemble sin, and as the sick person is healed so the sinful person is forgiven; nothing is driven away. Furthermore, much Jewish

---

[1] Cf. Robinson, p. 40.

[2] The attempt of Kallas, *The Significance of the Synoptic Miracles*, pp. 88 f., to see in every nature miracle an attack on a demonically-possessed universe stretches the evidence beyond breaking point.

[3] *The Significance of Satan*, pp. 14 ff.

[4] The corpse, though instanced by Ling, is not strictly a parallel; it would have been Jairus and his wife, not their dead daughter, who would have been defiled by contact with the corpse; but it was the daughter who was healed.

thought linked leprosy to sin, regarding it as a punishment for sin.[1] Thus we cannot link leprosy too closely to demonic possession; it might equally be related to sin.

Exorcism and the healing of sickness are often set side by side in statements about the activity of Jesus and his disciples (i. 32, 34; vi. 7, 13). But may not sickness be linked with sin? This is certainly the attitude of much modern psychology, which regards sickness as brought on by sin, for example, an ulcer by worry, which is lack of trust in God and consequently sin. Support for this point of view has been drawn from Mark ii. 1-12,[2] where sickness and sin are clearly related. It is very doubtful if we can accept the modern psychological theory that before the man in this story could be healed a guilt complex had to be removed by forgiveness. It is a modern theory: Swete in his commentary of 1898 does not mention it. It would hardly therefore have been a solution possible in the first century. It may be that Mark falls back here on the old view that sickness is a punishment of God; the man has sinned, God has chastised him with sickness, therefore he must first be forgiven and then healed. This is more probable than the view that the sickness is due to demonic powers, who would hardly have sent the sickness as a chastisement for sin. Where elsewhere these powers appear in the Gospel Jesus deals with them directly, speaking to them and ordering them to depart: here he speaks to the man himself and deals with him. If all sickness is to be traced to Satan, then this thought is not at all apparent at this point, and certainly we cannot draw the conclusion that the man's sin was due to Satan. How then must we interpret the incident? With Mark the argument is surely: since Jesus can heal the sick therefore he can forgive sins. He does the latter first; his power to do so is doubted; he performs the former to prove his power. It is an argument *a minori ad majus*. The power of Jesus is manifested in both actions; if the healings are a sign of the inbreaking of the Kingdom so also is forgiveness; healing and forgiveness are both expected in the Messianic time; they are present now in the life

---

[1] Cf. below, pp. 106f.

[2] Whatever the earlier tradition Mark took ii. 1-12 as one incident. In what follows I have drawn largely on an earlier article, 'Mark ii. 1-12', *Biblical Theology*, III (1953), 41-6. Cf. also R. T. Mead, 'The Healing of the Paralytic—A Unit', *J.B.L.* LXXX (1961), 348-54.

3-2

of Jesus. Looked at thus the incident as it appears in Mark obviously fits in with the early Church situation. A Christian evangelist begins to preach the forgiveness of sins; men ask him how he can be sure that God forgives sins now, so as proof of the power of God working through himself he heals the sick; if God can deal with the sickness of men, he can deal also with their sin. Since sin and sickness are related, in that both are forms of evil, this argument could be effective; sin would be the greater evil to the Christian but not necessarily to the bystander watching the miracle performed, for whom then it would not be an argument *a minori ad majus*. Thus we cannot conclude that when Jesus heals sickness he defeats demoniacal powers. Rather he may be dealing with sin.

Jesus also encounters evil in the hearts and minds of men as well as in their bodies. Their evil ways are attributed to hardness of heart (vi. 52, the disciples in relation to the miracle of the loaves and fishes, cf. viii. 17; x. 5, the Pharisees in relation to the relaxation of the law of marriage in regard to divorce by Moses, cf. iii. 5).[1] When Peter counsels Jesus to take some other way than that of the Cross his thoughts are described as 'human' (viii. 33). When the disciples are unable to stay awake and pray in the Garden of Gethsemane their failure is attributed to a weakness of the flesh, that is, as we have seen, a weakness not of the purely physical, but of the whole man (xiv. 38).[2] Men are described by Jesus as unbelieving and faithless (vi. 6; ix. 19). Sin originates from within man and not from outside; it is from within a man that evil thoughts go out (vii. 21–3). The disciples are commanded to beware of the leaven of the Pharisees and Herodians (viii. 15) and, while the precise reference of leaven at this point is not clear, it must imply thinking and acting as the Pharisees and Herodians do. One man can make another stumble and do evil (ix. 42). Likewise a man's own hand or eye or foot may lead him to sin (ix. 43–7). And while Mark quite clearly indicates by his use of Old Testament

---

[1] Mark uses two words, the root πωροῦν and σκληροκαρδία (x. 5). The former may mean 'blindness' rather than 'hardness'; cf. J. A. Robinson, *Ephesians*, pp. 264 ff. In either case blame attaches to the person; even if it is held that God has blinded or hardened the heart (cf. John xii. 40) the moral responsibility remains; cf. K. L. and M. A. Schmidt, *T.W.N.T.* v₄ 1024 ff.

[2] Cf. above, p. 30.

quotations that the supreme evil of the Cross was ordained of God, he also clearly traces it to the sin of men. This evil intent of the heart is seen as early in his narrative as iii. 1–6; it appears again in the hostile way in which the Jewish leaders seek to entrap Jesus with their questions so that he will stumble and put himself in their power to destroy him (xii. 13 ff.); the sin of the traitor in xiv. 17–21 may be also linked to the fulfilment of the divine purpose, but not in such a way that the human sin is excused. And throughout the Passion itself the evil of men's hearts is depicted in the way in which they ill-treat and abuse and mock Jesus. Thus he encountered the evil in the hearts of men.

At no point is this evil traced to the work of Satan or to demonic forces. The only apparent exception is viii. 33,[1] and this as we have already seen does not imply that Peter is the tool of Satan or that Satan is active at this point. In contrast Luke quite clearly makes the act of Judas in betraying Jesus an action inspired by Satan (xxii. 3), but this represents his general tendency to intensify the work of spiritual forces both good and evil; thus the denial by Peter is also traced to Satan (xxii. 31–4); this would again warn us against reading these forces back into the historical life of Jesus; they may rather represent interpretative elements of the early Church. In Mark the evil in men whereby they are led to oppose Jesus is consistently led back to the evil intent of their own hearts; it is from within man that evil comes and goes out from him both to render himself unclean and to injure others. The fact that men's culpable spiritual blindness (iv. 10–12) is traced to God shows how far Mark is removed from a Satanic explanation of evil—and from our ideas.

It might however be argued that Mark is simply repeating the tradition as he received it and that the common way of expressing the origin of evil was to trace it to men; Mark, while

---

[1] iv. 15 in the interpretation to the Parable of the Sower might also be regarded as an exception; but whatever the original meaning of the parable Mark clearly sees the attack of Satan in the interpretation as an attack on the followers of Jesus and not on Jesus himself. It is moreover interesting that only one of the three classes of failure is said to be attributed to Satan; the failure of the other two classes is attributed to tribulation and covetousness; it is unjustified to carry over the attribution to Satan in the first instance to the other two. This is just another example of the fact that Mark sees temptation coming from different sources of which Satan is one, but not the only one.

holding to another theory, the Satanic origin of temptation, does not vary the tradition. This is rendered most unlikely by two factors. (*a*) The attribution of evil to Satan is precisely the kind of matter which an editor could vary in the tradition without seriously affecting the main message of a pericope. That he would be likely to do so is evidenced by the fact that Luke did exactly this with the tradition in making Satan the author of Judas' betrayal and Peter's denials. Mark does not so vary the tradition. (*b*) Some of the passages to which we have drawn attention as evidence that for Mark evil begins in the heart of man are probably his own editorial insertions (iii. 6;[1] vi. 6; vi. 52, cf. viii. 17) and not derived from the tradition. Thus when Mark had an absolutely free hand he did not introduce the Devil as the origin of temptation.

Confirmation of this may be seen in the very different attitude which Jesus takes up to sin in men and to sickness or demonic possession. Sickness and demons are regarded as invading man from outside and must be driven out of him. Sin is too much a part of man to be dealt with in that way. We may begin by noting that when Jesus deals with a demoniac he addresses the demon and not the man who is possessed by it. Until the demon has been expelled the victim is passive in the interview. The sick many times come to Jesus requesting healing for themselves (i. 40; x. 47); Jesus himself speaks to the sick directly (ii. 5, 11; iii. 3; x. 51); he seeks their co-operation in their healing through their faith (v. 34; x. 52; cf. vi. 5, 6); sometimes it is the co-operation of others that leads to their healing (vii. 26–9; ix. 23, 24). This in itself then brings out a difference in the way in which Jesus deals with the sick from that in which he deals with the demoniac, suggesting that for Mark sickness cannot always be seen under the rubric of possession. In sickness the sick person is still a responsible agent able to take part in the healing. Jesus' approach to the sick is different from his approach to the demoniac.

When now we turn to consider how Jesus deals with the evil in the heart of men we see that this distinction is carried further; he is now concerned always to talk with the person himself and

---

[1] Dibelius, pp. 44 f.; Bultmann, p. 63, hold that it is Markan. Taylor; Knox, 1, 9, 11 f.; Lohmeyer; Schmidt, p. 100 consider it part of the traditional material.

induce his co-operation. We may examine his early encounters with opponents as Mark groups them together in ii. 1–iii. 6. Their opposition to Jesus is not necessarily outwardly spoken, but in each case Jesus deals with it by way of argument. On one occasion (ii. 25 f.) the argument is based on Scripture, but on each of the other occasions it reaches down to the true understanding of the relationship of man to God; in iii. 1–6 Jesus penetrates to the true meaning of the Sabbath; in ii. 15–17 he shows the full outreach of the love of God, which cannot be confined to the righteous; in ii. 1–12 he appeals to his opponents to realise the might of God in dealing with sickness and sin. In each case he is concerned, not to show them up in the eyes of bystanders, but to lead them to a fuller comprehension of the ways of God with men. He puts forward a genuine argument in which he attempts to win them over to his own position. The same is true where he encounters his opponents over clean and unclean foods (vii. 1 ff.) and over divorce (x. 2 ff.). It may seem in the series of debates beginning in xii. 13–40, concerning the payment of tribute to Caesar, the resurrection from the dead,[1] the nature of the greatest commandment, and David's Son, that Jesus is a little more abrupt with some of his opponents, seeking rather to show that they are in the wrong than to convince them of their errors. We would note first that these four incidents appear to form a stylised pattern based in part on the questions asked in the Passover Haggadah;[2] thus the main pattern with its rejection of the questioners is motivated by this underlying structure rather than by any sense that opponents are silenced like demons. Secondly, we must remember that the actual form of such a pericope as xii. 13–17, where Jesus seems to silence the Pharisees with a clever retort, lies in the nature of what is happening; stories told of great men always show them silencing their opponents with astute answers. Thirdly, in the passage Mark xii. 13–40 Jesus' somewhat

---

[1] Matt. xxii. 34 might provide an argument for a demonic understanding of these debates since here it is said that Jesus 'muzzled' (ἐφίμωσεν) the Sadducees; this verb is used of Jesus' exorcism of demons in Mark i. 25 (cf. iv. 39). If so this would be a Matthean heightening of the demonic; unfortunately for such a view Matthew does not use φιμοῦν in describing Jesus' exorcisms.

[2] Cf. D. Daube, *The New Testament and Rabbinic Judaism*, pp. 158 ff.

sharper tone may be accounted for by the fact that his opponents, with the exception of the scribe of *v.* 28, are out to trip
him in order to have an accusation against him, rather than
that they are genuinely seeking information. The same is true
of viii. 11–13. Thus nothing more than the normal sin of men
can be seen in xii. 13–40; Jesus does not treat his opponents as
he treats demons.

Now if it can be argued that the Markan Jesus seeks to enlighten his opponents with truth by his answers it must also be
said at the same time that he intends to puzzle them. This is
Mark's well-known secrecy motif. Jesus muzzles the demons
who would say who he is (i. 25; i. 34, etc.); he forbids the
healed to go round talking about him (i. 44; v. 43, etc.); he
hides himself from men (i. 35; iii. 7; vii. 24). In relation to his
teaching this comes out most acutely in the statement about
parables (iv. 11, 12): the mystery of the Kingdom is deliberately
hidden from those who are 'outside'. It is impossible to deduce
from this that those 'outside' are in any way demonically
possessed. Before they encounter him, the devils already know
the nature of his power and being; the sick in their encounter
become at least partly aware of these; those 'outside' are on the
other hand kept in ignorance; their knowledge is not silenced;
it simply does not exist, and it would appear the effort is made
to keep it from existing. We are not concerned with the question
of the genuineness of this saying about 'parables', nor with its
place in the teaching of the historical Jesus, but only with the
understanding which its present form gives us of Mark's
theology. It is probable that παραβολαῖς is not to be restricted
here to what we normally call 'parables', that is, illustrative
stories or similitudes.

Hence in the evangelist's vocabulary παραβολή was a comprehensive
term. It labelled forms of speech and actions in so far as both kinds
of activity were regarded as media through which the μυστήριον
of the kingdom of God was finding expression, though in such a
manner as to be hidden from οἱ ἔξω.[1]

Mark quotes here from Isa. vi. 9, 10 using a text similar to that
of the Targum. He applies the text to the unbelieving Jews of

[1] G. H. Boobyer, 'The Redaction of Mark iv. 1–34', *N.T.S.* VIII (1961),
59–70, at p. 64.

Jesus' time. These are kept in the dark as to the purpose of Jesus' coming so that they do not understand; matters are however explained privately to the disciples (iv. 33, 34). It is Jesus himself who acts and speaks in such a way that the outsider does not comprehend, and for the Evangelist this means that ultimately God is responsible for the way in which revelation is veiled. Thus it is not to any action of Satan that we should attribute the blindness of the Jews but to God himself.

There is consequently a twofold attitude of Jesus towards his opponents. On the one hand he attempts to enlighten them in argument and on the other he seeks to veil revelation from their sight. Looking at this from another angle we may say that men are both morally responsible and that at the same time they play a role in history determined by God. This appears most vividly in the case of Judas (xiv. 21): the Son of Man must be crucified because it is written, and therefore ordained of God, and yet Judas is fully responsible. This twofold character is probably also present at the back of the conception of 'hardness of heart' when viewed against its Old Testament origin.[1] The double attitude of Jesus in Mark may perhaps also be explained in another way. Where Jesus explains to men the error of their positions he is usually dealing with misunderstandings of already existing revelation in the Old Testament, for example the Sabbath law or the teaching on purity and uncleanness, but where he veils his true meaning it is in relation to his own purpose and the mystery of the kingdom.

When we examine the discussions Jesus has with his disciples, we find again that he attempts to explain difficulties to them; for example, he endeavours to dissipate their hardness of heart (viii. 14–21). To a large extent the twofold veiling and explanation of revelation disappears and the emphasis lies on the explanation. Thus the parables are explained to the disciples (iv. 34). When they do not understand the coming Passion he explains to them three times what is about to happen to himself (viii. 31; ix. 31; x. 33 f.). He even encourages them to say out plainly among themselves who he is, for he asks them that very question (viii. 29). Peter is only rebuked when he refuses to accept the revelation that is given to him (viii. 33), unlike the demons who are rebuked because they announce the revelation

[1] Cf. p. 36, n. 1 and K. L. and M. A. Schmidt, *T.W.N.T.* v, 1024 ff.

that should be kept quiet from men. Thus Jesus is ready to treat his disciples as full human beings who can come to a position in which they can know the truth of God; for their culpable ignorance he holds them responsible and does not blame any hidden demonic influence.

The final encounter of Jesus with evil takes place naturally in the Passion.[1] The whole Gospel builds up to this event. Here again we note the twofold character we observed earlier. On the one hand the Passion proceeds from the evil of men's hearts and on the other its happening is predetermined. The former of these elements begins early in the Gospel with the first sequence of encounters between Jesus and his opponents (ii. 1–iii. 6), which ends with their resolve that he must be put to death (iii. 6). This opposition mounts against him until it bursts in the plot of Judas with the priests and scribes to betray him to death (xiv. 1, 2, 10, 11). From now on at every turn evil appears; the disciples flee (xiv. 50); Peter denies him (xiv. 66–72); false witnesses are brought out against him (xiv. 56–9); he is mocked, spat on, humiliated (xiv. 65; xv. 16–20, 29–32); Pilate clearly designates the envy of the priests which has moved them to kill him (xv. 10). This evil is intensified by the clear indications of his innocence: true witnesses against him cannot be found (xiv. 55); Pilate asks what evil he has done (xv. 14); he is crucified between two obvious wrongdoers (xv. 27); the centurion who watches him die proclaims his innocence in announcing his true nature (xv. 39). What is the reaction of Jesus to this evil in the heart of man? Silence! (xiv. 60 f.; xv. 5). He who had rebuked the demons and told them to keep silence about his true nature now bears silently the evil of men; he who had carefully explained to men their failure to understand the purposes of God now offers no more explanations. The silence is only broken three times. Twice he clearly states who he is (xiv. 62; xv. 2); if previously he has explained men's errors in their interpretation of God's law and kept secret the nature of his person, the process is now reversed: for now he proclaims his own nature and refuses to protest against the injustice of his trial. The third time in which he breaks silence is the cry of dereliction; this however is not addressed to his opponents. Thus the whole attitude of Jesus is one of acceptance

[1] A fuller treatment of the Passion story is given later, pp. 89 ff.

towards the evil that crowds in on him; he does not fight against it but accepts it. This is congruent with that aspect of the Passion in which it is seen to proceed not merely from the evil in the heart of man but also from the inevitableness of the Cross. It has been prophesied by Jesus himself; all happens according to the Scriptures (xiv. 49) now that the hour is come (xiv. 41). Mark makes few direct quotations from the Old Testament, but his whole Passion narrative is full of allusions to it; this very allusiveness shows how deeply determination according to the Scriptures has entered into his view of the Passion. Thus there is no suggestion that behind all this in Mark there is an ever-active Satan leading men on to destroy the Christ so that he may be brought into his (Satan's) power. Men are evil in themselves, but they act in accordance with prophecy.

All this is external evil, coming from outside to assail Jesus, but we have already seen that in the Passion Jesus has to meet evil which begins within himself: xiv. 34–6. The words here are extreme; Jesus is horrified by the prospect of immediate death. His soul is cast down;[1] his will rebels against God's will. It is gratuitous to see at this point a return of the Devil to claim his prey. Jesus is terrified by death, the cup which he must drink, and not by the Devil. But through prayer the incipient weakness within himself is met and he goes to encounter that which he fears. The most terrible evil in the Gospel is not the demonic or sickness but the evil in the heart of man; it comes to its climax in the Passion and lays its hand even on the heart of the Christ himself. It is not diabolical but human.

To summarise, we may say: Evil meets Jesus from different sources in Mark; its origin may lie in demonic forces, in which case it is not moral evil; where Jesus is assailed by sin, this is seen to originate in the human heart; occasionally this is traced back to God's hardening of the heart; Jesus fights sin in men by seeking to lead them to truth and men are held morally responsible for their actions. The nature of the attack by Satan on Jesus is not made clear in the Temptation story; it may well have been temptation to sin. Consequently we may say that for Mark evil may originate with Satan or in the human heart, though not necessarily the heart of the person who is subject to

[1] Cf. Ps. xlii (xli). 6, 12; xliii (xlii). 5; Jonah ii. 8; iv. 9; Ps. xxii (xxi). 15; Ps. cxvi (cxiv). 3.

the temptation. The interpretation of the Parable of the Sower is a perfect illustration of the variety of sources from which temptation may come: Satan (iv. 15); persecution, that is, evil originating with other men (iv. 17); covetousness, that is, evil originating within the heart of the person who is tempted (iv. 19).

We must now go on to ask how this fits into the general biblical pattern. Where in the biblical and post-biblical material does sin get its grip on man? Is man continually tempted by a devil who is outside him and waits to lure him astray, or does temptation begin either with himself in his own heart or with others who lead him astray? Since we are primarily concerned with temptation it is unnecessary to widen our inquiry to seek the origin of sickness and physical evil of various kinds.

THE OLD TESTAMENT

Since our question is not, 'How did sin enter into the world?', but rather, 'Where does temptation to a particular sin begin?', we do not need to discuss in detail Gen. iii and its account of the Fall of man;[1] we may note that this has little influence on the Old Testament teaching about sin and temptation and that within the Old Testament period the serpent is not identified with Satan. But the story does show sin as coming to man from outside him; the serpent tempts Eve. We must recognise that within the biblical record this is a historical event, and not, as it is so often interpreted, a typical event showing how temptation and sin enter the life of every man. It cannot thus be taken as representing the beginning of temptation in each man; it is an individual event. But as such it shows that for the Old Testament the onslaught of temptation can be seen as coming from outside; but equally it comes from outside to Adam, who is tempted not by Satan but by Eve. Likewise Jezebel entices Ahab into sin (I Kings xxi. 5 ff.) and Potiphar's wife attempted to seduce Joseph (Gen. xxxix. 6 ff.). Thus temptation comes from

---

[1] Cf. C. R. Smith, *The Bible Doctrine of Sin*, pp. 37 ff.; W. Eichrodt, *Theologie des Alten Testaments*[4], II/III, pp. 278 ff.; N. P. Williams, *The Ideas of the Fall and of Original Sin*, pp. 12 ff., 39 ff.; F. R. Tennant, *The Fall and Original Sin*, *passim*.

fellow-humans. But it may also start within a man himself. Jeremiah's statement, 'The heart is deceitful above all things, and desperately corrupt; who can understand it?' (xvii. 9), may go further than much Old Testament teaching, but it is correct in seeing the origin of actual sin in the inner life of man. Thus Esau says in his heart that he will kill his brother Jacob (Gen. xxvii. 41) and God sees that the thoughts of man's heart are evil (Gen. vi. 5). This inwardness of the source of evil comes out more and more as we proceed through the Old Testament. We find it in the Deuteronomist (xv. 7, a hardened heart; viii. 14, an arrogant heart leading to rebellion against God), but more especially in Jeremiah and Ezekiel. For both the heart is the source of sin (Jer. iii. 17; xvi. 12, etc.; Ezek. vi. 9; xiii. 2, etc.) and the new man for the new age will have a new heart (Jer. iv. 14; xxiv. 7; xxxi. 33; Ezek. xi. 19; xviii. 31; xxxvi. 26—a heart of flesh instead of a heart of stone). The priestly writer testifies to the same (II Chron. xxv. 19; xxvi. 16; xxxii. 25; xxxvi. 13); and the idea is also found in the Psalms (li. 12, 19; xxxvi. 2–5; liii. 2) and Job (xiv. 4; xv. 14–16; cf. Prov. xii. 20).

There is also another element in the Old Testament which traces sin in men to evil spirits. We have seen that the Fall is not to be taken as in any way showing the general manner in which sin takes place as response to a temptation from the Devil, but there are perhaps other instances of this. There is the evil spirit from the Lord which comes on Saul and leads him to attempt to kill David (I Sam. xvi. 14; xviii. 10–12; xix. 8–10); we may note that this spirit comes from God and that it is regarded as 'possessing' Saul rather than as tempting him (cf. Judges ix. 23). The spirit is sent by God to punish (cf. also Hos. iv. 12; v. 4; Isa. xxix. 10; xix. 14; Num. v. 14).[1] The same idea underlies I Kings (xxii. 20 ff. where God wishes to lure Ahab to his destruction and one of the spirits of his council goes to lie to Ahab; this is not temptation. Nor strictly speaking is Job's encounter with Satan; Satan is sent by God to try Job; he never explicitly attempts to make Job sin; it is Job's wife who does this (ii. 9). In Zech. iii. 1, 2 Satan appears in his earlier role of 'accuser'. Perhaps the most interesting case is that of I Chron. xxi. 1 where Satan, through opposition to Israel,

[1] Thus Eichrodt, *op. cit.* p. 30. On 'temptation' in the Old Testament see C. R. Smith, *The Bible Doctrine of Grace*, ch. v.

entices David to number the people; in the earlier account
(II Sam. xxiv. 1 ff.) it is God who incites David because he is
angry with Israel; probably the later account must be read in
the light of the earlier and Satan be regarded as the tool of
God as in Job and not as acting independently. Thus we cannot
see in the Old Testament any clear place where Satan is
depicted as an independent tempter of men to evil, though the
support for such a view could be drawn from a passage like
I Chron. xxi. 1 once the role of Satan as tempter had been
clearly defined. Rather God through his spirit(s) may be
viewed as the author of temptation. The origin of sin thus
largely lies within man himself in the Old Testament; where he
is tempted from without it is not generally the work of Satan
but of other humans, or even of God.

THE INTER-TESTAMENTAL LITERATURE

Here we find exactly the same view. Men follow the evil that
rises within themselves (I Baruch i. 22; Tobit iv. 13; I Esdras
i. 46; Sir. xii. 16; vi. 2; v. 2; Wisd. iv. 12; I Macc. xi. 8; II
Macc. xiv. 3). In Sir. xv. 14 it is said that God created man at
the first and 'left him in the power of his own inclination', and
the context shows that this refers to all men and not to Adam
alone.

In Sirach and Wisdom the evidence, taken together, shows that the
two Sages believed that in a man's mind there are a number of
'desires'—some a-moral, some moral, some immoral—which all
somehow appeal to him to choose them, but *until* he chooses, he is
neither moral nor immoral. *When* he commits himself to a good
desire (and it becomes his motive), he is good; when he commits
himself to a bad desire, he is bad. The *will* is the organ of sin, and
in so far as a man *chooses* bad motives he is sinful. . . . Evil desires
are a man's own.[1]

But if men follow the evil within themselves they also may be led
to evil by the influence of others (Sir. xi. 29–34; vi. 5–13).
Apart from IV Ezra (= II Esdras) the origin of sin in the world
is not traced to Satan; in Wisd. ii. 24 death is so traced and in
Sir. xxv. 24 Eve is described as the beginning of sin, but there

[1] C. R. Smith, *The Bible Doctrine of Sin*, p. 85.

is no real doctrine of original sin. IV Ezra (iii. 21 f.; iv. 30; vii. 116–18) comes much nearer such a doctrine; through the sin of Adam man is given a powerful tendency towards sin, but each man remains free to sin or not to sin; he is accountable for his sin and the tendency within himself to sin is his own. Thus so far we have seen no evidence for the idea that temptation comes from Satan to man, apart from the once-for-all incident of Adam, and even in that case the role of Satan is by no means stressed (cf. especially the passages in IV Ezra). It is only made clear in Wisd. ii. 24; here the serpent may be, though not necessarily is, identified with the Devil;[1] the latter is opposed to God, and is probably no longer his agent. The very omission of reference to the Devil in the day-to-day tempting of men to sin is the more conspicuous.[2] Satan is not then in the Apocrypha the ordinary source of temptation.

Among the rabbis sin is connected above all with the evil impulse in man (יצר הרע).[3] This is probably the same as the *cor malignum* of IV Ezra and the διαβούλιον of Sir. xv. 14. Man has been created with the *yetzer ha-ra'*; it is there from birth having been placed in man by God.

The opportunity or the invitation to sin may come from without, but it is the response of the evil impulse in man to it that converts it into a temptation. It pictures in imagination the pleasures of sin, conceives the plan, seduces the will, incites to the act. It is thus primarily as the subjective origin of temptation, or more correctly as the tempter within, that the *yeṣer ha-ra'* is represented in Jewish literature.[4]

The evil impulse is not connected with the body or flesh in any dualistic fashion but following the general trends of Old Testa-

---

[1] Cf. Fichtner; Holmes (in Charles, *Apocrypha and Pseudepigrapha*), etc., *ad loc*. The reference may, however, be to the incident of Gen. iv (cf. Geyer; Gregg, etc., *ad loc*.): Cain's murder of Abel. If that view is taken we have here a case of temptation by the Devil.

[2] Sir. xxi. 27 does not necessitate a reference to Satan; cf. R.S.V. rendering. Tob. iii. 8, 17 refers to an evil demon who has slain men; there is no reference to temptation.

[3] Cf. Moore, I, 474 ff.; Strack–Billerbeck, IV, 466 ff.; W. D. Davies, *Paul and Rabbinic Judaism*, pp. 20 ff.; S. Schechter, *Some Aspects of Rabbinic Theology* (London, 1909), pp. 219–92; Williams, *The Ideas of the Fall and of Original Sin*, pp. 60 ff.; Tennant, *The Fall and Original Sin*, pp. 145 ff.

[4] Moore, I, 481 f.

ment and Jewish anthropology with the heart. We may recall how our examination of the Old Testament has shown how often evil begins within a man in his own heart; the Rabbinic conception of the evil impulse ties in with this. To balance the evil impulse man is given a good impulse (יצר טוב). The evil impulse may be defeated through meditation on the Torah and by the stirring up of the good impulse. Normally the evil impulse is impersonal, but it is frequently personified.[1] It may then be identified with Satan or with the angel of death. However, the Rabbinic references to Satan as the tempter of man are not themselves frequent; for the rabbis Satan is rather man's accuser before God than his tempter, though his activity as tempter is witnessed as early as R. Akiba (†135).[2] The emphasis which the rabbis lay on Satan is very slight compared to that which they lay on the evil impulse; this latter is mentioned again and again in their writings without any reference to Satan. The two ideas must have co-existed; temptation may come from without through Satan who appears, perhaps as a prostitute as in the cases of R. Akiba and R. Meir,[3] but temptation also comes, and more frequently, from within man, from the evil impulse created in him by God, there being no suggestion that this latter is excited by Satan.

In the writings of the Qumran community the Devil occupies a more prominent position than in the earlier Jewish literature; in this the Dead Sea Scrolls are closely linked to the Apocalyptic books, many fragments of which, of course, have been found in the caves. The Devil is normally called Belial; the names Satan and Mastema occur respectively three and four times;[4] the favourite Rabbinic designation, Sammael, does not occur at all. Even where Satan and Mastema are used it is not always clear if these denote the Devil. This is true also of Belial; on each occasion of its use we have to look carefully to see if it is a proper name or a noun.

The noun בליעל, which in the M.T. can mean 'wickedness, worthlessness' (Deut. xv. 9; Nah. i. 11) but also 'worthless,

---

[1] Moore, I, 492 f.

[2] Cf. Strack–Billerbeck, I, 139 ff.; III, 109 f., 372 f.; Foerster, *T.W.N.T.* II, 74 ff.

[3] Cf. Qid 81a, quoted in Strack–Billerbeck, III, 109 f.

[4] Cf. K. G. Kuhn, *Konkordanz zu den Qumrantexten.*

wicked men' in the phrases 'sons of Belial, men of Belial'
(Judges xix. 22; xx. 13; I Sam. i. 16; xxx. 22; I Kings xxi. 13;
Prov. vi. 12; xvi. 27), now becomes extended to represent a
power outside man and attacking him. But it can still occur as
an ordinary noun as in the M.T. (cf. 1QH iv. 10; ii. 22; vii. 3).
The difficulties of interpretation may be seen in the fact that
Kuhn[1] lists all the occurrences in 1QH as nouns, whereas
Mansoor[2] takes many of them as proper names, denoting the
Devil. In 1QM Belial, who has been created by God (xiii. 11),
appears clearly as the leader of the spiritual hosts of wickedness
with whom the community is engaged in an apocalyptic war.
He is here the enemy of the community rather than of the
individual, and is in no way associated with tempting men to do
evil, except at xiii. 11, 12 where he is said to seek to destroy
men, making them guilty;[3] this latter is also the passage in which
he is said to have been created by God, so that there is no
absolute dualism (cf. 1QS iii. 18 ff.); it is also possible that there
is here a reference to his fall, but the text is corrupt.[4] When we
turn to the other writings we find that his activities cover a
wider range, in large part the same as that of the two senses of
the Greek word πειράζειν, namely, 'testing, tempting'. This
is the age of Belial (1QS i. 17, 18; ii. 19; cf. 1QM xiv. 9) and
it is a period of stress and trial for the members of the community (1QS i. 17, 18). Those outside the community are the
men of Belial's lot (1QS ii. 4, 5), who oppose the sons of light
just as Belial raised up Jamnes and his brother to oppose Moses
and Aaron (C.D. v. 18, 19). Belial has been let loose (presumably by God) and uses his three nets of whoredom, wealth and
uncleanness to snare Israel (C.D. iv. 13–19), but since God lets
Belial loose for this purpose this must be a testing rather than a
tempting. Nor is the reference to the sins of Israel during the
ascendancy of Belial a necessary allusion to him as tempter
(1QS i. 23, 24); the Emperor Domitian would not be described
as tempting Christians because during the persecution he
instituted some of them apostasised. However, at this stage we

---

[1] *Ibid.*

[2] *The Thanksgiving Hymns*; cf. especially p. 108, n. 1.

[3] Three words are used שחת (Pi'el; this, however, may denote his own
destruction), רשע (Hiphil), אשם (Hiphil).

[4] Cf. J. van der Ploeg, *Le Rouleau de la Guerre, ad loc.*

are not far from the conception of temptation and it is at times difficult to draw a line between testing and temptation. The devices of Belial with which the writer of the hymns is assailed by men of deceit (1QH ii. 16, cf. iv. 12–14) bring us closer to temptation, though Belial may not here be a proper name. Again the writer is slandered by those on whom Belial has worked (1QH v. 26). Similarly in two passages from the fourth cave (4QFl i. 8, 9; 4QT 23) men of Belial ensnare others and make them stumble. We should notice that in all these references Belial does not attack the members of the community directly but through men who are already in his power; in that sense he is only a tempter at second hand. 1QH vi. 21 may seem to provide a case of certain temptation, but the text reads quite straightforwardly if we take Belial as a noun; it then says that a wicked counsel is in the heart of men; the same is true of 1QS x. 21. This shows the difficulty of being precise in an assertion that Belial tempts—or does not tempt; in these two passages, where we come nearest to the conception of Belial as the one who attacks in order to ensnare the soul, we cannot be certain that it is Belial as a personal being who is meant, and not just wickedness. Belial appears also as punishing men (C.D. viii. 2) and as destroying (1QH iii. 28, 29), and we may assume he acts therein as the agent of God. The case of a man who falls into the power of the spirits of Belial is regarded as possession and contrasted with sin (C.D. xii. 2, 3).

Mastema occurs four times; certainly at 1QM xiii. 4, 11 it is a noun and not a proper name, unless we are to regard Belial as the angel of Mastema, which is most unlikely. At 1QS iii. 23 it may be either noun or proper name; it appears in the passage about the two spirits, which we shall shortly see does show temptation as coming from a spirit.[1] At C.D. xvi. 5 Mastema may be a proper name; the angel of Mastema is said to leave a man when he takes seriously the Law of Moses; this appears to imply temptation, and we may note the similarity to the Q narrative of the Temptations of Jesus, in that the words of the Law defeat Satan. The name Satan occurs only in fragmentary portions of the Dead Sea Scrolls (1QHf iv. 6; xlv. 3; 1QSb i. 8) and it is not possible to draw any firm deductions from its use.

The passage on the two spirits (1QS iii. 17 ff.) is very relevant

[1] Cf. P. Wernberg-Møller, *The Manual of Discipline*, *ad loc*.

to our purpose, though it stands in some isolation from the rest of the Dead Sea Scrolls since the doctrine of the two spirits is not found elsewhere in the Scrolls; it may not then be normative. The Spirit of deceit, made by God, and apparently equated with the angel of darkness, rules the sons of deceit and attempts to make the sons of righteousness err; the latter are generally under the protection of the spirit of truth, or the prince of lights. The reign of the angel of darkness is the cause of all the sins, offences, guilt and iniquitous deeds of the members of the community; the spirits associated with him seek to make the members stumble (1QS iii. 22–4). At iv. 8–11 a long list is given of the sins caused by the spirit of deceit. We have then here a clear picture of an outside power attacking man in order to lead him to sin, that is, tempting him. There is a certain resemblance to the doctrine of the good and evil impulses in man as found in Rabbinism, in that, were it not for the mention of the angel of darkness, the spirits of truth and deceit could be seen as indwelling the hearts of members of the community like the good and evil impulses; but the angel of darkness implies an outside power. Thus in this passage definitely, and to some extent elsewhere, we find temptation viewed as coming to man from spiritual powers of darkness and not just as emerging from within man himself.

But we also find in the Qumran writings the predominant teaching of the Old Testament, namely, that evil starts within the heart of man. In the Thanksgiving Hymns the psalmist describes himself as 'the foundation of shamefulness, and the source of impurity; the crucible of iniquity, and the edifice of sin'[1] (i. 22, 23; cf. xii. 24, 25). Though this and similar statements are used by the writer of himself it may be assumed that they do not misrepresent the conception of the source of temptation among the community as a whole. So we find the hymn writer referring also to the (evil) devices of his imagination (v. 6), the lusts of the heart (v. 26). In the *Manual of Discipline* those who walk in the stubbornness of their hearts are continually rebuked (i. 6; ii. 14, 26; iii. 3; v. 4, 5; vii. 18, 19, 24; cf. C.D. ii. 18; viii. 19; xx. 9, 10). The eyes and the mind can lead astray (1QS i. 6; v. 4, 5; xi. 9; C.D. ii. 16). So also a man is led into evil by his spirit, whose desires he chooses (C.D. iii. 7, 11, 12; 1QS vii. 18, 19, 23; viii. 12). Men may be said to

[1] Mansoor's translation.

pervert themselves (1QS i. 24). A man may also be said to have a perverted spirit (1QH iii. 21; i. 22; xi. 12), and the human spirit is meant. The same phrase occurs at 1QH xiii. 15 where it is said that a perverted spirit has dominion over man; Mansoor[1] takes this to be an external evil spirit, but it might as easily be the man's own perverse spirit which rules him and leads him to evil.

The two conceptions of temptation as coming from outside and as beginning within man himself can sometimes lie close beside one another, as in 1QH iv. 12–15 (cf. v. 26), where men are said to plot the devices of Belial, but are then described as seeking God with a double heart, as having a root that breeds gall and wormwood in their thoughts and as going astray with stubborn hearts. This anomaly is removed if we take Belial here as a noun, 'worthlessness', rather than as a proper noun; but the co-existence of the two ideas is not impossible in so far as one may be seen to be the original conception of the Old Testament and the other as entering through Iranian influence.

It may also be that the conception of 'flesh'[2] in these writings suggests the origin of sin within man himself. In accordance with the general usage of *basar*, flesh is man in his humanity, often as opposed to God; but there are also references to 'flesh of sin, deceit, guilt' (1QS xi. 9, 12; 1QM iv. 3; xii. 12); flesh can be cleansed (1QS iii. 9; iv. 21). In regard to 1QS xi. 12 Kuhn says, 'Sin is brought about through "flesh" as that which qualifies human existence as such'.[3] In line with this is Mansoor's translation of 1QH x. 23, 'carnal intent thou hast not assigned for me'; the impulse (yetzer) of the flesh is sin. Flesh should not of course be equated with the body as if only sexual sins were meant; the wide meaning of flesh as man in his totality is always present. Sin can thus arise within man himself; there is no suggestion that the Devil takes hold of man through his flesh.

As in the Old Testament temptation can of course come from outside a man from other men, as distinct from spiritual powers

[1] *Ad loc.*
[2] Cf. K. G. Kuhn, 'New Light on Temptation, Sin and Flesh in the New Testament', and W. D. Davies, 'Paul and the Dead Sea Scrolls: Flesh and Spirit', both in *The Scrolls and the New Testament*, pp. 94–113, 157–82 (ed. K. Stendahl); Meyer, *T.W.N.T.* VII, 109–13.
[3] Kuhn, *op. cit.* p. 103.

of wickedness. Thus one man may be a snare to another (1QH ii. 8, 10, 11; 4Qp Nah. ii. 8). False prophets lead men astray (1QH iv. 16 f.; cf. C.D. i. 15; 1Qp Hab. x. 9); the hymn writer encounters opponents who would lead him into evil (1QH v.10, 11, 23–36). So certain men are excluded from the community because they may tempt others (1QS v. 14 ff.).

Turning now to the Apocalyptic writings we find that the spiritual powers of evil occupy an important place and that correspondingly the Devil has become more prominent. In the different writings he appears under various names, for example, Beliar, Mastema, Satan, Sammael; though in some writings he features rarely if at all.[1] He is often seen in the role of tempter in which we are interested; and he appears in this role in almost all the books in which he figures at all largely. Thus we find him enticing men in Jub. i. 20; x. 1; xi. 4, 5; Adam and Eve x. 4; I Enoch viii. 1 ff. (here it is the fallen angels who have the role); xix. 1; lxix. 4–6; T. Dan. i. 7; v. 6; T. Joseph vii. 4; T. Benj. vii. 1, 2; II Enoch xxxi. 6, 7.

Yet at the same time we find that men are tempted by their fellows; this appears particularly in these writings in the way in which women are regarded as enticing men to sexual sin: for example, Jub. xxxix. 5 ff.; T. Reub. v. 3. In Jub. xvii. 4 Sarah becomes jealous when she sees Abraham happy with Ishmael. There is one strange passage in which women are considered to tempt angels, I Enoch vi (cf. lxix. 4), the role of tempter being completely reversed. Concurrently with these trends tracing temptation to Satan and other human beings, we find that evil is also considered as beginning in men's minds. This may not be as prominent here as in certain other parts of the material we have examined; but it needs to be remembered that by the very nature of the case the Apocalyptic writings were not greatly taken up with actual descriptions of the way in which evil actions were conceived and performed but rather with supernatural forces as they appeared at the beginning and end of the world and with their effect on the course of history, individual and national. Yet we do find many statements that suggest that the authors had not abandoned the dominant trend of Old Testament thinking which saw evil as originating within man himself.

[1] In each of *Ass. Moses* and *Sib. Or.* one reference only and none in II Baruch.

In I Enoch xcviii. 4 it is said that sin has come from man himself and *v.* 12 of the same chapter speaks of men who love deeds of unrighteousness. In T. Reub. iii. 12 Reuben says that his mind led him to sin taking in the thought of a woman's nakedness. Many times men are spoken of as 'corrupting themselves' (Jub. v. 10, 19; xxxvi. 8). Men devise evil against others (Jub. xxxvi. 8; xxxvii. 12); a man may be evilly disposed in his heart towards another and so seek to slay him (Jub. xxxvii. 24; cf. *v.* 12; Mart. Isa. i. 12, 13). Men follow their own devices which are regarded as evil (T. Issach. vi. 2). The impulse of youth may blind a man's mind and lead him to sin (T. Judah xi. 1; xiii. 6; cf. xiv. 1 ff.). Sin and evil are attributed to the imagination and desire of men (Jub. vii. 24; v. 2). In the T. Asher i. 3 ff. we meet the two inclinations or impulses which figure so largely in Rabbinic thought on temptation. There are some strange phrases which suggest that Satan takes possession of a man after he has given his heart to evil; in Mart. Isa. ii. 4 Manasseh turns aside his heart to serve Beliar; here Beliar is conceived as a strange god rather than as devil. In T. Simeon v. 3 it is said that fornication brings a man nearer to Beliar, rather than that Beliar incites a man to fornication. In the vast majority of cases where evil is described in these writings (e.g. Jub. xxiii. 14 ff.; xxiv. 6; I Enoch xcv. 1 ff.; xcix. 1 ff.) it is neither attributed to Satan nor is it suggested that it began in man himself; but since the latter was the predominant view within Israel preceding the appearance of Satan on the scene, it must be assumed that where no mention is made of Satan then he is not to be implicitly supposed as active, but that the author held the view of the Old Testament which attributed temptation either to the man himself or to other men. In a number of passages the two ideas that evil begins within man and that it is incited in him by Satan are held in almost adjoining verses (Jub. vii. 24 and 27; T. Dan. i. 4, 7; T. Reub. iii. 1–11), thus showing that in this period no one point of view held sway.

Looking back now over the path which we have traversed from the Old Testament through late Judaism to the New Testament period we see that there are three ways in which a man may be incited to do evil: temptation may start within himself, it may start in the world around him and it may start supernaturally through an assault by the powers of evil (on rare occasions God is viewed as the author);[1] later Christianity crystallised out into the last of these three conceptions so that Satan is seen as the author of all temptation; we must not however read back developed ideas into earlier periods. Historically Satan as the author of temptation arrived late on the scene; it is not necessary to argue whence the idea came; it was presumably from Iranian sources. There is no systematic treatment of Satan in late Judaism which shows him as the author of all temptation; instead our survey of the sources, though brief, has been sufficient to show that the other two conceptions, which are found in the Old Testament, continued into the period of Judaism. Particular instances of sin are traced to Satan and the other supernatural powers of evil, but there is no general statement that in every case he is the tempter. Thus the three ideas exist in parallel, authors sometimes using one and sometimes another. At this stage the issue had not been clearly thought out. The argument that proceeds from the view that because Satan is later regarded as the source of all temptation therefore he must have been also so regarded in the Judaistic period shows a lack of historical sense; we must begin with the earlier period and work to the later and not work back from the later and impose its generalisations on the earlier. Nor can we argue from the conception that Satan tempts, which is perfectly true for this period, to the conclusion that all temptation is due to Satan. As yet in Judaism Satan is not integrated fully into theological thought and he occupies different places in different writings. Thus in the New Testament period we may expect to find varying conceptions of the origin of temptation lying alongside one another. We have already shown this to be so in the case of Mark and for the sake of completeness we proceed to show briefly that it is true also for the rest of the New Testament.

[1] 'We are very far from asserting that the beliefs in an interior innate corruption, and in an exterior personified power of evil, are logically irreconcilable or incapable of being simultaneously held by the same person; they were actually held together by the Jews of our Lord's day, with little attempt at harmonisation...', Williams, *The Ideas of the Fall and of Original Sin*, p. 109.

THE NEW TESTAMENT

In the Pauline and related writings the picture presented is not essentially different from that which we have observed in the preceding. Satan fights against God and seeks to draw men away from God. As tempter he appears most clearly in I Cor. vii. 5 (cf. I Tim. v. 14 f.); Eph. iv. 27; vi. 11; II Cor. iv. 4; II Tim. ii. 26; I Thess. iii. 5.[1] In almost all these passages we find that Satan has his grip on men only because they have first sinned;[2] in II Cor. iv. 4 he blinds the minds of unbelievers, that is, those who refuse to believe (cf. Eph. ii. 2); in I Cor. vii. 5 Satan only has his opportunity because husband and wife have decided to abstain from sexual intercourse and are consequently living under strain; he is not thought of as suggesting that they should stay apart from one another; in Eph. iv. 27 the believer is first angry and thus gives Satan his opportunity to lead him further astray. The idea of deception by Satan is closely related to temptation and is found in II Cor. xi. 14. In Eph. vi. 16 it is by no means sure that the 'fiery darts' of the devil are to be restricted to temptations nor in I Tim. iii. 7 is it certain that there is any reference to the Devil at all. There is no statement whatever that the Devil is responsible for all temptation.

It is consequently not surprising when we find that Paul sees evil as incited in men by other men, including the peril that comes from the tolerance of immoral men in the community (Rom. xiv. 13 ff., 20 f.; I Cor. v. 9; viii. 11; xv. 33; Gal. iii. 1; v. 7–10; Eph. v. 6). The passion of lust may lead a man astray (I Thess. iv. 5; II Tim. ii. 22). Marriage brings anxiety and so the possibility of sin (I Cor. vii. 33 f.). Temptation also begins in men. The beginning of evil against which God's wrath is manifested is in Rom. i. 21 laid at man's own door. To please ourselves (Rom. xv. 1) may be sin, when it makes others stumble. Knowledge puffs up and leads men into evil (I Cor. viii. 1). Men are said to desire evil (I Cor. x. 6). Quite in the manner of the Old Testament the sins of the Gentiles are attributed to their hardness of heart (Eph. iv. 17–24), and the Colossian believers (i. 21) are said to have once had minds estranged

---

[1] But Satan is here the one who tests, rather than tempts; the context speaks of the persecutions that assail the Thessalonians.

[2] Cf. Ling, *The Significance of Satan*, pp. 38, 47.

from and hostile to God by which they were led into evil. They run the danger of being puffed up in their sensuous minds (ii. 18). Minds can be corrupt and so lead to sin (II Tim. iii. 8; cf. Tit. i. 15; iii. 11). When Paul begins to write more systematically the source of sin in man is often the 'flesh' (Gal. v. 16, 24; Rom. viii. 4, 5), and the 'flesh' appears as a power to some extent independent of man yet never wholly disassociated from him and certainly never equated with the Devil;[1] in like manner 'sin' becomes a power outside man which makes him go wrong (Rom. vii. 8, 17) and 'law' itself may become the source of evil (Rom. vii. 5, 11), though 'law' is good (Rom. vii. 12, 14). Indeed it is a remarkable fact that if Paul held that Satan was the cause of temptation he succeeded in writing all his major passages about evil (e.g. Rom. vii) without reference to him. It remains only to note that twice God would appear to incite men to evil, namely, when he hardened Pharaoh's heart (Rom. ix. 18; cf. xi. 8 ff.) and when he deluded men in relation to the Parousia (II Thess. ii. 11).

In the Lukan writings Satan appears at the outset as the tempter of our Lord and it is implied in iv. 13 that he returned to tempt Jesus later.[2] At Luke xxii. 3 Satan is said to have entered into Judas so that he went to the chief priests and initiated the process that led to the betrayal of Jesus, and in Acts v. 3 Satan is said to have filled the heart of Ananias to tell a lie; both these appear rather more like cases of possession in which Satan enters a man than direct temptations in which he remains outside a man and leads him astray; but the idea of temptation certainly cannot be excluded. We encounter also the continuation of the Old Testament strain in which evil appears to begin inside a man himself. Many of the instances in Mark are repeated. In the non-Markan material we may notice the phrase in the story of the rich man who pulled down his barns and built bigger, 'I will say to my soul' (xii. 19) and the very similar phrases at xii. 45; xvi. 3; xviii. 4. The mouth speaks according as the heart is filled with evil or good (Luke

---

[1] If, however, the flesh is not taken as a personified power but as that through which the forces of evil attack man it becomes the channel rather than the source of temptation. But this takes us no further towards an identification of the forces of evil with demonic powers in temptation.

[2] Cf. p. 3, n. 2.

vi. 45). In the Book of Acts jealousy is a continual source of evil, for example, v. 17; xiii. 45; xvii. 5. At Acts xiii. 27 it is said that the Jews killed Christ because they could not understand the Scriptures. Acts vii. 39 repeats an Old Testament way of thinking in a passage retelling the Old Testament, but the same idea is independently present in Luke ix. 47. The Jews incite others to riot and so to sin against the spread of the Gospel (Acts xiii. 50; xiv. 19, etc.); thus the origin of sin lies in others, as we have also found it elsewhere. It is remarkable that although in Acts the Christians are continually seen as guided in all their activities by the Holy Spirit yet Satan does not occupy the corresponding position in respect of deception and temptation.

In the Johannine literature, including the Apocalypse, the spiritual powers of evil appear more consistently as in conflict with men. There is a close relationship between the Devil and the 'world' (I John v. 19; John xii. 31; xiv. 30; xvi. 11); the opponents of Jesus and of the Church are of the Devil (John viii. 44; I John iii. 8; ii. 13, 14). So the Devil is first said to put it into Judas' heart to betray Jesus and then is said to enter him (John xiii. 2, 27). Here Satan appears quite definitely as the tempter. It is doubtful if a reference to the temptations of Jesus should be seen in John xiv. 30 where our Lord says that the ruler of this world has no power over him; rather the general conflict of light and darkness is mirrored here.[1] In Rev. xii. 9; xx. 3 Satan appears as the deceiver of the world. In I John iv. 1 ff. the false prophets who lead men into error are themselves demonically inspired. Here temptation may be regarded as indirectly the work of the Devil. If thus the Devil appears as the tempter and deceiver of men evil is also seen to originate in their hearts. This appears clearly in John ii. 24, 25 where Jesus is said not to trust himself to men because he knew what was in man; this can hardly mean that Jesus knew that man was weak to resist temptation coming from Satan but that he knew men as evil within themselves and that from their own hearts they would plot his death. Nor is the relationship of men

---

[1] The accusation that Jesus has a devil (John vii. 20; cf. viii. 48; x. 20) is an accusation of mental disorder rather than a suggestion that the Devil tempted him to do wrong. Cf. Ling, *The Significance of Satan*, pp. 28 f.; Langton, *Essentials of Demonology*, p. 171.

to the Devil simply one in which he prompts them and so they do wrong; men themselves are ready before he comes to them to do what he wants; they are willing to do his desires (John viii. 44); they love darkness (John iii. 19). The Devil may deceive men, but they can also deceive themselves (I John i. 8). A man may shut up his compassion against a brother (I John iii. 17). Deception and temptation may also come from one man to another; II John 7 speaks of the deceivers who have gone out into the world; Pilate was made to sin through the pressure the Jewish authorities exerted on him (John xix. 12–15).

Matthew does not contain much material different from what we have already examined in Mark and Luke. There are a series of passages (v. 37, 39; vi. 13; xiii. 19, 38) in which πονηρός (-όν) is used and at times it is doubtful whether this is intended as neuter or masculine, and if the latter whether it describes either the Devil or an evil man. It is unnecessary to determine the precise meaning in most cases as the conception of temptation does not enter. The phrase in the Lord's Prayer, 'Lead us not into temptation, but deliver us from evil', may be taken as 'deliver us from the Evil One', but it is very doubtful if πειρασμός means 'temptation' and not rather 'affliction, tribulation, persecution'. In iv. 3 Satan is termed 'the tempter'; this is the nearest we possess to a general statement that temptations come from Satan; yet it does not imply that all temptation comes from him. The only absolutely general statement in the New Testament material is James i. 14 which implies the heart of man as the origin of all temptation. Most of the statements suggesting that the origin of temptation lies either within man himself or comes to him from other men which we have already encountered in Mark and Luke are repeated in Matthew; we need only draw attention to xii. 33–5 (cf. vii. 16–20; Luke vi. 43–5) where men are likened to trees and it is implied that because the tree is bad the fruit will turn out to be bad; the evil deeds of man are the result of the evil disposition within, rather than of the work of the Tempter. At xviii. 7 a woe is called down on the man who brings another into temptation and at xxiii. 16 the Pharisees are termed 'blind guides', since they lead others into sin.

The remainder of the New Testament does not contain much about the Devil. I Pet. v. 8 with its reference to the Devil on the prowl is concerned with persecution rather than temptation, though this may cause temptation. James (iii. 15) refers to the wrong kind of wisdom as devilish, but this again hardly seems to be temptation; probably however the call to resist the Devil at James iv. 7 is a call to resist him as tempter. But these epistles on the other hand contain clear reference to temptation as beginning in man. Noteworthy here is James i. 14, 'Each man is tempted when he is lured and enticed by his own desire'. This is almost a general statement implying that all temptation comes from man himself. James also sees the tongue as the origin of temptation (iii. 1–12) and the strife which exists among church members comes from their passions (iv. 1). The author of Hebrews speaks of the evil unbelieving heart which leads away from God (iii. 12) and goes on in Old Testament quotations and thoughts derived from them to instance the hardened heart which leads into sin (iii. 15; iv. 7; cf. iii. 10). The same author can speak of the deceitfulness of sin (iii. 13). As in James there are references in both the Petrine epistles to the passions as leading men astray (I Pet. ii. 11; i. 14; II Pet. iii. 3; cf. Jude 16, 18). Also in II Peter false teachers are viewed as enticing away the believer (ii. 1 ff.; ii. 14).

We thus find the same pattern appearing throughout the New Testament as we discovered in Judaism; temptation comes either from Satan, or from the man himself, or from other men. There is no statement which suggests that temptation originates with the Devil alone; he is never described as the sole author of temptation. Particularly in the Gospels of Luke and John we find that the activities of Satan centre on the Cross, but this is a development from Mark. We must also recognise that the evil of the Cross while it may be attributed in some way to Satan is much more commonly looked upon as a part of God's predetermined plan.

PART II

THE PASSION

So far we have looked somewhat negatively at the purpose of the ministry of Jesus. We have argued that he defeated Satan conclusively at the time of the temptation in the desert and that thereafter his activities against the demons were in the nature of mopping-up operations. We have further argued that evil in Mark is not conceived as basically demonic and that such a view is not out of step with current Judaism and the remainder of the New Testament. But if the whole purpose of the ministry is not the defeat of demonic forces and if these do not dominate the conception of evil in the Gospel, why then does Mark think Jesus lived and died? It is therefore necessary now to turn to a positive assessment of the ministry of Jesus as Mark conceives it.

CHAPTER III

THE MARKAN SEAMS

THE most obvious place to look for Mark's hand is in the words, phrases, sentences which join together the various incidents of the Gospel. The incidents themselves may or may not go back to Jesus himself, but they came to Mark as part of the tradition and he put them together. We turn now to examine these 'seams'. But we do not confine our attention to them alone; we need also to take into account any relevant editing of the material itself—by way of additional phrases or sentences which Mark has added. These are naturally more difficult to detect since statements which may seem out of accord either with the material or a place in the life of Jesus may well have been added before Mark's time and been taken over by him.

The first editorial statement of Mark is obviously his introductory verse (i. 1). The key-word is εὐαγγέλιον. This is defined as the Gospel of Jesus Christ. Is the genitive Ἰησοῦ Χριστοῦ to be taken as objective or subjective? Perhaps it may be allowed both senses, in that it is the Gospel which the exalted Christ proclaims through Mark to his church and also the Gospel which is about that same Christ.[1] That its content is the Christ appears through its paralleling with him in viii. 35; x. 29 ('for my sake and the Gospel's'). The two are again associated in xiii. 9, 10.[2] The Gospel is something which must be believed, and with this belief repentance is closely linked (i. 15; cf. vi. 12 where the content of preaching is repentance).[3] Repentance is not merely sorrow for sin but also a turning from it to goodness; but it is essentially related to sin as i. 4 shows. It is not then renunciation of the Devil but renunciation of sin. Marxsen[4] has shown that the Markan conception of 'gospel' is

[1] The most recent discussion is that of Marxsen, pp. 77–101. He holds that Mark introduced this word into the Synoptic material.

[2] Cf. Marxsen, pp. 79–83.

[3] E. Schweizer, 'Anmerkungen zur Theologie des Markus', *Neotestamentica et Patristica* (*Suppl. to N.T.* VI), pp. 36 f., shows that the content of 'preaching' (κηρύσσειν) for Mark is repentance.

[4] Pp. 91 f.

closely allied to the Pauline, though not directly dependent thereon. For Paul the Gospel is salvation from sin; it is defined in Rom. i. 16 as the power of God unto salvation and that salvation is set out in Rom. chs. v–viii as a deliverance from sin and its consequences.

Postponing the discussion of the titles 'Christ' and 'Son of God' until later we turn now to i. 14, 15 where Mark summarises the content of the message which Jesus preached. Obviously Mark composed this with an eye to the present condition of his readers and it need not be taken as a summary of the teaching of the historical Jesus. It is strongly coloured by the language of the early Church.[1] We have already looked at εὐαγγέλιον and seen that its content is Christ himself; it is thus related in its usage here to the preaching of the early Church. The same is true of κηρύσσειν.[2] To preach the Gospel is the activity of the Church in the post-Resurrection period. This is obviously so in xiii. 10 and xiv. 9. At i. 45; v. 20; vii. 36 preaching follows directly on exorcism and healing, as it must have done in the early Church; Christ was preached. John's preaching (i. 4, 7) is again for Mark a preaching of Christ; this is his function: to testify to Jesus. He does not occupy an independent position as a preacher of repentance as in Matthew and Luke. In iii. 14; vi. 12 the disciples are described as preaching within the lifetime of Jesus, but these references obviously look forward to and are coloured by the practice of the early Church; the apostles are examples for the activity of the early Church. In i. 38, 39 Jesus is himself described as preaching in the villages of Galilee; probably again Mark thinks of Jesus as preaching about himself. Thus we may conclude that at i. 14, 15 Mark envisaged the preaching of Christ as a preaching not merely by Christ but about Christ.

The phrase 'the Kingdom of God' almost certainly goes back to our Lord, but what content does Mark give to it? Does he regard it as a present reality or as belonging to the imminent future? The former is certainly true of Matthew and Luke who

---

[1] Lohmeyer, *ad loc.*; Lightfoot, *Gospel*, p. 20; J. Sundwall, *Die Zusammensetzung des Markusevangeliums* (Acta Academiae Aboensis, Humaniora, IX, 2, 1934), p. 8.

[2] See the very long note devoted to the word by Lightfoot, *History*, pp. 106 f.

speak of the exorcism of demons as a manifestation of the Kingdom (Matt. xii. 28 = Luke xi. 20; cf. Matt. iv. 23). That Mark however can regard the Kingdom as future appears in xv. 43 where Joseph of Arimathea is named as one looking for the coming of the Kingdom; here Mark may be indicating the attitude of the believer of his own time. The Kingdom is also viewed as future in Jesus' words that he would not drink of the fruit of the vine again until he did so in the Kingdom (xiv. 25). The strong statement of ix. 1 which says that some shall not die until they see the Kingdom of God come in power may imply that its coming will be soon, but it certainly implies that it is not yet. In three places in ch. iv the Kingdom of God is connected to parables. The first of these is the difficult passage iv. 11, 12. We are not concerned to find the original meaning of this logion and place it correctly either in the life of Jesus or in that of the early Church; there are good grounds to believe that its present position is a Markan creation.[1] We have, however, to interpret it within its place in this chapter. The disciples, and in the Markan context these must be understood to include the believers of his own day, are given (by God) the mystery of the Kingdom, but the parables in which it is unveiled to them serve to conceal its meaning from non-believers.[2] Something of the meaning of the Kingdom of God must therefore be given in the Parable of the Sower, and particularly in its interpretation, about which Mark will not have had the doubts we may have, and also, since the plural 'parables' is used, in the other parables of this chapter and especially those specifically referring to the Kingdom. Two parables are set out as Kingdom of God parables, namely, the seed growing secretly (iv. 26–9) and the mustard seed (iv. 30–2). In neither case is the Kingdom of God to be taken as like a man who scatters seed nor as the mustard seed; it is the whole action

---

[1] Cf. Jeremias, *The Parables of Jesus*, pp. 11 f.; Boobyer, 'The Redaction of Mark iv. 1–34', takes iv. 10–13 as a unit.

[2] The line of thought which Mark holds in regard to the parables in iv. 11 f. appears to be carried on by iv. 21–5 (a Markan insertion into the group of parables) and iv. 33 f. (*v.* 33 is certainly Markan; *v.* 34 may be also). It is difficult to accept the implication that ὁ λύχνος is here to be identified with our Lord who 'comes' (ἔρχεται) and is later made manifest. This may have been the meaning in the tradition, but it does not suit the Markan context.

of the parable to which the Kingdom of God is likened.[1] In each of these two parables there is a completed action, a tree in which the birds make nests and a crop being harvested; each of these is future to the first action of the parable—the sowing of the seed—and the emphasis lies on the completion of the action. The Kingdom belongs accordingly to the future though the steps which bring it in have already begun. Turning now to the Parable of the Sower this may have originally been a straight-forward parable about the Kingdom in which emphasis lay on a harvest: 'In spite of every failure the Kingdom of God comes at last.'[2] Mark has however transformed this by the addition of the interpretation: the Gospel is preached in the world and some men receive it, that is, to them the mystery of the Kingdom is revealed, and they bring forth fruit; others fail to receive it or receive it and lose it, that is, they lose their understanding of the Kingdom. This itself does not therefore tell us much about the nature of the Kingdom. There remain a number of passages in which men are spoken of as entering or receiving the Kingdom. At ix. 47 entering into the Kingdom must be interpreted in a future manner since it is contrasted with being cast into Gehenna. The phrase recurs in the discussion about the difficulties of the rich in entering the Kingdom of God (x. 23–5); this pericope begins with the arrival of the rich man who asks Jesus what he needs to do to inherit eternal life; eternal life is here understood as future (cf. *v.* 30) and not in the Johan-nine sense as a present possession. It is reasonable then to suppose that references to the rich as entering the Kingdom of God (*vv.* 23–5) are to be taken in the future sense; this is con-firmed by the final future reference of *v.* 30. It may not be however true that in their original context these passages had a future reference, and Jesus may originally have intended to imply the entering of the Kingdom as a present reality; but in the context they are given by Mark it is difficult to see anything other than a future reference. References to the Kingdom of God occur in the preceding pericope on the receiving of the little children (x. 13–16). Since at x. 15 Jesus speaks of receiving the Kingdom as a present possibility the present reference to it cannot be excluded in x. 14. The same is true of the scribe who

---

[1] Jeremias, *The Parables of Jesus*, pp. 89 f.
[2] Jeremias, *op. cit.* p. 92.

asked concerning the Great Commandment and who was told that he was not far from the Kingdom of God (xii. 34). These latter texts (x. 13–16; xii. 34) may represent the original trend of the teaching of Jesus which emerges despite the editorial work of Mark and the selective action of the early Church. However the main drift of the Markan interpretation of the Kingdom rests on its future nature. We may thus approve of the judgement of V. Taylor, 'in this Gospel (Mark) the main emphasis lies upon the Kingdom as future and, indeed, imminent, and as the community in which God's will is done'.[1]

Returning now to i. 15 we may see that whatever the underlying Aramaic may have meant, when Mark says that the Kingdom of God ἤγγικεν, he does not mean that it has arrived but that it is imminent. In line with this we have found no evidence that Mark connects the Kingdom with the demonic world and its defeat. The Kingdom is considered in terms of men. It is something which men receive or enter; when its accomplishment is considered, as in the Parable of the Mustard Seed, it is the birds of the air, that is, the Gentile nations, that come to it and are part of it.[2] The Parable of the Seed growing secretly up to its reaping in harvest (harvest with its implication of judgement on men) must lead to the same conclusion. And in so far as the Parable of the Sower is connected with the Kingdom it obviously concerns men. Thus the Kingdom of God for Mark is related not to the demonic world and its conquest but to the rule of God over men.

There is no evidence in Mark that Jesus is himself to be regarded as the Kingdom, a view which emerges in the other Synoptics.[3] When Mark says that the Kingdom of God is at hand he does not mean that this should be taken in a spatial sense: 'The kingdom of God has come close to men in the person of Jesus, and in his person it actually confronts them.'[4] This comment of Cranfield cannot be sustained in the light of Mark's general usage of the Kingdom. Mark equates Jesus with the Gospel but not with the Kingdom. The Gospel, that is,

[1] Pp. 114 f.
[2] C. H. Dodd, *The Parables of the Kingdom*, pp. 189–91; T. W. Manson, *The Teaching of Jesus*, p. 133, n. 1.
[3] Cf. K. L. Schmidt, *T.W.N.T.* I, 590 f.
[4] Cranfield, p. 68; cf. pp. 63–8.

5-2

Christ, must be believed because the Kingdom is close at hand. Here Mark is speaking to the readers of his own time and is setting before them a decision to be made. It is concerned with repentance and belief, an attitude towards God whose result will be entrance into a future Kingdom which God will bring. Negatively we must observe that Mark makes no reference to the subjection of demons nor to the healing of sickness; in relation to the Kingdom he neither says that Jesus did these things nor does he offer victory in them to the readers of his own time; they, the readers, are instead brought into a relationship towards God and promised a part in the final consummation. The purpose of the ministry of Jesus must then be the bringing of men into this relationship with God. As we proceed we will learn in more detail what this relationship is and how it is brought about by Jesus.

In the incident i. 21–8 it is difficult to determine the extent of the Markan editing. Verse 21 a with its reference to Capernaum and v. 28, which is in general terms, may certainly be ascribed to Mark. But can we also put down vv. 21 b, 22 to his hand? Verse 27 takes up again what is said in v. 22, and therefore if v. 22 is not part of the traditional material then perhaps we should argue the same for v. 27.[1] But vv. 23–7 read as a whole. Furthermore the reference in v. 22 to the scribes would seem an unlikely addition to a Mark finally compiled in Rome.[2] It is not then easy to conclude that the hand of Mark is to be detected in vv. 21 b, 22.[3] Yet v. 23 does read like a fresh beginning; καὶ εὐθύς is a favourite introductory phrase of Mark to a new pericope, and there is the second reference to the synagogue. Perhaps the easiest solution is to assume that vv. 21 b, 22 represent a fragment of traditional material which Mark has introduced at this point, observing that they make a suitable preliminary to v. 27.[4] By so doing Mark has emphasised Jesus as teaching men with power prior to his exorcism of

[1] So Bultmann, pp. 209 f.; Bundy, p. 77.

[2] Bussmann, I, 131 f. attributes the whole passage (vv. 21–8) apart from the reference to the scribes to his G; the reference to the scribes he ascribes to his Galilean redactor.

[3] Taylor takes vv. 21–8 as having come to Mark as a unit; Lohmeyer takes vv. 21 f. as Markan.

[4] The reference to the Sabbath in v. 21 is not followed up in vv. 23–7; contrast iii. 1–6.

demons with power: the word of instruction is prior to the word of exorcism and forms the basis for it. It is not then correct to take the first great act of Jesus as an exorcism; it is preceded by teaching, and indeed (*vv.* 16–20) by the powerful word which calls men to him.

i. 39 is another summary statement[1] of Mark describing the activity of Jesus. 'Both the vocabulary and style suggest that this summary statement was added by Mark either in composing the Gospel or at a still earlier stage.'[2] The last phrase of the verse καὶ τὰ δαιμόνια ἐκβάλλων is omitted in the Freer MS (W). Prior to the discovery of this MS, J. Weiss had suggested that it was a redactorial addition to Mark.[3] He argued: (*a*) the words are lacking in the Lukan parallel, and (*b*) in the immediately succeeding pericope describing activity in the sphere of Galilee healings and not exorcisms are described. These reasons do not appear sufficiently cogent to lead us to omit the phrase.[4] In *v.* 38, which would appear to be a part of the tradition received by Mark,[5] Jesus sets out his activity as preaching. Now in *v.* 39 Mark qualifies this by adding to it the phrase 'and casting out demons'. There has already been one exorcism (i. 23–7) and Mark is preparing for his explanation of exorcisms in iii. 22–7.

There seems less ground for taking i. 45 as the work of the evangelist. Without it the section i. 40 ff. lacks a proper climax. It may be however that the words from ὥστε to ἦν are due to Mark since they can be understood in line with his doctrine of a Messianic secret.[6] The close association of κηρύσσειν and λόγος in this verse may have been understood in the sense of the preaching of the Gospel by the early Church, but there is nothing here to help us to determine the content of the Gospel.

ii. 1, 2 certainly bear some signs of Markan editorial work. The anacolouthic εἰσελθών and Mark's favourite πάλιν are an indication of this.[7] But how far does this editorial work

---

[1] C. H. Dodd has argued that many of these summary statements once formed together an outline of the life of Jesus and that Mark has adapted his material to this outline. Cf. p. 112, n. 1.

[2] Taylor, *ad loc.*   [3] P. 151, n. 1.   [4] Cf. Schmidt, pp. 59 f.

[5] Schmidt, pp. 58 f., and the great majority of commentators take *vv.* 35–8 as part of the traditional material. Bussmann puts it in his G source. Bultmann regards all *vv.* 35–9 as a redactional summary.

[6] Thus Schmidt, pp. 66 f.   [7] Cf. Taylor, *ad loc.*

extend? Both Luke and Matthew have entirely different introductory sections to the incident of ii. 3–12; in the incident itself however they follow Mark very closely. This may suggest that practically the whole of ii. 1, 2 is Markan. The original incident may have begun with a simple statement 'He was at home (in a house, the house)'.[1] We are interested especially in Mark's statement that Jesus ἐλάλει τὸν λόγον. Qualified by τοῦ θεοῦ (κυρίου) this phrase was used in the early Church in the sense of the proclamation of the Gospel (e.g. Acts iv. 29, 31; viii. 25). Does it carry any of this significance at ii. 2? The particular phrase recurs at iv. 33 and viii. 32. λόγος by itself has quite obviously no particular reference to the Gospel in viii. 38; x. 24; xiii. 31, in all of which it is used in the plural, nor at v. 36; vii. 29, where it is used of the words of others than Jesus. At x. 22; xiv. 39 it refers to particular sayings of Jesus; elsewhere it has a variety of meanings (xi. 29; xii. 13; vii. 13). In the interpretation of the Parable of the Sower (iv. 14 ff.) it is used of the sowing of the word in the hearts of men and here it must have the sense of 'Gospel', if Mark viewed this interpretation as an explanation of the success and failure of the spread of the Gospel in his own day. This same meaning must appear at iv. 33 f.; the mystery of the Kingdom (iv. 11), which cannot be disassociated from the Gospel (i. 15), is made known in the parables; here in iv. 33 it is said that in the parables the word is proclaimed. This word must then be the Gospel. i. 45, 'he spread abroad the word', is less decisive and λόγος may easily here mean 'an account of what had happened'. At viii. 32 Jesus is himself said to speak the word boldly; this might be taken as a reference to his preceding prophecy of his passion and λόγος mean 'saying'; but it is surely difficult to avoid the meaning 'Gospel' at this point. If the Gospel is linked directly to the Passion, death and Resurrection of Jesus, of which he has just spoken, then Jesus proclaimed the Gospel in proclaiming his death and resurrection; and here moreover he is a pattern to the early preacher who must also proclaim this very Gospel 'boldly'. We now return to ii. 1. The absolute usage of λόγος[2] here then leaves it exceedingly probable that Mark had in mind

---

[1] So Schmidt, pp. 78 f.; cf. Lightfoot, *History*, p. 41.

[2] It is natural that when Jesus is the speaker λόγος should not be qualified with either τοῦ θεοῦ or τοῦ κυρίου.

the proclamation of the Gospel.[1] But what is it that is proclaimed in the succeeding verses? A sick man is brought to Jesus and the first thing he does is to speak a word of forgiveness. The content of the word which is to be spoken is not 'Jesus heals' but 'Jesus offers forgiveness', that is, the essential content of the Gospel is the forgiveness of sin and not victory over sickness (or the Devil). Had Jesus begun by healing the man the Gospel might have been viewed as victory over the demonic forces of the world, but the Gospel is related here to forgiveness. This also is the content of the Gospel that Mark himself would preach.[2]

The section ii. 1–iii. 6 is generally held to have come to Mark as a unit, a complex of conflict stories.[3] It cannot then include much editorial work apart from its beginning and end. The only verse which merits discussion is ii. 13.[4] This verse is completely omitted in Matthew, drastically shortened in Luke, contains Mark's favourite πάλιν and bears no particular relationship to vv. 14–17. Mark is creating a background for the incident that is to follow.[5] And in this background we observe how he presents Jesus as teacher, though the quantity of teaching that he gives from Jesus is small compared to that which we find in the other Synoptics. διδάσκαλος is the favourite address of others to Jesus in Mark. It is however when we look at the places where διδάσκειν and διδαχή are used in Mark that the importance of this root for him becomes apparent;[6] for these two words occur largely in the seams between incidents, where we are most likely to see the hand of Mark: thus διδαχή comes in i. 22, 27; iv. 2; xi. 18; xii. 38; but only i. 27 is integral to the incident in which it occurs. διδάσκειν is found in i. 21, 22;

---

[1] Cf. Lohmeyer; Hauck.

[2] At iv. 33 f. the content of the 'word' would appear to be the eschatological kingdom.

[3] So Dibelius, p. 219; Schmidt, pp. 103 f.; Knox, pp. 8 ff., etc.

[4] Cf. Taylor, ad loc.; Schmidt, p. 82. Whether Mark made other additions to this complex it is difficult to determine. ii. 15–17 may have originally lacked the introduction of ii. 14; but ii. 15 requires some explanation concerning whose house Jesus was sitting in and ii. 16 some preceding reference to publicans. Mark may have added ii. 21 f. or ii. 27 f. or they may have been a part of the existing tradition.

[5] Hauck.

[6] Cf. Schweizer, 'Anmerkungen zur Theologie des Markus', pp. 37 ff.

ii. 13; iv. 1, 2; vi. 6; viii. 31; ix. 31; x. 1; xi. 17 (perhaps only a conventional Markan expression[1]); xii. 35, all of which are probably editorial; more doubtful are vi. 2, 34. Only at xii. 14 and xiv. 49 is the word used in a way integral to the pericope; at vii. 7 it is in a LXX quotation; in vi. 30 it is used of the teaching of the disciples. Thus διδάσκειν and its cognates are favourites of Mark. If we examine in this way the 'seams' between the incidents then Mark leaves us with the impression that the main activity of Jesus was teaching; note especially x. 1, where teaching is said to be his custom; this appears much more regularly in the seams than does 'healing' or 'exorcism', and, whereas the incidents recording these gradually disappear towards the end of the book, the teaching of Jesus continues right through to the Passion itself. Probably no distinction is to be made between preaching (κηρύσσειν) and teaching. Preaching seems to be used more often of the activities of others about Jesus (i. 4, 7, 45; iii. 14; v. 20; vi. 12; vii. 36; xiii. 10; xiv. 9) than of the activity of Jesus himself (i. 14, 38). But the connection between the two is seen in the equivalence of such passages as vi. 12 and vi. 30. The content of the teaching of Jesus is not made clear; very often the reference to the teaching of Jesus is general without specific relation to what follows, or in the incident that follows the use of διδάσκειν, etc., no actual teaching of Jesus is given (i. 21, 22; ii. 13; vi. 34; x. 1). His teaching may be connected with the coming of the Kingdom (iv. 1, 2) which is made known through parables; it is directed against the Pharisees (xii. 38) and against the misuse of the temple as market (xi. 17); it sets him forth as greater than David (xii. 35); and, most noteworthy, two of the Passion predictions (viii. 31; ix. 31) are introduced as the teaching of Jesus. Thus Mark sets out Jesus as teacher and his teaching is certainly linked with the understanding of his death and resurrection.

While the failure of the disciples to understand Jesus has been a commonplace of Markan criticism since the work of Wrede, Ebeling[2] has shown how this failure is balanced by a corresponding attempt by Jesus to enlighten the disciples. We may note that iv. 13 is balanced at once by the interpretation of the

---

[1] Taylor, ad loc.
[2] Ebeling, *Das Messiasgeheimnis in den Evangelien*[2], pp. 146–79.

parable which the disciples had failed to understand; likewise their lack of understanding about the miracles of the loaves is followed by teaching (viii. 14–21); in the two incidents on the lake (iv. 35–41; vi. 45–52) the fear of the disciples for themselves, which is closely linked to ignorance of the nature of Jesus, is answered by a revelation of his supernatural nature. Peter's failure to understand his own confession of Jesus as the Christ is followed by teaching on what will happen to the Christ (viii. 27–33); the failure of the disciples to understand the way of service as that along which Jesus goes to the Cross (at ix. 33 ff. and x. 35 ff. following on the second and third prophecies of the Cross they are discussing their own greatness) is balanced with teaching by Jesus on the nature of service. Thus Mark sets out Jesus in his teaching as bringing to men a revelation of himself and of the necessity and nature of his death and resurrection. But we may note that it is not a revelation pure and simple but one linked closely to following Jesus, to discipleship. The way of service along which Jesus goes must also be the way for the disciples (x. 42–4); they have also to take up their crosses and go after him (viii. 34). The understanding only comes to those who go in the way of Jesus. Thus, if Mark sets out Jesus as one who reveals, it is not in the sense of one who admits the curious to see the mysteries of God, but of one who is only understood by his disciples as they enter on the hard path of discipleship.

iii. 7–12 is taken very generally to be a Markan construction. In it Mark sets out the activities of Jesus as twofold, healing and exorcism. We must ask how far this is a clearly Markan construction and how far Mark has used traditional material. If we do not go so far as Knox[1] in attributing this section to the 'Twelve-Source', yet we have to notice certain difficulties in the passage if it is entirely Markan. It is said that the boat is introduced in iii. 9 as preparation for iv. 1, but it seems a quite unnecessary duplication, particularly if iv. 1, 2 is itself a Markan construction; may it not have been a part of the tradition that Jesus taught from a boat at the lake-side, a tradition which Mark has made use of more than once? Further the geographical designations of *vv.* 7, 8 seem unnecessarily detailed for a Roman audience; this again suggests tradition. The early

[1] Pp. 17 ff.

73

Christian preacher must have said something about the life of Jesus and there would have been summary statements about his teaching and activity; cf. Acts x. 38 f. This is true whether or not we accept the view of Dodd that there was a summary outline of the life of Jesus.[1] Mark may have used such traditional material at this point. In particular he allows this material to make reference to exorcism because he is about to introduce the dispute of Jesus with the scribes on this very matter and the one exorcism which he has already related (i. 23–8) is not sufficient to create such a discussion. Noteworthy is the absence of reference to the teaching of Jesus. We have seen that this is a constant Markan theme in the 'seams'; this again suggests we are dealing with traditional material rather than a straightforward Markan construction. Possibly teaching is implied in the reference to the boat; ostensibly the boat is to prevent people jostling Jesus; but once he was in the boat what would he do except teach? This is the purpose of the boat in iv. 1.

There now follow a number of pericopae, the Markan connecting links between which contribute little or nothing to our inquiry. In some cases the seams are of the briefest possible nature, being just sufficient to set the scene, sometimes no more than a mere καί (iii. 13, 19b, 22, 31; iv. 21, 24, 26, 30, 35; v. 1, 21, 25). iii. 19b–34 appears to have been traditional material that came to Mark, perhaps already joined together, though the 'sandwich' (vv. 19b–21, 22–30, 31–5) suggests Mark's hand; in any case there are no seams within it of significance. Mark may have rewritten the material to bring out the meaning he desired; iii. 30 may well be his comment. We have, however, already examined this passage in detail.[2] iv. 1 is certainly Markan, and perhaps the seam also includes iv. 2; in it Jesus is depicted as teacher and the following passages show him as the teller of parables. iv. 11 f., 21–5, 33, 34 are Markan insertions into the parables with the intention of explaining their use; iv. 11 f., 21–5 probably utilise traditional material whose original setting has been lost; iv. 33, 34 would rather appear to be Mark's own conclusion to this passage of parables. There follow (iv. 35–v. 43) four δυνάμεις of Jesus. Then Mark brings him to his own village of Nazareth.

[1] Cf. p. 112, n. 1.　　　　　[2] Cf. pp. 10 ff.

vi. 1, 2 a would appear to be Markan. vi. 1 sets the scene for what follows and ἤρξατο διδάσκειν is a Markan phrase (cf. iv. 1; vi. 34; viii. 31) incorporating his favourite use of ἄρχομαι. The following verses (to 6 a) clearly contain traditional material emanating from a Galilean source which alone would have interest in the names of Jesus' brothers. Mark may have brought together two separate pieces of material.[1] In the pericope the villagers wonder both at the wisdom of his teaching and at the great works he has done. We are presumably intended by Mark to carry back the allusion to his mighty deeds to iv. 35–v. 43 in which Mark has recounted in detail four of them—though none of them was performed in Nazareth, Mark's readers still have them in the mind's eye. Since the traditional material also carried reference to his teaching Mark introduces Jesus as teacher in his connecting link (v. 2 a).

vi. 6 b is remarkable in that Mark here sends out Jesus on tour round the villages and states his activity as teaching alone; there is no reference to his healing activity or to exorcisms. Matthew corrects this by the introduction of reference to Jesus as healer; Luke has no parallel. The omission by Mark is all the more noteworthy because he proceeds directly to record the sending out of the apostles on a mission in which they heal and exorcise. The original story of the mission here will have probably contained a reference to the sending out of the Twelve followed by the instructions of vv. 8–11. To this Mark has added in v. 7 Jesus' bestowal on them of authority over demons and the whole of vv. 12, 13 recounting what the Twelve did.[2] This might appear to give a certain prominence to exorcism as an activity of the apostles since it appears in both v. 7 and v. 13. This needs to be seen in the light of two facts: (a) Jesus is described in v. 6 b by Mark as teaching, and not as exorcising; (b) Jesus gives authority to exorcise.[3] Thus Jesus is seen by Mark primarily as a teacher, but also as one who can delegate authority over demons because he already possesses that authority.

In vi. 14–16 we may again suspect the hand of Mark.

---

[1] Cf. Schmidt, pp. 152 ff.; vv. 2 b, 4 appear to be linked to Jesus' teaching as mentioned in vv. 1, 2 a, whereas vv. 2 c, 5, 6 may have formed a separate unit relating to his miracles. We note again that the Word (σοφία) precedes the healing (cf. ii. 1–12).

[2] Cf. Taylor.   [3] Cf. below, pp. 187 f. for a fuller discussion.

ἤκουσεν is left without an object; this may have been present in the original context which vi. 14 possessed in the tradition; if so Mark must have torn the passage from there and placed it here. Verses 14–16 are obviously intended as introductory to *vv.* 17–29, the account of the death of John. It is hardly likely, as some commentators suggest, that Mark introduced this merely to indicate the passing of time between the sending out of the disciples (vi. 7–13) and their return (vi. 30). There were presumably many other pericopae Mark could have introduced at this point to serve this purpose: his choice of this one is significant. The death of John foreshadows the death of Jesus; ix. 11–13 closely connects the two deaths.[1] vi. 15, 16 with their three different identifications of Jesus with Elijah, John and one of the prophets recall the scene at Caesarea Philippi (viii. 28); indeed it is possible that the construction of one may have influenced that of the other: '. . . in describing a new scene, he (Mark) sometimes repeats on an extensive scale words and phrases he has used in an earlier narrative'.[2] If vi. 15, 16 recalls the scene at Caesarea Philippi then let us remember that the identification there is quickly followed by the prediction of the Passion. Thus Mark is indicating to us in vi. 14–29[3] the final end of the forerunner's successor.

vi. 30–4 would appear to be an amalgam brought together by Mark.[4] With most of it we are not concerned since it describes the activity of the disciples rather than that of Jesus; *v.* 34 brings us to the latter. vi. 34*a* may have lain in the tradition, but 34*b* is a Markan construction and must be taken as qualifying 34*a*.[5] σπλαγχνίζεσθαι is also found in the doublet viii. 1–9. Either usage may have inspired the other, but since vi. 34*a* contains a biblical quotation and is not directly connected to the miracle of the feeding it would appear more likely that this has been formed by Mark using the key-word which he met in the other tradition. The sequence of thought in viii. 2 ff. seems

[1] Marxsen (pp. 22 f.); Lohmeyer, *ad loc.*, take the absolute use of παραδοθῆναι in i. 14 as a premonition of the Passion.

[2] Taylor, p. 53. Mark may have introduced *vv.* 15, 16 here as a deliberate parallel to viii. 27 f.; cf. Bundy.

[3] It is irrelevant whether we decide vi. 17–29 is bazaar gossip (Rawlinson) or an early Church creation; it came to Mark as part of the tradition; he uses it as a minor passion pointing to the greater Passion.

[4] So Schmidt, pp. 178–93; Taylor, etc.   [5] Note the use of ἄρχεσθαι.

more natural; Jesus feels compassion for the hungry crowd and so he feeds them. In vi. 34 Jesus sees the crowd as sheep without a shepherd and in his compassion teaches them; then the feeding follows almost as a separate incident.[1] But feeding is much more the task of a shepherd than teaching.[2] How do we explain the intrusion of teaching? The quotation is not a literal reproduction of any particular Old Testament text and may have been inspired by one or more of a number of places, namely, Num. xxvii. 17; III Kgdms xxii. 17; II Chron. xviii. 16; Ezek. xxxiv. 5; Judith xi. 19. Of these III Kgdms xxii. 17 = II Chron. xviii. 16 and Judith xi. 19 are the least likely to have been formative since they do not suggest Jesus as the new Moses, and Ezek. xxxiv. 5 combined with xxxiv. 23 would imply Jesus as the new David, or King of Israel (in the Markan Passion story Jesus is often referred to as the King of the Jews). Of these two the former appears preferable because it is possible to make some connection between Moses as lawgiver and teacher and Jesus as the shepherd who teaches (cf. Ps. cxix. 176). Moreover there is a link between Jesus as the new Moses and the Feeding of the Five Thousand; Jesus gives the new manna. Moses fed the people with God's teaching: for man does not live by bread alone but by whatever comes from the mouth of God (Deut. viii. 3, where there is a distinct reference to manna. In John x. 8, 16, 27 the sheep hear and heed the voice of Jesus, which must imply some reference to his teaching).[3] Perhaps then in *v.* 34 we may see a reflection of the view that Jesus feeds men with the word of God just as once he fed them with bread and fishes.[4] Some confirmation of this close relationship of the

[1] Lohmeyer alone of commentators appears to observe the strangeness of Mark's reference to the teaching of Jesus. Matthew changes the reference by linking Jesus' compassion to healing; Luke omits the quotation about the shepherd and the reference to the compassion of Jesus, but says that he taught and healed.

[2] On the biblical picture of the shepherd and his activities cf. Jeremias, *T.W.N.T.* vi, 484 ff.

[3] The Shepherd appears as teacher in post-canonical Christian teaching (cf. Jeremias, *op. cit.* p. 496); in Philo the Logos and νοῦς appear as shepherd (*ibid.* pp. 488 f.).

[4] In the Johannine eucharistic discourse Jesus says to the disciples who have found his statements difficult to accept, 'It is the spirit that gives life, the flesh is of no avail; the *words* that I have spoken unto you are spirit and life' (vi. 63).

teaching of Jesus to what he gave to the crowds in the two feeding stories is found in the very difficult passage which terminates his teaching on the understanding of these miracles, namely, viii. 14–21; this again would seem to be a Markan amalgam of traditional sayings.[1] There is continual reference here to the dullness of understanding of the disciples (*vv.* 17, 18, 21; cf. vi. 52); they had not been able to appreciate his teaching (the leaven of the Pharisees is interpreted in Matthew as their teaching: xvi. 11, 12). To return to vi. 34: Mark sets out Jesus as the shepherd who feeds his people with true teaching; from his supply there is more than enough to feed all their needs[2] (in the feedings there was food over and above what was necessary); but it is not always easy to understand (viii. 14–21); the parables, we may recall, also required their explanation (iv. 11, 12).

vi. 45, 46 do not show much trace of Markan style and are probably part of the tradition which he received; there is good reason to believe that they always adhered closely to *vv.* 35–44.[3] Verses 47, 48 show Mark's hand[4] and perhaps he has made the link at this point between the feeding narrative and the walking on the water, though the fact that the second feeding is also followed by a scene in a boat may imply that this connection lay deep in the tradition. Verse 52 is Markan and again serves to hold together the feeding and the incident on the lake.[5] What concerns us is the reference to Jesus as praying. Mark rarely shows us Jesus in prayer; only elsewhere at i. 35 and xiv. 35 ff. Luke, as is well known, extends these references (iii. 21; xi. 1, etc.). What is the significance of the prayer at this point? Lohmeyer sees a connection between the prayer and epiphany of Jesus to the disciples. May it not however represent the beginning of a new stage in the ministry? The prayer at i. 35 is followed by the decision of Jesus to widen his ministry into the villages around Capernaum, that is, into Galilee; associated with the prayer of Jesus at vi. 46 is the sending of the disciples out of Galilee (Bethsaida) and in the subsequent section (perhaps as far as ix. 30) the incidents largely take place

---

[1] Cf. Taylor; Klostermann; Dibelius, pp. 228 f.

[2] Cf. G. H. Boobyer, 'The Eucharistic Interpretation of the Miracle of the Loaves in St Mark's Gospel', *J.T.S.* III (1952), 161–71.

[3] Cf. Schmidt, pp. 193 f.

[4] Cf. Hauck, *ad loc.*: use of καί, etc.   [5] Lohmeyer.

outside Galilean, indeed outside Jewish territory. Both prayers are preceded by a great success and followed by movement away from that success.

vi. 53–6 appears to be a Markan summary based on tradition which he has received.[1] The fact of the presence of a place-name (Gennesaret) would emphasise Mark's usage here of tradition. In the passage Jesus is depicted as a popular healer as in iii. 7–13, and as in that pericope no mention is made of him here as teacher. Both these passages we have seen came from the tradition; Mark however continually in his own seams introduces Jesus as teacher. In that he would seem to be correcting the tradition he has received.

In vii. 1–23 Mark gives us a period of sustained teaching by Jesus. There may be Markan seams at vii. 1, 9, 14, 17, and vii. 3, 4 is probably a Markan explanatory addition, but in none of them is there anything which shows us how Mark regarded the activity of Jesus. There follow two miracles to which again there are brief connecting links but nothing of importance for us (vii. 24–30, 31–7). We have already dealt with the second feeding and the subsequent discussion in so far as it concerns us (viii. 1–21). The seam again at viii. 22 (the healing of the blind man of Bethsaida) has nothing to show us.

In the section viii. 27–ix. 1 there are a number of connecting links, namely, viii. 27, 31, 34; *v.* 30 may also be Markan, relating to the Messianic secret. Presumably the sections viii. 27–9, viii. 31–3, and viii. 34–ix. 1 came to Mark as units; the only doubt would lie in relation to the last of these whether Mark had built it up from separate sayings; since however it concerns discipleship rather than the activities of Jesus we need not enter into its analysis. The introduction of the crowd at viii. 34 suggests that viii. 34–ix. 1 did not originally belong with viii. 27–33; the whole point of the two earlier passages is that Jesus is alone with his disciples in an area where he would not be likely to have a crowd ready to hand. We may suspect that Mark has then added this section. For our purpose the question is much more interesting: has Mark brought together viii. 27–9 and viii. 31–3?[2] The use of καὶ ἤρξατο διδάσκειν, a favourite

---

[1] So Taylor; Schmidt, p. 195; Weiss, pp. 222 f., etc.

[2] Cf. Schmidt, pp. 217 f.; Lagrange; Weiss, p. 237; F. Hahn, *Christologische Hoheitstitel*, pp. 226–30.

editorial phrase, reinforces this suggestion. To make the link Matthew uses ἀπὸ τότε, a stronger phrase than καί; it implies a new state, and perhaps also a new time, in the teaching about the suffering of Jesus. It must also be noticed that this teaching bears a certain formalised character, being repeated twice more, and Mark may have regarded it as a formula to be inserted at suitable points.[1] On the other hand there is no need in Mark to give ἤρξατο the sense of 'began', as if a new start is intended at this point;[2] similar teaching is introduced with the same word at x. 32. Furthermore the appearance of Peter in both *vv.* 27–9 and 31–3 would have tended to draw these two pericopae together prior to Mark's time even if they were not originally one complete incident in Jesus' life. We must now look a little more closely at Mark's editorial references to the teaching of Jesus. We have seen that though Mark continually draws attention to the teaching of Jesus he gives little content to that teaching. The one place where we have found it strongly linked to actual teaching by Jesus is iv. 1, 2 in relation to the parables. What does the word 'parable' mean? If we trace behind it the Hebrew משל (Aramaic מתלא) with its meaning 'riddle', 'dark saying', and assume that Mark as well as his source understood it in this sense at iv. 11, 12,[3] then it may be possible to argue that where Mark refers editorially to the teaching of Jesus he has in mind teaching which is in riddles, difficult to understand, hard to accept. If we now examine his references to Jesus as teaching, we see that this is true of iv. 1, 2. His teaching in the synagogue of Nazareth causes offence (vi. 2). vi. 34 b is followed by the feedings which both crowds and disciples failed to understand (vi. 52; viii. 14–21). viii. 31 and ix. 31 precede predictions of the Passion, which the disciples again found 'hard sayings'. x. 1 is certainly followed by many sayings which it is hard to live out, even if their meaning is clear (x. 9, 21, 24);

[1] On the analysis of the Son of Man sayings about the Passion cf. F. Hahn, *op. cit.* pp. 46 ff.

[2] Cf. Howard, *Grammar*, II, 455 f.; Blass–Debrunner, §392.2; Taylor, pp. 63 f.; Turner, xxviii (1927), 352 f. ἤρξατο + infinitive is in Mark the equivalent of the imperfect. Cf. J. C. Doudna, *The Greek of the Gospel of Mark*, pp. 111–17.

[3] Cf. Marxsen, 'Redaktionsgeschichtliche Erklärung der Parabeltheorie des Markus', *Z.T.K.* LII (1955), 255–71; Boobyer, 'The Redaction of Mark iv. 1–34'.

observe how the disciples need an explanation of the saying about divorce (*v.* 10); how they find his attitude to the infants difficult (*vv.* 13f.); and their astonishment at his sayings about riches (*v.* 26). xi. 17 offends the priests and scribes so that they at once plot to kill him (xi. 18). xii. 35 is indeed followed by an enigmatic enough saying. At i. 21, 22 his teaching is with power and provokes great amazement. Further the references to Jesus as speaking the word have equally gnomic character at iv. 33 and viii. 32; at ii. 2 they are followed by Jesus' claim to be able to forgive sins, a claim which causes the scribes to stumble. It may then be that where Mark makes reference to the teaching of Jesus, either using διδάσκειν or λαλεῖν τὸν λόγον, he is drawing our attention to the difficulty of what Jesus says and does for those who are outside the Christian community; those within are given an explanation and understand. These matters are largely taken up with the eschatological nature of the Kingdom (iv. 1 ff.), the nature of the Eucharist (vi. 34 ff.), the meaning and necessity of his death (viii. 31; ix. 31), the claim that sins are forgiven through him (ii. 1 ff.), and certain hard points in Christian ethics (x. 1 ff.). The phrase 'Jesus taught' is to be understood in the sense of the addition 'in parables', which itself is to be understood in the sense of 'riddles, hard sayings, gnomic utterances', obscure to those outside, comprehensible to those within. Whether all this be accepted or not, Mark intends to set out Jesus as active in teaching, and not as an exorcist or as forcing men's minds. Teaching is his custom (x. 1).

The seams (ix. 2, 9, 14, 30) in the immediately succeeding material yield us little of interest; they are mainly geographical and temporal, adding in themselves nothing to our picture of the activity of Jesus other than that he and the disciples were continually on the move.[1] ix. 30–2 is a Markan construction, containing both the secrecy motif and the second prediction of the Passion, introduced by the reference to Jesus as teacher with which we have just dealt. ix. 33–50 is an amalgam of sayings held together by a number of key-words; the editorial connections in the sense of 'seams' hardly exist at all; the sayings themselves deal mainly with the lives of the disciples rather than with the activities of Jesus. Likewise in ch. x, describing Jesus'

[1] Cf. pp. 123 ff. below.

journey to Jerusalem, the seams are brief and mainly topographical (*vv.* 1, 2, 10, 13, 17, 23, 28(?), 32, 35, 46). Verse 31 may be an addition of Mark; he also appears to have brought together the sayings of *vv.* 41–5. We will return to *v.* 45 later: otherwise there is little here which deals with the activity of Jesus.

With the entrance of Christ into Jerusalem we come to a more closely connected sequence of events in the Markan narrative.[1] Whether they all actually occurred within the short space of a few days as Mark makes out it is not our purpose to inquire; it is very probable that Mark received the account of at least the main events of the last days in Jerusalem as part of the tradition. We need not therefore speculate whether the entrance into Jerusalem took place at the Feast of Tabernacles rather than at Passover-time and what Mark means by changing the festival. If Mark did make this change it was surely to heighten the tension of the crucifixion and the change of itself does not alter the picture which he presents of Jesus.

The topographical elements in the seams at xi. 1, 11 may have been supplied by Mark or derived from the tradition, but in either case they tell us nothing of the activities of Jesus. Taylor suggests that the words ἐφ’ ὃν οὐδεὶς οὔπω ἀνθρώπων ἐκάθισεν (xi. 2) may be an embellishment of the original story.[2] Bauer has made out a case to show that the πῶλος was not a young ass but a young horse.[3] It has been further suggested that Jesus in thus riding on an unbroken colt shows his mastery over the demonic.[4] This stretches things too far. Bauer has by no means proved his case,[5] and even if he had there is another possible explanation of the words; in Zech. ix. 9 (LXX) the πῶλος is described as νέος. Animals for sacrifice were not expected to have been used for domestic and farm purposes (Num. xix. 2; Deut. xxi. 3; Horace, *Epodes* ix, 21–2; Virg.

---

[1] On the section xi. 1–xiii. 37 cf. T. A. Burkill, 'Strain on the Secret: An Examination of Mark xi. 1–xiii. 37', *Z.N.T.W.* LI (1960), 31–46.

[2] Pp. 452 f.

[3] W. Bauer, 'The Colt of Palm Sunday', *J.B.L.* LXXII (1953), 220–9.

[4] G. B. Caird, *Principalities and Powers*, p. 71, n. 2.

[5] Cf. O. Michel, 'Eine philologische Frage zur Einzugsgeschichte', *N.T.S.* VI (1959), 81 f.; H. W. Kuhn, 'Das Reittier Jesu in der Einzugsgeschichte des Markusevangeliums', *Z.N.T.W.* L (1959), 82–91.

Georg. IV, 540; Ovid, *Metam.* III, 10–11), and this entry partook of the nature of a sacral event.[1] There is no need then to see in these words a Markan editorial reference to the demonic. Verse 10*a* may also be an addition to the tradition; if so it emphasises the coming of the Kingdom, rather than tells us about the meaning of the activity of Jesus. Jesus enters the city as king, and within the Passion story as told by Mark it is as king of the Jews that he is crucified (xv. 26, etc.). Thus the story here is tied to the Passion by this addition to the shout of the people. But *vv.* 9*b*, 10 also represent the worship of the Church for its exalted Saviour, and in that sense they would be taken by Mark's readers as representing their own worship and faith.[2]

In xi. 12–25 we have one incident sandwiched within another, a favourite Markan editorial trick (cf. iii. 20–35; v. 21–43). We may thus attribute to him the present arrangement. Simple temporal and topographical links at xi. 12, 15, 19, 20, 27 hold it together inwardly and join it to what precedes and what succeeds. The incident of the Cleansing of the Temple may well have been a piece of detached tradition.[3] It is differently placed within the Synoptic and Johannine traditions and taken by itself it was only a prophetic act, insufficient to trigger off the crucifixion.[4] The incident about the fig-tree, whether originally a prophetic and symbolic action or a development of the parable of Luke xiii. 6–9, must also have possessed at one time another place in the tradition; the parenthesis (again typical of Mark),[5] that it was not the time for figs, indicates a certain unhappiness about its present position.[6] It has been presumably placed there in order to imply the judgement of God over the Temple, the city, or Israel—there are many leaves, but no fruit. To this story Mark has appended a number of sayings on faith (xi. 22–5). In the account of the Cleansing of the Temple there

[1] So Taylor; Lohmeyer, etc.   [2] Cf. Lindars, pp. 171 f.

[3] Schmidt, pp. 291 ff. He quotes J. Weiss and Heitmüller writing respectively on Mark and John in *Die Schriften des NTs* (1907/8) and maintaining respectively that the Johannine and Markan datings are correct!

[4] Schniewind. Had Jesus driven out the priests themselves his action would certainly have been much more than prophetic.

[5] Taylor.

[6] This incident and the Entry may have taken place at the festival of Tabernacles; cf. C. W. F. Smith, 'No Time for Figs', *J.B.L.* LXXIX (1960), 315–27.

are a number of traces of Markan editing. Verses 18, 19 are omitted by Matthew and considerably altered by Luke so that the cleansing no longer provides the excuse for the plotting of the Jewish leaders. Quite clearly Mark however does intend us to understand that it did. The key verse is 17 which Mark introduces by a reference to Jesus as teaching. Bultmann conjectures that this replaces something more akin to John ii. 16;[1] a statement such as the latter would not have been enough to invite the Jewish leaders to plot the crucifixion. What, however, does Mark, with his solemn introduction, wish us to see in *v.* 17? Whose is ὁ οἶκός μου? In Isa. lvi. 7 it is Yahweh's house, but in Mark does it not read more naturally as Christ's own house? Even if the quotation as it stands in Mark represents what Jesus said and if we assume he intended a reference to God's house, that is no reason why the early Church should not have understood the μου of Jesus himself. If Jesus made this claim it does provide sufficient grounds within the Markan story for the plotting of the Jewish leaders (*v.* 18). Whether this be so or not we do have the close connection between οἶκος and the Church of God (Christ) for the early community (I Pet. iv. 17; Heb. x. 21, etc.). Now it appears that the part of the Temple which Jesus cleansed was the court of the Gentiles.[2] The People of God, the House, the Church, is not for Jews only, but, cleansed by Christ, is for all men. What Jesus accomplishes he accomplishes for all men, Gentiles as well as Jews. Thus Mark also depicts him as healing a Gentile (vii. 24–30) and feeding a Gentile crowd (viii. 1–10).[3]

There now follows a series of incidents (xi. 27–xii. 40) in which the differences between Jesus and the Jewish leaders are sharply defined. These differences are concerned with behaviour, authority and the interpretation of the Law of God. In them the tension between Jesus and his opponents is made quite clear so that the crucifixion becomes reasonable as their reaction

---

[1] P. 36.

[2] Cf. Lightfoot, *Gospel*, pp. 60–9. It is unlikely that the reference in *v.* 17 to the Gentiles is a post-Markan addition, though it is omitted by Matthew and Luke. It falls into line with Mark's Gentile interests.

[3] Cf. T. A. Burkill, 'Anti-Semitism in St Mark's Gospel', *N.T.* III (1959), 34–53. The cursing of the fig-tree would indicate the end of the place of the Jewish people in God's redemptive purpose.

to him; it emerges out of their refusal to accept his authority and guidance in the matters under dispute. There are few scholars who would maintain the view that all these incidents occurred on the third day of Jesus' visit to Jerusalem or that they all happened even in Jerusalem. They must have occupied a much longer time, and even if we allow that they took place in Jerusalem it may not have been during the last visit of Jesus to the city. It is difficult to say whether these incidents all formed part of a complex which came to Mark and which he introduced at this point or whether he himself has brought them together. The former has been maintained by Albertz, Taylor and many others. It has been criticised recently by W. L. Knox.[1] The stories do not form any easily recognisable pattern[2] nor do they rise to a climax; for this reason it is perhaps unnecessary to decide who compiled them.

It is possible that xi. 27–33 was always attached to the story of the Cleansing of the Temple.[3] The variation in the introductory formula by Luke, who attaches it to the teaching of Jesus, suggests rather that it may have been a piece of detached tradition that Mark brings in at this point. Bultmann[4] would limit the original tradition (whether coming from Jesus or from the Palestinian community) to *vv.* 28–30; but surely without *v.* 33 these lack a telling conclusion. Verses 31, 32 may well be additions of Mark to bring out the reason for the refusal of the priests and scribes to answer. The authority of Jesus is here linked to the baptism and the prophetic teaching of John the Baptist. Mark has not told us much about John, but what information he has provided concerns John as the forerunner who introduces Jesus and points out his significance. John is the messenger who declares that after him there comes one who is stronger and who will baptise with the Holy Spirit. John's baptism has the authority of heaven and in that baptism Jesus is recognised as the Son of God and the Spirit descends upon

[1] Pp. 85 ff.

[2] Daube, *The New Testament and Rabbinic Judaism*, pp. 158 ff.; 'Four Types of Question', *J.T.S.* II (1951), 45–8, indicates that in xii. 13–37 a Rabbinic scheme of questions is followed. If this is so this part of the complex will probably have been compiled prior to Mark during the Palestinian stage of the tradition.

[3] Taylor.   [4] Pp. 19 f.

him. In introducing John again at this point Mark is not merely arguing that Jesus' authority comes from God, as does that of John, but indicating that Jesus' authority is that of the one to whom the heavenly voice said, 'Thou art my beloved Son, with thee I am well pleased'. It is by this authority that Jesus does ταῦτα (v. 28), that is, it is as Son and as Messiah (both ideas seem to lie in the words of the heavenly voice) that he cleansed the Temple—and ultimately it will be because of these claims that he will be crucified.

In the next incident Jesus is clearly set out as the Son of God. The Parable of the Wicked Husbandmen (xii. 1–12) probably had another setting in the life of Jesus,[1] but by the time of Mark it had been adapted to give an interpretation of his death. The process of interpretation was still continuing in the early Church and we find that the allegorisation is given more exact detail in Matthew and Luke (cf. the parallels to Mark xii. 8). It is impossible to say with certainty if Mark was the first to begin this allegorisation, but probably he gave the parable its present position. xi. 27 and xii. 12, both Markan seams, show that it is directed against the leaders of the Jewish people. It sets out briefly the history of that people who are given a vineyard by God; they reject his messengers, the prophets; they reject his Son; so their leaders are rejected and the leadership is given to others. The Son who was rejected is now reverenced by the Church ('this is wonderful in *our* eyes', v. 11). The Church as a building and Christ as its foundation was a commonplace of the ideology of the early Christians (I Pet. ii. 4–8; I Cor. iii. 9–17; Eph. ii. 19–22). It was through the rejection of the Son of God that this new community of the Christian Church (including Gentiles) came into existence. So this passage is used by Mark both as a justification of the New Israel, built on the rejected Messiah, and as providing further grounds for the opposition of the Jewish leaders to Jesus (v. 12). The death of Jesus is given significance in this parable by the resultant creation of the new Israel.

The following three incidents (vv. 13–17, 18–27, 28–34) are juxtaposed with little editorial introductory material. The total

---

[1] Jeremias, *The Parables of Jesus*, pp. 55 ff.; C. H. Dodd, *The Parables of the Kingdom*, pp. 124 ff.; Wilson, *Studies in the Gospel of Thomas* (London, 1960), pp. 101 f., has pointed out that Logion 65 of Thomas contains the form of the parable thought to be original by Dodd and Jeremias.

effect is to show the discomfiture of those who approach Jesus; the third pericope in which there is some common ground between the scribe and Jesus is concluded with the statement that no one dared to ask him any more questions (xii. 34).

The last of these discussions between Jesus and his opponents (xii. 35–7a) is a question put by Jesus to them in which he confounds them; they give no answer. Whether this incident was originally told either to defend or to deny the Davidic lineage of Jesus does not concern us; Mark quite obviously assumes that lineage;[1] nor need we speculate whether the incident is a community creation[2] or a piece of genuine tradition.[3] In Mark it plays its part in leading to the rejection of Jesus by the Jewish authorities, who certainly could not allow the Christological claim inherent in it.[4] Jesus is here set out not only as Davidic King but as Kyrios. This is the favourite designation of the early community, though not often applied to Jesus by Mark.[5] At the moment of Mark's writing Jesus was sitting at the right hand of God: this was the belief of every strand of thought in the early Church. But are 'his enemies' yet put under his feet? And who are 'his enemies'? There is one line of thought which regards his enemies as powers and principalities and as already subject (I Pet. iii. 22; Eph. i. 20–2); in the other line of thought although he is already sitting at God's right hand he still waits for God to subject his enemies to him (Acts ii. 34 f.; I Cor. xv. 25; Heb. i. 13; x. 12 f.).[6] This latter appears to be the more primitive conception and failing any direct statement to the contrary is the natural conclusion to draw from the Markan passage: there is yet to be an eschatological fulfilment of the Lordship of Christ.[7] The Old Testament text recurs at xiv. 62, the confession of Jesus before the High Priest, where combined with Dan. vii. 13 it again possesses eschatological import. Here surely the High Priest must be included among the enemies of Christ who will be made subject to him. This is the only clue which Mark gives concerning whom he regarded as the enemies of the Lord who were to be made subject to him. The placing of the text in

---

[1] Cf. Lindars, pp. 46 ff. [2] Bultmann, pp. 51, 136 f.
[3] Taylor; Cranfield, in different ways.
[4] Cf. Hauck. [5] Below, pp. 166 f.
[6] Cf. pp. 184–6 below. [7] Cf. Lohmeyer.

xii. 36 where there is controversy between Jesus and the Jewish leaders might again suggest that the enemies are these leaders, that is, men and women. There is no indication that he included powers and principalities among the enemies of Jesus—or that he excluded them. For Mark the moment of subjection is neither cross, resurrection nor ascension. All these things have happened and the enemies are not yet subject. In particular the Cross is not the moment of subjection. If however we take the less probable interpretation of xii. 36, namely that in line with I Pet. iii. 22 and Eph. i. 20-2 it refers to powers and principalities as already subject, then this must be the subjection that took place in the binding of Satan in the Temptation.

xii. 37 b-40 continues the conflict between Jesus and the Jewish leaders; the crowd at this stage is not included among the enemies of Jesus as Mark makes clear by his 'seam' (37 b). The difference between the common people and the authorities is underlined in xii. 41-4, where the widow's mite is acceptable though the gifts of the rich are not.[1]

With ch. xiii, the Little Apocalypse, we are not concerned in detail. The connecting seams are brief and give no information about the activity of Jesus, other than that he is represented as teaching. But the final verse (37) is important: what Mark says here is for all Christians. Chs. xi, xii have been leading up to the Passion story, yet at this point (ch. xiii) the narrative seems to break off into another theme, the return of Jesus and the consummation of all. Here Mark sets out the subjection of his enemies to him which he has already indicated in xii. 35-7a. This is still future.[2] For the Christian believer there remain

---

[1] This pericope seems at first sight meaningless in relation to the main purpose of Mark. We only understand its importance when we link it closely to xiii. 1-4 (the chapter division at this point is most misleading). xiii. 2 predicts the destruction of the temple to which the woman has given her whole possessions. Jesus commends the woman and prophesies the destruction of that to which she has given her all! Surely this juxtaposition fits the situation of the readers: their world seems to be falling around them in the persecutions they are enduring; need they then give up the ordinary duties of morality and the upkeep of the Christian mission? Like the widow they must continue to give: despite the catastrophic conditions under which they live they must continue the ordinary duties of Christian service.

[2] In regard to what we may learn from ch. xiii about the return of Christ and Mark's editing, cf. Marxsen, pp. 101-40.

many hard days before that consummation. 'Chapter xiii is a great divine prophecy of the ultimate salvation of the elect after and indeed through unprecedented and unspeakable suffering, trouble and disaster.'[1] But it also serves to remind us before we come to the terrible narrative of the crucifixion of the nature of him who is to be crucified; the Jewish authorities did not understand whom they were putting to death; Mark makes sure we do. To reassure us of the ultimate solution Mark might well have put this section after the Resurrection, where it might seem to come logically, but he deliberately puts it earlier so that we see the whole Passion in the light of the ultimate victory of the return of Christ.

The Passion narrative in some form must always have been a part of the Christian tradition. It is difficult to see how the death of Jesus could have been referred to at all in preaching without some account being given of how it had taken place and an attempt made to show that Jesus was not guilty but innocent; moreover it is likely that from the beginning his death was shown as in accord with the will of God and also that men were held responsible for it.[2] If the Passion narrative was so used in the early community it is obvious that there are certain parts of it, for example the account of the Last Supper, which are not germane to this purpose and must have been added later. This additional material consists of two kinds: some of it, for example the account of the Last Supper, could be inserted at no other point in the total Gospel story than in the Passion narrative; some of it could have been inserted earlier in the Gospel but has been adapted to the Passion narrative, for example the Anointing (xiv. 3–9). We are not here making a judgement on the historicity of the material Mark used; even if it were argued that Jesus never kept the Last Supper with his disciples yet very early in the course of the tradition an account of this took its place closely tied to the death of Christ; from its first telling it can never have had any other place but in the

---

[1] Lightfoot, *Gospel*, p. 48. Cf. pp. 48–59 for a discussion of the detailed links which join ch. xiii to chs. xiv, xv.

[2] It is unnecessary to argue these points in detail: cf. Taylor, pp. 653 ff.; Dibelius, pp. 178 ff.; Schmidt, pp. 303 ff.; Knox, i, 115 ff.; Lightfoot, *History*, pp. 126 ff.; T. A. Burkill, 'St Mark's Philosophy of the Passion', *N.T.* ii (1958), 245–71.

context of the death of Jesus. Mark then had no control over the placing of this incident. We cannot however go on to argue that under no circumstances could Mark omit it from his account of the Passion; John succeeded in doing exactly that. Mark may be suspected of including it for at least two reasons: (*a*) as an account of the origin of the Eucharist; (*b*) for the light it throws on an understanding of the Passion. From these general considerations we must now turn to the narrative itself. It will be seen that the seams connecting incidents are of much less importance in the Passion narrative than elsewhere—by reason of the very fact that it was a connected narrative before Mark began work on it.

It is generally accepted that xiv. 1, 2, 10, 11 must have been the original beginning to the Passion narrative into which Mark has set the pericope of the Anointing.[1] This sandwiching of one event by another is a common Markan editorial device (cf. iii. 20–35; v. 21–43; xi. 12–25). The story exists in variant form in Luke vii. 36–50 and John xii. 1–8. It cannot thus have been firmly attached to the Passion. It may have been told earlier to set out the duties of almsgiving and worship over against one another,[2] but in Mark it is given a definite relation to the death of Jesus by *v.* 8*b*. In the light of the plots of the Jewish authorities it shows that Jesus was well aware of the closeness of his death, and since he accepts the anointing it implies that he accepts the death. He is anointed on the head (contrast Luke and John where the anointing is on the feet): such an anointing implies appointment to an office; it is thus as Messiah, the Anointed, that Jesus willingly goes to his death.[3]

If the account of the Last Supper is an interpolation in the Passion story as used in preaching, it is almost certain that *vv.* 12–16 which relate to the preparation for the meal are also

[1] Cf. Taylor; Dibelius, p. 180; Burkill, 'St Mark's Philosophy of the Passion', p. 246, etc.

[2] Burkill, 'St Mark's Philosophy of the Passion', p. 253.

[3] It is unnecessary for us to enter into the discussion of the meaning of εἰς μνημόσυνον αὐτῆς. Jeremias has held that this originally meant that God would remember the woman in the Last Judgement ('The Gentile World in the Thought of Jesus', *Bull. S.N.T.S.* III (1952), 21 f.; *Jesus' Promise to the Nations*, pp. 22 f.), but he admits that Mark (and Matthew) must have understood the saying as presupposing a world-wide mission which would remember the woman's action.

a Markan insertion at this point. There is however no editorial significance in its placement here; there is no other possible position for it in the whole Gospel. However it does make clear to us that Mark regarded the Last Supper as a Passover meal. There are indications in xiv. 2, where the Jewish authorities plot the arrest of Jesus before the Feast, that the original narrative adhered to the Johannine dating of the Crucifixion. It is unlikely that Mark made the change; there must have been a second stream of tradition from before his day from which he drew vv. 12–16 and in which it was maintained that the Last Supper was a Passover meal. It is sufficient for our purpose to realise that Mark's use of vv. 12–16 implies that he did not regard Jesus as the Passover lamb. This is a negative conclusion in regard to Mark's understanding of Jesus and yet not to be ignored for that reason. His more positive understanding of the death of Jesus in relationship to the Last Supper is obviously contained within that account itself (especially v. 24), and to this we shall have to return later.[1] However we may say here that just as the Jewish Passover in addition to commemorating a past event looks forward to a future deliverance, so the Christian Eucharist points forward, within the narrative to the death that is to follow and beyond the narrative to the consummation at the end of time.[2]

The account of the preparation for the Lord's Supper is not followed directly by the Supper account itself but there is interpolated the prophecy of the Betrayal. Here again we have Mark's sandwiching effect. The Betrayer is mentioned in vv. 10, 11; then comes the preparation for the Last Supper, vv. 12–16; then Jesus shows his awareness of the Betrayer's actions, vv. 17–21; and this is again followed by the account of the Last Supper vv. 22–5. (A kind of double sandwich.) If vv. 10, 11 with their announcement of the existence of the Betrayer were part of the original narrative then it is likely that vv. 17–21 were also. The story of the Betrayer answers the question how the enemies of Jesus came to be able to seize him; vv. 17–21 make us realise that Jesus was aware of what was happening and yet did nothing to prevent it. The double reference to eating in v. 18 and v. 22 reinforces the suggestion that in vv. 17–21 and vv. 22–5 we have two sources or traditions which Mark has

---

[1] Below, pp. 144 ff.   [2] Cf. Lightfoot, *History*, pp. 140 f.

brought together.[1] Within *vv.* 17–21 we may note the strong element of predetermination in regard to the death of Jesus (*v.* 21, 'just as it is written' and *v.* 18, if ὁ ἐσθίων is the correct text, is a quotation of Ps. xli (xl). 10).

Taylor suggests that *vv.* 26–31 are a Markan construction and this appears reasonable. It is noticeable that Mark sets the prophecy of the denial of Peter and of the scattering of the disciples on the way to Gethsemane, whereas Luke and John set it in the Upper Room. Mark's positioning brings sharply into contrast the disloyalty of the disciples to Jesus and his own loyalty to his Father. It serves thus to emphasise the evil in men over against which the drama of the Cross is played out. Verse 28 is exceptionally difficult. It can be omitted from the pericope without hindering the flow of thought in relation to the denial of Peter; we may thus assume its introduction by Mark. Set directly after a prophecy of the scattering of the disciples it must refer to their gathering again, and so to a new relationship of Shepherd and sheep which follows on the Resurrection. Whether this new relationship is to take place through the resurrection appearances themselves or through the Parousia has been disputed; the answer is closely linked to the understanding of the use of 'Galilee' in Mark.[2] Whichever of these two points of view be accepted[3] the verse is presumably inserted here, first, to set the Passion in the light of the eventual triumph of the Resurrection and/or Parousia and, secondly, to show that our Lord himself expected the continuance of the fellowship of the disciples both with himself and with one another. Out of the Cross there comes a Christ who will draw together again those who have failed him.

The incident in Gethsemane, *vv.* 32–42, reads like an amalgam of two separate accounts,[4] probably two separate narratives of the same incident. It begins by telling how Jesus

[1] Bultmann, pp. 265 f., 276.

[2] Lightfoot, *Locality*, pp. 111–26; Lohmeyer, *Galiläa und Jerusalem*, pp. 10–14, 26–36; Marxsen, pp. 36 ff.; M. Karnetzki, 'Die Galiläische Redaktion im Markusevangelium', *Z.N.T.W.* LII (1961), 238–72.

[3] We believe that the reference is to the resurrection appearances; cf. below, pp. 173 ff.

[4] Cf. Bultmann, pp. 267 f.; Bussmann, I, 193 ff.; Knox, pp. 125 ff.; R. Thiel, *Drei Markus-Evangelien*, pp. 23, 65–8; though these reach different conclusions as to the division of the material.

leaves his disciples and says that he is going to pray (*v.* 32). But he is then said to take the inner three, Peter, James and John, and he talks to them (*vv.* 33, 34*a*); these again he leaves telling them to wait for him (*v.* 34*b*). If we follow the narrative strictly only Peter, James and John will have been with him at the time of the arrest (*vv.* 42–3), yet in *v.* 50 'all' are said to flee, which suggests the whole company of the disciples rather than the three. There is again the paralleling of the passing of the hour (*v.* 35) and the taking away of the cup (*v.* 36). By the very fact that Mark feels compelled to bring together these accounts so that nothing is omitted he emphasises the importance of the incident. Certainly for the early Church a large part of this importance lay in the references to the correct attitude to trial —cf. *v.* 38, and the praying attitude of our Lord—but we may also discern both the incomprehension of the disciples even at this late hour concerning what is about to happen to their master and the attitude of Christ himself towards the fate that lay ahead of him. Whereas in the Temptation and the Baptism, where we might have expected Mark if he was at all biographically inclined to have said something about the struggle in the soul of Jesus, we do not find such, here we are given a glimpse. Mark, who at the time of writing will have known of the death of many martyrs, must have been very much aware of the difference in the attitude of Jesus and of those who like Stephen went most joyfully to their death. Despite the manner in which Mark has shown Jesus to be conscious of the necessity of his death he now shows him afraid before it.[1] This may appear an inconsistency; if so it is an inconsistency which must have been forced on Mark by the material itself. But it may not be an inconsistency. On the one hand Mark shows the death of Jesus as predetermined and on the other he shows sinful men engineering it. We see their sin not only in the plotting of the Jewish authorities but also in the incomprehension of the disciples; already we are aware that one of them will betray him and another deny him. These two lines of thought now come together in Gethsemane; Spirit[2] and flesh are opposed;

[1] We may note that Luke omits *v.* 33 and thereby reduces the fear shown by Jesus. We find it difficult to minimise this element in Mark as Ebeling does (*Das Messiasgeheimnis und die Botschaft des Marcus-Evangelisten*, pp. 174–8).

[2] We take τὸ πνεῦμα in *v.* 38 to refer to the Spirit of God; cf. above, p. 30.

God and man are opposed; evil now comes as close to Jesus as it possibly can; it attacks from within. At the conclusion of the incident the element of predetermination reappears, 'the hour is come' (v. 41) and Jesus hands himself over to 'sinners'. His destiny lies in their hands; their plots will now have their issue.

The next pericope, vv. 43–52, the arrest of Jesus, probably contains an original core, vv. 43–6, recounting the actual arrest, to which Mark has added various sayings and peripheral incidents. We observe that he describes Jesus again as teaching (v. 49). That there were many around the temple who needed healing is shown by the story of the crippled beggar at the gate (Acts iii), but there is no reference to Jesus as healing. His main activity is teaching.

Verses 53–72 are again a sandwich of which the central portion is the trial before the High Priest and the first and third parts concern the failure of Peter when put to the test of loyalty; this again suggests a Markan arrangement.[1] It is unlikely that the denial of Peter formed a part of the original Passion narrative, but some form of the trial must have appeared in order to show the innocence of Jesus and to make clear the grounds of his condemnation. This the present account certainly does. Jesus affirms that he is the Son of the Blessed, the Christ.[2] The impressiveness of this statement is driven home by the silence of Jesus before false accusations.[3] He however clearly attests his true being and this is followed directly by the statement that all held him worthy of death (v. 64). Whether Jesus

---

[1] It has been analysed in different ways; cf. Taylor; Bultmann, pp. 269–71; Knox, pp. 131 ff.; Bussmann, pp. 198 ff.; etc.; the trial may be a doublet of xv. 1. Dibelius (pp. 192 f., 213) rightly views the trial before the High Priest as the central action in the Markan account.

[2] The Markan text may have originally read σὺ εἶπας ὅτι ἐγώ εἰμι. Such a supposition accounts more easily for the Matthean and Lukan text and also takes account of the variation in the Markan textual tradition; cf. Taylor, *ad loc.* If so, the reply is not a direct affirmation; it implies that the statement is true with a different interpretation. Mark's readers would, of course, take it as an affirmation of Sonship and Messiahship. We do not need to inquire what the High Priest meant by his question (if he asked it in that form); Mark takes it in its full sense of 'sonship'. Cf. J. Blinzler, *Der Prozess Jesu*[2] (Regensburg, 1955), p. 76.

[3] Verse 58 is difficult. It may rest on a genuine statement of Jesus (so most commentators), but Mark clearly indicates it is a false accusation. It thus serves to highlight the true grounds of condemnation.

really maintained a secrecy about his own being or not, Mark draws out in unmistakable terms the nature of that being and the resultant necessity of death. Jesus is both Christ and Son of the Blessed, that is Son of God. Here come together two titles which have been chasing one another through the Gospel. From the beginning (even if the reading υἱοῦ θεοῦ is false in i. 1), Jesus has been set out as Son of God in the voice at the Baptism, at the Transfiguration and in the cries of the demons. He has been hailed as Messiah by Peter in the confession at Caesarea Philippi, in the entry into Jerusalem and in the Anointing (xiv. 3–9). Now Mark brings these two titles together. We tend to separate them in our discussions of their origin and probable meaning. It may well be that Mark did not see the distinction between them that we do but regarded them almost as interchangeable.[1] In any case it is because of the central picture of Jesus exemplified in these two terms that Mark has given us in his Gospel that he is put to death. Jesus continues after the affirmation of his nature and status to say that the High Priest will see his power. But when Mark writes the High Priest of that time is already dead. Mark must have also then seen meaning in this statement for his own readers. They will see the Christ in his glory. We are recalled here to the Little Apocalypse. The ultimate victory is as certain as the imminent death; and since the death has already happened Mark's readers may be assured that they will see the victory.[2]

xv. 1 gives in summary form the trial of Jesus before the Jewish authorities. They then hand him over to Pilate. Verse 2 reads as an addition to the original account; in vv. 3–5 Jesus is said to have answered nothing, yet in v. 2 he has spoken to Pilate even if it was only very ambiguously. Though xv. 2 is an addition to the account it is very unlikely that Mark of his own accord introduces Jesus at this point as the King of the Jews. The kingship motif sounds all through this stage of the Passion; cf. vv. 9, 12, 17 f., 26, 32. Though Mark has brought this title of

---

[1] Cf. Wrede, *Das Messiasgeheimnis in den Evangelien*, pp. 75–7; but see below, pp. 107 f., 165–73.

[2] Even if we accept the interpretation of J. A. T. Robinson, *Jesus and His Coming*, pp. 43 ff. (cf. Taylor), that the original reference in ἐρχόμενον (xiv. 62) related to the Son of Man's going to God, Mark will still have viewed it as a victory which his readers are to behold; the High Priest never saw it fulfilled; Mark's readers may.

Jesus into extreme prominence yet it will have lain in the tradition and may indeed go back to the inscription on the Cross: Pilate must have had some grounds for condemning Jesus. 'King of the Jews' is the political side of the Messianic title; that this is so appears in *v.* 32 where we have the variant, 'The Christ, the King of Israel'; here Jews speak; on the other occasions it was Gentiles who used the title, 'King of the Jews'. It is clear that Mark wishes us to see Jesus condemned and crucified as the Jewish Messiah. It is also clear that he does not wish this to be taken in a political sense. The political leader is Jesus Barabbas[1] who is set in contrast to Jesus the Christ. The ambiguous answer of Jesus to Pilate (xv. 2) implies that while Jesus accepts the title of King he queries the meaning Pilate reads into it. 'It is an affirmation which implies that the speaker would put things differently.'[2] Pilate quite obviously does not see Jesus as a dangerous political offender. Indeed the encounter with Pilate serves to underline the hostility of the Jews to Jesus in that it shows Pilate making some attempt to save him. Not only are the Jewish leaders now involved in this hostility but so also is the crowd (xv. 11 ff.). In contrast the innocence of Jesus is again shown clearly (xv. 14).

There follows the account of the mocking by the soldiers, xv. 16–20*a*, the theme of which repeats that of xiv. 65 and appears again in xv. 29–32. The humiliation of Jesus is heavily underlined in this threefold repetition. The evil in men is again displayed in the presence of the Messianic Son of God. It is probable that Mark has added each of these accounts of the mocking to the original Passion narrative.[3] In the first account certain anonymous people in the house of the High Priest mock him,[4] in the second, Roman soldiers, in the third, passers-by (i.e. presumably the 'crowd'),[5] the High Priests and scribes

---

[1] We assume, with most modern commentators, that the original reading in Matt. xxvii. 16 was Ἰησοῦν Βαραββᾶν and that Matthew copied this from an original Ἰησοῦς Βαραββᾶς in Mark xv. 7. στασιαστής, στάσις (xv. 7) suggest revolution. As against this view, cf. R. Dunkerley, 'Was Barabbas also called Jesus?', *E.T.* LXXIV (1963), 126 f.　　[2] Taylor, *ad loc.*

[3] So Taylor; Bultmann, pp. 271, 284; etc.; cf. P. Winter, *On the Trial of Jesus* (Berlin, 1961), pp. 21 f.

[4] It almost reads as if Mark intended us to view the High Priests as themselves carrying out the mockery; cf. Knox, p. 132.

[5] In Luke the crowd watches but does not mock.

and the crucified thieves. Thus no section of humanity stands apart from the general hostility. On each occasion the mocking attacks a claim that might be made for Jesus: the first, that he was a prophet; the second, that he was King of the Jews; the third, that he could save and that he was the Messiah. In the third we may note how the word σῴζειν is used; this cannot be detached from its soteriological reference; Jesus as Messiah is the one who saves men; this is why he dies. Here Mark is implicitly setting out the purpose of the life and death of Jesus and it is connected to his relationship to men, not his relationship to the demonic world.

The section xv. 20b–32 describes the actual carrying out of the crucifixion. Probable Markan additions within it are the reference to Simon of Cyrene (v. 21), the notice of time (v. 25) and, as we have already mentioned, the mocking (vv. 31, 32). Apart from their role in the mocking Mark makes no explicit use of his mention of the two thieves, though the later textual tradition makes clear reference to Isa. liii. 12. So many of Mark's Old Testament references are indirect that it is possible, though not likely, that he intended such a reference here.

xv. 33–41 describes the incidents attending the death of Jesus. In particular we may notice the darkness (v. 33), his great cries (vv. 34, 37), the rending of the temple veil (v. 38) and the confession of the centurion (v. 39). All these are in some sense signs of the tremendous event that is taking place. Which part of this material was original to the Passion narrative and which has been added by Mark is not easy to determine. It is easy to say that the references to the darkness and the temple veil are legendary, but that does not mean that they had not been added to the account prior to Mark. It is possible also to argue that the two references to a great cry by Jesus (vv. 34 and 37) are doublets (Luke gives the great cry in another form xxiii. 46), but again we cannot be sure that Mark has added one or other.[1] We may assume that the original Passion account has under-

---

[1] For an analysis of xv. 33–41 see the various commentators, Bultmann, pp. 273 f.; Knox, pp. 142 ff.; F. C. Grant, *The Earliest Gospel*, pp. 175, ff. Taylor, pp. 649–51, 653–64 is particularly valuable. Schreiber, p. 157, n. 5, gives an analysis different from that usually found, holding that Mark added vv. 34b–36, 39–41. Details of his analysis are lacking, but are apparently to appear in a future work.

gone modification and that Mark agrees with the form of it
which he produces. There is then first the strange natural
portent of darkness; this cannot be taken other than as a
cosmic event. There are many references to natural portents
accompanying the death of great men[1] and this may well be
the present intention of the reference. But the darkening of the
sun is also a sign that judgement is taking place (Amos viii. 9;
Jer. xv. 9; Mark xiii. 24).[2] This judgement is not however a
judgement on nature or the powers of evil but on men, the
darkness signifying the moment of enactment. We may observe
that Matthew increases the cosmic emphasis in the sense that
he records further unusual events, namely the earthquake, the
split rocks, opened tombs and the reappearance of dead saints
(xxvii. 51–4). This by no means implies that Matthew takes a
more 'cosmic' view of the death of Jesus, in the sense that it
has to do with the defeat of cosmic powers, than Mark does.
The recording of unusual events, as the darkness, is not then
necessarily a sign that the powers of evil are being judged. In
Matthew and in Mark it is men who are being judged and the
darkness is a sign of this. If this is the interpretation it coheres
with the rending of the veil in that both denote judgement on
Israel[3] (in both Amos viii. 9 and Jer. xv. 9 it is the chosen people
or Jerusalem that is judged) and Mark has prepared us for this
judgement on Israel by the way he has shown the continued

---

[1] Virg. *Georgics* I, 466 ff.; Diog. Laert. IV, 64; Plut. *Pelop.* 295 A (31, 2);
cf. Strack–Billerbeck, I, 1040–2.   [2] Cf. Iren. *Adv. Haer.* IV, 33, 12.

[3] While it is probably true that for apologetic reasons Mark with the other
evangelists attempted to lay the blame for the death of Jesus as far as possible
on the Jews (Winter, *On the Trial of Jesus*, stresses this much more than
Blinzler, *Der Prozess Jesu*[2]), it must not be overlooked that this was also a
theological tendency within his work; Jesus is at issue with the Pharisees
from the beginning (iii. 6); the Cross is judgement on Judaism (the rending
of the veil, the darkness, the destruction of the temple and its rebuilding in
three days). Judaism must therefore be shown to be fully involved in the
crucifixion.

This does not imply that Judaism alone came under judgement. We
must remember: (*a*) Pilate is in part responsible for Jesus' death and
therefore under judgement; (*b*) many Jews, for instance the disciples, are
not under judgement but through the Cross have become members of the
new community which replaced Judaism; (*c*) the Jews come under judgement principally because they have been God's People; judgement must
begin at the House of God, but it does not end there.

opposition of the Jews to Jesus. The veil may be either that separating the Holy of Holies from the Holy Place or that separating the Holy Place from the outer courtyard. If it was the outer veil its rending must indicate a judgement on Judaism;[1] if it was the inner this element of judgement will still remain but there will be added to it the sense of open access to God (cf. Heb. vi. 19 f.; ix. 8; x. 19 f.).[2] Into this same complex of ideas it would seem we must also fit the mocking of the passers-by who repeated the false accusation that Jesus would destroy the Temple and build it again in three days (xv. 29; xiv. 58). The rending of the veil is in effect the destruction of the Temple. It will be rebuilt in three days—with the Resurrection the new community will be formed (xvi. 7). The conception of the Christian community as the temple was a commonplace of early Christianity, a temple not made with hands but spiritual.[3] Whatever the original intention of this accusation this reference to the destruction of Israel and the creation of the new community through the death and Resurrection of Jesus would appear to be Mark's aim in recording the words as part of the mocking at this point.[4] If the rending of the veil indicates judgement on Israel's exclusive way to God and the removal of a barrier preventing access to him it is also appropriate that it is immediately followed by the confession of the Gentile centurion that Jesus is the Son of God.[5] This title has played too big a part in the Gospel for it to be taken at this point as the testimony of an eye-witness to the courageous death of a martyr; such may be the Lukan interpretation (xxiii. 47), but

---

[1] Jesus' judgement on the Law is earlier emphasised by Mark (ii. 23–iii. 5; vii. 1–23, especially vii. 19b). This element in Mark is played down by Matthew; cf. Bornkamm in Bornkamm, Barth and Held, *Tradition and Interpretation in Matthew*, p. 31, n. 2. The rending of the veil is also found in Gnosticism; cf. R. McL. Wilson, *The Gospel of Philip* (London, 1962), pp. 139 ff., 189 ff. The theme connected to it is not usually 'judgement'.

[2] Cf. Test. Levi x. 3 f.; Test. Benj. ix. 3 f. On the variant tradition in the Gosp. Heb., cf. Klostermann, *ad loc*. It seems too fanciful to connect the rending of the veil with the rending of the heavens at the Baptism as Lightfoot, *Gospel*, pp. 55 f.; Yates, *The Spirit and the Kingdom*, pp. 232–7.

[3] Cf. Best, *One Body in Christ*, pp. 160 ff. and the references given there.

[4] Cf. Lindars, pp. 66 ff.

[5] Cf. Lohmeyer. It would be to go too far to take the rending of the veil as the removal of a covering which permits the true Son of God to be seen in the crucified Jesus; the veil rent, the centurion sees and believes.

in Mark it is clearly a confession of faith. In Matthew (xxvii. 54) the centurion utters his confession on seeing the earthquake and darkness; in Mark he makes it on hearing the final cry of Jesus and observing his death.[1]

It has been suggested that the strong cry, which is mentioned twice (*vv.* 34, 37), is surprising in a crucified man, who would normally die slowly from exhaustion,[2] and must therefore be given special significance as a cry of triumph. But Jesus died unexpectedly early for a victim of crucifixion who usually lingered many days in his agony; this is recognised in Mark in Pilate's amazement at Jesus' early death (xv. 44). It is possible that the great cry was the immediate cause of his death in using up his available reserves of strength. Obviously we are concerned only with the second great cry (*v.* 37)—the first (*v.* 34) is the cry of dereliction and cannot contain the thought of triumph. The two cries were probably originally doublets, though Mark will not necessarily have regarded them as such. Yet if the second great cry is to be taken as different in content from the first we might expect some clear indication of its meaning. Schreiber[3] suggests that we should see it as the cry of victory in exaltation since it is immediately followed by the confession of the centurion, who uses the words that apply to the exalted one, namely, the Son of God (cf. Ps. ii. 7). But it is difficult to see in Mark sufficient grounds for identifying the moment of death with that of exaltation.[4] Moreover alternative explanations of the great cry are possible. Luke (xxiii. 46) and John (xix. 30) both give interpretations of it in which they take it as a cry of triumph in the sense that the task set to Jesus by God has been completed; what has been predetermined throughout the whole Gospel, his death, has now been brought to its end in obedience. Such an explanation may be traced in Mark's view of the centurion's words as his recognition of Jesus as Son of God. If, as we believe, there is a close connection

[1] The text of Mark is difficult at this point, but probably originally contained a reference here to the 'cry' of Jesus; thus Taylor; Cranfield; Lohmeyer; etc., reading κράξας (or ἔκραξεν καί) before ἐξέπνευσεν.

[2] Cf. Klostermann; Lagrange; Wellhausen; *ad v.* 39.

[3] P. 163. Cf. H. W. Bartsch, 'Historische Erwägungen zur Leidensgeschichte', *Evangelische Theologie*, xxii (1962), 449–59.

[4] Cf. below, pp. 130 ff.

between this title and the sacrifice by Abraham of Isaac then the centurion's confession of him as Son may be linked to the great cry in that it is the cry of triumphant obedience to the sacrifice required and signifies willing acceptance of it. No ram is forthcoming to replace the Son on the Cross and he now accepts that there is no deliverance for him.[1] We are not then required to see in the great cry a shout of victory over opposing spiritual powers. The very fact that it is a man, the centurion, who confesses Jesus in the moment of death, and not a cosmic power which bends the knee to him, shows that Mark is seeing the death of Jesus firmly in relationship to men: it is an event whose significance exists for man, rather than for nature or the spiritual powers.

Lastly we must look at the content of the earlier cry, the cry of dereliction (v. 34). Mark underlines its importance, first by quoting the Aramaic, the actual words of Jesus,[2] and then giving a translation, and secondly by recounting how the group around the Cross misunderstood it. It comes at the end of the period of darkness and yet within that period; if that darkness signifies judgement then Mark is indicating that Jesus is, as we might say, at the wrong end of judgement. If Israel is judged and forsaken by God (the veil of the Temple is rent) then in Jesus that judgement is seen executed; there are places within the Gospel, the Temptation, the Baptism, where Mark appears to look on Jesus as Israel; this may be another such passage. It is probably also to be linked to Gethsemane: Jesus encounters the evil within and outside the soul of man; only evil could drive God away from man.

The second piece of mockery in this passage, when Jesus' words on the Cross are misunderstood and he is offered a drink to prolong his life so that the spectators may see if Elijah will come to his aid (xv. 35 f.), must underline the sacrifice of Jesus.[3]

[1] Perhaps the first great cry (v. 34) might then refer to his disappointment that God had not produced the necessary ram. God had not forsaken Isaac but provided the substitute. Here there is no substitute provided; the Son must be the sacrifice.

[2] We need not delay to argue whether Jesus spoke Hebrew or Aramaic; obviously Mark understood him to speak Aramaic, witness to which are the other Aramaic phrases preserved in the Gospel.

[3] It may represent the combination of two traditions, 35, 36b and 36a; cf. Taylor.

Elijah, =John the Baptist, has already come and suffered a
Passion. Though popular Jewish belief looked on Elijah as one
who would come in the hour of need,[1] he has already come,
been rejected and cannot come again. Perhaps there is deeper
irony: Elijah's coming was to be associated with judgement
(Mal. iii. 1 ff.); judgement is now being suffered by the one
whom Elijah would have expected to execute it.

In the last two verses xv. 40 f. of the section on the death of
Jesus Mark mentions the women who watched the crucifixion.
He names women again in the next section concerning the
burial (xv. 42–7) and again in the story of the empty tomb
(xvi. 1–8).[2] It may be that he wishes to emphasise them as
eye-witnesses, but the threefold repetition of the names suggests
rather that he is putting together three sections which were once
separate. Whether this is so or not there is nothing in xv. 42–7
which concerns us. xvi. 1–8 is the necessary completion to the
story of the Cross: necessary because in the Markan predictions
of the Cross the Resurrection has always been mentioned; it is a
part of that which is determined beforehand. Whatever the
significance of *v.* 7 it means that Jesus is raised for the benefit
of his followers: they are to see him again in Galilee.[3] Thus the
meaning of the Cross and Resurrection is again tied down to its
relationship to the believer rather than given a cosmic setting
in relation to the subjection of evil powers. Out of the event of
death and resurrection the new community emerges.

[1] Cf. Strack–Billerbeck, IV, 769 ff.

[2] The Western text omits the women at xvi. 1 and may be original.

[3] On Galilee cf. below, pp. 173 ff. xvi. 7 is probably a Markan addition,
cf. Bultmann, p. 287; Johnson (*ad* xiv. 28); Burkill, 'St Mark's Philosophy
of the Passion', p. 271, etc.

CHAPTER IV

THE SELECTION OF THE MATERIAL

WHEN we ask why Mark has chosen the particular pericopae which we find in this Gospel we meet an initial difficulty: we do not know what material was available to him out of which he could select. If we knew that Mark had a great amount of material about the teaching of Jesus, say a 'copy' of Q and only three exorcism accounts, and chose to omit most of the teaching and put in all three exorcisms, this would obviously lead us to conclude that for him exorcisms were most important. Equally had he at his disposal only the teaching of Jesus which he has inserted and a hundred exorcism stories from which he selected the present three then we would come to quite a different conclusion about the importance of the exorcisms for Mark. Unfortunately we are not in a position to draw either conclusion. We may note that most of the expansion of Matthew and Luke is in the direction of giving fuller teaching by Jesus; in proportion there are not added as many new pronouncement stories and miracles as direct teaching. This would suggest that Mark used most of the available material about the activities of Jesus, other than about his teaching. We must not therefore assume that Mark had unlimited material at his disposal (cf. John xxi. 25) from which he made a judicious or injudicious selection. The early Church may already have trimmed down the amount of available material and left Mark with little from which to select. That Matthew and Luke give more teaching of Jesus does not mean that Mark deliberately eliminated most of this material as if suggesting that Jesus was a man of action rather than of speech; it may not have been available to him; in any case we have seen how in his editorial seams Mark has stressed the fact that Jesus taught.

But even if Mark was fairly well confined to certain material and did not have an unlimited choice we may still ask why he has included the material that he has. There was naturally no radical cleavage between Mark and the early Church in which he found the material and he will have included it for very similar reasons to that which led to its preservation, or creation, within the Christian community. He may also have had additional private reasons of his own, as we might say, but he will hardly have greatly disagreed with the reasons of the early Church. To look at the material itself may give some indication of the reasons for its inclusion. To ask why a particular incident has been included might be answered formally by saying that the evangelists included it because it happened. But many things happened which they have not included. Jesus must have eaten every day of his ministry, but they do not record these meals; yet certain meals are recorded: a meal with Levi, because of the sayings about the purpose of the ministry to which it leads (ii. 13–17); a final meal with his disciples, because in it the early Church (including Mark) saw the basis for its own celebration of the Eucharist (xiv. 12–25); and two mass feedings (vi. 30–44; viii. 1–9). These are all recorded because they have greater significance than other meals which were eaten only with the intention of nourishing the body.

We may begin by looking at what we may term the 'mighty works' of Jesus, the miracles and healings.[1] And since we have already mentioned the two mass feedings we commence with them. They are obviously linked through their wording with the Eucharist; they are also connected with the Old Testament manna feedings in the wilderness and seemingly thereby with the expected eschatological meal. But we must not forget that they show us Jesus as the wonder-worker who is able to supply the needs of men; he has compassion upon them (viii. 2). Men should open their eyes to behold in the giver of food for the thousands the one who can supply all their needs.[2] We have already seen[3] that by his linking of the feeding incidents to vi. 34b and viii. 14–21 Mark indicates that one of the needs of

---

[1] G. H. Boobyer, 'The Redaction of Mark iv. 1–34', has argued that in iv. 12 τὰ πάντα includes not only the strictly so-called parables but also the δυνάμεις and διδαχή of Jesus. We have ourselves seen (pp. 80 f.) the connection between Jesus as teacher and mysterious sayings, i.e. παραβολαί. If the δυνάμεις, as seems likely, are also to be included among the παραβολαί then they must be carefully examined for the meaning they reveal to the eye of faith.

[2] Hunger need not necessarily be for material food but can be given a spiritual turn, e.g. Amos viii. 11; Isa. lv. 1; Ps. xlii (xli). 2–4; Matt. v. 6.

[3] Pp. 76 f.

the soul which Jesus meets is that of true teaching. Jesus may then, in the Markan interpretation, be seen as the one who brings spiritual understanding to men; if they will but look at what he, the wonder-worker, has done, they will understand (viii. 17, 18, 21). This would represent the Markan interpretation as distinct from, and over and above, that of the early Church.

Closely allied to the two feedings are the two accounts of storms on the Sea of Galilee (iv. 35–41; vi. 45–52);[1] indeed Mark has deliberately linked the second to the first feeding (vi. 52).[2] In both instances the astonishment of the disciples serves to underline the greatness of their master; there is no situation in which he is not supreme. There seems no reason to doubt that the traditional interpretation of the second of these passages is basically correct, namely that in moments of testing the Christ will come to the ship of the Church and bring calm. This may be conceived both as a present coming of the risen Lord in every emergency[3] and also as his once-for-all coming in the Parousia to bring final deliverance. The same thought of deliverance from times of testing lies in the first account (iv. 35–41),[4] but here the storm that has come on the Church is regarded as of demonic origin: it is rebuked in very similar words to those in which demons are rebuked (i. 25).[5] Accord-

---

[1] Whether they are parallel accounts of one incident and what measure of historical kernel they contain it is not necessary for us to determine.

[2] Verse 52 is a Markan comment; it is omitted by Matthew.

[3] This story may either have received colouring from the resurrection narratives or itself been originally a resurrection narrative transferred to the pre-resurrection period; cf. C. H. Dodd, 'The Appearances of the Risen Christ: An Essay in Form-Criticism of the Gospels', in *Studies in the Gospels* (ed. D. E. Nineham), pp. 9–35. Loisy views it as a symbolic representation of the Resurrection itself.

[4] P. J. Achtemeier, 'Person and Deed. Jesus and the Storm-Tossed Sea', *Interpretation*, xvi (1962), 169–76 considers that the stilling of the storm depicts Jesus as the one who turns chaos into order. The sea represents the power of chaos; but in the Old Testament (Ps. lxxiv; Isa. li. 9 f.; etc.) 'God's work of creation and his work of redemption are...closely linked'. Thus the stilling of the storm is an act of redemption. Similarly, we might add, to walk on the sea (vi. 45–52) is a sign of his power over demonic chaos (cf. Job ix. 8; Ps. lxxvii (lxxvi). 20).

[5] Hoskyns and Davey, *The Riddle of the New Testament*, pp. 69–71 have shown the inner Old Testament links which connect iv. 35–41 and v. 1–20.

ingly Jesus is depicted as the deliverer of men from evil, including that which may be directly traced to the activity of evil supernatural powers. Jesus is present in the Church, the ship; so believers need not be afraid in the midst of persecution. This takes us on to the exorcisms in which again we see Jesus as the deliverer of men from demonic forces. The early Church continued to practise exorcism (Acts xvi. 16–18; cf. xix. 13), and certainly one factor in the preservation of these stories will have been that of example: this is how to carry out an exorcism (cf. ix. 29, a verse omitted in Matthew and Luke; indeed in this whole pericope the method of Jesus is contrasted with the method, or the lack of it, of the disciples; there is on this occasion no confession of Jesus by the demon and no instruction to silence by Jesus). Two peculiarly Markan factors enter into the exorcism accounts: the confession by the demons of the Divine Sonship of Jesus (i. 24, 34; iii. 11; v. 7) and the testimony that a successful exorcism gives to the fact that Jesus has already conquered Satan (iii. 27). Possibly the command to silence laid by Jesus on the demons should also be listed here as a Markan factor, but it is part of a more general command to silence about his healing activity. The exorcism stories therefore both bear witness directly to the being of Jesus and to his activity in his already accomplished victory over Satan and his continued ability to deliver men from Satan's underlings.

In all the remaining healing stories Jesus is again set forth as the one who performs mighty works.[1] They are recounted because they show us Jesus as the mighty deliverer of men, this time from sickness, and because they are examples to the early Church of how to carry on healing activity. Various types of healing are signs of the eschatological age—though this appears more clearly in Matthew (xi. 5) and Luke (vii. 22). We have already seen that Mark makes in ii. 1–12 a strong connection between the forgiveness of sin and the healing of sickness.[2] The same is true of the preceding miracle (i. 40–5), where a leper is

---

[1] But the miracle stories are not told merely to show Jesus as wonder-worker (iv. 41). The ancient world knew too many such wonder-workers to be easily convinced by the wonders of another that he was the Son of God. Cf. A. Richardson, *The Miracle Stories of the Gospels*, pp. 20 ff. Mark makes this clear at viii. 11 f.

[2] Pp. 69 ff.

cleansed;[1] leprosy was sometimes a punishment for sin (Miriam, Num. xii. 10; Gehazi, II Kings v. 27; Uzziah, II Kings xv. 5);[2] the leper is excluded from the worship of God and when he is accepted as clean it is on the presentation of a sin offering and guilt offering (Lev. xiv. 10 ff.).[3] The same word καθαρίζειν is used of the removal of sin (Acts xv. 9; II Cor. vii. 1; Eph. v. 26; I John i. 7, 9, etc.) and of cleansing from leprosy (i. 40, 41, 42).[4] Leprosy is then a type of sin. But more generally sin and sickness are related. This may be seen in the LXX translation of Isa. liii. 4 where חֳלִי is rendered by ἁμαρτία—a fact of which Matthew makes use (viii. 17). In the LXX rendering of Isa. liii. 3, 4 the servant is said to bear both μαλακία and ἁμαρτία, implying their equivalence; μαλακία may mean 'moral weakness', but in Hellenistic Greek certainly means 'sickness' (cf. Matt. iv. 23; ix. 35; x. 1). A similar connection to that between leprosy and sin may exist also in the case of the woman with the unclean issue of blood (v. 25–34), for those so afflicted were also excluded from Jewish worship (Num. v. 2 ff.).[5] Into the valediction of Jesus, 'Go in Peace', may be read a deeper meaning; peace is not merely health but peace with God, through the reconciliation that has taken place with him in healing and therefore in the restoration to the congregation of Israel.[6]

The healings testify not only to the power of Jesus to forgive sin but also to certain other closely related activities. He gives sight to the blind (viii. 22–6; x. 46–52). Blindness in Mark is not mere pardonable ignorance but culpable rejection of the truth; so the power of Jesus to give sight to the blind lies close

[1] Cf. Lightfoot, *Gospel*, pp. 25 f.

[2] The rabbis also looked on leprosy as a punishment for sin; cf. Moore, II, 149, 248; Strack–Billerbeck, IV, 747 ff.

[3] Richardson (*The Miracle Stories of the Gospels*, p. 61) goes beyond the evidence when he argues that Jesus in touching the leper takes on himself the burden of defilement and is revealed thereby as the sin-bearer. This may be true, but there is no indication in Mark that he wishes us to make this deduction. Jesus often touched the sick in healing.

[4] F. Hauck and R. Meyer, *T.W.N.T.* III, 416 ff. To connect 'cleansing' the leper with sin seems as valid as to connect it to 'unclean' spirit: and so make it 'demonic' as Ling does (*The Significance of Satan*, pp. 14 ff.).

[5] Cf. Richardson, *The Miracle Stories of the Gospels*, p. 61.

[6] Cf. Schniewind, *ad loc.*

to his power to forgive sin. The first of these accounts, the restoration of sight to the blind man of Bethsaida, is closely linked to the blindness of the disciples; in viii. 18 they have been accused of having eyes but not seeing; in the immediately succeeding pericope (viii. 27–30) Peter 'sees' Jesus as the Christ. Lightfoot[1] has drawn attention to the close parallels between viii. 22–6 and viii. 27–30, implying that Mark has deliberately placed this healing story in order to underline the confession of Peter. But the blind man receives his sight in two stages; Peter in viii. 27–30 does not yet 'see' fully; he sees Jesus as Messiah, the first stage, but is unwilling to accept what the Messianic ministry involves for Jesus, the second stage. It will require the Resurrection before he is completely restored; hence Peter's confession is followed by the story of the Transfiguration (ix. 2–8).[2] At x. 52 the second blind man who is healed immediately becomes a disciple and follows Jesus on the way to Jerusalem and thus on the way to the Cross:[3] receiving his full sight all at once, he takes up his cross (viii. 34) and follows Jesus in the manner which Peter was bidden but rejected; Peter had had his sight only partly restored. The giving of sight to the blind was an eschatological sign (Isa. xxxv. 5 f.; xxix. 18 f., etc.) as was also the making of the dumb to speak and the deaf to hear; this is explicitly brought out in the story of the healing of the deaf man with the impediment in his speech (vii. 32–7, see especi-

---

[1] *History*, pp. 90 f.

[2] Johnson, *ad loc.* A. Kuby, 'Zur Konzeption des Markus-Evangeliums', *Z.N.T.W.* XLIX (1958), 52–64, holds somewhat similarly that in the first part of the Gospel (up to viii. 21) the disciples do not understand Jesus, from viii. 27 onwards they understand he is great but misunderstand the nature of his greatness, i.e. they receive their true knowledge of Jesus in stages. viii. 22–6 is thus a transition section; cf. x. 46–52; xiv. 3–9. A. M. Farrar, *A Study in St Mark*, pp. 105 ff. sees similar significance in the two stages of recovery of sight in viii. 22–6.

[3] Note the use of the title 'Son of David' in x. 46–52 and in the succeeding sections (xi. 9 f.; xii. 35–7), and of the almost equivalent 'King of the Jews' in the Passion story. Cf. Kuby, 'Zur Konzeption des Markus-Evangeliums'. J. B. Tyson, 'The Blindness of the Disciples in Mark', *J.B.L.* LXXX (1961), 261–8 holds that the original disciples never did come to understand correctly the meaning of Jesus' death and that Mark is writing in conscious opposition to them. Under the influence of Paul he has come to see both its necessity and redemptive significance, to which the Church in Jerusalem still remained blind.

ally *v.* 37). In the raising of Jairus' daughter[1] (v. 21–5, 35–43) the claim is quite obviously made that Jesus has power over death; those believers who have lost loved ones should remember that they are but asleep and that Jesus, who is himself the risen Lord, will raise them.[2]

There are two key-words which run through almost all the healings of Jesus and are closely related to the theme of redemption, namely σώζειν and πίστις. The first of these possesses the double meaning, 'heal', 'save'. As alternatives ἰᾶσθαι or θεραπεύειν could have been used. The former of these is indeed used once by Mark (v. 29); it is more frequent in the other New Testament writers, and in Jewish Greek and the Apostolic Fathers does attain the same double sense of 'heal' and 'save'.[3] It also possesses this double sense at times in the New Testament (e.g. Matt. xiii. 15). θεραπεύειν does not anywhere have the double sense; it is used by Mark at i. 34; iii. 2, 10; vi. 5, 13. It is significant that every one of these instances except iii. 2 occurs in summary statements of the healing activity of Jesus. In the stories which tell the great deeds of Jesus Mark uses σώζειν. iii. 2 occurs in what is a Pronouncement Story rather than a healing account. The summaries may emphasise only the great healing activity of Jesus, but the accounts of particular healings take us into the second meaning of σώζειν; this confirms our analysis that in them we are to see indications of the redemptive power of Jesus. We must now look more closely at those passages in which σώζειν has the meaning 'save' so that we may learn from another angle what is the inner meaning of the healing miracles. It is interesting to observe that the word is featured in two of the healing stories (v. 25–34; x. 46–52) in which the redemptive significance is otherwise less obvious. That Mark is aware of the redemptive meaning given by the early Church to σώζειν appears clearly at viii. 35; x. 26; xiii. 13, 20. Most interesting

[1] Whether this was originally a story of restoration of life or not need not concern us; for Mark it was such.

[2] Certain other miracles of Jesus are told with emphasis solely on the lesson to be drawn from them and not on the element of great power in Jesus; e.g. the man with the withered hand in the synagogue (iii. 1–5) and the Syro-Phoenician woman's daughter (vii. 24–30).

[3] Cf. Bauer, *Wörterbuch*.

is xv. 30, 31. This has obviously undergone Christian redaction. In *v.* 30 σῶσον will be taken in the sense of 'preserve thy life' and can represent an original comment of a mocker, but in *v.* 31, 'He saved others; himself he is not able to save', we may discern the modification or creation of the early Church. If we take the sense of 'preserve life', the second clause could be a true comment, but it is unlikely that the High Priests said that Jesus preserved the lives of others; for taken in relationship to the accounts we have this must refer to saving from death and only Jairus' daughter was so saved. If, however, 'save' means 'heal' in the first clause, which the priests might admit, it cannot mean such in the second. It is easier then to see this as a Christian comment on the crucifixion put into the mouths of the scorners.[1] Jesus is able to save men, but the divine necessity requires that he does not save himself. The reader will connect the 'save' of the first clause both to its occurrences within the Gospel in relation to healing and to his own experience of salvation; he will thus see the first as a pattern for the second.

The second key-word which sounds throughout the healing accounts is πίστις (ii. 5; v. 34; x. 52; cf. iv. 40; πιστεύειν in v. 36; ix. 23, 24; ἀπιστία in vi. 6). But this word, just as much as σῴζειν, is a part of the Christian redemptive vocabulary. The healing stories with the stress they lay on the necessity of faith in God's power working through Jesus are examples to the Christian of the need for faith if he is to be redeemed.

Thus we may conclude that Mark in no way intends us to see the mighty works of Jesus as merely mighty works so that we are only impressed by the miraculous. He uses them to teach about redemption. The element of greatness is not to be ignored: they do set forth the mighty Son of God, but they set him forth as the Redeemer.

When we turn to the other types of material which Mark uses the reason for their inclusion is normally much more obvious. The teaching of Jesus contains within its own content the reason for its selection. It may deal with problems of Christian conduct (xii. 13–17; ii. 18–20; ii. 23–iii. 5, etc.); with difficulties raised for the Christian believer by outsiders (xii. 18–27); with the beginning and nature of discipleship (i. 16–20; ii. 13 f.; x. 17–22; viii. 34–ix. 1; ix. 33–7, etc.); with the nature of

[1] So similarly *vv.* 29*b* and 36 reflect Christian views.

Christian belief (e.g. the parables of the Kingdom; the Parousia, ch. xiii); with the nature of Christian worship (the Last Supper, and possibly x. 13–16 in relationship to the admission of infants to the Church). But in using this material Mark has also given it particular slants of his own; for example, in using the parables he has taken up and emphasised, or created, a theory of the blindness of the crowds and of the disciples. The teaching of Jesus is given with authority (Mark i. 21–8); Mark wishes us to see it as a mighty work; in it we see Jesus' glory just as much as in the miracles; for all who come to him he has the answer which cannot be gainsaid (ii. 1–iii. 6; xi. 27–xii. 37). Moreover the teaching, as the mighty works, is redemptive because in it men's minds are opened to see the truth. Within the teaching there are statements by Jesus about the purpose of his ministry: these we shall treat later.[1] The remainder of the material largely consists of narrative portions telling us who Jesus is (Baptism, Transfiguration, etc.) and the connected story of the Passion which we have already considered in some detail.

[1] Ch. VI.

CHAPTER V

THE ORDER OF THE MATERIAL

WE turn now to the order in which Mark has put together the material he has selected. It must be realised that Mark was not completely master of the situation. The story of the Passion could not be put at any other point than at the end of his book; likewise the account of John's preaching and baptism of Jesus must come at the beginning. Between these two fixed points it is a matter of conjecture how far genuine biographical considerations ordered the material.[1] Mark's plan of the ministry in which Jesus does not appear in Jerusalem until the last few days would not appear to be borne out by the evidence from the other Gospels. But if Mark has decided that there is only one short period of ministry in Jerusalem then all the material concerned with Jerusalem must appear at that point. There is another way in which Mark may not have been fully master of the order of his material. Whereas some of it may have come to him as individual pericopae which he was free to insert where he wished, some of it also came to him as complexes (i. 16–39 or ii. 1–iii. 5) either in, or apart from, written sources and he appears to have kept together at least some of the material that came to him in this way; at any rate, if he did not, then it would be impossible today to detect the pre-Markan complexes.

The most striking feature of the Markan arrangement is the disproportionate amount of space given to the death of Jesus. This dominates the whole Gospel, being indeed a case of the tail wagging the dog.[2] Whether or not the thought of the

---

[1] It will be seen that we side with Professor Nineham rather than with Professor Dodd on the nature of the order of events in the Gospel of Mark. Cf. C. H. Dodd, 'The Framework of the Gospel Narratives', *New Testament Studies*, pp. 1–11, and D. E. Nineham, 'The Order of Events in St Mark's Gospel—an Examination of Dr Dodd's Hypothesis', in *Studies in the Gospels* (ed. Nineham), pp. 223–39. Cf. also H. Sawyerr, 'The Marcan Framework', *S.J.Th.* XIV (1961), 279–94; H. A. Guy, *The Origin of the Gospel of Mark*, pp. 20 ff., 48 ff.

[2] M. Kähler's often-quoted dictum is apposite: 'Passionsgeschichte mit ausführlicher Einleitung.' Cf. Dehn (p. 15), 'Es (the Gospel) ist der weitere Rahmen zu Tod und Auferstehung Jesu'.

Suffering Servant is contained in the words of the Heavenly Voice at the Baptism, the element of opposition to Jesus has certainly entered the Gospel by ii. 1–12 and is explicitly seeking his death by iii. 6. From then on it never disappears. The death and Resurrection of Jesus are thus Mark's main subject. In the Passion then we must seek the meaning of Jesus for Mark. In his scheme the Cross is no chance happening. The subtle allusions to the fulfilment of the Old Testament in the Passion story[1] (ix. 12; xii. 1–12, etc.), the sense of divine necessity (viii. 31, 33; xii. 11; xiv. 36), Jesus' own deliberate purpose to go to his death (x. 32–4; xiv. 36) combine to illuminate the Cross as predetermined plan. Yet, as we have already seen, men are not excused their share of guilt,[2] and Mark draws out how they conspired to put him to death led on by their own obstinate rejection of the truth (iii. 1–6; xiv. 10, 11, 17–21, 55; xv. 15). At the same time the innocence of Jesus is maintained (xiv. 55–6; xv. 14); the accounts of the great deeds of Jesus earlier in the Gospel serve this same end in that they have depicted him going about and doing good. In part then this detailed account of the Passion and the underlying currents that led up to it answers the question which must have been often asked in the early Church, Why did Jesus die?[3] From the beginning the Cross was a stumbling-block to the Jews and an offence to the Greeks, and part of the emphasis on the Passion in the Gospel is an attempt to meet this criticism. But the Cross had not merely to be explained as fact, it had also to be given meaning; if it was part of the divine plan, for what purpose had God designed it? Or, to put it another way, what did Jesus achieve for men, for the world, when he died and rose again? What theological interpretation does Mark put on his death?

We may now begin to trace, somewhat hastily, the course of events as narrated by Mark. Obviously much of what Mark records will not throw direct light on our central problem of the soteriology of the Gospel and we shall only pause where we feel that light is thrown on this by the order of the material.

Mark begins (i. 2, 3) by linking his Gospel firmly to the Old

---

[1] Cf. Burkill, 'St Mark's Philosophy of the Passion', *passim.*

[2] Cf. above, pp. 36 ff.

[3] Cf. J. H. Ropes, *The Synoptic Gospels*, pp. 10 ff.; F. C. Grant, *The Interpreter's Bible*, VII, 633.

Testament.[1] This is the only place in the Gospel where he quotes by name from the Old Testament. Elsewhere his Old Testament references either occur in the teaching of Jesus or they are not explicitly introduced as from the Old Testament. This first quotation must then be seen as the conscious linking of what follows to the Old Testament. Though *v.* 1 has spoken of a beginning, the sequel is to be read in the light of Old Testament categories. The bridge between the old and the new is John the Baptiser, who is Elijah (cf. the description of *v.* 6 and the explicit identification of ix. 11–13). John's function is to testify to Jesus; this he does, saying not only that Jesus is the greater (*v.* 7), but also that he will perform a greater ministry, baptising with the Spirit, whereas he John himself baptises only with water. Thus at the outset we are faced with a prophecy that Jesus has come to act on behalf of men. To its meaning we shall return later.[2] The 'Coming One' is now identified, first as the man Jesus from Nazareth and then in his baptism as the Son of God.[3] We postpone until later a fuller consideration of the content of the Heavenly Voice, in particular whether it intends the equation of Jesus with the Suffering Servant.[4] Identified as Son he is given the Spirit; he who is to impart it must first receive it. This Spirit then leads him into conflict with the Devil. The latter comes to tempt him, seeking to intervene and prevent the ministry which is beginning. He suffers, however, a crushing defeat (cf. iii. 27). The Devil now disposed of, Jesus begins to preach.

Up to this point Mark had probably not much choice in the ordering of his material. The Old Testament must come before

[1] It is doubtful if the quotation from Malachi in *v.* 2*b* should be read. The original reading in *v.* 2*a* refers to Isaiah alone; Matthew and Luke use only the quotation from Isaiah, omitting the remainder. This might be the correction of an obvious mistake on Mark's part, but it is more likely that the quotation from Malachi is an early gloss. Contrast Schreiber, p. 160. Because Mark ties his Gospel thus firmly to the Old Testament at the beginning and continues to reinforce the tie with Old Testament allusions we must contest Bundy's statement (p. 42) that what Mark narrates 'does not emerge from the stream of history'.

[2] Below, pp. 134 f.

[3] Whatever the primitive Church may have believed, the words of the Heavenly Voice are not for Mark an adoption formula but an announcement or revelation of who Jesus is. Cf. Mauser, p. 96, n. 3.

[4] Below, pp. 148 f., 167 ff.

the New Testament. John must precede Jesus and testify to him; the Baptism must precede the ministry. The temptations alone might have been delayed or spread throughout the ministry. Since the Devil tempts other men continually it would have appeared *a priori* probable that Mark would have regarded Jesus as continuously tempted. This we have found he did not do. Mark deliberately places the Temptation before Jesus moves out to meet men, confirming the earlier analysis we had made of its meaning for him.

From now on he is freer to place his material in the order he chooses. i. 16–38 (39) was probably in existence in its present form prior to Mark. Sometimes it is said that Mark sets it where he does as illustrating a typical day in the activity of Jesus. This may have been the original reason for its compilation, though it is difficult to see how Jesus would have called disciples every day. It is much more likely that he follows the statement of the preaching activity (i. 14, 15) of Jesus with a verification of its effectiveness (i. 16–20) and then the remainder of this complex perforce follows. We have seen that i. 14, 15 reflects the terminology of the early Church and that Mark thinks of the preaching of the Gospel which is Jesus Christ rather than of preaching by Jesus.[1] The proclamation of the Gospel is immediately followed by the response of men—as it was in the early Church.[2] The Gospel, to Mark, includes the whole activity of Jesus, in particular his Passion, which occupies so much of his book, and his Resurrection. The preaching of the Gospel by the early Church thus leads to the formation and growth of the Church itself. The result of the Cross is the existence of the Church. One of the things which Jesus does for men is to create the Christian community. And this community must be self-perpetuating. Those who are called are themselves to be fishers of men. Jesus has preached and has netted men; they in their turn must now go and fish. This theme is repeated in ii. 13–17. Jesus calls Levi (v. 14) after he has taught (*v.* 13) and Levi begins the process of catching men by inviting publicans and sinners to his house to meet Jesus (*v.* 15),[3] and this leads on to a statement by Jesus of the purpose of his ministry,

---

[1] Above, pp. 64 ff.
[2] The disciples are here typical believers rather than Apostles; cf. Bundy, pp. 71 f.   [3] We assume that Levi gave the feast.

namely, to call sinners (*v.* 17). We shall have to return to the nature of the Christian community which Mark views as created through the ministry of Jesus;[1] it is sufficient now to see how Mark by the ordering of his material views its creation as a result of the preaching of the Gospel, the Gospel which is Jesus Christ himself in his life, death and Resurrection.

Within the complex i. 16–38 the next event is the first account of an exorcism by Jesus. This follows appropriately near to the Temptation. Because Jesus has won his victory in the conflict with Satan he now conquers Satan's subordinates, who in the process acknowledge the person of Jesus (i. 21–8). Matthew destroys this sequence and Luke delays considerably the account of the exorcism; this they may do because for them there is not the same close association of it with the Temptation. There follow the healing of Peter's mother-in-law as in the original complex (i. 29–31) and a summary statement of healings and exorcisms which obviously depends on the fact that a sample exorcism and healing have just been recounted (i. 32–4).

At the conclusion of this complex Mark adds on another healing account, that of the leper (i. 40–5), before taking up and following through the next complex (ii. 1–iii. 6). As we have seen leprosy is a type of sin,[2] and in the first story of the next complex (ii. 1–12) the theme of sickness and sin is continued.[3] Thus at the first available point[4] Mark indicates that the healing activities of Jesus are a type of his work in saving men from sin, and in this light we have to read the remainder of the healing accounts. After this Mark continues with the complex ii. 1–iii. 6 with its mounting tension and its conclusion that Jesus must be put to death. We may note that before Mark indicates the determination of the Jewish leaders to eliminate Jesus he has already shown Jesus' awareness of the need for his own death (ii. 19, 20), and he sets out the nature of the

---

[1] Ch. VIII. [2] Pp. 106 f. above.

[3] J. Sundwall, *Die Zusammensetzung des Markusevangeliums*, pp. 11 f., shows that certain verbal links exist between i. 40–5 and ii. 1–12 and concludes that Mark intended them to be taken together.

[4] He would have had to break the complex i. 16–38 (it is tightly sewn together with temporal notes) if he had inserted the account of the cleansing of the leper earlier; or else he would have had to rewrite i. 29–31 entirely, a course also probably not open to him.

salvation which Jesus achieves in his death, that is, redemption from sin, both by explicit statement (ii. 17) and under the type of healing (i. 40–ii. 12). The complex thus contains the story of the Gospel in miniature, ending with the Passion (iii. 6).

iii. 6 almost demands that the account of the Passion should follow directly. But there is a sudden change of theme: the popularity of Jesus. This theme had already been present in i. 16–39; now it reappears contrasting strongly with the hostility of the Jewish leaders. And with it occurs a second theme which also had appeared in i. 16–39—the new community. There we had seen the call of the first disciples (i. 16–20); now we see further steps taken in the creation of the new community, namely, the appointment of the Twelve (iii. 13–19). Even though death comes there will be a continuing community,[1] and the community will not be a disorganised body but one in which there will be those appointed to special positions. Though Mark may not give to 'apostle' a technical sense we cannot deny that in the appointment of the Twelve there are the rudiments of organisation. This organisation would seem to be linked also to the twelve tribes of Israel, so that the new community is the new Israel. In between these two items about the crowd and the appointment of the Twelve there is another reference to exorcism and the confession of Jesus by the devils (iii. 11, 12). Thus over against the threatening Cross we see the goodness of Jesus to men testified by his popularity with the crowd, a supernatural confession of his true being by the demons, and his own preparation for the period after his death.

With iii. 20–35 the theme of conflict returns. His own family[2] and the scribes now together join in criticism and their criticism is concerned with 'possession', a theme which arises naturally out of the preceding accounts of exorcism (i. 21–8; iii. 11, 12). Jesus answers with 'parables' (iii. 23–7) which

[1] Cf. Dehn, p. 74. However, Dehn's suggestion that the crowd of iii. 7–12 represents the true Israel is unlikely. In Mark the crowd is an amorphous and anonymous background generally expressing wonder or amazement at the actions of Jesus; cf. B. Citron, 'The Multitude in the Synoptic Gospels', *S.J.Th.* VII (1954), 408–18.

[2] In the opposition of Jesus' own family we see in microcosm the rejection by the nation.

those who have eyes to see (iv. 11, 12) can understand; he is 'possessed', if he is 'possessed', by the Holy Spirit alone, in whose power he defeated Satan and now expels demons. We are made aware again of the believing community which is present and does see—the true family of Jesus (iii. 33–5). We also learn something more of the nature of the new community called into existence by the Gospel, namely, its members do the will of God. But also they have eyes to see the inner nature of all the activities of Jesus, and so we pass naturally to the Markan account of the parables in iv. 1–34.[1] Already in his Gospel Mark has drawn attention to the 'secrecy' motif: the demons are silenced (i. 24, 25; iii. 11, 12); the cleansed leper is forbidden to speak about his healing (i. 44). But those who are 'with Jesus' (iii. 14) are given understanding (iv. 11, 12); to them not only his acts but also his mysterious words testify to his true nature. Within the first parable itself, that of the Sower, two attitudes to Jesus are set out, that of believing acceptance (the new community) and that of temporary and partial acceptance (the crowds, if not also the Jewish authorities). These parables have also their place in asserting the ultimate victory of the Gospel; despite opposition the Kingdom will come and the stand of the community for Jesus will be justified.

iv. 35–v. 43 consists of four mighty works each recounted in detail.[2] Thus Jesus is again set out as the mighty Son of God, who can save (v. 23, 28, 34). Leaving apart what inner meaning these stories possess we can say they depict Jesus as mighty over against both the opposition of men and demonic powers and as over against the humiliation of the Cross which has been already indicated and is shortly to be formally announced (viii. 31).

From this manifestation of his saving power we are transferred at once by Mark to another reminder of the opposition:

[1] On the connections here see Boobyer, 'The Redaction of Mark iv. 1–34'.

[2] It has often been held that iv. 35–v. 43 was a complex taken over by Mark: thus Taylor, pp. 94 f.; Schmidt, p. 135. Against this may be argued: (a) The Greek of v. 25–34 is different from that of v. 21–4, 35–43 (cf. the participles of vv. 25–7), indicating different sources (cf. Lohmeyer, ad loc.). (b) The insertion of one incident inside another is a favourite Markan editorial device. Cf. Sundwall, Die Zusammensetzung des Markusevangeliums, pp. 32–5.

Jesus is rejected by his own village (vi. 1–6a).[1] There is a certain vagueness in the way in which Mark introduces this incident: Jesus comes εἰς τὴν πατρίδα. It is only as the incident progresses that we realise Nazareth (cf. i. 9) is intended. This vagueness suggests the possibility that here we have a minor 'rejection'. Jesus' own πατρίς is also Jerusalem; when he goes there he will again be rejected by his own people (cf. John i. 11). Already we have learnt that his true family are those who do his will (iii. 35). The Jews reject him and the new family of the Church takes their place (cf. xii. 9). Returning to vi. 1–6a and Nazareth we find that to its people he is but the son of Mary; envy corrupts their hearts so that they stumble. Thus we can see Mark setting fairly and squarely on the shoulders of men their rejection of Jesus. Where there is this unbelief Jesus is powerless. Then once again we swing from rejection to hope for the future: the Twelve are sent out to their mission (vi. 6b–13), and they return from it filled with success (vi. 13, 30).

At this point a new stage opens in the Gospel in which Jesus is continually on the move (vi. 14–x. 52). It begins with a miniature passion—that of John the Baptist (vi. 14–29).[2] At first sight it is peculiar that such a story is told in detail; all that is needed for the subsequent narrative (viii. 28) is a mere reference to the death of John; instead we are given a full account. John and Jesus suffer comparable fates (ix. 11–13). The account of the death of John ends almost precisely as that of the death of Jesus—disciples come, obtain the corpse and bury it (vi. 29; cf. xv. 42–7). For Jesus there is a sequel—the Resurrection (xvi. 1–8); but resurrection is not omitted in the case of John; it is only one who has risen from the dead who could work the mighty works of Jesus (vi. 14). Now these works are still found in the early Church; the account of what the

[1] Lightfoot, *History*, pp. 184 ff., sees in this account a parallel and contrast to i. 21–8. We have two synagogue scenes, one at the beginning and the other at the end of his Galilean ministry, implying his rejection in Galilee.

[2] It may be that Elijah is mentioned before Moses in Mark's account of the Transfiguration, ix. 2–8 (contrast Matthew and Luke), because Elijah = John the Baptist who suffers and dies, and is therefore for Mark a more important figure than Moses. Cf. A. Feuillet, 'Les perspectives propres à chaque évangéliste dans les récits de la transfiguration', *Biblica*, XXXIX (1958), 281–301.

Twelve do encases this story of John the Baptist (vi. 6*b*–13 and vi. 30); in the mighty works of the early Church is to be seen the presence of the risen Christ. Thus though the passion of John has no resurrection we are made aware that the Passion of Jesus will have such a Resurrection. And again as in the conflict with the Jewish authorities (ii. 1–iii. 6) and in Nazareth (vi. 1–6*a*) we see evil arising in the heart of man and bringing opposition and death, for doubtless Mark sees the court of Herod as wicked and Herod himself as skilfully manœuvred by an evil woman.[1]

We now come to two sections which have long been recognised as to some extent parallel (vi. 30–vii. 37 and viii. 1–26). Each section begins with a feeding, contains the account of a voyage, has statements about the lack of understanding of the disciples, speaks of controversy with the Jewish leaders and ends with a miracle in which a dead faculty (hearing, eyesight) is restored. Mark may either have composed these two sections from separate pericopae or he may have found them in existence (in part or in whole). The latter is more probable; he will then have modified them to suit his purpose by additions, and possibly subtractions. Thus he may well have added a considerable part of the discussion with the Pharisees in vii. 1–23 and the whole incident with the Syro-Phoenician woman (vii. 24–30). This latter, following directly on the controversy with the Pharisees about uncleanness, may be Mark's way of saying that Jesus finding opposition among the Jews turned to the Gentiles —a common pattern in Acts (xiii. 46; xviii. 6). The Cross does not hang as obviously over these two sections as over some of the earlier, but its presence is perhaps felt in the two accounts of feeding the multitudes which the early Christians saw as prefigurations of the Eucharist, and this is strongly tied to the Death of Christ. The compassion of Jesus towards men is emphasised (vi. 34; viii. 2), and his power in the miracles he works. To his goodness and greatness are opposed the scheming of the Jews and the obstinate stupidity of the disciples. But the removal of their lack of understanding is signified in the two miracles of the restoration of men's senses (vii. 32–7; viii. 22–6).

---

[1] The difficult references to the Herodians at iii. 6 and xii. 13 may bear some relation to the place of Herod in this minor Passion, since Herod plays no part in the Markan story of Jesus' own Passion.

On the placing of the latter we have already commented:[1] it is a suitable introduction to the confession of Peter, and its use in this way may have led to the placing of the whole complex. The entire passage vi. 14–viii. 26 deals largely with a journey in Gentile territory and therefore instances Jesus' relationship to the Gentiles, indicating that the Gospel is also for them.[2]

With viii. 27 we appear to enter a new atmosphere in which the Cross is no longer a remote threat but looms a terrifyingly short distance ahead. Whether the confession of Peter was a turning point in the life of Jesus himself we need not stop to examine; certainly it represents a turning point in the narrative of Mark. The Cross is now explicit; the crowd largely disappears; the disciples are prominent; the mighty works, with the exception of teaching, recede. We are instructed in the nature of the ministry of Jesus and in the meaning of discipleship. The section lasts until x. 52, where Jesus reaches Jerusalem and the events of the last week begin. It is conceived as a journey towards Jerusalem and death, and the instruction is given to the disciples on the journey.[3] Discipleship is a pilgrimage. Here we have an approximation to the theme of the Epistle to the Hebrews; there, however, the emphasis is laid on a pilgrimage towards the heavenly city and rest; here the pilgrimage is towards suffering, persecution and a Cross. Discipleship is not static but dynamic. This appears not only from the layout of the whole passage (viii. 27–x. 52) but in the individual pericopae where it is regarded as 'following' Jesus (viii. 34).

We commence with the confession of Peter, who begins to see (cf. viii. 22–6). Mark shows that Peter does not see clearly; Jesus announces his Passion and Peter refuses to believe it (viii. 31–3). We have reason to believe that Mark may have brought together these two incidents,[4] and if he has not done so he has certainly emphasised their connection by his use of διδάσκειν. In v. 31 it is the Son of Man who it is said must suffer; in v. 29 Peter has confessed Jesus as the Christ. The abrupt transition from one term to another suggests that for Mark the two mean the same person. It may be noted that in

---

[1] Pp. 107 ff. above.   [2] Cf. Schmidt, pp. 208 ff.
[3] The sense of movement is continually present: viii. 27; ix. 2, 9, 14, 30, 33; x. 1, 17, 32, 46.   [4] Pp. 79 f. above.

the other predictions of the Passion Mark also uses the term 'Son of Man'. T. W. Manson has argued that 'in Mark it is possible to trace a gradual narrowing of the denotation until at the last the term has become a name for Jesus alone. The point in the Markan narrative at which this takes place is significant: it is at the Last Supper.'[1] It is not clear from this whether Manson means that it is only at the Last Supper that Mark identifies Jesus with the Son of Man or whether it is only at that point that we can discern in the Markan narrative that Jesus identified himself with the Son of Man. The former would hardly appear to be true. We have already pointed to the quick change of term from Christ to Son of Man (*vv.* 29, 31). Peter's rebuke and Jesus' reply in the Markan narrative would again suggest that Mark understood Jesus as referring only to himself in *v.* 31. There is also the unique position that Jesus gives to himself in *vv.* 34–8; the disciples may have to suffer, but if so it is for the sake of Jesus and it is Jesus whom they follow. ix. 9 would also appear in Mark to be a reference to the personal Resurrection of Jesus and not to that of a corporate Son of Man, whatever the original reference may have been. In x. 33 f., the third prediction of the Passion, the details are so approximated to the actual Passion story as told by Mark that there is no room for doubt that here Mark took the Son of Man to be Jesus himself. At ii. 10 the Son of Man is said to be able to forgive sins; at ii. 5 Jesus has just done this very thing. At xiv. 21 it is the Son of Man who is to be betrayed into the hands of sinners, but a few verses earlier (xiv. 18) Jesus had spoken of himself as about to be betrayed. At xiv. 24 and x. 38 we have two sayings about the suffering of Jesus which are cast in the first person; Mark only envisages in God's plan the suffering of one man; this again implies the identification by Mark of the Son of Man with Jesus. There is indeed no point in the Markan account where difficulty is caused by assuming that Mark identified the Son of Man with Jesus, and there is much that causes difficulty if we suppose that Mark held that the Son of Man was someone other than Jesus or that he was a corporate person. To say this is not, of course, to make a decision on the use by Jesus of the

---

[1] 'Realized Eschatology and the Messianic Secret', in *Studies in the Gospels* (ed. D. E. Nineham), p. 215. Cf. his *The Teaching of Jesus*, pp. 211–34, for a fuller discussion of his doctrine of the corporate Son of Man.

term; there are indications in Mark that Jesus' usage was not as simple and direct as Mark implies.

To return to the Markan narrative. In viii. 27–30 Peter has said that Jesus is the Christ; in viii. 31–3 Jesus goes on to say that to be the Christ means to suffer; in viii. 34–ix. 1 he adds further that to be a Christian means to suffer. From the prediction of the Passion we move directly to the nature of discipleship. And we find that the same is true of each of the other predictions. After the second (ix. 31) Jesus teaches that discipleship means service (ix. 33 ff.) and the same theme reappears after the third prediction (x. 33 f. and x. 35–45). The nature of discipleship is thus set in the light of the Cross; the understanding of discipleship proceeds from an understanding of the Cross. Thus we see again how closely Mark links the death of Jesus to men; its primary importance lies not in a conquest of demons but in the creation of true disciples. The nature of discipleship and the distinction between it and the ministry of Jesus concerns the details of the pericopae rather than their order and we shall return to it later.[1]

The first prediction of the Passion and the teaching to which it leads on discipleship is followed by the account of the Transfiguration. The latter is closely linked to the preceding by a stated time interval[2]—a most unusual procedure for Mark outside the closely woven Passion narrative: the Cross is to be succeeded by glory. We are thus again sharply reminded of the nature of him who suffers. He is God's Son, superior to all that belongs to the Old Testament dispensation. Perhaps it is also an indication to disciples that if they take the Cross they also will attain to glory (cf. Rom. viii. 17). Though for a moment Mark lifts us to glory, we do not long escape the Cross, and the disciples coming down from the mountain are reminded of its proximity (ix. 9–13). John the Baptist, that is Elijah, did not restore all things; he was killed. What else may they expect for the Messiah? Then again we move back sharply to the might of Jesus: he heals the epileptic boy whom the disciples had failed to restore: the goodness of Jesus is set against the Cross and his power to save against the weakness of death.

The pattern continues in ix. 30–x. 31 and in x. 32–52, namely, a prediction of the Passion with a following discussion

---

[1] Pp. 154 ff. below. [2] Cf. Mauser, pp. 111 f.

of discipleship in its light. There are of course variations. In x. 2–12 a discussion with the Pharisees and disciples about divorce is introduced. This may be either because as Jesus nears Jerusalem the pattern of conflict begins to reappear, the conflict that will eventually lead to his death, or it may be that in this teaching Mark sees Jesus as performing here a mighty work, teaching with authority (i. 22). There follow two apparently very different passages on discipleship: the first (x. 13–16) suggests that discipleship is a matter of reception: the second (x. 17–22) suggests the need for effort. As Wellhausen[1] has pointed out this is the antinomy of discipleship that finds classical expression in Phil. ii. 12, 13. The third section on the Passion and discipleship ends with a mighty work, the healing of blind Bartimaeus (x. 46–52); but perhaps more important than its significance in showing the greatness of Jesus is the fact that Bartimaeus becomes the disciple of Jesus; he follows him into the city (xi. 1 ff.); he thus, as it were, takes up his cross in the wake of that of the Lord.[2] As the three sections on the Passion and discipleship were preceded by the healing of a blind man who received his sight in two stages, here a blind man is healed all at once and becomes the true disciple who follows Jesus towards the Cross; unlike Peter he sees fully.[3]

The remainder of the Gospel we have already examined in

---

[1] *Ad loc.*

[2] Indeed he is the only person whom Jesus cures who follows him as his disciple; cf. Bundy, p. 410.

[3] Wellhausen, p. 66, has argued that in this section (viii. 27–x. 52) the idea of repentance which was prominent earlier in the Gospel in relation to discipleship is now abandoned and that of 'following' Jesus substituted. 'Following' is not the only conception of discipleship in this section: there is also ministry, self-denial (which is closely related to repentance) and being as a little child. Alongside 'repentance' in the earlier part is also set 'belief in the Gospel' (i. 15); the Gospel is Christ himself, and in the context of the whole book this must be the Christ of the Cross. Discipleship in viii. 27–x. 52 is, as we have seen, also set in the light of the Cross; it is not mere imitation of Christ; this is excluded by viii. 35, 38 where Christ is given a unique position. The two conceptions of 'following' and 'repentance' are held together by the Cross. We meet repentance first in the Gospel because repentance is necessarily prior to following. Repentance implies following since repentance is never merely sorrow for sin but also a turning from it to good: following is based on repentance since we cannot go on the new way until we have turned from the old.

more detail[1] and it is only necessary here to redraw the main lines. Mark has apparently decided to have only one Jerusalem ministry and so material appears here which may have belonged to other periods in the life of Jesus. The conflict stories of xii. 13–40 are no more acute than those of ii. 1–iii. 6, but Mark must have needed some conflict stories at this point to bring out the opposition between Jesus and the Jewish leaders, and so he now uses these. The sequence begins with the setting out of the authority of Jesus in the royal entry into Jerusalem, the cleansing of his own house, the Temple, and the proclamation of judgement in the cursing of the fig-tree. It is not then surprising that in xi. 27–33 the question of the authority of Jesus is directly taken up. And the nature of Jesus as the Son of God is clearly set out in the parable of the vineyard (xii. 1–12). Mark will leave us in no doubt as to the being and authority of him who is to suffer. At the same time he under-lines the guilt of those who bring about the Cross (xi. 18; xii. 12). There follows the sequence of conflict stories (xii. 13–40), in which again he emerges as mighty in word and as the master in speech of all who come to him. On this there follows the Little Apocalypse and again we are reminded who is the one who will die on the Cross. The Passion narrative itself (chs. xiv, xv) has already been discussed in some detail. Mark had here least control over the ordering of his material. The lines were already set and he had to follow.

This would seem the point to examine the view of Schreiber who finds an overall pattern in the Gospel in that Mark pro-claims the Hellenistic kerugma in terms of the tradition about Jesus. He finds this Hellenistic kerugma principally in Phil. ii. 6–11, to which he allies I Cor. ii. 8; these with the kerugma have come under the influence of the conception of the θεῖος ἀνήρ and the Gnostic Saviour myth. The hidden Saviour is crucified by the powers that do not recognise him, but in so dying he conquers them and saves men (cf. I Cor. ii. 8).

Mark's Gospel is a Passion history with a detailed introduc-tion because the Cross was the decisive event for the Hellenistic kerugma.[2] The journey to Jerusalem (viii. 27–x. 52) shows Jesus as the hidden servant who humbles himself in obedience

---

[1] Pp. 82 ff. above.   [2] Pp. 156–9.

to death but is exalted in his death (Phil. ii. 8 f.).[1] Mark has set
out Jesus in i. 2 as the messenger of God who comes to the
Temple (Mal. iii. 1) and in the Gospel he spends almost all
the time of his visit to Jerusalem in the Temple.[2] xi. 1–11, the
triumphal entry into the city, would be seen by the Hellenistic
Christian as the heavenly greeting to the already exalted
Saviour.[3] This Saviour has already been seen in the Transfiguration (ix. 2–8) which took place six days after Peter's confession
—a similar period to that which Jesus spent in Jerusalem
beginning with the confession of the crowds and ending with his
death; the death must then also be the exaltation.[4] The title
Son of God is the most important for Mark, and after Jesus'
death he is so addressed, indicating that the crucified is the
exalted and enthroned Son of God (cf. Ps. ii. 7 where the king
is enthroned).[5] In the title Son of Man the ideas of humiliation
and exaltation are united; it is noticeable that in viii. 38;
xiii. 26; xiv. 62 there is no mention of judgement though
Christ's return is indicated; judgement has already taken place
through the Cross.[6] In conformity with the Hellenistic kerugma
and the Gnostic Saviour myth Mark sets out the pre-existence of
the Son of God in the Parable of the Vineyard (xii. 1–12), where
God sends his only Son.[7] Closely allied to the Saviour are the
saved, the Christian community which Mark views as knowing
the Messiah hidden from the world and which has been created
by the exalted Lord, in conformity with the Gnostic myth of the
Saviour and the saved.[8] This theory of exaltation on the Cross
fits in with his account of Jesus as journeying only once to
Jerusalem: as the divine Saviour can only once ascend to the
heavenly Jerusalem so Jesus can only once go up to the earthly
Jerusalem.[9] But if the Cross is the moment of exaltation then
what of the Resurrection? Mark gives no account of resurrection appearances.[10] In ix. 2–13 he binds closely together the
Ascension (ix. 2–8 speaks of the exalted Christ), the death
(ix. 12, 13) and the Resurrection (ix. 9, 10); what happened
secretly on the Cross is seen openly by the believer at Easter.[11]
An analysis of xvi. 1–8 confirms this view. The women alone

---

[1] Pp. 160 f.   [2] P. 160.   [3] P. 161.
[4] Pp. 161 f.; cf. H.-W. Bartsch, 'Historische Erwägungen zur Leidensgeschichte'.   [5] P. 163.   [6] Pp. 164–6.   [7] Pp. 166 f.
[8] Pp. 167–70.   [9] Pp. 170 f.   [10] P. 173.   [11] Pp. 173–5.

are given the message of the Resurrection because they alone followed Jesus to the Cross; this is in conformity with Mark's general view that only he shares in salvation who takes up his cross.[1] xvi. 7 is a Markan insertion, but refers neither to the Parousia nor to the Resurrection but to the exaltation; in Galilee of the Gentiles, that is on the Gentile mission, the Church will see its exalted Lord.[2] Here Mark carries further his campaign against Peter and the Jewish-Christian kerugma which has no place for the Gentile mission. The leaders of the Jewish-Christian Church (Peter, James, John) did not obey the Lord (ix. 6) but were blind and did not go to Galilee.[3] In his as yet unprinted dissertation, *Der Kreuzigungsbericht des Markus-evangeliums. Eine traditionsgeschichtliche Untersuchung von Mk. xv. 20b–41*,[4] Schreiber has analysed in detail the account of Jesus' death and claims to have found there evidence that the moment of death was the moment of ascension. Mark has combined two ancient traditions, one of which sets out the Cross as world judgement (in *vv.* 33, 37, 38). In so weaving them together he has modified them to show the death of Jesus as both judgement and salvation, the former to unbelievers, the latter to believers.

In this view of Mark there are many valuable insights, but we cannot accept its central thesis that the moment of death is also that of exaltation and victory over the demonic powers. However, before we examine this, we may take leave to doubt if Schreiber has correctly stated the Hellenistic kerugma and if the Gnostic Saviour myth and the θεῖος ἀνήρ conception have affected this kerugma and Mark as much as he argues.

Schreiber bases his account of the Hellenistic kerugma principally on Phil. ii. 6–11. We may allow that this is a pre-Pauline passage, but there are also pre-Pauline passages in the Apostle's letters which stress other aspects of the death of Jesus, for example I Cor. xv. 3 f.;[5] Rom. x. 9;[6] Rom. iv. 24b, 25;[7]

[1] Pp. 175 f.   [2] Pp. 176 f.   [3] Pp. 177 f.

[4] A reference to this is given on p. 157, n. 5. I have no knowledge of the dissertation itself.

[5] Cf. Bultmann, *Theologie des Neuen Testaments*, p. 82; A. M. Hunter, *Paul and his Predecessors*, pp. 15 ff.

[6] Bultmann, *Theologie des Neuen Testaments*, p. 81; Hunter, *Paul and his Predecessors*, pp. 28 ff.

[7] Hunter, *Paul and his Predecessors*, pp. 30 ff.

Rom. iii. 24–6;[1] I Thess. i. 9, 10.[2] Now if it is objected that some if not all of these passages are to be traced back to the Palestinian community, it may be answered that the distinction between the Palestinian kerugma and the Hellenistic may not be as great as Schreiber makes out, but that the latter is a continuation and development of the former.[3] More particularly it may be answered to Schreiber that if the Palestinian kerugma is to be found in Q as he alleges[4] then Q takes no account of the death of Jesus and gives no interpretation of it, and these passages cannot then belong to the kerugma of that community. Thus we may conclude that these passages bear witness to the kerugma of the Hellenistic Church, and that they set out the death of Jesus as a death for the sin of men. This conception of the death of Jesus as an offering for sin was present in the early Hellenistic community, as Bultmann has shown in detail.[5] The Hellenistic kerugma contained therefore a much wider conception of the death of Jesus than is revealed in Phil. ii. 6–11.[6] It is not our purpose to argue that the two conceptions (e.g. Phil. ii. 6–11 and I Cor. xv. 3 f.) are reconcilable (we may observe that Paul apparently found he could use both), but to determine how far Mark is governed by either, by both, or by some other conception. Before leaving this we may note that in the passages to which we have drawn attention the Resurrection of Jesus is either set out in parallel to his death (I Cor. xv. 3 f.; Rom. iv. 25) or occupies the central position (Rom. x. 9). For the Hellenistic community belief in the Resurrection, which may have been identified with the

[1] Bultmann, *Theologie des Neuen Testaments*, p. 47; Hunter, *Paul and his Predecessors*, pp. 120 ff.

[2] Cf. Neil, *Thessalonians* (Moffatt Commentary), *ad loc.* Contrast J. Munck, 'I Thess. i. 9–10 and the Missionary Preaching of Paul', *N.T.S.* IX (1963), 95–110.

[3] Thus e.g. Hunter traces I Cor. xv. 3 ff., *Paul and His Predecessors*, p. 17.
[4] Pp. 172 f.   [5] *Theologie*, pp. 84–6.
[6] There may have been two formulations of the Hellenistic kerugma: I Cor. xv. 3–5 would be the example of one type and Phil. ii. 6–11 (cf. I Tim. iii. 16) the example of the other; cf. E. Schweizer, 'Two New Testament Creeds Compared', *Current Issues in New Testament Interpretation* (ed. W. Klassen and G. F. Snyder), pp. 166–77. The first creed almost certainly originated in Palestinian Christianity but was carried over into Hellenistic Christianity; the second originated in the Hellenistic atmosphere. Cf. Leivestad, *Christ the Conqueror*, pp. 288 ff.

to substantiate the view that the Cross is the victory over the forces of spiritual evil.

At the same time we must conclude that Mark is not dominated by the kerugma of Phil. ii. 6–11. Mark in the course of his narrative does not depict Jesus as the humble servant.[1] There are passages in which this idea is found, for example x. 35–45, but the general impression that Mark leaves is of a strong Son of God who has authority. Whatever Jesus may have been in reality, to the readers of Mark's Gospel he is the Son of God with power, so announced at the beginning (i. 11, if not i. 1) and so depicted throughout in his mighty works.

[1] Cf. below, pp. 140 ff.

CHAPTER VI

THE WITNESS OF JESUS AND OTHERS TO HIMSELF

WE now consider those verses within the material in which statements are made either by Jesus or others concerning his function and activity and the purpose of his work. We do not now look at the seams or the order of the material but into the material itself. This may have undergone some editing at the hands of Mark; if we can show such in any of the statements to be considered it will of course be primary evidence for the Markan view. Most of the statements however came to Mark in the material and his inclusion of them is at least secondary evidence for his own point of view; if they had definitely cut across it he would either not have included them or would have modified them. It could be argued that he might have permitted an occasional statement which was at variance with his own main theology through loyalty to the material transmitted to him or because he did not himself realise its divergence from his main position. We shall find however that there are a considerable number of statements all conveying more or less the same view, one not out of harmony with what we have already learnt; so this possibility is excluded.

We begin with the statements of John the Baptist about Jesus, i. 7 f. Mark appears to have used traditional material without modification here.[1] There are two significant phrases: Jesus is described as ὁ ἰσχυρότερος, and he is said to baptise with Holy Spirit.

In the use of ἰσχυρός Grundmann[2] claims to detect a very primitive Christology in which Jesus is set out as the 'stronger' conqueror of Satan, who is the 'strong one', and his hosts (cf. Luke xi. 20–2). It is not our purpose to dispute this claim but only to indicate our doubt that it formed part of the Markan Christology. Mark makes no use of the 'stronger' conception

---

[1] Schmidt, pp. 18–22; Bultmann, pp. 245–7; cf. Taylor; Lohmeyer; Klostermann, *ad loc.*

[2] *T.W.N.T.* III, 402–5.

in his discussion of the defeat of Satan (Mark iii. 27: his parallel to Luke xi. 20–2). Moreover, Mark does not depict Jesus in i. 7 as stronger than Satan but as stronger than the Baptist. Thus this suggested primitive Christology is not present here in the mind of Mark. But what does he mean by saying that Jesus is stronger than the Baptist? Lohmeyer[1] suggests that ὀπίσω should be understood spatially rather than temporally; we would expect the one who follows John to be his servant or disciple, but in fact he is the greater; John would loose his shoes: in this lies the paradox. ὀπίσω is also used by Mark to indicate the place of the disciple in respect of Jesus (i. 17, 20; viii. 34). John precedes Jesus to death, and as we have already seen John's Passion is an indication of the Passion of Jesus;[2] Jesus precedes his disciples to death (viii. 34); the contrast lies in this—the disciples are less than Jesus but Jesus is greater than John. None of these explanations makes it entirely clear why Jesus is 'stronger' than John, and perhaps the original allusion is lost. Mark certainly indicates by the word the superiority of Jesus to John; the remainder of the Gospel makes clear in what this superiority lies.

The Baptist also contrasts himself with Jesus in respect of baptism: Jesus will baptise with Holy Spirit. It is impossible to enter here into a full discussion of the origin of this logion and of the difference between it and the Q form. Elsewhere I have attempted to show that both the Markan and the Q sayings are variants of an original word of the Baptist that Jesus would baptise with wind and fire, and that the reference in the Markan form is to Pentecost (cf. Acts i. 5).[3] If this is so then the reference is here to the gift of the Spirit by the exalted Christ to the Church. Part of the achievement of Jesus is to have given to his Church the Spirit. Unfortunately, Mark includes very little material which tells us in detail what the Church of the Spirit is like, though we do learn that through the Spirit the members of the Christian community are able to stand firm in persecution and to witness therein (xiv. 38; xiii. 11).

i. 16–20 has already been considered in relation to the

---

[1] *Ad loc.* 　　　　　　　　[2] Pp. 119 f. above.
[3] Best, 'Spirit-baptism', *N.T.* IV (1960), 236–43. For the reasons advanced there the contentions of Yates, *The Spirit and the Kingdom*, pp. 22 ff., are to be rejected.

arrangement of material in the Gospel;[1] it however also contains a statement in which by implication Jesus sets out his own purpose: He calls disciples to send them out as fishers of men. If their purpose is to fish for men at his command, then his purpose must also be to fish for men—both directly and through them. That is to say, his objective is men; it is not the defeat of Satan, though this may be involved, but the creation of a community of men who are his disciples. It is towards men that his activity is directed.

In i. 24 there is a statement about the purpose of Jesus made by one of his enemies, the demon who is being exorcised, and who alleges that Jesus is come to destroy demons.[2] This certainly describes the activity of Jesus in relationship to the evil powers, but it would be wrong to extend it so as to take it as a statement of the whole purpose of Jesus.[3] It must be held within its context, that of an exorcism, and it must be remembered that it is the statement of an enemy who looks at things from his own limited point of view. We may not then take this as a statement of the full activity of Jesus or even as a part of the central activity unless there is corroborative evidence elsewhere.

i. 38 forms the conclusion to the passage i. 35–8 which we have accepted as part of the tradition received by Mark.[4] Our concern is with the final clause εἰς τοῦτο γὰρ ἐξῆλθον. Is this merely a reference to Jesus' departure from Capernaum or is deeper meaning to be seen in it? The preceding narrative seems to imply that Jesus went out to avoid the crowds of sick who were pressing him and to pray in quietness to his Father. Yet *v.* 38 implies that he came out in order to go and preach in other towns; and at ii. 1, 2 he is back preaching in Capernaum. It is these slight discrepancies that have made many commentators[5] assume that Mark intends us to see here a deeper

---

[1] Cf. pp. 115 f. above. i. 16–20 is again a passage which came to Mark in the tradition.

[2] The phrase may be read either as a question (so most of the English Versions) or as a statement; for our purpose it is unnecessary to decide between these alternatives.

[3] Cf. Kallas, *The Significance of the Synoptic Miracles*, p. 78.

[4] Cf. above, p. 69.

[5] E.g. Lohmeyer; Lagrange; Klostermann; Rawlinson; Schniewind; Swete; Hauck (?); Schmidt, p. 58; Lightfoot, *Gospel*, p. 24; Bundy, pp. 85 f.; etc. Contrast Taylor; Dehn; etc.

Christological meaning: a coming out from God into the world to preach. Certainly this was the view of Luke, the earliest commentator (cf. Luke iv. 43). In the praying of Jesus we are deliberately brought back to the God from whom he came forth. Perhaps there is a deliberate correction of the assertion of the demons (i. 25) that Jesus is come to destroy them:[1] preaching is rather his true activity. And 'preaching' in the eyes of Mark's readers will obviously mean the whole content of the Gospel: Jesus Christ crucified and risen, together with the meaning that they put on his death, which is, as we are seeing, that Jesus died for men who are sinners.

In ii. 10 the activity of Jesus is described, and therefore indirectly his purpose. We have already seen how in this passage forgiveness of sins precedes healing and dominates it.[2] At ii. 10 the Son of Man, who for Mark is Jesus himself, says that he has power on earth to forgive sins.[3] Probably Mark's readers when they read of Jesus forgiving sins would think of him as continuing to possess this power in his exalted state and as forgiving their sins. It is not, however, directly indicated in this passage how he is able to forgive, but the use of the title 'Son of Man' in relationship to the forgiveness of sins may imply a link with the Passion. It is this title that is used frequently in the predictions of the Passion (viii. 31; ix. 12, 31; x. 33 f., 45; xiv. 21, 41). There may thus, then, be an implicit reference at this point to the Passion. This in itself may throw light on another problem: to those who view Mark as a strictly historical book in which the story of Jesus is told there is the difficulty that Jesus forgives sins here by word and prior to his death; the early Church, however, appears to have accepted the view that forgiveness came through the death of Jesus (I Cor. xv. 3). If, however, Mark was thinking primarily of the activity of the exalted Christ,[4] who has passed through the Passion, and if he

---

[1] Cf. Lohmeyer.   [2] Pp. 35 f., 69 ff.

[3] The exact significance of ἐπὶ τῆς γῆς is difficult. Textually its position is uncertain. It may mean that the Son of Man while on earth had power to forgive sins (and the early Church would add, 'as he now has in Heaven'), or it may mean that the Son of Man has power to forgive sins on earth, i.e. before the final judgement, while the sinner is still alive on earth.

[4] 'Son of Man' is also used of the risen and exalted Christ (ix. 9; xiv. 62); Mark possibly uses this term here because it suggests both the crucified and the exalted Lord.

shows the connection of forgiveness to the Passion by means of the title 'Son of Man', this will have been no problem for him. The problem may have existed for the underlying tradition, but it did not arise for Mark.[1] Before passing from this verse we may note finally that there is no exclusive activity of Jesus set down here, nor is the forgiveness of sin said to be his main purpose.

The connection of his coming with men's sin does however appear to be his main purpose in the next verse at which we must look, ii. 17, 'I am not come to call righteous but sinners'. The whole passage ii. 15–17 bristles with difficulties: has ii. 15–17 been added to ii. 14 in the tradition or was it originally connected to it? In whose house did the meal take place, Levi's or Jesus'? Does καλέσαι mean 'call' or 'invite'? Is ii. 17b an interpretative addition to ii. 15–17a? We do not need to answer all these questions. It is probable that the material as it came to Mark in the complex of conflict stories (ii. 1–iii. 6) already joined together ii. 14 and ii. 15–17a and contained ii. 17b. The introduction of the proper name Ἰησοῦς in v. 15b probably indicates that Mark took the earlier αὐτοῦ as referring to the house of Levi. Luke by his addition of εἰς μετάνοιαν at the end of v. 17 certainly took καλέσαι to mean 'call' rather than 'invite'; the application to table fellowship within the Christian community, an issue of which Acts shows that Luke was very much aware, cannot therefore have appeared to him as prominent in the Markan account; we may thus doubt if it was important for Mark himself, though we may not deny that overtones are present. The addition of Luke thus probably represents the Markan point of view.[2] Within the saying δικαίους occasions difficulty, whether the saying be taken as originating with Jesus or not. Neither he nor the early Church would have allowed that there were righteous who did need to be summoned to repentance. Presumably then a certain amount of irony must underlie its use here.[3] Lastly, who are

[1] The original incident may never have contained the words ἵνα...γῆς (v. 10); this clause may either be a comment of the early Church or of Mark himself (so Cranfield, ad loc.).

[2] It may, however, have been the interest in table fellowship which led to the preservation (Taylor) or creation (Bultmann, pp. 92, 105) of this pericope in the early Church. [3] So Taylor; Rawlinson; etc.

the ἁμαρτωλοί who are summoned? In ii. 15, 16 they are set in parallel with the τελῶναι; these latter were despised not only by good Jews but throughout the ancient world.[1] The ἁμαρτωλοί are either those of immoral life or the 'am ha aretz who were defiled by association with Gentiles; since the 'am ha aretz would probably have included the τελῶναι, ἁμαρτωλοί should be given the sense of 'immoral people'. However, in ii. 17b we find ἁμαρτωλοί alone; no longer are tax-collectors and sinners set in parallel. Does it then continue to have the same meaning? It seems very probable that it has now slid into the Pauline sense (Rom. v. 8, 19; Gal. ii. 17) and means 'sinners'; all men are sinners and Jesus calls all. For Mark's Roman readers there would have been little interest in the 'am ha aretz; and, if ἁμαρτωλοί means 'immoral people', why should the parallel τελῶναι be dropped, since these were despised in the Gentile world as much as in Judaism and would have been considered as equally in need of the call of Jesus? Thus we take ἁμαρτωλούς in v. 17b to mean 'sinners' in the religious sense for Mark and his readers.[2] Since in v. 17b ἦλθον must definitely be given the sense of 'purpose', that is, Jesus has come into the world in order to call, we see the saying as a statement of the purpose of Jesus—to call sinners. Here is a quite simple statement of the object of his activity. There is, of course, no relationship made between this call of Jesus to sinners and his death, though the whole complex ii. 1–iii. 6 bears a Passion reference implicitly in its recital of 'conflict' stories and explicitly at ii. 20 and iii. 6.[3]

The predictions of the Passion do not tell us anything about what was achieved in the Passion. They make clear its import-ance: it was a divine necessity (δεῖ viii. 31, cf. ix. 12). This divine necessity did not lie in the other events in the life of Jesus; he might have healed other sick people than those he did

---

[1] Cf. Cicero, De Off. I, 150; Aristophanes, Eq. 247 f.; etc.

[2] Our analysis might be used to suggest that ἁμαρτωλοί in v. 17b, standing by itself, originally meant the 'am ha aretz, whereas in vv. 15, 16 it meant 'immoral people' in parallel with τελῶναι. Verse 17b thus might have been a saying of Jesus, or certainly have originated on Palestinian soil, inde-pendent of vv. 15–17a, and later have been attached thereto. This might account for the difficulties of associating v. 17b with vv. 15–17a as indicated by Dodd, The Parables of the Kingdom, pp. 117 f.

[3] Cf. pp. 116 f. above.

heal, or called another twelve than the Twelve he called; but it was necessary that he should die and rise again. He might well have said 'I am come to suffer, die and rise again'. The statements do not themselves reveal the meaning of the 'coming'; for this we must look to other statements of Jesus and to the other evidence of his activity that we have been considering.

We encounter another text about the coming of the Son of Man in the celebrated 'ransom' saying of x. 45. Its context is service. The sons of Zebedee have sought a reward for their discipleship; the other disciples complain about the ambitious Zebedees; Jesus tells them that true greatness does not lie in superior position but in service; from this he goes on to say, 'the Son of man did not come to be served but to serve, and to give his life a ransom for many'. Mark again undoubtedly equates Jesus with the Son of Man. What Jesus teaches in the first part of this logion is both for himself and his followers: both his mission and theirs is to serve and not be served. But the second part of the logion is peculiar to Jesus alone; it particularises the nature of his service—to give his life a ransom for many. Much has been written concerning the authenticity of this saying. Three positions are possible: (a) it is a genuine logion of Jesus; (b) it was created in the early Church and came to Mark as part of the tradition; (c) we owe it to Mark or the particular community in which he wrote. If this last was true then it would be especially valuable in fixing the Markan doctrine of the purpose of Jesus. But the evidence suggests that one or other of the first two views is more likely, and for our purpose it is unnecessary to determine which; for in either case the saying will have come to Mark in the material he received.

The claim for the Markan authorship of the saying is usually based on two grounds: (a) its omission in Luke; (b) resemblance to Pauline theology.[1] As against these we may argue: (a) The Lukan passage, xxii. 24–7, shows the influence of the Hellenistic Church organisation of the later part of the first century (cf. νεώτερος, ἡγούμενος) and is thus not in its present form original; the Markan saying has been modified to suit the Lukan context of Church discipline; to this Mark x. 45 b was

[1] Rashdall, *The Idea of the Atonement*, pp. 29 ff., 49 ff. Bultmann, p. 144; Klostermann; Branscomb, *ad loc.*

irrelevant, and it was therefore dropped.[1] (*b*) Paul does not make use of the concept of λύτρον but rather of ἀπολύτρωσις which has its roots in the Exodus experience.[2] If Mark x. 45*b* reflects a servant Christology which is found also in Paul, then it may be argued that the servant Christology found in Paul already lay in the tradition which he accepted,[3] and since it lay in already existing material, therefore its presence in Mark is not necessarily a sign of Pauline influence. It is also sometimes argued that x. 45*b* does not follow directly from x. 45*a* but takes us into a new world of thought;[4] this does not appear an insuperable objection to its existence prior to Mark; if Mark could make the jump, then someone earlier could have made it; the new step only particularises what the διακονία of Jesus was. Finally, it may be said that positive explanations of the saying, basing it either on a servant Christology or on the Maccabean martyrs, set it firmly in a Palestinian context and therefore as pre-Markan. We are thus left with two possibilities: either the saying is an authentic word of Jesus or it came into existence in the Jewish Christian Church as the comment of a preacher on x. 45*a*. Between these we do not need to decide. It is probable that x. 41–5 is a Markan composition in which he has put together traditional sayings of Jesus.[5] We may note the use of καί at the beginning of each of *vv.* 41, 42, 44, 45. Some of the sayings of the passage appear in variant form and differently arranged in Luke xxii. 24–7. If Mark in any way put together *vv.* 41–5 then he added *v.* 45, or at least there was the real possibility open to him of omitting it, as Luke did. Hence we may argue with confidence that it is important for his understanding of the death of Jesus.

From this we must turn to consideration of the meaning of the logion. Whether accepted as genuine or not, the vast

---

[1] Cf. R. H. Fuller, *The Mission and Achievement of Jesus*, p. 57; Büchsel, *T.W.N.T.* IV, 343.

[2] Cf. Fuller, *The Mission and Achievement of Jesus*, p. 57; Feine, *Theologie des NTs*[8], p. 109; Taylor, pp. 445 f.; Taylor, *Jesus and His Sacrifice*, pp. 99–105.

[3] Jeremias, in W. Zimmerli and J. Jeremias, *The Servant of God*, pp. 88 f., 93 (= *T.W.N.T.* V, 703 f., 706); A. M. Hunter, *Paul and his Predecessors*, pp. 31 f., 141 f.

[4] Wellhausen, *ad loc.*

[5] Cf. Taylor; Lohmeyer; Hauck.

majority of commentators have found the background to the saying in the concept of the Suffering Servant. This has now been severely challenged by Professor Barrett[1] and Miss Hooker.[2] We feel that their points are well taken. Briefly they are: (a) In the Isaianic passages which describe the Servant he is set forth as the Servant of *God*, that is, basically he serves God; but in Mark x. 44 f. the service is that of *men*; Jesus who might technically claim to be the ruler of the disciples as their master sets himself out as their servant. (b) Linguistically Mark x. 45 uses διακονεῖν, a word which with its cognates is very common in the New Testament, but which is rarely used in the LXX and never used in reference to the Servant of God (παῖς and the word-group δοῦλος are found).[3] (c) Mark's phrase ψυχὴν διδόναι is too common in Jewish and secular Greek to be necessarily traced back to παρεδόθη εἰς θάνατον ἡ ψυχὴ αὐτοῦ (Isa. liii. 12). (d) אָשָׁם (Isa. liii. 10) and λύτρον are not linguistic equivalents; the former is never rendered in the LXX by the latter or any of its cognates; the latter never renders the former nor any of its cognates. (e) אָשָׁם and λύτρον do not carry the same connotation. The former is the sacrifice offered at the same time as restitution is made for a wrong done (Lev. v. 14–19); it is not itself restitution, nor is there any idea of compensation or equivalence involved in it. The latter contains the idea of equivalence, but the word-group associated with it is often used of God's redemption of Israel without any suggestion that he makes a payment. (f) The main verbal link between Isa. liii and our logion is the use of πολλοί; this occurs three times in Isa. liii. 11 f.; but the word is too common for a serious argument to be based on it. (g) The first part of our logion provides a strong contrast in the opposite ideas of serving and being served. If the saying is conceived in terms of the Suffering Servant it is a 'little precious'[4] to suggest that the Servant did not come to be served, but it fits in admirably

---

[1] 'The Background of Mark x. 45', in *New Testament Essays*, ed. A. J. B. Higgins, pp. 1–18.

[2] *Jesus and the Servant*, pp. 74–9. Hahn, *Christologische Hoheitstitel*, pp. 54 ff., defends Isa. liii as the background of x. 45b and xiv. 24.

[3] Cf. J. A. Emerton, 'Some New Testament Notes', *J.T.S.* XI (1960), 334 f.

[4] Barrett, 'The Background of Mark x. 45', p. 8.

with the contemporary apocalyptic conception of the Son of Man who came to rule.[1]

If then we reject the explanation of Mark x. 45 in terms of the Suffering Servant, how are we to understand it? Here Dr Hooker and Professor Barrett part company. She, following the connection of the word-group associated with λύτρον, takes it in the general sense of redemption. The death of Jesus is the redemption of men. Sin is thus not emphasised but is certainly implied since it renders redemption necessary. Professor Barrett, however, points out that λύτρον is followed by ἀντί and that this suggests some idea of equivalence.[2] He finds this conception of the equivalence of one man's death to the life of others in the contemporary Jewish idea of the death of the martyr (II Macc. vii. 37 f.; IV Macc. vi. 27 ff.; xvii. 22; xviii. 4),[3] where the self-sacrifice of the martyrs means deliverance and purification for Israel. In itself this is but an example of the more widespread conception in the Old Testament and Judaism of the One and the Many; the One takes the place of the Many, as their representative. But the idea of the Suffering Servant is itself a part of the conception of the One and the Many and the Maccabean martyrs may themselves have been influenced by it. We cannot therefore ignore the indirect influence of the Isaianic Servant passages on Mark x. 45 even if their direct impact is denied. Barrett's derivation seems preferable to Miss Hooker's and yields a closer connection between the death of Jesus and sin.

If however these arguments are not thought sufficiently

---

[1] This argument is to some extent nullified if 'Son of Man' did not retain for Mark its full apocalyptic significance but was becoming one among a number of interchangeable titles used of Jesus.

[2] Cf. L. Morris, *The Apostolic Preaching of the Cross*, pp. 26–35.

[3] λύτρον does not occur in these passages, but the idea which it represents is present, being expressed by ἀντίψυχον (IV Macc. vi. 29). On the place of expiatory suffering in Rabbinic thought cf. Moore, I, 546 ff.; J. Downing, 'Jesus and Martyrdom', *J.T.S.* XIV (1963), 279–93. F. C. Grant, 'Biblical Theology and the Synoptic Problem', in *Current Issues in New Testament Interpretation* (ed. W. Klassen and G. F. Snyder), pp. 79–90, taking a similar point of view to Barrett, lists also Pal. Sanhedrin, 11.30 c, 28, 'The drops of blood which fell from those righteous men (I Kings xx. 35–7) made atonement for all Israel'. C. Maurer, 'Knecht Gottes und Sohn Gottes im Passionbericht des Markusevangeliums', *Z.T.K.* L (1953), 1–38, rejects the reference to the Maccabean martyrs.

strong to lead to the rejection of the Suffering Servant idea as basic to Mark x. 45, then we still move in somewhat the same territory in that in Isa. liii the death of the Servant is definitely a death for the sin of his fellows.[1] The meaning is well expressed in the words of Rawlinson: 'The phrase sums up the general thought of Isa. liii, and expresses the idea of a vicarious and voluntary giving of life, with the thought also implied that the sacrifice was in some way mysteriously necessitated by sin.'[2]

Finally we may observe that there is no suggestion in the saying that the λύτρον is paid to the Devil: nor is it stated in so many words from what the Many[3] are freed. Neither are these matters made precise in the Maccabean passages to which we have drawn attention; since in Mark the death of Jesus is a divine necessity it is probable that if he were pushed to the point of saying to whom the ransom was paid, he would say 'to God'.[4] If the Suffering Servant conception lies behind the logion then the guilt offering was definitely paid to God. There is thus no reason to find a reference to the Devil here.

The Markan passage (xiv. 22–5) about the Last Supper is relevant to our inquiry. It is obviously not our concern to decide whether the Markan account is prior to the Pauline nor to determine which of them more accurately represents the original words of Jesus. It is highly unlikely that Mark interfered with the words of institution as they came to him in the tradition.[5] Liturgical texts are normally treated with great reverence. It seems very likely that the references to the

---

[1] It may be that either through the Maccabean martyrs or through the Suffering Servant we should see here a connection with the sacrifice of Isaac; cf. below, pp. 169 ff.

[2] *Ad loc.*

[3] That πολλῶν is used in place of, and means, πάντων accords with a common Semitic idiom; cf. Jeremias, *T.W.N.T.* VI, 536 ff.

[4] Cf. Büchsel, *T.W.N.T.* IV, 345 f.

[5] Jeremias, *The Eucharistic Words of Jesus*, pp. 118 ff., has drawn attention to the many Semitisms in the Markan account. He considers that the position of μου in the saying about the cup would have been impossible in Aramaic. J. A. Emerton, 'τὸ αἷμά μου τῆς διαθήκης: The evidence of the Syrian versions', *J.T.S.* XIII (1962), 111–17, rightly disputes the conclusion of Jeremias; cf. Dalman, *Jesus-Jeshua*, pp. 160 f. If Jeremias is correct then, τῆς διαθήκης must have been added on Hellenistic soil; however, the connection of διαθήκη with the Supper is found also in Paul and may therefore be assumed to be primitive and have belonged during the Palestinian period.

covenant and to the pouring out of blood in the saying attached to the cup are interpretative additions to the original words of Jesus, but they will have been in the text before Mark received it. If of course they were Markan additions then they would emphasise strongly the view that Mark was putting out on his own a doctrine of the death of Jesus which connected it to the sin of men rather than the defeat of the Devil. We, however, assume that Mark did not add them; but in using them in the account he presumably agreed with their interpretation of the death of Jesus. It is important for the understanding of the Markan account that we realise that it was a Paschal meal at which the Eucharist was instituted (xiv. 12, 14, etc.). Mark may or may not have known of the alternative tradition which made Jesus die at the time of the slaughtering of the Passover lamb and thereby made the Last Supper take place prior to the Passover, but he clearly excludes it by his careful description of the preparation for the meal. The account is also firmly held within the Passion story; there may be allusions to the Eucharist in the feeding accounts, but the institution is tied to the night before the death of Jesus, and accordingly must be interpreted in the light of that death.

The saying about the bread is left without interpretative addition and whatever meaning we give to it must be read out of the total context, or out of the meaning of σῶμα itself, or out of its parallelism with the saying about the cup. It is almost certainly erroneous to derive the meaning of the bread logion from the fact of its fraction, that is, that as the bread is broken, so Christ's body is broken in death. The breaking of bread was a normal part of the action of asking a blessing on a meal,[1] and the actual words, 'This is my body', are connected in the account to the distribution and eating of the bread and not to its breaking.[2] Equally the saying about the cup is not to be connected to its pouring out but to the participation in it; the saying actually follows the participation. If the bread logion is taken by itself, and we shall see that this is more probable, then σῶμα probably has the meaning of 'self'—the body is the outward expression of the self and cannot be detached from the

---

[1] Cf. C. F. D. Moule, *Worship in the New Testament*, p. 19; A. J. B. Higgins, *The Lord's Supper in the New Testament*, pp. 51 f.

[2] Cf. Jeremias, *The Eucharistic Words of Jesus*, p. 142.

self.[1] To eat the bread which is Christ himself is then to participate in Christ, and the saying will be interpreted along the lines of I Cor. x. 16 f.[2] Naturally the Christ in whom the Christian participates is the crucified Christ, but this of itself does not tell us anything about the meaning of the death of Christ. For an interpretation of this we must turn to the saying associated with the cup.

When we now consider this we are forced, as in the case of x. 45, to accept the argument that there is not sufficient evidence to show formative influence from the Servant concept.[3] It is possible to link the usage of covenant with the Servant concept through Isa. xlii. 6; xlix. 8,[4] but the theme of the covenant is so general in the Old Testament that it is impossible to tie it down to these two texts, especially since it is here connected to the shedding of blood, of which there is no mention in the Servant passages; moreover in the Isaianic passages the Servant is himself the covenant. It is much more natural then to see in the cup-logion when it speaks of the covenant a reference to Exod. xxiv. 8 or Zech. ix. 11 under the influence of Jer. xxxi. 31 ff.; or to circumcision. The use of πολλοί is again as in x. 45 too widespread a Semitic idiom to ensure a connection to Isa. liii. 11, 12; and ἐκχύννειν has no place in the Servant imagery. The most difficult phrase in the saying is τὸ αἷμά μου τῆς διαθήκης. As it stands this would normally refer in Judaism to the blood of circumcision.[5] This hardly seems possible in the present context. Blood and the institution of a covenant are also associated in Exod. xxiv. 8; if this connection is accepted, then Jesus would be understood as instituting a new covenant, διαθήκη, carrying within itself the concept 'new',[6] and this saying would be brought into line with the

[1] Cf. Pedersen, *Israel*, I–II, p. 171, cf. pp. 171–81; Best, *One Body in Christ*, pp. 215 ff.

[2] Cf. F.-J. Leenhardt in Cullmann and Leenhardt, *Essays on the Lord's Supper*, pp. 41–3.

[3] The majority of commentators appear to accept the influence of the Servant concept. It is rejected by Hooker, *Jesus and the Servant*, pp. 80–3, and doubted by Behm, *T.W.N.T.* II, 136.

[4] Fuller, *The Mission and Achievement of Jesus*, pp. 72–5.

[5] Jeremias, *The Eucharistic Words of Jesus*, p. 134.

[6] In the Qumran writings there are many references to the 'covenant'; normally 'the new covenant' is intended though the adjective 'new' is

strategy. On July 26, 1948, by executive order, he established a review appeal board to oversee federal-hiring discrimination cases and appointed another committee to begin desegregation of the armed services.

In courting Jewish votes, Truman revealed the same pattern of drift followed by decisive preelection action. Large numbers of Jewish voters in key states such as Illinois, New York, Ohio, and New Jersey fervently supported establishment of an independent state of Israel. The United States, they demanded, should endorse this goal. Zionists in the United States pressed the White House for action, but Truman had other factors to consider: the actions of the British and future access to important oil reserves in Arab territories. When order broke down in 1948 because Palestinian Arabs refused to participate in a partition of the region, Truman decided upon recognition of the state of Israel. Israel proclaimed itself an independent state on May 15, and Truman almost immediately preferred United States diplomatic recognition. He extended this diplomatic shield later in the spring when Arabs attacked the new nation. By threatening sanctions, the President secured an uneasy armistice. While these actions did not win Truman the election in 1948, they did help him squeak to victory in key states such as Ohio.

Truman took another step toward victory by calling a special session of Congress on July 16, one day after the Democratic convention. This astute move diverted attention away from the terrible divisions in the Democratic party that the convention had revealed. Unable to influence the choice of a candidate, Democratic liberals, led by Hubert Humphrey, of Minnesota, forced through a tough civil rights plank. Southern Dixiecrats walked out of the party convention and met in Birmingham, Alabama, to form the States' Rights Party. Nominating Governor Strom Thurmond, of South Carolina, for president, the party dedicated itself to one particular right of states—the right to discriminate against black citizens. On the left, the Progressive party nominated Henry Wallace for President. Challenged on both sides, Truman picked his fight with the Republican congress, largely ignored Thurmond, and questioned the loyalty of Henry Wallace. The Republican congress obliged the President. Dubbed the "Turnip Day" special session, it passed almost none of the proposals made by Truman: antiinflationary legislation, comprehensive housing, aid to education, extension of social security, and repeal of the Taft-Hartley

Act. After two weeks, Congress adjourned: only controls on credit and housing construction legislation had passed. The Republicans had handed Truman a perfect issue, a do-nothing Congress, and a lackluster candidate in Governor Thomas Dewey of New York.

The official campaign began in September—an uphill struggle for Truman. This was, however, his sort of fight. Rolling up his sleeves and delivering rapid punches to the conservative Wall Street lawyer image projected by the Republicans, Truman criss-crossed the nation, stopping in small towns, but also carefully aiming his campaign at big labor centers. In an extravagant populist idiom, Truman lambasted the class-conscious Republicans and promised a revival of the New Deal. If the mantle of Roosevelt hung loosely around his smaller shoulders, many voters failed to notice it. Contrary to the confident predictions of the polls, the President won a small plurality of around 2 million votes and a significant electoral majority. Strom Thurmond received 39 electoral votes, all in the South, and Wallace gained none. More importantly, a decisive Democratic majority swept into the House and Senate, bringing with it a new generation of liberals; among them, in the Senate, were Hubert Humphrey, Paul Douglas, and Estes Kefauver and, in the House, Eugene McCarthy, Sidney Yates, and Abraham Ribicoff.

With his victory, Truman had revived the New Deal coalition of labor, urban residents, Catholics, farmers, and black voters. He accomplished this by protecting the gains of the 1930s, not the achievements of the 1940s. Truman had secured legislative reorganization in 1946 and unification of the armed forces in 1947, as well as centralization of overseas spying operations in 1947. The Hospital Survey and Construction Act of 1946 passed as well as a Federal Airport Construction Act. But these were not the stuff of liberal reform; indeed, most of Truman's proposals had fallen on deaf congressional ears.

Buoyed by his victory, however, Truman proposed an ambitious social reform program. In a rousing State of the Union message in early 1949, he suggested major innovations in medical care, housing, and farm policy. This "Fair Deal" agenda was designed by administration liberals and direct descendants of the New Deal. At its heart stood a farm program created by the new Secretary of Agriculture, Charles F. Brannan. The Brannan Plan proposed to maintain farm income through direct subsidies to farmers while allowing commodity prices to rise or fall. Enthusiastically greeted by labor and some farmers, the program encountered fatal opposition from Republicans, the powerful Farm Bureau Federation, and southern congressmen, who opposed the limitations placed on cash benefits to large farming operations.

Weak congressional leadership jeopardized other Fair Deal projects: a national health insurance program, repeal of Taft-Hartley, and the creation of a Fair Employment Practices Committee all failed. Only in the areas of Social Security benefits and housing did the President achieve legislative victory. The Social Security amendments of 1950 extended coverage and benefits, and the Housing Act of 1949 provided for construction of 810,000 low-cost housing units and loans and grants to cities for slum clearance.

On another count, the President scored a substantial victory. In April 1950, Senator Robert Kerr, of Oklahoma, introduced a bill exempting natural gas from federal price regulation. Squelched in the House by Speaker Sam Rayburn, of Texas, liberals belatedly mounted opposition in the Senate, but they failed to stop the bill. Urged on by liberals, Truman decided to veto the measure. Likewise, in 1952, Truman successfully blocked the Tidelands Bill, which would have turned over title and control of offshore oil deposits to shoreline states. The effect of this bill would have been to leave private oil companies unregulated by friendly or weak state governments.

During his second term of office, Truman learned one of the most important truisms of American politics: victory at the polls does not always translate into legislative success. A coalition of Southern Democratic conservatives and Republicans stymied liberal legislation. His electoral coalition had neither strength nor coherence enough to achieve new legislative victories. While it may not have been apparent at the time, Truman's tough stands on foreign policy matters and his vociferous antagonism to Communism may have helped explain his surprise victory in 1948. Indeed, Truman benefited from America's desire for security as much as from its need for change in 1948. And most of his attention after 1948 went toward foreign policy.

By 1948 and 1949, the Cold War threatened to engulf the world in military struggle. The borders of China and Eastern Europe became serious trouble spots. Disputes in these areas had been building since the end of the war, and they worsened because the superpowers failed to settle problems raised by the defeat of Germany and Japan. Shifts in power that accompanied the war rupted traditional relations in Europe and Asia, and neither the United States nor the Soviet Union was willing or able to make compromises that would have stabilized those areas.

In Europe, the contradiction between American and Russian interests loomed dangerously—Germany being the most contentious problem. The Russians believed that only their hegemony over Eastern Europe could prevent future threats from Germany. They had three possible means to achieve such a goal. They could continue the wartime alliance with the United States and agree on a friendly division of Europe into spheres of interest. They could continue military occupation of Eastern Europe. Or, they could transform the societies on their borders into Communist states and integrate them into the Soviet political and economic system.

From the vantage point of Western Europe, the United States had much the same choice: it could guarantee peace by agreement with the Russians, continue to build up military occupation forces, or promote capitalist social and economic organization in friendly nations. While none of these options was ever completely rejected by either side, the exercise of social and economic hegemony became more and more the recourse of both superpowers. Moreover, failure to settle outstanding issues intensified the commitment to rearmament on both sides. When the Russians successfully tested an atomic weapon in 1949, they broke the short-lived United States nuclear monopoly. From then on, a balance of terror reinforced the balance of power.

Truman's first meeting with Stalin at Potsdam in 1945 decided the early course of American-Soviet relations. From hindsight, Truman claimed that he decided two things about the Russians at this conference: they believed that the United States was headed for a postwar depression and therefore needed Russian trade; and they sought control over Eastern Europe. The President bluntly deduced that "Force is the only thing the Russians understand."

Truman and Stalin failed to agree on the position of the German-Polish border or on a peace treaty with Germany. Lack of accord on the future of Germany and Eastern Europe led to a gradual division of Europe into two armed camps. This did not occur immediately; there were even moments when a shift in policy seemed possible, but the general course of events flowed toward confrontation. Germany was almost immediately divided into two, not four zones. This policy of "bizonia," advocated by General Lucius Clay, split the conquered nation into a Russian zone and a joint French-United States-British area. Competition for peripheral areas also increased; countries occupied by Soviet troops gradually reorganized along Communist lines, ending in February 1948 with the Communist coup d'état in Czechoslovakia.

Similar pressures and competition also played on the stage of Western Europe. United States involvement in the Greek civil war in 1947 resulted from the exhaustion of the British. In September 1946, a much-contested plebiscite returned King George II to power in Greece. Opposition to his conservative government quickly heated up into armed struggle. By the winter of 1947, Britain, which had been supplying arms to the Greek royal government, could no longer sustain the endeavor. Truman had to decide: either enter the fight in a significant way or risk a victory by Communist-supported insurgents. The President chose the first option and, upon advice from Dean Acheson and Republican Senator Vandenberg, appeared before Congress with a message designed to persuade—and frighten—that body into appropriating aid. Truman's address to Congress on March 12, 1947, worked. In many ways, his speech galvanized anti-Communist opinion as effectively as had Churchill's "Iron Curtain" address a year earlier. By the middle of May, Congress had voted substantial aid. Including both Greece and Turkey under the umbrella of United States power, Truman admitted that these governments were not perfectly democratic. But, he argued, as friends of the United States, they were allied to democracy and the ideals of a free press, a free radio, and personal liberty.

Problems of reconstruction and stability in Western Europe preoccupied policymakers in early 1947. A new plan was sketched first by Dean Acheson and then dramatized by Secretary of State George C. Marshall in a commencement address at Harvard. Secretary Marshall's plan for European aid went to Congress in 1947 and eventually passed in April 1948. The European Recovery Act, or Marshall Plan, provided $17 billion in assistance to Europe. It might not have passed, however, had it not become an obvious Cold War act. Over the summer of 1947 in Paris, Marshall Plan negotiations were held that included the Soviets and their allies. The Russians, however, rejected the strings that the aid program would attach to their economy, and they walked out, forcing Czechoslovakian representatives to follow suit. Assured that Communist nations would not benefit from American aid, Congress more willingly appropriated money for the program.

eepening economic and political division of Europe even-
lidified into military alliances. In the spring of 1948, the
United States moved to create an anti-Soviet European defense
pact and an official state of Western Germany. When a new West
German currency was introduced inside the western sector of the
shared city of Berlin, the Russians responded with a total blockade
of traffic via road and railway into the city. Faced with a number of
possible responses, Truman chose to airlift supplies to Berlin, and
the Russians balked at shooting down American cargo planes. After
a number of grim months, the Soviets relented and allowed normal supply routes to operate. But the bad feelings engendered by
this confrontation worked their mischief. Congress swallowed its
objection to foreign aid and entangling alliances and ratified the
North Atlantic Treaty on July 21, 1949, creating a military alliance
including the United States, France, Britain, the Benelux countries (Belgium, the Netherlands, and Luxembourg), Canada, Portugal, Denmark, Norway, Italy, and Iceland. Point Four Aid
passed on June 5, 1950, extending American aid to friendly Third
World countries. By 1951, thirty-three nations had assistance
agreements with the United States under the act.

If anything, events in Asia were more unsettled after World War
II than in Europe. In Southeast Asia, American policymakers
acquiesced in the reintegration of Java into the Dutch empire
and Indochina into the French empire. In China, Roosevelt had
banked on the survival of Chiang Kai-shek, the corrupt but
clever leader of the recognized Nationalist regime. During the
war, the Japanese conquered much of China, but Chiang
seemed more interested in battling Communist insurgents led by
Mao Tse-tung than in engaging the invading armies of the Axis
power.

If Roosevelt had unrealistically committed himself to the fortunes of Chiang, Truman had to preside over the consequences of
this policy. For almost forty years, the United States had supported a strong, friendly China, but by the late 1940s, this policy
was obviously stalemated. Immediately after the war, Truman
tried without success to secure a truce between warring Chinese
factions, largely because Chiang refused to end his attacks on the
Communist insurgents. By the summer of 1946, fighting had
broken out over a broad area of China. General George C. Marshall, who had been dispatched to negotiate with Chiang, returned
home, convinced that the Chinese leader would never institute

reforms or broaden his political base. Truman realized the United States could do little except watch in frustration as the Chinese Nationalists lost the civil war.

In 1948 and 1949, the tide of battle turned, and Chiang's forces rapidly lost control of their strongholds in southern China. Anticipating a defeat, Truman approved publication of a "White Paper" blaming Communist victory in China on the corruption and inefficiency of Chiang. On December 8, 1949, Chiang fled to the Chinese island of Taiwan with the remnants of his army and supporters. At the same time, the State Department rejected tentative feelers from the important Chinese Communist leader Chou En-lai, suggesting that he and other factions in the revolutionary leadership desired friendly relations with the United States.

Korea was a danger spot on a smaller scale. Unable to agree on a joint settlement with the Russians, who occupied the northern half of that nation, the United States allowed the right-wing leader Syngman Rhee to set up a Republic of Korea in 1948 in the south. The Russians countered with the creation of the Democratic People's Republic of Korea under Kim Il Sung. Both major powers then withdrew their troops in 1949, leaving the two small states to confront each other across the thirty-eighth parallel.

These events raised a din of fury from Republican enemies of the Truman administration. Attacking Truman, the New Deal, and "Communists in government," members of the Republican party led by the "China Lobby"—a group of pro-Chiang congressmen—pilloried the Democratic administration. Their special target was Dean Acheson, now Secretary of State. Dean Acheson's remarks to the National Press Club in January 1950 did not help the administration's cause. The Secretary of State noted that the United States defense perimeter did not include Korea or Taiwan.

The Republicans claimed this speech to be an invitation for attack. But when the North Koreans did invade the South in June 1950, no such simpleminded reason could explain their act. Following previous skirmishes and a heated-up propaganda war between both sides, armed hostilities were as much caused by local events as they were by outside encouragement.

The beleaguered Truman administration acted swiftly to prevent its South Korean ally from falling. The President dispatched the 7th Fleet to protect Taiwan from conquest by the Chinese Communists, and, taking advantage of the Soviet boycott of the United Nations, secured a Security Council resolution condemning the invasion and calling for armed resistance. Truman also announced on June 27 that he would take measures to aid French military forces in Indochina attempting to quell a rebellion there. It seemed that confrontation with Communism had arrived at last.

Yet, like everything else in the Cold War, the Korean adventure proved frustrating and indecisive. It quickly became apparent that the U.N. resolution principally meant United States aid to South Korea. Other nations provided only token support. To save Syngman Rhee, Truman dispatched American ground forces to Korea on June 30. By late summer, General Douglas MacArthur, head of the U.N. command, had rebuffed the North Korean armies at Pusan on the southern tip of Korea. Then, on September 15, he launched a counterattack behind enemy lines at Inchon. Within two weeks the tide of battle had turned; United States forces retook Seoul, the capital of South Korea, and Truman permitted MacArthur to cross the border at the thirty-eighth parallel in pursuit of the North Korean armies. Had he been satisfied, the President might have declared an end to the conflict, thus restoring the prewar status quo. But, encouraged by his advisers, committed to reunification, and barely able to restrain MacArthur, Truman allowed the invasion, insisting that non-Korean troops be kept away from the Chinese borders. In October, Truman flew to Midway Island in the Pacific to talk with his headstrong military commander. MacArthur assured him that neither China nor the Russians would intervene.

Although the Indian ambassador to China warned that the Chinese would enter the war if non-Korean troops passed far beyond the thirty-eighth parallel, Truman chose to ignore him. Promising to bring United States troops home by Christmas, MacArthur pushed the retreating North Koreans toward the Yalu River, threatening Chinese bridges and hydroelectric plants. Chinese reaction was swift and surprising. On October 26, Chinese troops intervened, defeating advance United States forces, driving them back toward the thirty-eighth parallel. MacArthur demanded more troops and urged help from Chiang Kai-shek. Truman refused to grant his general's request to escalate the war for fear of widening the conflict into a world conflagration.

By early winter, Truman's commander was still losing ground, but he was sounding all the more like a policymaker. On March 7, 1951, he issued a statement ridiculing Truman's concept of limited war. Two weeks later, the President ordered his general to keep

The Korean War, 1950–1953

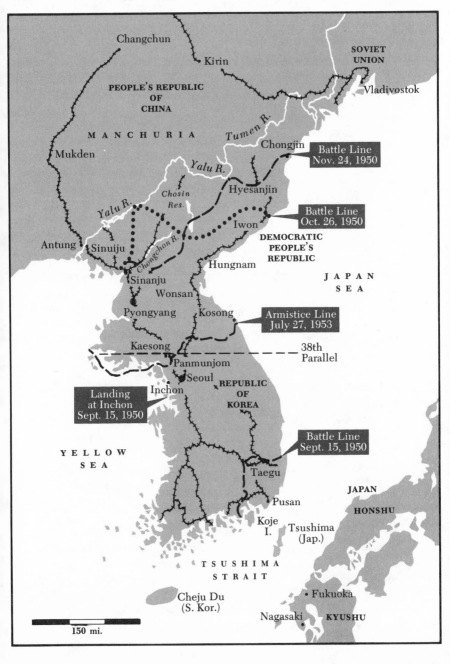

silent on foreign policy matters. But MacArthur persisted, sending off a critical message to Representative Joseph W. Martin, which the Republican released to the press. Faced with insubordination, the President had no choice. He relieved MacArthur of his command on April 11. The disgraced general flew home to the cheers and plaudits of Truman's critics. Yet a political movement never solidified around him or his desire for a wider war, and after a period of glory, MacArthur suffered the fate he predicted would be his: "Old soldiers never die," he told a reverential Congress, "they just fade away."

If the war in Korea caused a constitutional showdown between the President and his military field commander, the backlash from the war and mounting foreign policy failures fed into a domestic crisis that left ugly stress marks on the nation for several decades. Failure to win the unwinnable Cold War or to end the hot war in Korea touched off an ideological cannibalization of the federal government that decimated the ranks of liberals in office. It engendered scapegoating at a crucial turning point in foreign and domestic policy when new and creative thought was most necessary. When the ideological bloodletting known as McCarthyism finally passed, the feverish anti-Communism of the nation subsided, but the problems and reversals of Cold War policy remained like rocks after a receding tide.

Agonizing over statements of American prisoners of war in North Korea supporting their captors, a special report of the U.S. Defense Advisory Commission in 1955 declared: "The battlefield of modern warfare is all inclusive. Today there are no distant front lines, remote no man's lands, far-off rear areas. The home front is but an extension of the fighting front." For many Americans, the Cold War demanded a total, national ideological mobilization. Support in the struggle came from everywhere. Even American comedians Lou Costello and Bud Abbott wrote to the President in early 1953, offering to contribute anti-Communist jokes for Voice of America broadcasts.

President Truman shared the anti-Communist convictions of most of his critics. But, as the American leader during the darkest days of the Cold War, his task was to moderate between extreme opinions and to offer guidance in protecting the rights of citizens to free speech and freedom from intimidation. Once out of office, Truman assessed his record on civil liberties in the most positive terms. Charging the Republicans and Senator McCarthy in particular with outrageous violations of individual rights, he argued in his *Memoirs* that his strongest commitment as president had been to protect freedom of speech.

The truth, however, is more complicated than his partisan declaration. Of course, some members of the Republican party—Congressman Richard Nixon, of California, and Senators McCarthy, of Wisconsin, Karl Mundt, of North Dakota, and William Jenner, of Indiana—used the "Communist" issue to smear opponents. But Republicans were certainly not alone in creating a national obsession with ideological purity. Labor leaders, liberals, Democrats, Republicans, and leading newspapers and journals all contributed to defining rejected ideas as treasonous acts.

It is more accurate to say that Truman used the anti-Communist issue with more discretion than his Republican opponents—but he still used it. In 1946, he established a Temporary Commission on Employee Loyalty. When the commission reported, he accepted their suggestion of a loyalty program for federal employees. On March 22, 1947, the President asked his attorney general to draw up a list of subversive organizations. He established federal departmental loyalty boards and pre- and post-employment security checks. By March 1952, 20,733 employees had been investigated. Over 11,000 were cleared; almost 3,000 initially okayed stood under review; about 2,500 left service on their own accord; and about 400 were dismissed.

Truman also allowed the activities and budget of the FBI to increase, augmenting the power of J. Edgar Hoover and adding more agents to his tightly run private army of crime-stoppers and ideological watchdogs. Congress stepped up its investigations of Communism, with diverse committees conducting as many as eighty-four inquiries between 1945 and 1952. Led by the House Committee on Un-American Activities (HUAC) and the Senate Internal Security Subcommittee, Congress held extensive hearings into the film industry (helping to generate a blacklist of Hollywood writers and stars suspected of leftist sympathies) and the federal government. Very little legislation came from these investigations. Instead, their rather clear purpose was to provide a forum for attacks on liberalism and the New Deal.

Only one piece of legislation dealing with the Communist issue passed during the acrimonious days of the second Truman administration: the Internal Security Act of 1950. An administrative nightmare, the law required the Justice Department to register the names, finances, and memberships of all Communist party and designated front organizations. All of their literature was to be labeled: Communist. Known Communists were denied passports out of or visas into the United States. And provision was made to intern suspected disloyal Americans in time of emergency, much as thousands of Japanese had been placed in camps during World War II. Truman dispatched a vigorous veto message saying that the act would throw away the ideals of "our free society." He added that he already possessed most of the powers granted by the act and had been using them for several years. Nonetheless, Congress overrode the veto, and the act became law.

Truman was right; he had been fighting suspected Communists on several fronts. The loyalty program was in full swing. Several individuals were denied passports (the most famous would be Paul Robeson in 1952), and the federal government indicted and secured the conviction of Communist party leaders under the Smith Act. But nothing defused the Communist issue in Congress. Truman's efforts appeared halfway measures at best—if not downright suspicious—to those who believed that radicals had infiltrated the administration. The perjury trial of Alger Hiss in 1949 and the 1950 espionage trial of Julius and Ethel Rosenberg, accused of passing atomic secrets to the Russians, seemed to confirm the worst accusations about security lapses. In fact, these trials proved the opposite—how little justified were fears of Communists operating at the core of government, passing secrets to the Soviets. Yet, both became a kind of public exorcism of frustration with failures of America's Cold War policies.

Whatever else, Alger Hiss was a stereotypical New Dealer, bright, well educated, well connected, and sometimes carelessly arrogant. Not a real member of F.D.R.'s inner circle, Hiss had run afoul of James Byrnes and of Adolf A. Berle in the State Department during the 1930s, and both of these men developed strong antipathies to him, if not suspicions about his loyalty. After helping to organize the U.N. Conference at San Francisco, Hiss was edged out of the State Department by Truman. In February 1947, with the sponsorship of John Foster Dulles (later Secretary of State under Eisenhower), Hiss became president of the Carnegie Endowment for International Peace.

His retreat from government service, however, did not protect him from attack. Self-confessed Russian agent Whittaker Chambers testified before HUAC, accusing Alger Hiss of passing secret documents to the Russians. "Mr. Hiss," the witness later declared, "represents the concealed enemy against which we are all fighting and I am fighting." Hiss vehemently denied charges that he had passed secret documents to Chambers; indeed, he claimed he did not recognize his accuser. When Chambers repeated his attack on NBC's *Meet the Press*, Hiss sued for libel. Then, on December 3, 1948, Chambers led HUAC investigators to his farm in Maryland, where he produced microfilm copies of the documents in question hidden in a pumpkin patch. This dramatic turnabout led to the indictment and conviction of Hiss on two counts of perjury in 1950.

Although Hiss did not tell the truth on several counts—he did know Chambers, for example—it is not clear to what extent, if any, he had consciously worked for the Russians or what was the value of the documents that he had allegedly passed in the 1930s. But questions of this sort were irrelevant to Republicans, like Richard Nixon, who used the issue to blast the administration for leaks and intrigue. Truman ineptly and irrelevantly counter-charged the Republicans with weakening his struggle against Communism.

The next trial was even more bitter and had grave consequences for the defendants. In 1950, Klaus Fuchs, a nuclear physicist and confessed spy, initiated a chain of revelations leading to Julius Rosenberg and his wife, Ethel. Both Rosenbergs were active Communists; both were children of immigrants; both were Jewish. And, in some ways, all three of these identities stood in the docket in 1950. With some substantial evidence against Julius, the FBI also had Ethel indicted, probably in hopes of making her husband reveal other members of an atomic spy ring. Neither defendant would confess, even after their convictions, even when the government offered clemency if they would name names. On June 19, 1953, the accused were executed at Sing Sing prison. This sorry end, after countless pleas, stays of execution, and interminable waiting, shocked much of the world, but satisfied those who demanded stern measures against Communists. Perhaps not the martyrs pictured by their staunchest defenders, the Rosenbergs were nonetheless the hapless victims of national outrage.

Senator Joseph McCarthy, the junior Republican Senator from Wisconsin, turned this frustration into political capital. Coming from one of the most liberal states in the union, McCarthy nonetheless articulated the fears and suspicions of a part of this constituency. Boosted by such newspapers as the *Chicago Tribune* and conservative elements in the Catholic Church, McCarthy also found approval in the Republican party. Senator Taft, majority leader in the Senate, made McCarthy head of the Government Operations Committee in 1953. From this position, the senator flung down his accusation of Communist infiltration into government.

McCarthy's first visible attacks on Communists in government came in late 1949 with a speech to the Young Republicans, charging infiltration of enemy agents in the State Department. In February 1950, at Wheeling, West Virginia, he accelerated his attack, claiming 205 Communists in the employ of the State Department. On February 20, McCarthy read a revised number of enemy agents—only fifty-seven—into the *Congressional Record*. Working down his list of suspected individuals and illustrative events, McCarthy honed in on the real target of his remarks, Secretary of State Dean Acheson. "This pompous diplomat in striped pants, with a phony British accent," had defended the character of Alger Hiss—and perhaps worse.

Although some observers reacted in disbelief that such wild charges could be believed, they were quickly disabused. McCarthyism, if perhaps not McCarthy himself, was deadly serious. A senate committee dominated by Democrats, called to investigate his charges, exonerated the State Department, but Republican members and McCarthy refused to accept the results. Despite the vigorous opposition of some Republican senators led by Margaret Chase Smith, of Maine, who issued a Declaration of Conscience, the Republican party allowed the Communist issue to become a partisan charge against the Democrats. And Truman, unable or unwilling to see beyond immediate issues, defended his administration in partisan terms. Nonetheless, the Communist issue hurt the Democrats. In the 1950 election, several liberal Congressmen (among them Claude Pepper, the liberal senator from Florida) fell victim to an anti-Communist crusade.

Relations between the administration and Congress after 1950 thickened with acrimony, charges, and countercharges. With the Korean War continuing relentlessly and McCarthy riding high in Washington, Truman's position disintegrated further with the discovery of corruption in his administration involving Attorney General J. Howard McGrath and with suggestions of gangster influence in Democratic-controlled cities uncovered by the Kefauver

Committee investigating organized crime. Compromised by his angry and unconstitutional seizure of the steel industry during a summer strike in 1952 and threatened with another split in the Democratic party, Truman's position looked bleak. Despite his achievements, he was not a popular president, and this unpopularity tarnished the whole Democratic party. Unable to create a coalition around anything but his own reelection, Truman failed in his ambitious Fair Deal. In foreign policy, he pursued aims that led to frustration and then war. The result was a loss of direction and control in government. Perhaps inevitable, it came when the times demanded the subtlest and most innovative political skills, which Truman, unfortunately, did not possess.

5 Cities and Suburbs

In his cellar room at the edge of Harlem, under the glare and warmth of 1,369 electric light bulbs, the "invisible man," the hero of Ralph Ellison's great novel of the same name, shouted his refusal to remain hidden and ignored. "Perhaps that's my greatest social crime," he pondered, "I've overstayed my hibernation, since there's a possibility that even an invisible man has a socially responsible role to play." Ellison's autobiographical novel chronicled one of the great American migrations of the twentieth century: the flood of blacks from the rural South into northern cities like New York City. Searching for jobs, social opportunity, and political freedom, these new urbanites transformed American city life. And, in the 1950s, they demanded recognition and new responsibilities.

Another major migration occurred simultaneously in the 1950s and 1960s, out of and beyond cities like New York City and into the suburbs and the Sunbelt. The escape predominantly of white Americans from high-rise cities to low-density suburbs occurred along a system of roads built under the greatest public-works project ever undertaken in this country. These projects came from the fertile imagination of men like Robert Moses, Park Commissioner and Planning Commissioner of New York City. Operating atop a financial pyramid of toll bridges and roads, Moses invested state funds in a system of highways connecting parks, city, and suburbs into a vast grid of endless motion.

Both Ellison and Moses can be seen as symbols of two divergent populations that participated in the relentless movement that transformed American cities and suburbs after World War II. These two populations helped create a civilization that not only looked different (it could be seen best from the air or photographed through a wide lens), but thought differently about itself.

The revolution in urban and suburban life and the drain of

population into the South and West extended a process of demographic dispersal already well under way before World War II.
America had become a predominantly urban society in the 1920s
but simultaneously began to abandon its central cities for the suburbs. The Depression of the 1930s retarded this motion, but it
resumed after World War II. By 1974, about three-fourths of the
population of the United States lived in 250 standard metropolitan
areas (comprising central cities and their satellite suburbs). Thus,
urban life had two phases: the dense population of the central
cities and the sprawl surrounding them, the one contracting and
the other expanding. The declining percentage of population in
central cities relative to their suburbs reveals the extent of change.
In the greater Baltimore, Maryland, area, the city proper fell from
67.6 percent of total population in 1950 to only 43.7 percent in
1970. In Detroit, during the same period, the decline was slightly
steeper, from 61.3 percent to 36 percent. Practically every other
American central city experienced the same phenomenon.

This shift is not hard to explain: population simply followed jobs,
housing, shopping opportunities, and roads. The changing economic base that stimulated population dispersal also shifted the tax
base and available public services. And, again, these changes
affected the demography of cities and suburbs: who lived in them,
their race and ethnic origin, family size and income, and age.

Overall, economic activity in the nation's twenty-five largest
metropolitan areas increased rapidly after World War II. From
1948 to 1963, employment in manufacturing went up by 16 percent, in trade by 21 percent, in services by 53 percent. But growth
was differential; the central cities lost 7 percent of the jobs in the
first two categories and increased service employment only by 32
percent. In the suburban areas, however, manufacturing employment went up 61 percent, trade increased 122 percent, and service jobs boomed by 135 percent. In the same metropolitan areas,
the central cities lost about 300,000 jobs, while employment increased by almost 4 million in outlying areas. By the end of the
1960s, suburban areas had more manufacturing jobs than the central cities.

Inside the city, the nature of work changed. From 1960 to 1970,
101 central cities lost over 800,000 blue-collar positions, but
gained 500,000 white-collar jobs. In surrounding areas, both categories increased, but new white-collar jobs doubled the number of
positions in manufacturing. Urban work, in other words, in-

Central Expressway, Dallas, Texas, 1972. Expressways and limited-access highways, often built with federal financing, transformed the appearance of American cities. Growth in Sunbelt boom towns such as Los Angeles, Dallas, and Houston was particularly affected by dependence upon the automobile.   (Bob W. Smith/EPA Documerica)

creasingly became dominated by service, administrative, and information industries rather than manufacturing.

The flow of business outward from the central cities enormously stimulated the suburban housing market, creating the postwar boom in housing starts predicted by business leaders during the war. New housing units in suburbs sprang up at a rate almost three times faster than in central cities. Federal Housing Authority and Veterans Administration loan programs brought new, cheap homes within the reach of millions of Americans who previously had to settle for urban apartment living. As a result, the percentage of Americans who owned their own homes rose by 30 from 1940 to 1970. Property values also reflected this shift in population pressure; from 1960 to 1970, city housing prices increased slightly compared to rapidly increasing values of suburban property. Along with housing went the appurtenances of new suburban life: new schools and roads, shopping centers, religious and recreational facilities.

The outward shift of population shrank the potential fiscal resources of central cities. Measured by retail sales, economic activity in most major cities expanded very little in the ten-year period between 1958 and 1967, while outlying areas shot up in total sales. Typically, in the city of Chicago, sales increased only 5 percent over the ten-year period, while suburban trade went up almost 87 percent. Los Angeles experienced more balanced growth, but even there, within the city limits, sales showed a 22 percent rise compared to 75 percent in suburban areas.

Compared to earlier periods, the economic position of the central cities had greatly deteriorated. In 1932, American cities together collected more tax revenues than either the states or the federal government. In 1959, however, city revenues amounted to only about one-half the total collected by the states and approximated only 15 percent of federal income. This trend was not readily apparent until about 1950, for city financial resources peaked immediately after the war. By the mid-1950s, however, the situation became obvious and serious. Tax revenues shrank as the tax base declined. By 1967, the median income of city dwellers fell to almost $2,000 less than that of suburbanites.

The diminished economic opportunity of the central city reflected the changing racial and class basis of the urban population. The influx of black and poorer Americans into the central cities and the outflow of white, wealthier residents constituted a demographic upheaval that shook every population group loose from traditional residential patterns. After a period of little change during the 1930s, the rural population of the United States resumed its rush into urban areas. From 17.5 percent of the total population in 1945, the rural share diminished to only about 5 percent in 1970. The racial complexion of this exodus proved even more remarkable. From 1960 to 1970, the white population on farms decreased by about 33 percent, but the black population declined by more than 60 percent.

Population of Standard Metropolitan Statistical Areas
(By Region, Size, and Race, 1950 and 1970)

		Inner City	Outside* Central City	Black Pop. as % of Inner City	Black Pop. as % of Suburbs
1950	White	43,001,634	33,248,836		
	Black	6,194,948	1,736,521	12.5%	4.9%
	Other	216,210	102,531		
1970	White	49,430,443	71,148,286		
	Black	13,140,331	3,630,279	20.5%	4.8%
	Other	1,226,169	843,303		

*Suburbs.
Source: Historical Statistics of the United States, Bicentennial Edition, Vol. I, p. 40.

Housing and job segregation filtered this population flow. Up to 1948, the courts enforced restrictive covenants in house sale contracts. Thereafter, the practice continued informally. New suburbs employed restrictions and pricing policies that excluded most black Americans, and occasionally other ethnic or religious minorities. In inner-city areas, whites sometimes turned to violence to prevent integration of their neighborhoods. During the 1950s, house bombings, and sometimes riots, occurred in major cities like Chicago, Los Angeles, Dallas, Atlanta, New York City, and others.

Occasionally, city governments acted to preserve racial and ethnic separation by placing public-housing projects in areas away from white populations, or sometimes they voted not to build them at all. Nonetheless, by the early 1960s, inner-city black ghettos emerged as large centers of social problems. Black city dwellers became more visible in their dependence upon shrinking social services. By 1968, many American city school systems had more than 50 percent black students, with much higher percentages in Washington, Baltimore, Chicago, Detroit, St. Louis, and New Orleans.

☆   ☆   ☆

Compared to the rural poverty of the Deep South left behind, the city represented a vast improvement. Yet, at the same time, the disparities and inequities the new black urbanites suffered became more obvious. Rural unemployment was easier to overlook than urban unemployment. The bonds of custom in small towns disintegrated in the cities of the North. Inadequate schools in rural areas went unnoticed; overcrowded, segregated northern schools became a persistent social problem. Increasing pressure on social services, while the tax base was eroding, exhausted urban resources. The suburbs needed schools, roads, and medical, recreational, and religious facilities, and they got them. The cities found themselves overburdened and overwhelmed.

Cities occupy a paradoxical place in the American imagination. Acknowledged centers of sophistication, commerce, culture, and government, they have the most visibly heterogeneous populations, where ethnic group bumps against ethnic group, where work and daily life mix and filter diverse populations. Yet, many Americans feared urban life because it was so visibly changeable and integrated. For those who wanted to start over, to flee crowded apartments, close neighborhoods, heat, slums, and dirt, the suburbs and the new communities of the Sunbelt exercised a dramatic attraction. As cities, particularly in the North, changed rapidly after World War II, becoming the focus of racial problems and concentrated centers of poverty, they came more and more to symbolize an older America, representative of old problems, not new opportunities.

The population shift out of the industrial North into the Sunbelt responded in part to stimulation provided by the federal government. Powerful southern senators and congressmen, who dominated defense and appropriations committees, secured large defense

Net Migration by Color
1940–1950 and 1950–1960*

1940–1950

Region	White	Nonwhite
Northeast	− 173 (− 0.5%)	+ 483 (+34.3%)
North Central	− 948 (− 2.5%)	+ 632 (+42.0%)
South	− 583 (− 1.7%)	−1,597 (−16.0%)
West	+3,181 (+23.8%)	+ 323 (+60.5%)

1950–1960

Region	White	Nonwhite
Northeast	− 206 (− 0.6%)	+ 541 (+26.0%)
North Central	− 679 (− 1.6%)	+ 558 (+23.8%)
South	+ 52 (+ 0.1%)	−1,457 (−14.1%)
West	−3,518 (+18.7%)	+ 332 (+23.6%)

*In thousands and percentages.
Source: Statistical Abstract of the United States, *1963, p. 39.*

contracts for industries in their states. As late as the mid-1970s, the pattern of net outflows of federal expenditures remained favorable to the South and West.

In some Southern states, right-to-work laws, legalized by the Taft-Hartley Act, enticed important industries such as shoe manufacturing and textiles into the South. Given available cheap labor, and legally and politically armed against unions, states such as North Carolina, South Carolina, and Texas picked up the remnants of the declining Northeastern clothing industry. Enormous federal sums expended for roads and airports gave these new manufacturing regions greatly improved access to markets.

New industry and transportation pulled population south and west. All regions of the United States gained population from 1940 to 1970, but the West grew twice as fast as the Northeast. The South also increased at a faster pace than either the Northeast or the north central section, signaling a relative decline of the old manufacturing states of the East and Midwest. In political terms, this shift cost older areas votes in the presidential electoral college.

For example, in 1940, New York State cast 47 votes in the electoral college; by 1970, it had only 41. In 1940, California had 25 votes, but in 1970, it increased to 45.

California exhibited the most rapid population rise. From the fifth most populous state in 1940, it rose to first place in 1963. About 5 percent of the American population lived within its borders in 1939; by the 1960s, this figure had multiplied to almost 10 percent. After World War II, most of the new population settled in the suburbs, making California one of the most suburbanized regions in the world. Even while rapidly urbanizing in this period, California witnessed a decline in population density in its most crowded areas.

Every poll asking Americans where they would prefer to live and travel invariably finds California as first choice. This is not surprising, for California has been a trend setter in establishing the

Population in Selected Central Cities, 1960–1970
(Changes in per annum white and nonwhite populations)

	White Pop. Change % per Annum	Nonwhite Pop. Change % per Annum
Bridgeport, Conn.	+ .4	+ 5.6
Chicago, Ill.	− 2.0	+ 3.1
Dayton, Ohio	− 1.9	+ 2.6
Detroit, Mich.	− 3.4	+ 3.2
Los Angeles, Calif.	+ .5	+ 4.3
Milwaukee, Wis.	− 1.1	+ 5.3
Montgomery, Ala.	+ .2	− .6
New York, N.Y.	− .9	+ 4.4
St. Louis, Mo.	− 3.7	+ 1.7
San Francisco– Oakland, Calif.	− 1.9	+ 3.4
Washington, D.C.	− 4.9	+ 2.7

Source: Statistical Abstract of the United States, *1975, pp. 887 ff.*

Net Flow of Federal Expenditures Over Taxes by Region (1975)

Region	Net Flow (in millions of dollars)
Northeast	− 762*
Mid-Atlantic	− 10,013
East North Central	− 18,618
West North Central	− 1,456
South Atlantic	+ 4,986
South Central	+ 6,536
Mountain	+ 3,631
Pacific	+ 7,008
Washington, D.C.	+ 8,690

*Per capita diffferentials are even more striking.
Source: National Journal, June 26, 1976, Government Research Corporation (quoted in Statistical Abstract of the United States, 1977, p. 257).

culture of modern work and leisure. As the center of the film and television industries and the backdrop for countless advertising campaigns, California became the stage for realizing the consumer dreams of millions of Americans. Not just the most populous, most suburbanized state in the union, it also strongly influenced national fashions, art, dress, housing, and life-styles.

The most popular situation comedy in television history, *The Beverly Hillbillies* (1962–1972), captured this westward shift and satirized the clash of cultures in California. When the hillbilly Easterners, with country manners and language, confronted the slick, new consumer world of California, the potential for comedy became unlimited. In exaggerated form, this represented the experience of millions of Americans who moved to the Golden State during the same years.

This transformation in demography and culture would not have been possible without the automobile. Throughout the period, the rapid construction of freeways, availability of cheap gasoline, and general affordability of cars transformed the American city and countryside in an unprecedented fashion. Dependence upon the

The Edsel, produced for a few years in the mid-1950s. This experiment by the Ford Motor Company, intended as a new family car that would appeal to the unconscious motivations of buyers, failed to attract a significant number of purchasers. (Library of Congress)

car changed what people ate and where they ate it; where they lived, worked, and vacationed; what sort of air they breathed; and what their houses, public buildings, and cities looked like. As never before, the health of the economy depended upon the restless and anarchistic energy of the automobile. As one of America's wisest critics, Lewis Mumford, put it, "We have been living in a fool's paradise . . . the brave new, simplified, automatic world of the machine."

Propagandists for the great American road system were anything but hesitant in their assessment of this paradise, however. Bernard De Voto, critic and interpreter of American culture, writing for the Ford Motor Company in 1956, rhapsodized that "A highway is not only a measure of progress, but a true index of our culture." A complex new system of highways, he said, would unbind "the giant" American nation. Undoubtedly, most Americans agreed with De Voto.

Modern automobile culture existed on an infrastructure of new federal highways and bridges. Following the opening of the limited-access Pennsylvania Turnpike in 1940, New York, Indiana, New Jersey, and Ohio constructed successful toll highways. California constructed an elaborate system of freeways financed by its own tax revenues. Nonetheless, early in the Eisenhower administration, it became clear that neither tollways nor state-financed expressways could relieve the congestion on the nation's highways. As a result, Eisenhower appointed General Lucius Clay in September 1954 to chair a committee to propose a new federal system of interstate roads. Representatives of the Teamsters Union and businessmen associated with the construction and automotive industries joined the resulting National Highway Program Committee. When the group reported in 1955, it outlined a massive building program justified by traffic tie-ups around American cities and by the need for rapid evacuation of urban areas in case of nuclear attack.

As passed in 1956, the Highway Act planned the construction of approximately 41,000 miles of interstate and defense highways, of which 5,000 miles would be urban freeways. The 90 percent federal share of construction costs would come from the Highway Trust Fund, accumulated through taxation on road usage and gasoline. The states were to contribute the other 10 percent of the costs. Original estimates pegged the total cost at $27 billion, although this forecast rose to $50 billion by 1970. In addition to periodic estimates and surveys of the system, the act required public hearings for any federally aided highway bypassing or traversing a city, town, or village

The direct consequences and multiplier effects of this system and other road-building projects undertaken in the 1940s and 1950s greatly intensified America's commitment to a car-centered culture. Automobiles competed successfully with all other forms of transportation, delivering a *coup de grâce* to an already moribund passenger rail system. By 1970, less than 1 percent of intercity passengers traveled by railroad. Automobile registration leaped from 27 million in 1940 to almost 90 million in 1970, more than tripling in thirty years. Of the twenty-fold increase in energy generated over the period, automobile traffic consumed a large share. More people possessed more cars and traveled farther, until by 1970, the average car owner went 10,000 miles per year in his automobile.

The automobile transformed America's living spaces. Los Angeles devoted about 50 percent of its total land area to streets and parking lots, although other cities limited this percentage to around 30. Shopping centers, "freeway industries," such as electronic companies, and housing developments sprang up along urban highways and clustered at the exchanges of beltways. Motor-home sales boomed, and after 1950, large chains of motels dotted the interstate landscape. The new drive-in way of life sharply differentiated urban from suburban living. The uncongested thruways sped cars between cities, national parks, suburbs, and the countryside. They made the United States accessible to its citizens in a way unheard of before World War II. But they also stimulated traffic, speed, and accidents until motor-vehicle deaths became America's fourth leading cause of death through the 1970s. And, over all of America's metropolitan area, a pall of smog accumulated.

Only in the 1960s did significant hesitations about this system begin to surface. Passed under President Kennedy, the Highway Act of 1962 sought to soften the inconvenience of road building by providing displacement aid for families moved out of the path of expressways. It granted power to the Secretary of Commerce to ensure that urban highway projects coincided with local city plans. Citizens groups began successful organization against the proliferation of highways. Residents of New York City, already choking on gasoline pollution, defeated a proposed lower Manhattan expressway. Perhaps the most remarkable confrontation, however, occurred in New Orleans, where the demands of the highway builders clashed with the traditions that gave the city its unique character.

From the motorist's perspective, the worst traffic problem of New Orleans was the Vieux Carré, the old French Quarter and tourist center. Plans to alleviate traffic in the area had long been on the drawing board. In 1946, New York City's planner Robert Moses submitted an "Arterial Plan for New Orleans" to the State Highway Department, featuring an elevated expressway between the Mississippi River and the edge of the Quarter. Several plans and years later, the city decided to construct a Riverfront Expressway. In 1965, the (renamed) Riverfront and Elysian Fields Expressway became I-310, a projected part of the Interstate Highway System. At an estimated cost of $40 million, the roadway would have eliminated through-traffic in the Quarter, but would have erected a towering, noisy barrier between the city and the river. Proponents contended that they could construct lighting and fences to preserve the character of the Quarter, but the prospect of a massive rush of traffic cordoned off by wrought-iron gates satisfied no one who loved the old section. Despite enormous local pressure for the highway, national architecture and preservation groups finally stopped it in 1969, when the Secretary of Commerce exercised his power under the new Highway Act of 1966 to halt any highway project that threatened the destruction of an historic site. The worst excesses of the highway barons were halted.

Yet, automobile traffic profoundly shaped the new urban and suburban landscapes of the postwar period. The universal architecture of billboards and fast-food drive-ins in the suburbs and the massive, opaque glass-and-steel skyscrapers punctuating every American downtown depended on an automobile culture that viewed buildings from a moving perspective. The modern office building, devoid of traditional ornaments, stated its purpose clearly. The clean, cool lines created by the great architectural firm of Skidmore, Owings and Merrill; the dreary bureaucratic tombs of Washington, D.C.; and the stylish massiveness of the "new brutalism" repeated the same message: function dominated form. Grandiose and overpowering, modern American urban architecture followed the specifications of space, materials, cost, and parking access. It expressed a valid but self-absorbed optimism about the future of American society, and, sometimes, a contempt for its urban or natural surroundings.

One of America's most renowned postwar architects, Ludwig Mies van der Rohe, once wrote that "Architecture is the real battleground of the spirit." During the 1950s and 1960s, this battleground became the suburban environment. At the cutting edge of American civilization after World War II, the suburban culture set off controversy, for the architecture, social life, and culture that grew up in the suburbs seemed to contradict traditional American ideals of individualism and self-help.

Perhaps the most renowned suburbs were the three Levittowns constructed in New York, New Jersey, and Pennsylvania during the 1940s and 1950s. Mass-produced communities had long been an idea dear to American social planners. During the 1930s, the New Deal built demonstration Greenbelt cities in Maryland, Ohio, and Wisconsin. But the ventures of William Levitt broke new ground, because they illustrated the profitability of sophisticated tract-housing projects when combined with town planning.

During the Depression, Levitt had made a fortune in real estate, and during the war, he gained valuable experience in constructing Navy housing. After 1945, he turned to tract housing. His first Levittown, on Long Island, constructed in 1947, conformed to a relatively traditional subdivision style with schools, churches, and businesses added after residences. His second experiment in planning proved more radical. His firm planned a new town in Bucks County, Pennsylvania, in 1951, with shopping centers at the edge of residential districts. Levitt found, however, in this and the first experiment, that placing social services after housing was completed caused serious problems. His third experiment in Willingboro, New Jersey, organized houses in neighborhoods or superblocks centering around schools and other social services. Land was set aside for religious structures.

Levittown houses were detached but mass-produced. The manufacturer offered several styles: the Cape Code, the Rancher, and the Colonial. Color variation ensured that every structure looked different. Architectural designs were eclectic—that is, with features mixed without much regard to continuity or purpose. Wishing his houses to be superficially different on the outside, Levitt wanted relative uniformity in his residents. Homeowner manuals warned against erecting unauthorized fences or changing house colors without permission. No washing could be hung outside on weekends, and from April to November, owners promised to cut the lawn once a week. Levitt also used house prices to funnel residents into his community. The New Jersey town offered relatively expensive houses to attract a somewhat higher class of resident. The New York Levittown excluded prospective black buyers with a restrictive covenant that read: "No dwelling shall be used or employed by members of other than the Caucasian race, but the employment and maintenance of other than Caucasian domestic servants shall be permitted." When the courts declared such restrictions unenforceable, Levitt instructed his salespeople not to sell to blacks. Overt discrimination finally ended by court order in 1960.

Levittowns and other new suburbs were no more exclusive than the town and city communities from which their populations came, but their homogeneity showed more visibly through countless picture windows. Residents resembled each other in race and classs, but not in ethnic group and religion. For example, in 1967, the New Jersey Levittown was 47 percent Protestant, 37 percent Catholic, and 14 percent Jewish. Residents tended to be young, with a high percentage married; almost no older people or single people lived in the community. The population enthusiastically supported their churches and civic organizations. Sociological surveys concluded that they had moved to the suburbs because they sought the leisured life, the open space—sometimes the exclusiveness—and the psychological benefits that home ownership bestowed on them.

These were sufficient reasons to persuade many Americans to migrate to the suburbs, but they worried a growing chorus of critics who denounced the social and cultural sterility of suburban living. From novels like John McPartland's *No Down Payment* (1957) to the serious philosophic work of Hannah Arendt, the growing sameness of American society distressed commentators. Widespread belief in the homogeneity of American culture emerged from many factors: the mass media; enlarged federal government participation in the economy; the bureaucratization of American business; political and social conservatism; and McCarthyism. And it seemed most rampant in the conformist life-style of the suburbs.

Exposés exaggerated and sensationalized the faults of suburbia. Paper-thin walls, barbecues, all-night dancing-and-drinking parties, and wife- and husband-swapping became clichés in satiric novels of the suburbs. Popular journals and sociological essays discussed the "suburban captivity of the churches," the relentless organizing of clubs and kaffeeklatsches, the identity changes of

Democrats into Republicans, vengeful and frustrated suburban mothers, tacky houses, flocks of bored children, and fathers whose only real function was home repair.

Even serious works sometimes shared this hyperbole. The most astute analyses of suburban life came from two sociologists, David Riesman and William Whyte, Jr. Riesman entitled his analysis of modern American life *The Lonely Crowd* (1950), a title as suggestive and powerful as the argument of his book. Declaring the existence of a new mass form of society, he sketched a progression of character changes he thought typified traditional societies, "inner-directed" societies (the Victorian Age), and "other-directed" societies (the 1950s). The great transformation of the modern age, he proclaimed, replaced inner- with other-directedness. "Inhibited," "self-willed," "aggressive," "aggrandizing," "creative," and "destructive" were words he used to describe the inner-directed man, a person who listened to his conscience and followed a self-constructed gyroscope to direct his life. His personality perfectly suited the heyday of finance capitalism and the rapid growth of population in the late nineteenth century.

For Riesman, modern consumer capitalism demanded a revision in personality structure to conform to the demands of bureaucracy and efficiency. In this type of personality, human motivation moved out of the conscience to reside in the peer group. To please others, to conform to superficial niceties, to be congenial and easy to get along with—that is, to be shallow—these were the demands of a society whose principal activity had turned from work as production to work as the manipulation of people. Inner-direction sought success; other-direction pursued security.

Looking back on his work a few years after he published it, Riesman said he had been much misunderstood and misinterpreted. He did not intend to argue the superiority of inner-direction (as so many readers seemed to think) nor did he mean to imply that such personalities, as he sketched them, really ever existed; they were convenient sociological straw men. He and his fellow researchers, he claimed, were not "conservatives harking back to a rugged individualism." Yet, for all his protests and disclaimers, Riesman's interpreters and critics rightly sensed the overtones of criticism. He did seem to prefer the inner-directed Victorian.

The ambiguity of Riesman's work did not characterize William Whyte, Jr.'s *Organization Man*, published in 1956. This brilliant and caustic attack on the ethics of peer group culture is decidedly conservative. Building on Riesman's insights, Whyte examined modern corporate work and the new corporate suburb Park Forest, Illinois. In the background of this critique lay a cherished memory from his own first days in business. As a young salesman in training, he entered Vicks Chemical Company's School of Applied Merchandising. There, in the rough-and-tumble world of production and selling, he learned aggressiveness and independence. It was a test for the survival of the fittest, and he survived. Modern rites of passage into business, however, had nothing of the ruthless honesty of such old-fashioned competition. The man who joined the modern corporation passed not through the jaws of competition, but over bureaucratic hurdles of personality tests. These entrance examinations, administered in leading corporations, identified the requirements of a modern business career. These included conformity, getting along with a group, approval from others, and further personality skills. Especially outrageous, Whyte argued, was the role of social science, which worked hand in glove with employers seeking to enforce this code.

Just as bureaucracy seduced the ethos of the workplace, conformity had conquered the suburb. Rootless, but with an insatiable desire to belong, the organization man and his wife behaved at home as if in training for corporate jobs. Suburban education taught "sociability" to their children. The norms of the neighborhood substituted for individual taste. Across the United States, Whyte found, from "the courts of Park Forest, the patios of Park Merced in San Francisco, Philadelphia's Drexelbrook, the New Levittown, Pennsylvania—there is an unmistakable similarity in the way of life."

Both Riesman and Whyte described the most menacing form of mass society, but sociologist Vance Packard, in his bestselling book *The Hidden Persuaders* (1957), tried to explain how that new society had emerged. In doing so, he exonerated the American public and blamed the manipulations of advertisers. Motivational researchers in the 1930s and 1940s had taught advertisers that consumers acted from nonrational motivations. They bought images of an idealized self when they purchased clothing; they acted to quell insecurities or to affect a high status, but they almost never selected a product for its real qualities. Packard argued that advertisers exploited this new knowledge and created a world of symbols in which food, cigarettes, clothing, and automobiles defined success and happiness. His most striking example came from the Chrysler Corporation. Dr. Ernest Dichter, a motivational researcher, convinced the corporation to redesign its automobiles. His study, "Mistress Versus Wife," argued that men were drawn to auto showrooms by convertibles, which they unconsciously associated with possessing a mistress. But they purchased a four-door sedan—or wife. To combine these two urges, Dichter suggested a union of the images, the four-door hardtop—a product that became a best-seller for years.

Packard's most serious point warned about the perils of motivational research in politics. Politicians could use psychological manipulation to sell shopworn and obsolete ideas. While this public relations approach to politics was still relatively rare in the early 1950s, a few politicians, most notably Richard Nixon, had begun to realize the potential of a practice that became widespread by the 1970s.

Riesman, Whyte, and Packard raised fears about the direction of mass culture; they worried about its tendency to commercialize and vulgarize. Their readers, already nurtured on lurid images from George Orwell's *1984*, published in 1949, imagined that they saw the same tendencies in McCarthyism and the drab sameness of life in the "Little Boxes" of Marin County, satirized in Malvina Reynold's song of 1963. But, suburbia was not the cultural desert or the malevolent blight that many critics claimed. Much like the city dwellers who had been their forefathers, suburbanites neither became instant vulgarians nor switched to the Republican party nor joined vapid, optimistic social religions. Instead, the suburbs illustrated and sometimes exaggerated already existing racial and class distinctions in American society.

Americans have traditionally regarded their urban populations with suspicion. In the early part of the century, millions of immigrants took up residence in the centers of industrialism and commercialism, where they became the subject of countless reform movements. After World War II the cities became the focus of America's racial problems. City governments, therefore, welcomed new tools of urban renewal granted them by the Taft-Ellender-Wagner Housing Act of 1949. The act aimed to ensure "a decent home and a suitable living environment for every American family." Specifically, it granted cities the power of eminent domain to condemn blighted areas and gave them federal funds to raze buildings there. These cleared properties could then be sold at a lower price to developers for construction of new housing or offices. With slum-clearance laws in force in about twenty-five states already, this legislation dictated a more coherent and homogeneous approach to urban renewal.

Another provision of the 1949 act expanded federal loans and subsidies for local low-rent public housing. The number of units constructed in any one year remained flexible, between 50,000 and 200,000, so that the president could employ the money in a countercyclical fashion. Public-housing rents, furthermore, were pegged at 20 percent below similar private units to eliminate competition with profit-making rental properties. Subsequent modifications of the program in the Housing Act of 1954 emphasized rehabilitation of neighborhoods and provided federal grants for comprehensive city planning.

Although this program promoted some public housing (much of it initially in the form of skyscrapers), it also displaced thousands of urban residents and subsidized the private reclamation of commercial areas. Relocation proved costly and difficult, so that urban renewal in some cities merely moved poor people from one section of the city to another, without improving their housing opportunities. Increasingly, poor, black urbanites occupied public projects, thus intensifying city ghettoization. While thousands of citizens moved into better housing, much of this new construction quickly deteriorated because of poor management, spotty upkeep, and abuse by residents.

Opposition to renewal projects gathered quickly. Antagonists protested the wholesale destruction of neighborhoods and architectural treasures. Writers, such as Jane Jacobs in her *Death and Life of Great American Cities* (1961), condemned slum clearance, calling it a profit-making shift of the poor from one section of the city to another, without dealing with the problems that created or increased urban blight. Martin Anderson's *The Federal Bulldozer*, published in 1964, blamed Washington for much of the destruction of cities. In response to such criticisms, the 1961 Housing Act—and the Demonstration Cities programs carried out later under President Johnson—modified slum clearance and required more comprehensive planning. But, even these improvements and growing willingness of city governments to hear out citizen opposition to renewal projects did not begin to solve the problems of slums, segregation, and the economic decline of the central cities. Slum residents had neither the political nor economic power to assert control over local governments more generally attuned to property values than to urban sociology.

Local governments reacted slowly to housing problems and city blight, in part because the victims of urban decay were generally poor and black. Traditional American attitudes toward the poor assumed that this population lacked the means to adjust to a complex industrial society. The Victorian Age had talked of an absence of willpower, immorality, and alcoholism as the causes of poverty. Post–World War II observers tended to emphasize shortcomings in education, inadequate health care, and segregation. No one in the 1950s denied that inequality could intensify poverty, but a new and widely held theory explained the behavior of urban blacks in terms of cultural deprivation. As Ralph Ellison wrote, even a sympathetic critic, like Gunnar Myrdal, defined black culture as a product of "social pathology." According to this theory, the American Negro was nothing but a shadow of white America.

This notion of cultural deprivation became a full-blown sociological theory by the 1960s, partly in response to the slow motion of urban reform. Borrowing the concept "the culture of poverty" from the anthropologist Oscar Lewis, writers such as Nathan Glazer and Daniel Moynihan felt they detected a similar culture in America's urban slums. In the isolated and degrading atmosphere of the ghetto, they argued, black culture operated to prevent successful integration of its residents into the rest of the society. This emphasis upon isolation and the disjointed culture of urban slums merged into a larger debate about the nature of American culture: was it one rich and variegated culture or two separate ones? This attitude, based upon comparison of black Americans with immigrant ethnic groups that had previously flowed into the cities, focused upon economic mobility.

At the same time, however, Americans increasingly recognized black culture as a major component in mainstream culture—from the important novels of Ellison and James Baldwin to the popular arts. The black ghettos of postwar society increasingly set trends in American mass culture. The identities of black and white culture have never been strictly segregated; even in the early nineteenth century, under the slave system, powerful interchanges flowed both ways. Nonetheless, black Americans, particularly in music, developed separate variants of songs, orchestrations, and rhythms that periodically merged into and refreshed the larger surrounding culture, splitting off again in new directions.

Chuck Berry. One of the early rock stars. Berry was a virtuoso guitarist and compose who wrote such famous hits as "Maybelline." His career was marked by heights of success and wealth as well as scandal and jail. (UPI)

The beginnings of rock-'n'-roll.

Pat Boone. In the mid-1950s, Pat Boone took songs written by black artists and cut his own recordings of them. These modified and "sanitized" versions helped popularize rock-'n'-roll in the white community. Boone's career was a model of teen-age propriety. In 1959 he was voted "Father of the Year."   (UPI)

In the 1950s, the impact of black music repeated old patterns but established new relationships. During the 1920s, white musicians in places like Chicago heard the astounding sounds and virtuosity of black jazz players, and they adopted and transformed that sound for white audiences. Throughout the period and into the 1930s, jazz and the blues existed at two levels, in the black community, where "race records" featured popular black artists like Bessie Smith, and in performances and recordings made by white jazz players for white audiences. George Gershwin and Darius Milhaud, the French composer, adopted the jazz idiom because its sounds and rhythms seemed uniquely modern and urban.

While jazz arrangements and sounds influenced every element of American music, the position of black artists remained ambiguous. Many black players and composers performed at exclusive, white nightclubs; sometimes they scored and played music for Hollywood films; but, in general, they did not receive full credit or reward for their efforts. For example, the great black composer Duke Ellington performed a Carnegie Hall concert in January 1943, but not before white jazz players, like Benny Goodman, had already appeared there.

In the 1940s and early 1950s, the introduction of rhythm and blues, a new urban music that also emerged largely in the black community, repeated the same patterns. White audiences became aware of this new danceable beat when disc jockey Alan Freed (who took the name Moondog) played it on the radio in Cleveland in 1951. In 1954, Freed moved his show to New York City. By then a number of popular black groups had emerged. White artists like Pat Boone began to cut sanitized "cover records" of the same songs to capitalize on their success. Other cover groups, like the "Crew Cuts," appeared. Their versions of rhythm and blues and a further evolution—rock and roll—quickly made the top-ten yearly sellers.

The explosion of rock and roll was also visual: the film *Blackboard Jungle*, released in 1955, used Bill Haley's rendition of "Rock Around the Clock" as background to a story of high school juvenile delinquency. This association with delinquency, sexuality, violence, and alienation made the film and the music more inflammatory. Teenage audiences leaped into the aisles to dance to Haley's music, and newspapers all over the country reported riots, fights, and vandalism incited by the movie.

By the middle 1950s, Chuck Berry, one of the most versatile black artists, and Elvis Presley, the "white man who had the Negro sound and the Negro feel," emerged as leaders in popular music. Working first for Sun Records in Memphis, Tennessee, Presley became a new kind of recording star, who openly exploited the sexuality and rebelliousness associated with this music. His music also added a strong ingredient of country-and-western sound. By the end of the 1950s, rock and roll had transformed popular music. The radio-TV series, the *Hit Parade*, born in the heyday of big bands, died in 1959. This ultimate in "cover" performances could not reproduce the excitement, rhythm, and sexual thrust of the new music. Dick Clark's *American Bandstand*, from Philadelphia, replaced it as the showcase of popular music. Much more attuned to the teenage audience, it emphasized dancing and original recording artists. By 1957, the show was seen nationally on television. Perhaps most significantly of all, black artists who wrote, played, and recorded popular music for a national audience began to emerge as celebrities. As the popularity of cover records declined, these artists established their own reputations and fortunes. The new urban popular culture had firmly established itself.

Adverse reaction to rock and roll came partly from its association with delinquency and juvenile misbehavior and partly from its reputation as black music. In return, rock artists gleefully satirized middle-class norms. The lyrics of Chuck Berry's "Roll Over Beethoven" (1956) illustrate the defiance and humor of this new music:

Well, I'm gonna write a little letter, gonna mail
   it to my local D.J.
Yes, it's a jumpin' little record I want my
   jockey to play
Roll over Beethoven, I gotta hear it again
   today
You know my temp'rature's risin' and the juke
   box blowin' a fuse
My heart's beatin' rhythm and my soul keeps
   a singin' the blues
Roll over Beethoven and tell Tchaikovsky
   the news.

Parents' groups, law enforcers, churches, and newspapers rarely saw the humor. Major American newspapers, such as the *New York Daily News*, throughout the 1950s predicted the imminent and hoped-for demise of rock and roll. Angry parents blamed the music for an outbreak of misbehavior at home, and some newspapers even printed stories claiming that popular music was an integrationist plot organized by the NAACP.

In 1959, public outrage against rock and roll reached Congress, and the House Committee on Interstate and Foreign Commerce held hearings to investigate "payola" (lucrative arrangements between disc jockeys and record companies). Although Alan Freed, one of the principal witnesses, was never convicted of accepting bribes, his career was ruined. The committee's assumption was clear: rock and roll was too vulgar and degrading to be popular; audiences had been "misled as to the popularity of the records played." Committee members even attacked Dick Clark for slighting crooners Bing Crosby and Perry Como.

The impact of this new music represented something rather different, however. This burst of energy from America's black ghettos illustrates the changing nature of American culture. The transformation of inner cities into degrading slums did not speak the whole truth about the urban experience of the 1940s and 1950s. Crime, violence, juvenile delinquency, and cultural impoverishment did not constitute the sole result of this experience. Ralph Ellison was right about his invisibility: it was time to become visible. Not just in culture, but in all elements of life, black Americans demanded integration into the mainstream. In the years of the Eisenhower administration, the rest of society began to grant reluctant recognition to these demands.

6 Republican Era

Author and playwright Thornton Wilder dubbed the 1950s the "Silent Generation" in an epithet accusing Americans of smugness and inaction. To *New York Post* columnist Murray Kempton, America came "of Middle Age" between 1950 and 1962. Both characterizations protested the bland politics of these years, and both blamed the central political figure of the era: Dwight David Eisenhower. To many observers, Eisenhower's middle-of-the-road Republican presidency represented a distasteful compromise in an era of recurring dramatic possibilities. It defined a policy born out of the cautious conservatism of the suburbs and the security-minded politics of old-fashioned morality.

Eisenhower's age (he was sixty-two when he took office) and appearance suggested that the reins of government had slipped into the control of the older generation. To *The New York Times*, Ike resembled "everybody's grandfather." Eisenhower, the oldest man yet to be elected president, served an American population that, in spite of the baby boom, had the oldest median age in the twentieth century. A far friendlier evaluation came from Republican Senator Everett Dirksen, of Illinois, who in eulogizing Eisenhower, construed his conservatism differently: "Perhaps there are times when a Nation needs brilliance in diplomacy, skill in administration, in-depth background in legislative needs," he admitted. "But there are also times when a Nation needs an abiding father with the wholeness approach of a national leader. . . ."

Eisenhower conservatism frustrated both Democratic liberals and right-wing Republicans, but it pleased an enormous majority of the American electorate who gave the former general two resounding victories despite the electoral unpopularity of his own party. Expectations for the new Republican administration differed widely. A few Republican party ideologues hoped the new president would break the icy truce with the Russians and initiate hot pursuit of Communism. Some voters hoped that in clearing up "the mess in Washington," the Republicans meant purging liberal insiders who had supported New Deal reforms and the Russian-American alliance of World War II. But an overwhelming majority probably supported him for opposite reasons: he promised to end the war in Korea, and he assured Americans he would consolidate, not reverse, the reforms of the 1930s.

For the eight years of his administration, Eisenhower pursued compromise, failing to consolidate his viewpoint in the Republican party. After his departure as president, the moderate, eastern Republicanism he represented wilted quickly in the heat of Sunbelt conservatism. Unexpectedly called to preside over the first small retreats of Jim Crow and segregation, his cautious enforcement of the *Brown* v. *Board of Education* desegregation decision of 1954 pleased almost no one. His defense budget conservatism and his blustery but inconclusive foreign policy roused criticism from all sides. Yet, in this time of immoderate choices, Eisenhower proved to be precisely what most Americans wanted.

Dwight Eisenhower was born on October 14, 1890, in Denison, Texas, and grew up in Abilene, Kansas. His family had a long ancestry, but uncertain standing in the small pioneer plains village. Led by Jacob Eisenhower, a minister and leader in the Protestant sect of the Lykens Valley River Brethren, the Eisenhowers had made their way to Kansas in 1878 from Delaware. Unlike the rest of his family, Dwight's father, David, tried his hand at engineering school. At Lane University, he met and married Ida Stover, of Virginia. But neither engineering nor merchandising, which he took up briefly, could support his growing family. By 1890, David was working on the railroad.

Despite the visible poverty of Dwight's family—in his fourth-grade class picture, he is the only boy wearing farm overalls—Dwight's childhood was generally a happy one. Ignoring his mother's professed pacifism, young Dwight earned a reputation as a skillful fighter and the nickname "Little Ike." Later recollections pictured his family days as warm, loving, and tinged with strong religious faith. His father constructed an immense chart of biblical history, on which the children could see the historical chronology of the Bible in 10 feet by 6 feet hieroglyphics.

Ike was not a studious boy, although he enjoyed history and the action of classic battles. His real interests focused on the playing field, and in high school he became an accomplished athlete. Still, he scored well on the United States Military Academy's competitive exams, and in 1911 he received an appointment to the academy. Handsome, athletic, with a mischievous grin and sandy blond hair, Eisenhower arrived at West Point to join the very special society that embraced his life for the next forty-one years. As a plebe football star, Eisenhower suffered a knee injury that forever ended his athletic career. Known as a maverick and prankster, he earned poor marks in discipline and graduated with a moderate standing in his class. He had not been an obvious success.

Out of school and serving with the infantry in San Antonio, Texas, however, Eisenhower began a rapid, careful ascent through army ranks. While in Texas, he met and married Mamie Geneva Doud, a wealthy and popular young beauty. By 1917, when World War I finally engulfed the United States, Ike had become a skillful organizer with important friends to advise him with his career. After the war, Eisenhower moved steadily upward, joining the Army General Staff in 1925 and attending Command School. At the same time, he wrote a military guidebook of American battlefields of World War I, without visiting Europe.

Congenial and with impressive competence in organizing and leadership, Eisenhower was dispatched to England to head American forces in the European theater during World War II. Work with troublesome French and British allies proved difficult, but Eisenhower emerged as a popular, politically skilled head of the victorious Allied armies on the western front. Long wartime absences from Washington and his wife, Mamie, took their toll on his marriage. Rumors of an affair with his driver, Kay Summersby, spread to Washington. If Ike was tempted to put personal happiness before duty, he quickly gave up dreams of a permanent liaison with Summersby. He had been in the army too long. Rejoining Mamie in Washington after the war, he planted his feet firmly on the track that led eventually to the presidency.

Appointed Chief of Staff in Washington after 1945, Eisenhower, like two other generals, had a political future. The others were George Marshall, later the controversial Secretary of State under Truman, and Douglas MacArthur. Both political parties courted Eisenhower as a presidential candidate. In 1947 and 1948, the Democrats made overtures to him, and the Republicans nominated him in 1952. From 1948 to 1952, Eisenhower bided his time, accepting an offer from Columbia to become president of that university. An improbable choice, Eisenhower remarked, "I told them they were talking to the wrong Eisenhower," indicating that his brother, Milton, a well-known educator and government consultant, would have been a better candidate. No doubt, he was right. He was unpopular with Columbia's liberal faculty and ran his office through a general staff. Fund-raising proved to be an unpleasant chore. Yet, this academic interlude did nothing to diminish his political prospects. He pushed no policy or party, and even when he rejoined the Army to command NATO forces in late 1950, he avoided close identification with the Truman administration.

Without apparent political debts to pay, Eisenhower was a perfect presidential prospect. In April 1952, he announced his candidacy for the Republican nomination. Nonetheless, Ike had serious opposition. After the electoral disaster of 1948, the Republican conservative wing, led by Senator Robert Taft, of Ohio, made a strong bid to control the party. Solid among state organizations, Taft seemed to promise what many regulars wanted: defeat of the Democrats, a hard-line foreign policy, and an end to social reform.

Robert Alphonso Taft, son of the late President William Howard Taft, was born and bred to Republican party politics. Yale-educated and a Cincinnati lawyer, Taft emerged in the late 1930s a leading critic of the New Deal and an opponent of the liberal-labor coalition that underwrote the Democratic party. An enigmatic, distant man, Taft inspired staunch loyalty from Republicans who opposed the social reform and wartime alliances of the Roosevelt and Truman administrations. Republican right-wing adherents hoped he would reverse the liberal and internationalist policies of twenty years of Democratic rule.

While his candidacy sat well with party regulars in 1952 and was greeted with rapturous accolades by conservative newspapers like the *Chicago Tribune*, Taft's career was strewn with inconsistencies that frightened potential followers. His toleration of Joseph McCarthy and his use of the Communist-in-government issue eliminated some support. Generally committed to unilateralism in foreign policy, he struck curious and sometimes inconsistent positions. He opposed NATO, the Marshall Plan, the Truman Doctrine, and the International Monetary Fund as needless foreign entanglements. Yet, deferring to the bipartisan policy of the Republican party, he voted for these policies in the Senate. An intelligent critic of postwar internationalism, who doubted the wis-

Dwight D. Eisenhower.   *(National Archives)*

dom of much Cold War policy, he sometimes found himself supporting measures that violated his principles.

Taft's power at the Republican convention in Chicago during early July ran down the Midwestern backbone of the party into the shadow Republican organization of the South. Many of his supporters were driven by the accumulated bitterness of twenty years of frustration, focused on Dewey's narrow defeat in 1948. Senator Dirksen, of Illinois, vented this anger during a crucial credentials floor fight, when he pointed to Dewey, standing in the midst of the New York delegation and shouted: "We followed you before and you took us down the road to defeat." Dirksen and the Taft forces, however, were brushed aside by the Eisenhower bandwagon, which picked up disputed delegates in Texas, Georgia, and Louisiana. Even warm support from keynote speaker Douglas MacArthur could not prevent Taft's defeat. The Eastern wing, led by Dewey and Henry Cabot Lodge, had triumphed. But party leaders tendered the vice-presidency as a compromise. Both factions agreed on Richard Nixon, senator from California. Nixon was a shrewd and fateful choice. Armed with a wide reputation inside the party as an opportunist, Nixon was a tough fighter—a California McCarthy—and thoroughly acceptable to party conservatives. But Nixon had also ingratiated himself with Easterners such as Dewey. The match was ideal: a presidential nominee who seemed above politics, a vigorous vice-presidential candidate, and a party platform narrowly based on Republican conservatism. A three-month Republican crusade against traitors "in high places," against Communism, Corruption, and Korea, began, led by a man who abhorred ideologies and political brawls.

The Democrats had to choose between improbabilities in 1952. President Truman considered a third term, but after a disastrous showing in early primaries, he turned from front-runner to kingmaker. Senator Estes Kefauver, of Tennessee, widely known for his Senate investigations into organized crime in 1950 and 1951, entered the race, but Kefauver's investigators had discovered embarrassing ties between Democratic city bosses and the underworld, and the party organization blocked the senator. Despite early victories in primaries, Kefauver's candidacy gradually sank as that of Governor Adlai Stevenson, of Illinois, rose.

Stevenson had long-standing ties to Democratic politics. His grandfather had been a congressman and then vice-president in 1892 during the Cleveland administration. After an Eastern education at Choate, Princeton, and Harvard, Adlai returned to the Midwest to work as a journalist and a lawyer. During World War II, he joined the office of the Secretary of the Navy. Sent to San Francisco as an adviser to the American delegation to the United Nations Conference in 1945, he continued as adviser to the American delegation to the U.N. in 1946 and 1947. Serious politics began in 1948 when he won the governorship of Illinois. His four years in office were competent, but uneventful.

By temperament a witty and urbane man, Stevenson was a political moderate and a strong anti-Communist. Yet circumstances made him a lightning rod for liberalism; he both attracted and dispersed hopes for vigorous reform. His elegant speeches and affirmation of the New Deal invited scurrilous attacks heaped on him by conservative newspaper columnists, giving him a reputation he did not entirely deserve. But, he was a candidate Truman could support, and he was acceptable to the liberal wing of the party and the South.

To win in 1952, the Republicans merely needed to last out the campaign without committing serious gaffs. Stevenson had the unhappy task of running for and against the Truman administration. The best theme the Democrats could muster was "You never had it so good," an unfortunate slogan that newspaper cartoonists gleefully satirized. Stevenson tried to establish political breathing room by moving his headquarters to Springfield, Illinois, but Truman insisted on entering the campaign anyway, undercutting the candidate's independence with a last-minute, whistle-stop defense of his administration in October.

Within the Republican party, Eisenhower had to make peace with Taft and then defend his lead in opinion polls. His presidency, he announced in Boise, Idaho, in August, would seek the "middle road." By this course, he hoped to steer between liberal Democrats and the conservative wing of his own party. Embracing the activist Republican heritage of Lincoln and Theodore Roosevelt, he defended federal intervention into the economy to preserve the market economy. He promised to maintain the "solid floor that keeps all of us from falling into a pit of disaster." He would not campaign against the welfare state.

In foreign policy, conservatives had more to praise. Eisenhower agreed with their firm opposition to Communism and he accused the Truman administration of errors and appeasement. The slurs and broad charges of McCarthy and Senator William Jenner, of

This cartoon appeared on the front page of the Chicago Tribune *on August 6, 1952.*
During the election campaign of 1952, a majority of American newspapers supported
the Republican ticket, urging a change in political party leadership for the first time
in twenty years. The Tribune *was among the most active and vociferous critics of*
Democratic rule. (Reprinted courtesy of the Chicago Tribune. *All rights reserved.*)

Indiana were, however, another matter. Unwilling to voice his distaste for these men, Eisenhower backed into endorsing their candidacies. This accommodation cost Eisenhower personally, in- itially preventing him from defending his old friend, General George Marshall, of charges of being soft on Communism. Con- demned by anti-Communist crusader McCarthy for "surrendering" China to the Communists, the general was ridiculed and smeared during a campaign that charged the Democrats with "twenty years of treason." Eisenhower's bargain with anti-Communist activists in his party on the vice-presidency risked his election for a short time. On September 18, the *New York Post* uncovered a secret $18,000 slush fund provided by wealthy California businessmen to Richard Nixon, catching the Republican apostle of ideological pur- ity with political grime on his face. Several newspapers in the Eisenhower camp, like the *Washington Post* and the Republican *New York Herald Tribune,* called on the Californian to quit. Eisenhower remained ominously silent, signaling Nixon to clear himself.

On September 23, the Republican vice-presidential candidate explained his finances to a national radio and television audience. In the most famous political speech of the decade, Nixon mixed mumbled humility with belligerent innuendo. Using the irresisti- ble intimacy of television, he portrayed himself as the victim of a smear. He acknowledged the existence of the fund used to pay office expenses, but claimed that he personally had received nothing. In a long, pensive introduction, he counted the roads to corruption he might have taken: to put his wife on the payroll ("She's a wonderful stenographer"), to sell his influence, or to ex- ploit family riches—if he had them. Then, in embarrassing detail, he outlined the family finances. He was satisfied with his success; unlike mink-clad Democrats, his wife, Pat, accepted her "respect- able cloth coat." He had received a gift—a dog named Checkers, beloved by his children—but there was nothing wrong with this. He would keep the dog.

The speech was both disingenuous and prophetic. The candidate never squarely faced the meaning of the slush fund. More pecu- liarly, in an uncensored moment, he thought out loud about some of the very forms of corruption he later pursued in his own pres- idency. But, the performance was a masterful stroke of public relations. Favorable telegrams poured into the national Republican headquarters. Nixon secured his position but undercut his relationship with Eisenhower. From that moment on, Nixon fruitlessly sought what he could never acquire: the consistent friendship and support of the general.

Despite a comfortable lead in the polls, the Republican campaign only caught fire on October 24, when Eisenhower suddenly announced in Detroit that he would visit Korea. Vague as it was, this promise suggested that the candidate would seek a quick peace to the seemingly interminable war. This announcement raised the odds even more against Stevenson. He could neither restore the Roosevelt coalition with fire-and-brimstone New Deal rhetoric nor divorce himself from the unpopular Truman administration. Even so, the November results were surprising. Eisenhower swept 34 million votes to only 27 million for Stevenson. More striking, the Republican mustered considerable strength in the South, taking Texas, Virginia, Tennessee, and Oklahoma. Elsewhere, the ticket slashed into the urban-ethnic coalition of the Democrats. The congressional Republicans fared less well, squeaking by in the House with a majority of ten and in the Senate only with Vice-President Nixon voting to break a deadlock.

The president-elect began immediately to summon his Cabinet and his staff, and quietly fulfilled his principal campaign pledge. Together with General Omar N. Bradley and future Cabinet members Herbert Brownell (Attorney General) and Charles E. Wilson (Defense), he slipped away under tight security to visit Korea for several days in November. Conferring there with American generals and Korean Premier Syngman Rhee, he emerged with no new policy, but he had kept his pledge.

Unlike subsequent presidents, Eisenhower relied heavily upon the advice of his Cabinet. Secretary of the Treasury George Humphrey, a conservative industrialist from Cleveland, emerged as his closest adviser. Secretary of State was John Foster Dulles, a personal friend and an experienced diplomat. Ezra Taft Benson, a Taft supporter, became Secretary of Agriculture. Dewey's supporter, Herbert Brownell, was appointed Attorney General. In 1953, when Congress created the Department of Health, Education, and Welfare, Eisenhower selected Oveta Culp Hobby, former commander of the Women's Army Corps, as Secretary. Martin Durkin, head of the Plumbers Union, became Secretary of Labor, a post he shortly relinquished to James Mitchell, a vice-president of Bloomingdale's department stores. The Cabinet carefully balanced the ideological wings of the Republican party and represented

Election of 1952

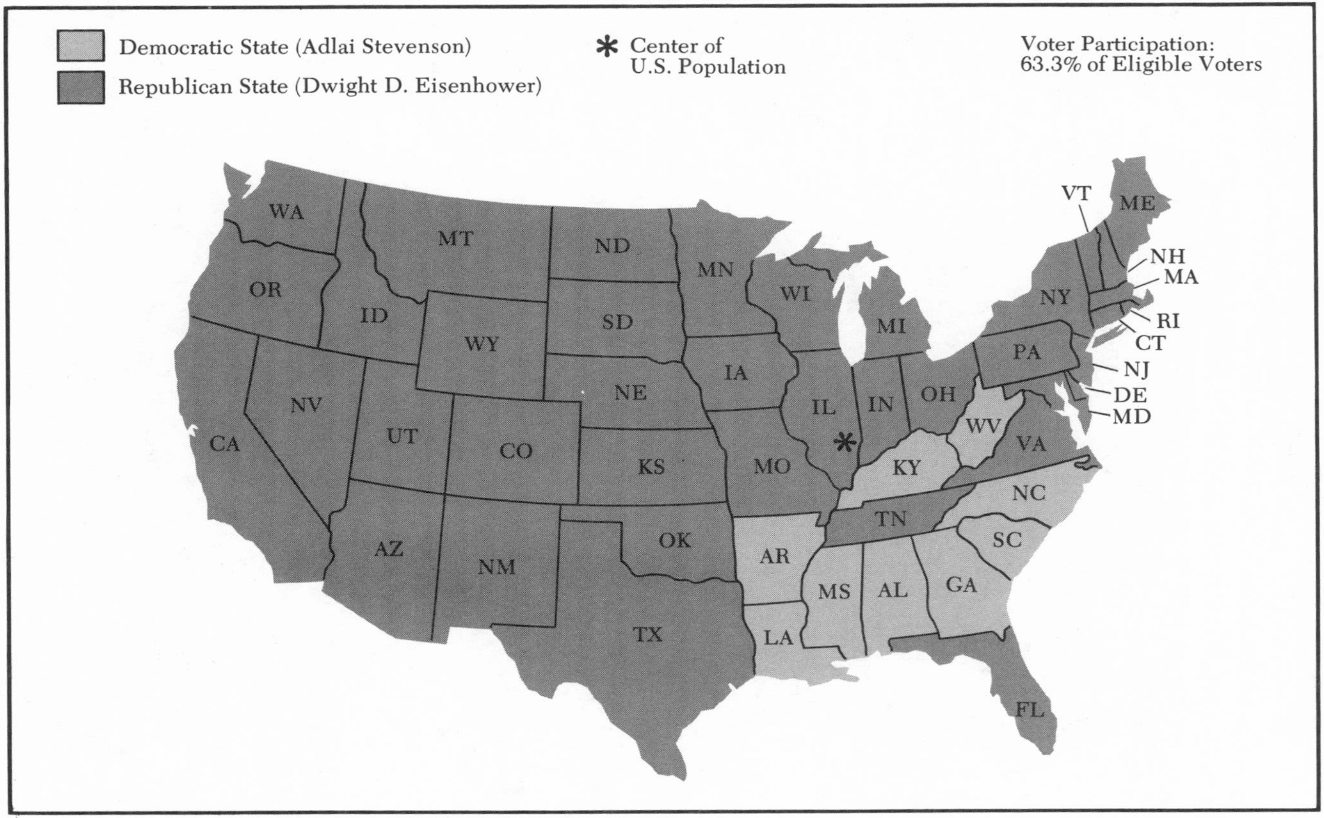
Democratic State (Adlai Stevenson)
Republican State (Dwight D. Eisenhower)
* Center of U.S. Population
Voter Participation: 63.3% of Eligible Voters
WA
OR
CA
ID
NV
MT
WY
UT
AZ
CO
NM
ND
SD
NE
KS
OK
TX
MN
IA
MO
AR
LA
WI
IL
MI
IN
KY
TN
MS
AL
OH
WV
VA
NC
SC
GA
FL
PA
NY
VT
ME
NH
MA
RI
CT
NJ
DE
MD

established wealth and economic power. This was certainly no departure from tradition, but Eisenhower chose his appointments from large commercial or manufacturing establishments. Except for Dulles, none belonged to the influential group of corporate lawyers that had advised Truman. In addition to the Cabinet, Ike appointed Allen Dulles to head the Central Intelligence Agency. Operating in tandem, the two Dulles brothers commanded the open diplomacy and clandestine operations of the American government.

Eisenhower's appointments appeared to underscore his commitment to the status quo. His inaugural address of January 20, 1953, was a platitudinous example of what theologian Will Herberg named "civic religion." Eisenhower had even penned his own prayer for the occasion. Two weeks later, he and his wife joined the National Presbyterian Church as full communicant members. In public, he acted as a spiritual leader, using the presidency as the ceremonial chief of staff of the Republic. Eisenhower was careful not to detract from his public image as a man above party, committed to traditional values of honesty, integrity, family, and simplicity in office. In part, too, the new president recognized the pervasive sentiment against strong, activist leaders. He was the first man to serve under the new Twenty-second Amendment to the Constitution, ratified in 1951, which limited all presidents following Harry Truman to not more than two terms.

There was, however, another side to Eisenhower—intelligent and sensitive to the burdens of leadership. In a diary entry early in the summer of 1953, the President privately ruminated about the difficult job he had undertaken. So far, his administration was immobile: the Korean War and Senator McCarthy still dominated the news. The United States, he worried, faced an unresolved crisis, a shortage of wisdom and common sense. "Daily I am impressed by the shortsightedness bordering upon tragic stupidity of many," he wrote, "who fancy themselves to be the greatest believers in and supporters of capitalism." Class struggle and revolution would never touch the United States, he assured himself. Yet, the extremes of selfishness that made revolutions possible existed in the United States. Americans, he hoped, would commit themselves to long-term goals, not short-term profits. The United States must promote equitable trade and industrialization in the "free world" and protect its access to raw materials. But, to sur-

During a visit to Korea in November 1953, Vice President Richard Nixon stands at attention while the national anthem is played. (U.S. Army Photograph)

vive, the nation also had to dedicate itself to a religious faith of unselfishness and cooperation.

In public pronouncements defining middle-of-the-road Republicanism, Eisenhower steered a course between political extremes. Obviously shocked by the proposals of some liberals, he also recognized challenges from his own party's conservatives. He firmly committed his administration to a balanced federal budget, with a small and efficient military establishment relying upon nuclear weapons. The danger, he told a news conference in 1953, lay in creating a militarized society: "We don't want to become a garrison state. We want to remain free."

The immediate background of these remarks was probably the administration's still-born "Operation Candor." Set up in April, a group of advisers prepared background material for a major address on atomic warfare. Several unacceptable drafts later, the President abandoned his proposal to speak frankly to Americans about "the age of peril." Such strong language and frightening prospects, he decided, would shove the nation toward the militarized psychology he opposed.

Up to his farewell address, in which he eloquently warned of excessive Cold War zeal, Eisenhower opposed the creation of a large military establishment. Nonetheless, his toleration of Republican extremists tugged him in another direction. The breaking point was Senator McCarthy. Ike had to encourage him or destroy him. The Wisconsin senator seemed to insist upon this extreme choice himself.

McCarthy and Eisenhower had already skirmished over the reputation of the President's friend George Marshall. In 1951, Marshall had been the subject of a poisonous book by McCarthy called *America's Retreat from Victory*. Distasteful as it was, Eisenhower supported McCarthy in 1952, even while he tried to rescue Marshall's reputation. And, after the election, compromise with the right continued to be Eisenhower's policy. Indeed, he allowed John Foster Dulles to hire former FBI agent and current McCarthy supporter Scott McLeod to investigate security risks in the State Department.

Still, McCarthy refused to relent. Driven by an insatiable urge for publicity and encouraged by conservative followers, the Wisconsin senator lambasted the federal government from his position on the Senate Government Operations Committee. During the summer of 1953, McCarthy and his aides, Roy Cohn and David

Schine, investigated overseas State Department libraries, finding works by philosopher John Dewey, historian Henry Steele Commager, critic Bernard De Voto, and poet W. H. Auden, whom they declared to be unacceptable politically. With this in mind, Eisenhower denounced "book burners" on June 14, 1953, at a Dartmouth College graduation ceremony. Almost immediately, however, he backtracked, assuring reporters that he didn't mean free speech for Communists.

The President cut off this confrontation for several reasons. In part, he feared McCarthy's popularity. Even his own advisers disagreed over how to handle the anti-Communist crusader. Moreover, the Republicans controlled the Senate by only one vote. Up to a point, Eisenhower agreed with McCarthy. He resolutely believed in the guilt of Julius and Ethel Rosenberg and refused to pardon them or commute their sentences, allowing them to die in the electric chair on June 13, 1953. Later in the year, on the basis of rumor, Eisenhower blocked J. Robert Oppenheimer, a distinguished nuclear scientist, from access to classified research materials. Charges that Oppenheimer was a security risk, because of his wife's politics and some earlier associations, played a role in this affair, but the scientist's most serious misstep was opposition to building the hydrogen bomb.

Although Eisenhower clearly understood the dangers of excessive anti-Communism, he resisted action until the anti-red tide began to break on the outer banks of his own administration. In early 1954, Senator McCarthy began his fateful television investigation of the United States Army. The ensuing Army-McCarthy hearings, beginning on April 22, focused first on an Army dentist accused of subversive beliefs, but quickly deepened into a challenge to the top brass of the military establishment. Understandably, the President recognized this as a veiled attack on his own career.

When it finally occurred, McCarthy's demise was a public suicide. His bluster, bad manners, and heavy sarcasm beamed daily into American living rooms, deeply embarrassing the Senate. And, McCarthy was outwitted by Army lawyer Joseph Welch. Unable to intimidate witnesses and confused about the purposes of his pursuit, the Senator was first brutish and finally boring, his decline mercilessly exposed by television cameras. In August, the Senate appointed a committee to study censure charges. Safely after mid-term congressional elections, the chamber, in Decem-

ber, voted to condemn him. McCarthy sank slowly and uncere-
moniously from public sight, condemned by rumor and innuendo,
dying on May 2, 1957. Some of the excesses of anti-Communism
also passed into obscurity with him, but neither the Congress nor
the administration admitted the origins of McCarthyism in a
national—and their own—obsession with ferreting out subversive
ideas. As if to confirm this impression, in 1954 Congress passed,
and the President signed, the Communist Control Act, requiring
the American Communist party to register as the agency of a "hostile foreign power."

Eisenhower emerged stronger from his two-year maneuver with
McCarthy, but he also established his independence from the Re-
publican right in foreign policy. This was no easy task, for the
Republican platform of 1952 contained a ringing denunciation of
Truman's policy of containment. Moreover, Secretary of State
Dulles advocated the "liberation" of Eastern European countries
from Soviet hegemony and the roll back of the "Iron Curtain."
Dulles's memorable slogans drew upon his evangelical belief in the
American economic and political system. In practical terms, Dul-
les suggested that a rejuvenated Germany and Japan could create
the western and eastern poles of a tight net of collective-security
pacts to ring the Soviet-Chinese worlds. However, if this sounded
like the confrontation demanded by some extremists, it was not.
When opportunity came to undo Communist gains in Eastern
Europe, Dulles refused to act. In mid-June 1953, Soviet armed
forces repressed East German workers, who rioted against the
Walter Ulbricht regime. The United States did little more than
deplore the action. The policy of "liberation" proved to be rhetor-
ically aggressive, but, in fact, it was another version of containment.

Eisenhower's containment policy became clearer in Korean
peace negotiations, although at the same time, the State Department fired George Kennan, the author of the doctrine. Eisenhower renewed talks at Panmunjom with the People's Republics of
North Korea and China. The repatriation of thousands of captured
Communist prisoners of war proved to be a major snag. Many told
their captors they refused to return home. Working quietly, Dulles passed word to the Chinese and Koreans that the United States
would lift all restrictions on the weapons of war—meaning the
atomic bomb—if satisfactory progress toward a settlement did not
occur. By June 8, 1953, both sides agreed on a tentative agree-

ment, but South Korean President Rhee objected and tried to scuttle the accord by releasing 27,000 POWs, most of whom disappeared into the South Korean population. Nonetheless, the agreement held, and Rhee had to back down. On July 26, 1953, Eisenhower announced an armistice. The costly three-year struggle ended without any resolution of the issues: the map of Korea looked very much as it had in 1950, divided between two hostile forces.

Clearing the boards of the Korean War freed Dulles and Eisenhower to implement their foreign policy. Their general strategy was to protect and extend world-wide United States interests through "massive deterrence"—the threat to use atomic weaponry—a policy of maximum effect and minimum cost. Coupled to this were collective-security alliances. Powerful nations, organized into groups such as NATO, hopefully could prevent limited aggression from becoming permanent gain. Massive deterrence, announced by Dulles in a speech on January 12, 1954, made possible a small federal budget while exploiting American nuclear weapons superiority. To avoid open intervention, the Central Intelligence Agency (CIA), headed by Allen Dulles, intervened surreptitiously in situations that required deception and minimal force.

The administration's shadow foreign policy apparatus sometimes worked against the interests of its open diplomacy. The Central Intelligence Agency evolved from World War II intelligence operations. The National Security Act of July 26, 1947, defined the basic structure of this new agency. Provisions of the law organized intelligence operations into one body, which reported to the National Security Council (made up of the President, Vice-President, Secretaries of State and Defense, the Director of the CIA, the Chairman of the Joint Chiefs of Staff, and the Assistant to the President for National Security Affairs). Exempted from public scrutiny of budgeting, purchases, hiring, and funding by the Central Intelligence Agency Act of 1949, the body escaped public accounting and control. During the Eisenhower administration, it sometimes pursued clandestine operations that undercut the stated foreign policy of the government. Under Allen Dulles, the operation expanded beyond traditional espionage in a great many foreign nations, operating inside the United States as well.

In one instance, the agency's operations touched the private interests of the Dulles brothers. In 1952, President Jacobo Arbenz

Guzmán, of Guatemala, expropriated United Fruit Company properties in his nation, and the company demanded a steep compensation. With rumors of rebellion circulating in 1954, the small country turned to the Communist bloc for arms and political support. John Foster Dulles (whose law firm, Sullivan and Cromwell, had United Fruit Company accounts) and Allen Dulles (who once sat on the board of directors of the company) met with the President and Latin American experts. Allen Dulles convinced Eisenhower to approve a clandestine operation against Arbenz Guzmán. With this go-ahead, a secret army quickly prepared for an invasion. When it landed in June, it quickly overcame the Arbenz Guzmán forces. The newly installed President Castillo restored United Fruit properties and eliminated his political opposition. To bolster the new government, the United States sent in large amounts of economic aid.

Nowhere were CIA operations more extensive or important than in Southeast Asia. Having struggled for eight years after World War II to regain their colonial position in Indochina, the French, in 1954, were exhausted. Worse, they committed a military blunder of enormous proportions. Early in the year, they gathered a large army at the fort of Dien Bien Phu, hoping to attract and then destroy their opponents. Instead, they found themselves surrounded by a larger army of Viet Minh insurgents. Led by Ho Chi Minh, this movement had sought independence for Vietnam since the early 1940s; now victory was close. After a fifty-five-day assault, the French surrendered. During this time, Dulles and Eisenhower weighed several responses. Already providing most of the military supplies to the French, the administration hinted at direct intervention, but met an outcry of displeasure. Air Force Chief of Staff Nathan Twining suggested using small atomic bombs around the fortress, but Eisenhower rejected this as well as conventional air strikes. Fear of involvement in another Asian war tied the hands of the President. On April 7, 1954, Eisenhower expressed his frustration with the situation when he enunciated a new theory, "what you would call the 'falling domino' principle": when one state falls to Communism, it will cause neighboring states to fall. Any thoughts of direct involvement evaporated after Pierre Mendès-France, the new French premier, negotiated a peace agreement with the Viet Minh in late July. According to the treaty signed in Geneva, Switzerland, Vietnam would be divided temporarily into two administrative units, in the north and south, until elections reunified the nation. The Viet Minh, Great Britain, France, the Soviet Union, and the People's Republic of China initialed the accords, but the United States refused.

Unable to prevent the fall of the French, the Eisenhower administration worked to deprive the Viet Minh of the fruits of victory. In September, the United States convened a conference in Manila to create the Southeast Asia Treaty Organization. Consisting of Great Britain, France, Australia, New Zealand, Thailand, Pakistan, and the Philippines, this defense organization was designed to prevent further decay of European and American influence in Southeast Asia. Inside Vietnam, the United States quietly replaced the French. Supporting Ngo Dinh Diem, who had close ties to the CIA, the administration bypassed the French in the south. Bolstered by American military and economic aid, Diem rose to prime minister. Holding a referendum, he stripped the French-supported emperor of Vietnam of his last pretense to power. Then, operating on the fiction that South Vietnam was a permanent nation-state, he consolidated his rule. At the same time, the CIA, operating inside various cover organizations, like the United States Information Service, worked secretly to improve South Vietnamese administration and to pacify the countryside. When Diem refused to hold scheduled reunification elections, the United States agreed with his position. Eisenhower himself felt that Ho Chi Minh would have won a national election.

Unable to do anything but hold the line in Southeast Asia, the Eisenhower administration confronted a new crisis in September 1954. The People's Republic of China suddenly began shelling offshore islands still held by the Chiang Kai-shek forces. Ultimately indefensible and probably of little importance, Quemoy, Matsu, and Tachen nonetheless became symbols of resistance to Communism. The United States responded with a mutual-defense treaty with the Nationalist government. In the Formosa Resolution, passed by the Senate in early 1955, the President received unspecified powers to protect Formosa and the Pescadores Islands between Formosa and the coast of China. This assignment of war powers by Congress allowed the President more latitude in initiating action in Asia, a power that some critics believed could lead to adventurism in this unstable part of the world.

In Europe, Eisenhower and Dulles tried to firm up alliances around Communist power centers. Success hinged upon a revitalized and rearmed Germany. While the United States could agree with the Soviet Union, in 1955, to neutralize the former Axis ally Austria, no such accord was possible in Germany. Eisenhower insisted upon a free Germany reunited by elections in all of the occupied zones. The resulting nation should then, he determined, be entitled to sign defense pacts and enter alliances of its own choosing. If the Russians refused, as they most certainly would, then Western Germany should be integrated into NATO.

Although Germany remained an unresolvable point of contention, the United States and the U.S.S.R. paid considerable attention to disarmament. The enormous cost of nuclear weaponry and upgraded conventional armaments threatened to distort Eisenhower's parsimonious "New Look" military budget. For the Russians, rebuilding wartime damage, while supporting a sophisticated military establishment, constituted a terrible burden.

Eisenhower first elaborated his disarmament policy in December 1953, in an address to the United Nations on peaceful uses of atomic energy. He proposed a United Nations stockpile of atomic materials and controlled destruction of atomic weaponry. The Russians responded by calling for complete and unconditional banning of all nuclear weapons. As it unfolded, the argument between the two sides revived positions first raised around the Baruch Plan of 1946. The United States insisted on controlled disarmament and unlimited inspections to monitor compliance. The Russians demanded total disarmament and no inspections. In the spring of 1955, however, the Soviets amended this stand to agree to surveillance and a more limited, four-phase schedule of disarmament. The United States postponed its reply until July, when Eisenhower had a planned conference with Russian leaders, Prime Minister Edgar Faure, of France, and Anthony Eden, of Britain, in Geneva.

The Geneva Conference marked a turning point in foreign affairs. More optimistic about negotiating with the Russians than Secretary of State Dulles, Ike remained adamant on reunification of Germany and its integration into NATO. The Russians were just as firm in opposing anything but the permanent neutralization of their former enemy. On disarmament, Eisenhower made a public bid on July 21, addressing delegates to the convention. His "Open Skies" proposal, prepared several months in advance, suggested opening both the Soviet Union and the United States to air inspection. Both nations would exchange military blueprints and other information. A possible step toward mutual understanding, the

Open Skies proposal did not represent a significant disarmament plan. Moreover, it would have favored the United States more than the Russians. Although no substantial agreement occurred, the American press spoke of the "spirit of Geneva." By this, they meant the possibility of more cordial relationships. Perhaps this was an exaggeration, but the United States and the Russians had at least determined to accept the status quo. The United States had become more interested in negotiating on such issues as disarmament, and, in turn, the Soviets recognized they could do little to prevent the independence and western orientation of West Germany.

Eisenhower's moderate success in softening the Cold War with the Soviet Union matched his modest achievements at home. The President's view of office differed considerably from the activism of his predecessors. The administration operations followed a military model, with chief of the White House staff, Sherman Adams, in command. Eisenhower's goals were also different; he hoped to reduce expenditures and balance the federal budget, yet he promised to preserve popular social legislation and expand capital projects in transportation. Obviously, he needed the close cooperation of Congress. A slim Republican majority in 1953 and 1954 made this possible, but after the Democratic sweep of the mid-year elections in 1954, Eisenhower's task became more difficult. Never again did the administration have a friendly Congress, although Eisenhower worked successfully with Democratic party leaders, such as Lyndon Johnson. Nonetheless, in the last years of his administration, the President found himself locked in a struggle against new social legislation and large proposals for defense spending generated by congressional Democrats.

Despite problems with Congress, Ike achieved moderate success in budget-balancing. Federal receipts exceeded expenses in 1956, 1957, and 1960. Deficits in 1954 and 1958 were insignificant. Moderate imbalances appeared in 1953 (Truman's budget) and 1955. Only in 1959, during the severe slump, did imbalance become serious. This general fiscal conservatism, coupled with relatively stable international prices for raw materials and a favorable United States trade position, helped control inflation. Measured by the wholesale price index, yearly inflation during the Eisenhower administration hovered around 1 percent.

In farm policy, Eisenhower agreed with Secretary of Agriculture Ezra Taft Benson that federal crop price supports should be lower.

New Deal and Fair Deal policy set high commodity prices by purchasing surplus grains and produce. In the Truman administration, the federal government established a 90 percent parity, or price supports to guarantee 90 percent of the earning power of agricultural products keyed to the 1910–1914 period. To maintain high prices, the government purchased vast quantities of grain, tobacco, and cotton. Benson persuaded Congress, in 1954, to lower parity to 70 percent on most commodities except tobacco. While this created more price fluctuation, it did little to solve the problem of high farm productivity and low prices. Nor did it help reverse the decline of the family farm.

If farm policy seemed a step toward orthodox free enterprise, Eisenhower took several strides in the opposite direction of the welfare state. In 1954, he signed a bill adding millions of self-employed workers to the Social Security system. He supported a higher minimum wage and new public-housing programs. Two large capital programs heavily involved federal financing. On May 13, 1954, he signed a bill to construct a St. Lawrence Seaway, joining the Great Lakes to ocean shipping through the mouth of the St. Lawrence River. The vast public-works project to build an interstate system of limited-access highways, which passed in 1956, further established Eisenhower as a president who had a Republican vision of the welfare state.

Eisenhower's most serious domestic problems were partly a consequence of his appointment of Earl Warren (formerly attorney general and governor of California) to the Supreme Court. Almost immediately after his confirmation as Chief Justice in 1953, Warren faced a decision on five segregation cases pending before the Court. All five cases challenged state and District of Columbia practices of school segregation. NAACP lawyers, led by Thurgood Marshall, argued that the old doctrine of "separate but equal" constituted inevitable discrimination. The practice of separation, they continued, established a psychology of inferiority independent of the physical condition of the schools. Conscious of the enormous step they proposed to take, the Court justices required a unanimous and forceful decision. Warren's installation as Chief Justice made this possible. On May 17, 1954, the Court declared school segregation unconstitutional in *Brown* v. *Board of Education of Topeka, Kansas*. Accepting Marshall's psychological argument, it ordered desegregation in 1955 "with all deliberate speed."

Eisenhower regarded this decision with initial ambiguity and then hostility. He had allowed the Attorney General to file in support of the NAACP, but, according to Warren, he personally implied that the Court should be lenient with school segregationists. After its announcement, Eisenhower refused to speak in defense of the decision. Thereafter, relations between the President and his Chief Justice cooled. In the remaining six years of his tenure, Eisenhower never proposed implementing the Warren decision, nor did he defend the Court from outrageous attacks mounted by members of his own party. First the John Birch Society, a right-wing fringe group, attacked the Chief Justice. Then, after the *Watkins* v. *U.S.* decision in 1957, defending the Constitutional rights of persons accused of subversive beliefs, even members of the American Bar Association bitterly attacked Warren. Ike was silent.

Criticism of the Court's desegregation decision accused the judicial branch of making decisions with wide legislative and executive implications. The Court was overstepping tradition to act as legislator and executor of controversial policies. To a degree, this reaction was accurate, although abundant precedents for Court activism exist in its long history. On the other hand, the Supreme Court had acted to defend the civil rights of black citizens that had remained flagrantly unenforced since the Civil War. Controversial though it was, the desegregation decision set irreversible forces into motion that eventually destroyed legal segregation in America.

By the summer of 1955, Eisenhower's moderate Republicanism was well established. Away from the din of partisan politics, the middle way he chose depended entirely upon his own leadership and popularity. But suddenly this proved to be fragile. On September 24, in Denver, Colorado, the President suffered a serious heart attack. His illness required complete bed rest for several days. Although he recovered speedily, he was struck with ileitis, which required corrective intestinal surgery, during the spring of 1956. Neither of these illnesses permanently disabled the President, but they did rouse talk about Vice-President Nixon's role and the possibility that he would have to step into the presidency. During the summer of 1956, although Ike's renomination was assured, party members discussed removing Nixon from the ticket. Much to the Vice-President's dismay, Eisenhower remained mute, although when the replacement movement fizzled, the President warmly endorsed Nixon.

As a campaign orientation in 1956, the President's philosophy of modern Republicanism had little impact on the party. With Eisenhower's official endorsement, Arthur Larsen discussed modern Republicanism in a campaign book, *A Republican Looks at His Party*. The author argued that on fundamental national issues, "we have greater agreement than ever before in our history." This new consensus, he argued, synthesized two contradictory political tendencies: the conservative Republicanism of 1896 and the radical liberalism of 1936. The pivotal election of 1956, he proclaimed, would reaffirm the basic moderation of most Americans, who wanted to avoid the Scylla of liberal projects to redistribute income and the Charybdis of conservative unregulated competition. The new Republicanism, he hoped, would attract millions of voters. It did—at least for the Presidential ticket. But, the Republicans continued to be a minority party in the Congress.

The ticket of Eisenhower and Nixon perfectly suited the inertia of the mid-1950s; the Democrats, with few new ideas, called again upon Stevenson. Stevenson departed from custom to allow the convention to select a vice-presidential candidate, but to some observers, this seemed a cavalier act of nonchalance. The delegates at the convention in Chicago did not enhance the ticket when they selected Estes Kefauver, one of the most liberal senators and a man repugnant to much of the party establishment. Stevenson and Kefauver tried to define real issues and differentiate clearly between the two tickets, but they failed to convince the electorate. Stevenson's discussion of nuclear fallout from testing fell on deaf ears. Even his last-minute warning about the health of the President backfired. Eisenhower and Nixon captured 57 percent of the vote, with 457 electoral votes to 73 for the Democrats. In the South, the Democrats won only Alabama, Arkansas, Georgia, Mississippi, Missouri, North Carolina, and South Carolina; the once-dependable South now split its votes. Nonetheless, in the Senate and House of Representatives, the Democrats increased their majorities. If modern Republicanism expressed the desire of Americans for a national consensus and unified purpose, the congressional elections revealed a desire for change and continued reform. This paradoxical voting pattern of the American electorate remained characteristic of every subsequent contest through the 1970s, thereby allowing a shrinking Republican party to contest the presidency successfully despite overwhelming Democratic party registration.

As in 1952, foreign policy issues were decisive in this election. Despite Secretary Dulles's 1955 threat to go "to the brink" of war with the Russians, events prior to the election evoked caution. In October 1956, Hungarians, caught up by the impulse of de-Stalinization sweeping Eastern Europe, rose against the repressive, Soviet-backed regime in their country and installed Imre Nagy as premier. At first, Nagy extended political and economic freedoms, which the Russians tolerated, but when he declared his nation's withdrawal from the Warsaw Pact, the Soviet Army acted quickly. On October 30, Russian tanks and troops streamed into Budapest, arrested Nagy, and crushed further opposition, installing a new government headed by János Kádar. From the beginning, Dulles and Eisenhower indicated that they would not intervene. Despite broadcasts of encouragement by CIA-sponsored Radio Free Europe, no American help materialized.

Just a few days later, the United States found itself allied to the Soviet Union against France, Britain, and Israel. Over the summer of 1956, relations between Egypt and the Western powers deteriorated. The new revolutionary regime of Gamal Abdel Nasser applied for United States loans and expertise to build a huge power and irrigation facility at Aswan. John Foster Dulles, however, finally rejected the project, and Nassar turned to the Soviet Union for help. To finance his industrial and military projects, Nasser nationalized the Suez Canal, built by the British and the French. Dulles hoped to pressure Nasser into some compromise, but the British and French demanded immediate retaliation. When Israel attacked Egyptian forces on October 29 in the Sinai Desert, the French and British used the flare-up as a pretext to intervene. On November 5, Anglo-French troops landed at Port Said. At this point, the Russians insisted on immediate withdrawal, threatening to send volunteers to aid their new Egyptian ally. Dulles and Eisenhower abandoned England and France, voting with the U.S.S.R. for a U.N. Security Council cease-fire resolution. Facing an impossible alliance of two superpowers, the French and British withdrew, thus ending their last grand imperial adventure.

Dwight Eisenhower's second presidential term was unique in American history, because he was the first president who by Constitutional amendment could not serve more than two terms. Nonetheless, he continued to pursue the goals of modern Republicanism, a balanced budget, and increased peace initiatives with the Soviet Union. Despite his distaste for the *Brown* decision, Ike moved cautiously toward limited integration goals. In 1955, he appointed Frederic Morrow, the first black American on the presidential staff. More importantly, he actively supported a civil rights voting bill in Congress. The act languished until August 1957, when Lyndon Johnson, the majority leader in the Senate, cajoled his fellow Southerners into allowing passage of the bill. Somewhat watered down, the act created the Civil Rights Commission and the Civil Rights Division of the Justice Department. It also strengthened voting rights. Most importantly, the law represented the first positive civil rights act since the end of Reconstruction.

Unwilling to speak in favor of school integration, the President found that events in 1957 compelled him to enforce it with military power. The stage for the nation's first great confrontation over integration was set in 1955 when the school board of Little Rock, Arkansas, submitted a plan for gradual desegregation to the courts. Most of the elected officials in the city supported the proposal, but Governor Orval Faubus suddenly intervened to prevent its implementation. The courts insisted, however, and the schools planned desegregation for September 3, 1957, at the opening of a new school year. Governor Faubus acted to stop integration. Calling up the Arkansas National Guard, he ordered troops to prevent black children from entering Little Rock Central High School.

The Governor's action turned a local incident into a challenge to national power, forcing the President to act. Meeting with Faubus on September 17, Eisenhower thought he had obtained assurances that the Governor would moderate his stand. But, he was wrong. On September 20, after a federal injunction forced Faubus to allow integration of the school, he withdrew his troops. At the same time, he warned black parents to keep their children away from school. These inflammatory remarks turned a bad situation worse, and when the school attempted to open on September 23, angry mobs of whites rioted. Little Rock's mayor, Woodrow Wilson Mann, appealed to the President for help. Finally, on September 24, Eisenhower dispatched troops to the riot-torn city, appealing at the same time on national radio and TV for calm. His actions were a small, reluctant step forward, but the walls of southern school segregation did not crumble for another decade.

The year 1958 represented the nadir of Eisenhower's presidency. Earlier, in 1957, the economy began to slip into serious recession. The downturn lasted until 1958, with industrial production remaining sluggish until the middle of the year. Unemployment rose from slightly more than 4 percent to around 7 percent in 1958. Recession stretched the length of unemployment so that 30 percent of those out of work were without a job for more than fifteen weeks. As in any recession, nonwhite workers were hardest hit, with official statistics recording almost 13 percent seeking work.

Deepening recession and unemployment stimulated demands for a Keynesian solution, a tax cut, and public-works projects. Eisenhower instinctively opposed both proposals, although the Cabinet discussed a tax cut in May 1968. In April, the President signed the Emergency Housing Bill, designed to pump money into federal programs, like the Veterans Administration house mortgage program. In general, however, Republican policy was to sit out the slowdown.

Scandal close to the heart of the administration rocked the party just before the congressional elections of 1958. On June 16, a House Legislative Oversight Committee accused Sherman Adams, the President's chief of staff, of maintaining an illegal business relationship with textile manufacturer Bernard Goldfine. In exchange for intervening with the Federal Trade Commission in his interest, Goldfine had given gifts to Adams and paid some of his hotel bills. Adams denied the charges. Even after the committee exonerated him, Adams was a liability to the President. Something of a martinet, Adams' unpopularity with congressmen made his departure inevitable. Reluctantly, Ike accepted his resignation on September 22. Then, on November 26, Eisenhower suffered a mild stroke, one more grim event in this difficult year. Although he quickly recovered, the permanent effects of hesitant speech thereafter marred his news conferences and speeches.

To the Republican party, the elections of 1958 were a disaster. Distance between the President and the party was never greater. The Democrats increased their congressional majority significantly; in the House, they held 283 seats to 153, and in the Senate, they gained 64 to 34 for the Republicans. Such lopsided results signified more than frustration at the economic downturn or scandal in the administration. They proved the failure of modern Republicanism to inspire either the party or the public.

One of the hardest-fought issues of the congressional campaign focused on America's defenses. Eisenhower's New Look military budget was conservative and cautious, susceptible to attack from Democrats who proposed extraordinary largesse with public money for missiles and bombers. In 1955 and 1956, leading Democrats had belabored a "bomber gap," a fictitious Russian lead in nuclear weapons delivery systems. The issue was relaunched after October 4, 1957, when the Russians successfully tested their first *Sputnik* space satellite. Lacking a parallel success, the United States suddenly discovered its vulnerability despite its ring of bomber bases circling the Soviet Union.

Senate Democrats directed charges of waste, inefficiency, and poor planning at the administration. To calm fears, Eisenhower went on television, November 7, to defend American science and his defense policies. During his speech, he announced the appointment of James Killian, President of MIT, as assistant for science and technology. Yet, on the same day, the President received more bad news. An advisory committee, headed by H. Rowan Gaither, Jr., of the Rand Corporation and later of the Ford Foundation, delivered its report on American defenses to the National Security Council. While the President and his Cabinet could accept some of its conclusions, they firmly rejected others, like the call for a massive civil defense program. Because of the implicit criticism of his policies, Eisenhower decided not to publish the report. Nonetheless, bits and pieces of the report leaked to the press; more than ever, it appeared that the United States had fallen behind in the arms race. Eisenhower still refused to release the document, invoking the executive privilege of his office. He did, however, finally agree to allow the members of Lyndon Johnson's Subcommittee on Preparedness to examine it in secret session.

As Dr. Killian later explained, Eisenhower's reluctance to increase defense spending came from his desire to negotiate seriously with the Russians. But there was another reason why the President was confident but unrevealing in his assessment of Russian defenses: he knew about, but could not release, information gathered by secret U-2 overflights, demonstrating Soviet military weaknesses. Caught in this position, the President was understandably troubled by the extensive advertising campaign conducted by arms manufacturers. In the end, he did authorize more defense funds. In 1958, National Science Foundation grants (some used in military research) rose to $50 million, and then to $136 million in 1959. On September 2, 1958, he signed the National Defense Education Act, providing about $1 billion in loans and scholarships for students in math, languages, and the sciences. In early 1958, Killian's Science Advisory Committee suggested consolidation of space research and operations. The result was the National Aeronautics and Space Administration (NASA), created on July 29, 1958.

Early in 1958—and none too soon for national prestige—the United States achieved several space successes: the launching of *Explorer I* on January 31 and the successful test of Atlas ICBM systems. While quieting some fears about Russian weaponry, these achievements did not eliminate the defense issue in the 1960 election. Claiming a "missile gap," the Democrats blamed Eisenhower's relatively low defense budget for alleged Russian superiority. In the long run, however, the greatest impact of *Sputnik* and its aftermath was probably on American education. Funds flowing into mathematics, sciences, language training, and engineering mounted rapidly as educators successfully convinced the public that there was also an "education gap."

Cut loose from any real future in his party, after 1958, Eisenhower tried to make his personal mark in history through foreign policy initiatives. But his strategy lacked clarity. He pursued a contradictory policy that found him edging toward closer relations with Nikita Khrushchev, the new premier of the U.S.S.R., only to be undercut by the secret activities of the CIA that he had approved. The area of nuclear testing did seem potentially one for agreement, however. Russian and American tests were belching huge quantities of radioactive material into the atmosphere, and scientists and the public worried increasingly about the effects.

Three days after he took office in March 1958, Premier Khrushchev announced suspension of open-air testing and urged the United States to follow his lead. In late August, Eisenhower promised to terminate American open-air testing once the current series ended. Early in November, the Russians resumed with a short series of test devices, but the United States continued its moratorium, and the Russians again suspended tests. Informal actions, however, did not lead to a permanent agreement, and in 1961, the Soviets resumed testing, followed by the United States in early 1962.

With the exception of flare-ups in the Middle East (the United

States landed troops in Lebanon in the summer of 1958) and continued acrimony over Quemoy and Matsu, the United States and the U.S.S.R. cautiously moved toward substantial negotiations in 1959. Like so much else in the Cold War, this relaxation of tension began in hostility. In March 1958, Khrushchev demanded normalization of the city of Berlin. By this, he meant a treaty to turn over access to West Berlin to his East Berlin allies. The result would be *de facto* recognition of East Germany, a possibility Eisenhower resolutely refused to consider. Khrushchev stiffened his demands by setting May 27, 1959, as a deadline for acceptance of his plan.

When spring of 1959 approached, the deadline slipped by as Eisenhower and the Russian premier embarked on a more concentrated phase of personal diplomacy. Eisenhower invited the Russian leader to visit the United States in September, and Khrushchev reciprocated with an invitation for 1960. Even this phase of relations began on a sharp note. In late July, Vice-President Nixon guided Khrushchev through an American exhibition in Moscow, during which the two leaders engaged in a running debate about the relative merits of American and Soviet societies. Because Nixon and Khrushchev stood arguing in front of stoves and refrigerators, American newspapers dubbed this the "kitchen debate." The Russian sharply denounced America's obsession with consumerism and homemaking. Nixon retorted: "I think that this attitude toward women is universal. What we want to do is make easier the life of our housewives." Khrushchev replied that Russian women were different.

Beneath his critical exterior, however, Khrushchev was ambivalent about America's consumer society. He rejected the gadgetry and materialism but promised to build more and better consumer items for Russian citizens. This attitude of awe and criticism also characterized Khrushchev's tour of the United States, beginning on September 15, 1959. For ten days, the Russian party, including Mrs. Khrushchev, followed an itinerary through American cities, California's Disneyland, and a farm in Iowa. Immense security problems and scattered incidents along the way did not detract from the success of the tour. Final negotiations at Camp David, Maryland—Eisenhower's retreat in the Catoctin Mountains— brought a postponement of the East German peace treaty. The two leaders also set plans for a spring summit meeting of the Big Four powers.

Shortly before Christmas, Eisenhower embarked on his own goodwill tour, visiting eleven countries in Asia, Europe, and Africa. By including India and Afghanistan, in addition to NATO countries, the President signaled a new attitude in American foreign policy toward neutral countries. This change was easier, in part, because John Foster Dulles retired as Secretary of State in early 1959, but it was also a logical extension of Ike's domestic policy of placing himself above the disputes and wrangling of politics.

Just as this policy seemed to open up prospects for peace, the President suddenly became mired in the unseemly business of espionage. Long eager to open the skies over the U.S.S.R.—with or without Russian approval—Eisenhower had authorized secret aerial surveillance of the Soviet Union. Utilizing the U-2 aircraft, which flew above the normal Russian missile range, these flights returned useful photographic reconnaissance materials. Of course, the Soviets knew about them, but could do nothing—that is, until shortly before the scheduled Paris summit in the spring of 1960, when they downed one of the spy planes. Official United States explanations at first claimed that a weather plane had strayed into Soviet air space. When Khrushchev produced the pilot and spy equipment, captured 300 miles inside the Soviet Union, its purpose became apparent. Rejecting the chance to blame subordinates, Eisenhower accepted personal responsibility for the overflights on May 9. In doing so, he probably doomed the summit meeting scheduled for one week later. When Khrushchev arrived at Paris, he seemed determined to explode the meeting, demanding a personal apology from the President. Failing to get it, he withdrew his invitation to Eisenhower to visit the Soviet Union.

Ninety miles from home, Eisenhower agreed to another CIA intervention that turned to fiasco. In early 1959, Fidel Castro led a successful revolution against the ruthless, but pro-American dictator of Cuba, Fulgenico Batista. During the 1940s and 1950s, Batista had transformed Cuba into a vacation and gambling center linked to the American underworld. Given its close proximity and single-crop agriculture (sugar), the island nation, outside the hotels of Havana and seaside resorts, continued to be an impoverished colony of the United States. Castro determined to change this. Beginning in the summer of 1959, the Cuban revolution deepened. Castro's government expropriated American industrial and agricultural property. When the Cubans signed a trade pact with the Soviet Union in the spring of 1960, Eisenhower agreed to a CIA plan to train and land rebels, hoping for a quick repeat of earlier intervention in Santo Domingo. Using open diplomacy, the Eisenhower administration tried to convince the Organization of American States to isolate Cuba, but the larger, more independent Latin American nations refused. With only a few months left to his administration, Eisenhower put the invasion off, leaving its timing and responsibility to his successor.

☆   ☆   ☆

To the very end of his term, Eisenhower remained popular with the American electorate. For Republicans this presented a problem: was popularity transferable? Vice-President Nixon hoped it was, and he eagerly courted Ike's support for the nomination. But, the President was less than encouraging. Indeed, shortly after Nixon won the Republican presidential nomination, reporters asked Eisenhower what Nixon had contributed to his administration. "If you give me a week, I might think of one," responded the President. "I don't remember." Subsequent warm endorsements did not reverse the impression that Ike hesitated to pass his mantle on to Nixon.

Eisenhower's most significant policy statement came in retrospect, as if to assess the lessons he had learned in office. On January 17, 1961, he delivered his farewell address, warning Americans to beware of the growing military-industrial complex. "This potential for the disastrous rise of misplaced power exists and will persist," he declared. Arms manufacturers and their clients in defense and the military constituted a powerful interest group that threatened American democracy. A secondary and equally ominous nexus of federally sponsored scientific research threatened to choke off intellectual freedom. "The prospect of domination of the nation's scholars," he said, "is gravely to be regarded."

Eisenhower's words went largely unheeded during the next few years, except by Americans already convinced of their truth, and he did nothing to follow them up. Like much else in his administration, his best sentiments received no second; no motion followed. Whatever Eisenhower understood about the perils of excessive defense spending, based on his anger at the huckstering merchants of arms, never got translated into policy. Some of his best initiatives in foreign relations were undercut by the latitude he allowed to Allen Dulles. Domestically, Eisenhower played the same role. Unwilling to take a stand against McCarthy, he prolonged the agony of anti-Communism. His refusal to promote the Supreme Court decision on school segregation doubtlessly intensified later struggles. He did act with restraint and intelligence in a world that demanded thoughtfulness. But, even to his warmest supporters, Eisenhower's years seemed to be an interlude, a respite from the normal turbulent tides of American politics. And, after eight years of his presidency, the nation and the world seemed as much as ever precariously balanced between the forces of destruction and the energies of creativity.

7 The Automatic Society

In his memorable farewell address of early 1961, Dwight Eisenhower evoked the image of American society squeezed in the grasp of a technocratic and military elite. His warning about the military-industrial complex beamed a spotlight on a debate about the direction of social and economic change growing since World War II. For a decade, sociologists, economists, and historians had puzzled over an apparent quantum leap in the development of American capitalism. Americans often appeared unsure about these changes. Sometimes, they seemed to prefer the simple homilies of Dwight Eisenhower or looked back to Harry Truman's blunt, homespun ideals. At other times, they preferred the rhetoric of technology, development, and growth. Applications of scientific, informational, and managerial innovations seemed to occur faster than society could smoothly absorb them. Stress points erupted around the impact of automation, the uses of new energy sources, the effects of information tools, like computers and television, and new corporate forms of economic organization. These issues became the focus of imagination and worry over the nature of modern society.

Concern about the deployment of technological ingenuity, ranging from nuclear energy to the smallest calculator chip, did not preoccupy just intellectuals and politicians. Even in the popular culture of the day, particularly science fiction, which enjoyed an immense boom in the 1950s, the same issues appeared in costume dramas removed to other planets and other times. But the preoccupations of popular culture were as timely and immediate as the tracts of sociologists and economists. How could modern men and women control the forces unleashed by modern industrialism? they all asked. What was the future of industrial society?

In 1950, Isaac Asimov, a widely respected science popularizer and science fiction author, published a remarkable book called *I*,

Robot. This collection of incidents dramatizes the problems of controlling robots, but its real subject is modern technology. Asimov's three "Laws of Robotics," printed as a foreward to the stories, define the relationship between humans and the machines they create. Robots are programmed not to injure humans. They have to obey humans, unless such actions bring harm. And, they are to protect their own existence, unless it means destruction to human beings. As the reader soon discovers, these laws are riddles with exceptions and contradictions. Asimov appears to be saying that these axioms, designed to guide advanced industrial technology, are inappropriate. They break down, because, in reality, no rules governing technology can anticipate human choices. This message is ironically underscored in the last story. An electronics expert called in to fix the central world computer, which has been sending signals to slow down the earth's industrial output, discovers that this programmed retreat is purposeful. Machines have taken over for the good of the human race and turned back the economic clock to a more primitive time.

This pessimistic but characteristic view of the automated society challenged optimistic, popular futurology, exemplified by a pamphlet on automation published in 1954 by the National Association of Manufacturers. Defending technology as the door to a "golden tomorrow," the NAM called automation a magical key to creativity. "Guided by electronics, powered by atomic energy, geared to the smooth, effortless workings of automation, the magic carpet of our free economy heads for distant and undreamed of horizons. Just going along for the ride will be the biggest thrill on earth," proclaimed the pamphlet.

In these incautious predictions and countless variations on the same theme, Americans celebrated the present and anticipated future successes of technological ingenuity. Stimulating their speculations were three great economic changes in the era: rapid technological advance, a revolution in the workplace, and consolidation of corporate structures. Several unique features in the period sharpened these changes. From the end of World War II until 1966 or 1967, American workers increased their productivity by a healthy percentage. Industry took advantage of low-priced and plentiful energy sources in the form of coal, natural gas, and oil. The period after the war was marked by sustained growth and high employment. Despite recessions in 1948–1949, 1953–1954, 1957–1958, 1960–1961, and 1973–1975, the traditional twenty-year

A 1950s conception of automation. At this Ford engine plant in Cleveland, Ohio, several functions, such as machining aluminum pistons, were carried out automatically. Pistons were transferred by conveyor belts to machines for processing.   (National Archives)

cycles of boom and bust leveled off into smaller peaks and troughs. In this era, America rose to unprecedented political, economic, and military predominance in the world. Exploiting this power, American enterprise penetrated and captured foreign markets and made huge overseas investments. By the late 1960s, the transformation of technology, the organization of work, and corporate consolidation had spread, creating a new economic order in much of the rest of the world. The American system was very much a world system.

The postwar technological revolution depended upon a massive application of energy to production, the discovery and use of new materials and manufacturing processes, and a burst of inventiveness in the field of communications. Together, these factors increased the productivity of workers, transforming factory and office and spurring the consolidation of industry. They also put the potential for destructiveness—as well as for creativity—at the fingertips of political and military leaders.

Production increases in the United States after 1945 depended upon substituting cheap fossil energy for human labor. From 1947 to 1975, output per hour of labor increased by almost 120 percent, while output per standard unit of energy increased by only about 23 percent. This disparity underscores the fact that the efficiency gained came through the application of more energy to production: in effect, electricity-, gas-, and oil-consuming machines replaced workers. At the same time, the efficiency of energy production remained relatively smaller. The consumption of gasoline by automobiles (a major consumer product and the chief means of transportation of the period), illustrates this fact. From 1945 into the 1970s, the efficiency of automobiles in moving passengers remained almost constant, indicating that technological improvements in the industry generally went into design and production, not performance. For all motor vehicles running on petroleum products, the average fuel efficiency per mile actually declined slightly between 1945 and 1970.

In the same period, energy necessary to generate a kilowatt of electrical power decreased by only about 33 percent. Thus, efficiencies in coal, oil, and natural gas generators accounted for only a part of the vast increase in electrical power produced by the United States from 1945 to 1970. Most of the increase came from burning greater amounts of fossil fuels and building new plants. Until the late 1960s, when sudden increases in the prices of oil and

natural gas spurred a substantial inflationary spiral, this dependence on cheap fuels had no serious side effects apart from environmental degradation.

Immediately after the war, the United States led the world in
development of new materials and ingenious uses of aluminum,
plastics, and a long list of alloys and rare metals. More efficient
machine tools revolutionized the basic manufacture of autos and
steel, although by the end of the period, the United States lagged
behind Japan and Germany in the application of advanced processes to steel production. In agriculture, mechanization, in the shape
of new harvesting machines and larger tractors; and chemistry, in
the guise of better fertilizers and sprays; and new strains of plants
and animals increased output dramatically. From 1947 to 1966,
total work hours in the United States spent in agriculture fell from
19.2 percent to only 7.5 percent. But output per acre increased by
33 percent. Moreover, the vertical integration of much agriculture
into production, processing, and marketing units, or agribusi-
nesses, revolutionized the nature of farming.

American inventiveness measured the dominance of the United
States in technology. From 1955 to 1973, American scientists and
workers developed over half the world's significant inventions,
although this rate declined somewhat after 1974. Inventions transformed whole industries. For example, in 1952, a new Ford plant
in Cleveland, with automatic machine-drilling capacities, could
turn out 154 engine blocks per hour using only 41 men, whereas
formerly it required 117 workers.

Particularly in communications—the transmission, storage, and
manipulation of information—the new technology impinged on
public consciousness. Television and computers symbolized the
new ability to distribute and store information. Television had existed prior to 1945 as a potential, but after the war, the technology
of transmitting pictures advanced rapidly. From a mere 6,000 re-
ceivers produced in 1945, the new television industry built 7 million sets in 1950, maintaining high production until saturation of
the market and foreign competition reduced domestic production
in the late 1960s. This new industry called upon scores of innovations and new processes, from transistors to printed circuits. Improvements also allowed color transmission, while videotape and
other developments in filming technique increased the mobility
and speed of camera work. In a single generation, 99 percent of
American homes acquired this electronic window to the world.

The industrial impact of computers was even greater, although home use of these instruments only began at the end of the period. The earliest computer technology emerged from the efforts of IBM (International Business Machines) and other companies to develop code-breaking machines and to ease war-related problems, such as measuring ballistics trajectories. One of the largest machines inspired by wartime demands was the ENIAC machine (Electronic Numerical Integrator and Calculator), installed at Aberdeen Proving Ground in Maryland in 1947. An enormous, energy-hungry conglomeration of 18,000 vacuum tubes and 70,000 resisters, it covered 1,500 square feet of space. After the 1940s, IBM and Sperry Rand (which hired Douglas MacArthur as board chairman in the mid-1950s), competed for a growing market in computing machines.

The federal government provided much of the impetus for the computer industry. In 1951, Washington used three machines to compute the 1950 census returns. By 1966, the federal government had almost 2,500 computers in use; at the same time, 226 insurance companies were employing 700 electric computers. In 1966, over 30,000 computers were on-line in every facet of American industry and commerce. Improvements in size and capacity and lower costs were remarkable. By the late 1970s, a five-dollar micro-processor had twice the capacity of the enormous and expensive machines constructed at the end of World War II, making it possible to automate an incredible range of home and industrial activities formerly done by human memory and computation.

The capacity to store and evaluate information meant that computers attached to feedback sensors could monitor practically any form of industrial process. Programmed to react to production errors or slippages, the computer system could issue instructions to reverse a malfunction. In 1956, such computers controlling industrial production had been tested only in a few spots, such as automobile plants, but by 1960, the chemical and petroleum industries and electric, steel, cement, and paper producers had all begun to adopt computers. In the late 1960s, tentative experiment had become accepted practice.

Advances in communications technology, together with the spur of competition with the Soviet Union, fulfilled ancient aspirations and enabled the United States to complete the Apollo moon-exploration series in the late 1960s and early 1970s. In July 1969, the *Apollo II* spaceship circling the moon launched a smaller craft

Neil Armstrong, the first moon walker, photographed his fellow astronaut Edwin Aldrin on the lunar surface, July 20, 1969.   (UPI)

that touched down on the moon's surface. Astronaut Neil Armstrong emerged and, then, Edwin Aldrin—the first men to walk on the moon. This striking success, coming after President Kennedy's proposal of a crash effort in May 1961, reaffirmed America's faith in its technological leadership. It also created a media event minutely recorded by television, down to the carefully chosen, impersonal words of Armstrong when he touched the surface of the moon: "That's one small step for man, one great leap for mankind." Monitored and planned to the point where crew members were more passengers than explorers, the moon probe represented a triumph of mechanical ingenuity. Nonetheless, the very high costs—NASA spent about $33 billion on various projects from 1961 to 1969—ruled out more distant, manned flights after 1972.

☆ ☆ ☆

Scientific advance also generated weapons of enormous power and intimations of destruction. In 1964, Stanley Kubrick produced *Dr. Strangelove*, an outrageous film satirizing the American military establishment, the reliance on atomic bombs, and the fail-safe computer technology possible in nuclear warfare, a predicament he would dramatize again in 1968 in *2001: A Space Odyssey*. Ku-

Fastest-growing Industries, 1950 to 1966

| Ammunition |
| Cathode-ray Picture Tubes |
| Semiconductors |
| Computing and Related Machines |
| Guns, Howitzers, and Mortars |
| Tufted Carpets and Rugs |
| Small Arms, 30 mm. and under |
| Electronic Components |
| Primary Nonferrous Metals |
| Optical Instruments and Lenses |

Source: *U.S. Department of Commerce*, Chemicals, Petroleum, and Rubber and Plastics Products (*1969*), *p. 9*.

brick saw human beings trapped by the destructive power of the technology they had created. Having discovered this power, Americans seemed bent upon employing it. Kubrick's fascinating films focused on the somber side of technology during the 1950s and 1960s: its power to destroy.

Evidenced by the ten fastest-growing industries from 1950 to 1966, the technology of annihilation developed as rapidly as the products of consumption. After World War II, the American arms industry continued to be a principal element in the economy. Its importance can be measured by the large percentage of American exports deriving from military production—as high as 20 percent in 1953. Thereafter, percentages declined, but their share remained significant. Defense spending and military production absorbed a major share of federal funds. Money earmarked for defense, excluding Atomic Energy Commission and space expenditures, accounted for a huge proportion of research and development appropriations.

Total defense appropriations, again excluding space research, declined sharply as a percentage of the national budget immediately after the war, but then spurted upward because of the Korean

Federal Funds for Research and Development, 1947 to 1970

Year	Total ($ millions)	Defense ($ millions)	Percentage for Defense
1947	619.5	469.3	76%
1950	972.6	599.7	62
1953	3,106.0	2,577.2	83
1956	2,988.2	2,267.6	76
1959	6,693.5	5,161.6	77
1962	10,289.9	6,722.9	65
1965	14,614.3	6,796.5	47
1968	15,921.4	7,709.3	48
1970	15,340.3	7,360.4	48

Source: Historical Statistics of the United States, *Bicentennial Edition*, *Vol. II, p. 966.*

conflict, remaining high until the end of the Vietnam War in 1973. During the 1950s, defense drained the federal budget of as much as 65 percent of its revenues; between 1952 and 1959, it constituted more than 50 percent of the total budget, although this figure fell to only 23.3 percent in 1978. This extraordinary commitment rapidly accelerated the destructive capacity of the American army, navy, and air force. Productivity in destructive capacity increased exponentially with the mammoth firepower of atomic and hydrogen bombs.

The United States and the Soviet Union (after 1949) designed nuclear weapons whose power dwarfed the explosions of Hiroshima and Nagasaki. By 1961, the Soviet Union had tested an H-bomb with 3,000 times the power of the first primitive weapons dropped on Japan. In the early 1970s, Russian and American intercontinental ballistic missiles could deliver this explosive power with great accuracy and by remote control. By then, three other nations had broken into the nuclear cartel: France, Great Britain, and the People's Republic of China.

The rapid proliferation of weapons demanded a new attitude toward military strategy. Despite limited agreement by the United States and the Soviet Union in 1963 to cease open-air testing, disarmament remained elusive. The atomic race had a logic of its own, limited by available resources and technology, not by common sense. Having the ability to destroy each other several times over, the two superpowers reached a parity of terror in the late 1960s, each one glaring at the other over a stockpile of unusable doomsday weapons.

The pursuit of security through nuclear terror made weapons development a priority and the potential use of weapons a matter of policy. A few groups, such as the Committee for a Sane Nuclear Policy, founded in 1957, questioned this commitment, calling for limited disarmament and an end to nuclear testing. They raised serious questions about the effects of radioactivity released in tests. Their criticism, however, had little effect. Even government scientists in the Atomic Energy Commission, who understood some of the potential danger, refused to warn residents living near test sites in the West.

Politicians and government scientists could quiet public discussion of atomic warfare, but they did not satisfy deep public suspicions about nuclear fallout. Instead, these fears were diverted into a fantasy culture in popular magazine stories and science fiction

"*I could see the bones in my hand like an X-ray,*" *said Paul Cooper, a soldier stationed a short distance from an atomic test like this one, which occurred at Camp Desert Rock, Nevada, on August 7, 1957.* (*U.S. Army Photograph*)

films portraying atomic Armaggedon. In January 1952, the editor of *Galaxy Science Fiction* magazine noted that over 90 percent of the recent stories submitted to his journal discussed atomic or bacteriological warfare, devolution, or mutant children. Beginning in the early 1950s and extending into the 1960s, science fiction films presented the effects of nuclear fallout in scores of ways—none of them positive. Some of these movies were clumsy horror films, but the best gave substance to problems that politicians avoided. Produced primarily in the United States and Japan, their appearance probably also released unarticulated public guilt and horror at the American atomic bomb blasts at Hiroshima and Nagasaki. The most frightening of all was *Them,* produced in 1954, depicting the power of radioactivity to produce genetic changes. The movie's monsters were giant ants. The success of this film and other films like it unleashed a Hollywood menagerie of destructive insects and animals on American cities and small towns—creatures who avenged humanity's discovery of atomic secrets.

Other versions of the atomic horror film urged world cooperation and the control of nuclear technology, as in *The Day the Earth Stood Still* (1951). In the film, a galaxy representative, Klaatu, and his powerful robot visit earth to demand that nations stop nuclear testing. Unheeded by all but a family that befriends him, he is assassinated, and his robot begins to destroy the earth. Only intervention by those who believed him stops the robot, who then resurrects his master. In this adapted parable of Christ's sacrifice and resurrection, the message is clear: stop testing or destroy the world and face God's wrath. On the whole, however, these movies rarely confronted the real issue: the immediate danger of nuclear warfare, perpetrated not by spacemen or preposterous monsters, but by real people. Of the few that attempted to be realistic, *On the Beach*, produced in 1959, bleakly depicted the last days of the human race.

Public discussion of survival in a nuclear war finally surfaced in the bomb-shelter controversy of the late 1950s. To construct shelters suggested that they would be used. The American public, after debating the issue for several years, rejected plans for underground bunkers. In effect, Americans preferred to ignore the possibility of life after nuclear warfare than to prepare for it.

Public understanding of the probable impact of atomic warfare emerged slowly in the late 1940s and early 1950s. A Boy Scout "Family Be Prepared Plan," of 1951, issued instructions far more appropriate to World War II air raids than to nuclear warfare. The Scouts advised families to stockpile food and keep doors and windows shut during an actual atomic blast. In a companion manual, the Scouts promised to provide messenger services for civil defense authorities. During the mid-1950s the newly created Civil Defense Administration devised more sophisticated warning systems, like Conelrad on AM radio. Val Peterson, the federal Civil Defense Administrator, promoted an evacuation program as the only effective means to escape atomic blasts. But, while the federal government did adopt a partial evacuation program (the 1956 Highway Act promised roads to make evacuation possible), most major evacuation routes in the East and Midwest led toward other threatened cities. Adoption of a limited national shelter policy for federal buildings in 1958 acknowledged the impossibility of effective evacuation.

Indecisiveness in federal civil defense policy came from public ignorance about the effects of radiation, from the assumption that early warning and subsequent evacuation were possible, and from President Eisenhower's opposition to an extensive shelter program. Government public relations events, such as "Operation Cue," an atomic test blast of 1955, covered by radio and television, confused Americans about radiation effects. Two hundred associations and companies contributed consumer items to the blast area to test their durability. Television commentators, volunteers, and trade association members, like Arthur F. Landstreet, the president of Hotel King Cotton in Memphis, Tennessee, crouched in "Position Baker," a trench cut only 10,500 feet from "ground zero." As Landstreet wrote afterwards, "Everyone is happy now and those who were privileged to participate in Baker feel that they were among the selected few."

Effective pressure to build shelters began after the Russians launched *Sputnik*, for the powerful rocket that lifted the world's first satellite into orbit could also deliver bombs to American cities. Experts realized the futility of early-warning systems in an age of intercontinental missiles. Eisenhower reacted to pressure by reorganizing the civil defense bureaucracy in 1958, but he did little more than centralize this function in the executive branch. Rejecting suggestions in the Gaither Report for a crash shelter program, he pushed a voluntary program of federal "stimulation, leadership, guidance, and example." But, without funding, this program accounted for very few shelters by the end of 1960. There

Nelson Rockefeller posed inside a prototype bomb shelter to publicize the civil defense program he promoted while governor of New York.   (Walter Sanders/LIFE Magazine, © Time, Inc.)

were other points of resistance too. Even in states like New York, where Governor Nelson Rockefeller pushed for an extensive program, the state legislature balked at such huge new appropriations.

Important opposition to shelters came from the military establishment, which was divided on weapons systems. For example, General Curtis LeMay, of the Air Force, criticized an expensive shelter program, fearing it would undermine support for the Air Force program of "counterforce," designed to knock out enemy missiles before they could be launched. A large civil defense budget would starve such projected weapons systems of funding.

Strong support for shelter construction did develop in strategic political sectors, however. The AF of L-CIO strongly endorsed a program, undoubtedly because of potential jobs. Organizations, such as the American Medical Association, approved it. In 1962, the American Institute of Architects held a national competition for the best blast-proof school building, awarding its first prize of $15,000 in December of that year. The most effective lobbying came from the new Kennedy administration, which supported larger arms budgets and a more aggressive foreign policy. Twice, Kennedy asked Congress for large increases in the civil defense budget. In May 1961, he requested tripling the budget but received only $86 million, or about half the sum appropriated in 1960 under Eisenhower. In July, he asked for $207.6 million more to designate shelters in public buildings. Despite strong opposition in the Senate from Wayne Morse, of Oregon, Stephen Young, of Ohio, and Ernest Gruening, of Alaska, the appropriation passed.

The administration tried again in 1963 for new shelter appropriations, but Congress remained reluctant to appropriate large sums for civil defense. By this time, the administration itself had split over how to convince the American people to support such a program. Of the $695 million requested, only $113 million survived congressional budget-cutting; quite clearly the issue had died.

Civil defense failed because most Americans refused to accept its necessity. As the shelter debate heated up, many citizens expressed horror at the statements of civil defense advocates. Despite extensive positive coverage in the press and on radio and television, few could be convinced that shelters were safe or desirable. Even the works of Herman Kahn, the Rand Corporation's expert on nuclear warfare, did more harm than good to the argument. Kahn's book *On Thermonuclear War,* published in 1960, tried to persuade Americans that limited casualties of 10 or 20 million people were reasonable. Of course, "tragedy" would increase, but "the increase would not preclude normal and happy lives for the majority of survivors and their descendants," he concluded. To many who read his books, this seemed a monstrous prospect.

As the public argument over shelters continued, moral and ethical issues became clearer and absurdities abounded. For example, in September 1961, *Life* magazine ran a cover picture of a fallout suit, although no such protective covering existed. Newspapers reported that a wealthy horse lover built an elaborate fallout shelter for her champion horses. Reports from Nevada claimed that citizens of that sparsely settled state were prepared to shoot Californians fleeing populated cities in the event of nuclear warfare. Probably the most controversial sentiment came from the Reverend L. C. McHugh in his article, "Ethics at the Shelter Doorway," published in September 1961 in *America,* the Catholic magazine. Reverend McHugh justified armed self-defense against neighbors: "I doubt that any Catholic moralist," he wrote, "would condemn the man who used available violence to repel panicky aggressors plying crowbars at the shelter door . . ." On the contrary, many Americans, including other Catholic moralists, did condemn such extreme behavior. In fact, recognition that nuclear war would destroy the fabric of ethics and society explained the passive resistance of most Americans to the shelter proposals of the 1960s.

☆   ☆   ☆

Americans in the 1950s and 1960s worried almost as much about the creative prospects of great technological change as they did about the destructive powers of nuclear warfare. Abundance was not without its perils. A. J. Hayes, president of the International Association of Machinists, stated this point forcefully: "Automation presents the United States—and eventually every country—with a threat and a challenge second only to the possibility of the hydrogen bomb." The force of technology, symbolized by automation, challenged traditional thinking about economics, the organization of work, and leisure.

In the 1950s and 1960s, labor unionists, politicians, scientists, corporate executives, sociologists, and religious leaders debated the contemporary problems of automation, as well as its benefits and difficulties in the future. As a concept, automation symbolized the possibilities of a revolution in work and social relations. Yet, words like "automation" and "cybernation" were frequently employed during these years with a degree of confusion. As originally defined in 1946, "automation" had at least two different meanings. Used by D. S. Harder, a Ford Company executive, it meant the automatic handling and transfer of parts between successive stages in production—in effect, a more complicated assembly line. But when the management consultant John Diebold wrote his report for Harvard University, "Making the Automatic Factory a Reality," he used "automation" to designate machine tools that could carry out a variety of processes in one place. During the 1950s, the term expanded, taking on new overtones because of the strides in computer technology. By the 1960s, "automation" also meant a factory in which machines replaced human labor and supervisory intelligence.

As the term "automation" stretched to fit new possibilities, mathematician Norbert Wiener coined a new term, "cybernetics." Wiener used "cybernetics" to suggest the relationship of computer technology to production. "Cybernetics" referred to the feedback and information-processing capacities of modern computers and machines. Information gathered by sensory monitors enabled a computer to maintain a manufacturing process according to a predetermined program of instruction. To Wiener, however, the implications of "cybernetics" went far beyond the computer-controlled factory. When he discovered that computers could "learn" to defeat their programmers at checkers, he wondered if decision-making computers could ever be controlled. Attached to a fail-safe atomic weapons system, for example, a computer might "win a nominal victory on points at the cost of every interest we have at heart, even that of national survival."

For labor unions, "automation" meant bread-and-butter issues. Early experiments in automation, particularly in the auto industry, and the enthusiasm of management for technologies that replaced workers convinced many labor unions that automation would be turned against them. In 1955, the first fully automated engine-factory machine tools drilled, bored, and constructed without constant human surveillance. Walter Reuther, the head of the United Auto Workers, proclaimed this new technology to constitute "the second Industrial Revolution." Reuther's fears about automation emerged in a dialogue that he repeated after inspecting acres of machines at the Ford engine plant in Cleveland. His management guide prodded him: "Well, you won't be able to collect dues from all these automated machines." Reuther replied: "You know, that is not what is bothering me. What is bothering me is, how are you going to sell cars to all of these machines?"

As a union leader, Reuther focused the automation debate on jobs, work rules, and wages. Trade union advances in controlling the workplace during World War II and afterwards had been impressive, and labor leaders were not prepared to sacrifice these gains. In his thinking, Reuther reflected the experience of bitter organizational struggles during the Depression of the 1930s. He calculated that industrial progress, if not properly anticipated, might cause dislocations as serious as the economic downturn after 1929. The economy would have to be tuned to absorb the rising productivity of American workers. As he told the Joint Congressional Committee on the Economic Report in 1955, rather than current rises of 3 to 4 percent, automation might push productivity increases to 5 or 6 percent a year. This immense jump in output threatened a severe underconsumption of goods and services if wages did not also rise rapidly.

☆   ☆   ☆

Mechanization—if not automation—rapidly altered American labor after World War II. It disrupted established patterns of work, intensifying alienation, unemployment, and problems of retraining. The largest single private employer in the United States in 1954, and one of the leaders in automation, was the Bell Telephone conglomerate, with 600,000 operating employees. In this industry, automation of communications equipment appeared early, and wholesale replacement of human operators began in the late 1940s. Joseph Beirne, president of the Communications Workers of America, reported that "the real drama of automation" was its effect on skilled operators. Transferred to new, unfamiliar forms of work, many women broke down emotionally or lost confidence. Although Beirne conceded the company's right to improve technology and even to eliminate workers, he wanted changes to be carried out in an orderly and open fashion, with union participation.

As it has always done, mechanical innovation disrupted established work patterns, dislocating workers and creating what economists called "technological" or "frictional" unemployment. Simply put, it meant unemployment caused by inadequate education and training. Automation procedures in manufacturing industries, coupled with intensive investment and development in consumer production and services diminished blue-collar employment while increasing white-collar jobs. This effect only increased labor union fears about automation, for they correctly saw their organizational base among manual workers and the unskilled shrinking. In the period from 1945 to 1970, jobs in manufacturing and construction increased only about 35 percent, while available positions in government and the retail, finance, and insurance sectors rose by more than 200 percent. During the same years, trade union membership increased slowly, so that in 1970, the percentage of workers in unions remained only about what it had been in 1946.

New opportunities for white-collar employees and upgraded minimal skills put pressure on colleges, universities, and junior colleges to train what some economists called a new "white-collar proletariat." The average years spent in educational institutions during these years reflected the impact of automation and demands for more extensive training. In 1952, the median year of education of an adult American was 10.9 years; in 1975, it had risen to 12.6 years.

While junior colleges and vocational institutions accommodated more students, elite universities transformed themselves into research centers for the development of further technological innovations. In 1959, Clark Kerr, head of the University of California, suggested naming the modern university a "multiversity," proposing that modern institutions of higher learning become knowledge factories devoted to training engineers, scientists, doctors, and social scientists for service in an advanced technological society.

Management considered the rapid growth of white-collar work and the upgrading of skills a perfectly natural and gradual progression in American capitalism. Testifying before Congress and writing articles for business periodicals, management representatives explained that automation had only good effects. The adaptation of automatic processes, an executive of the Ford Motor Company told Congress in 1955, "will be an evolutionary and not a revolutionary process." It would only gradually shift employment from unskilled, backward production to new growing industries.

In certain industries, automation brought new approaches to

collective bargaining. During the 1960s, a few unions, such as the Electrical Workers in New York, secured a twenty-hour work-week, although many of these workers spent their spare moments in overtime. George Meany, head of the AF of L-CIO, occasionally pressed employees to shorten the workweek to thirty-five hours in order to spread available work. But, despite scattered protests, many unions, including Reuther's UAW, negotiated productivity agreements with corporations during the 1950s and 1960s, trading jobs for higher wages. An example of this development was the 1959 Armour pact with two meatpacking unions. Part of the contract designated a company "Automation Fund" of $500,000. Using this money, an "Automation Committee" composed of labor, management, and neutral observers studied technological displacement and suggested experimental remedies.

Another 1959 agreement, the "Kaiser Steelworkers Long Range Sharing Plan," emerged from the long and costly steel strike of that year. The program promised to pass on a portion of profits gained from increased productivity. If an employee lost a job due to automation, the company promised to place him in a reserve labor pool and pay his average hourly earnings for at least a year. The UAW, in particular, proposed a shorter workweek and guaranteed annual salaries for workers instead of weekly wages, but only in the construction trades did the shorter week become the rule. And none of the automation agreements seriously challenged management prerogatives to apply advanced technology to work.

As in other areas, the federal government acted as referee in the automation debate. The Employment Act of 1946 committed the federal government to pursue full employment for the nation's laboring population. Beginning in the mid-1950s, Congress aired the problems of automation in extensive, frequent hearings. Operating through the Joint Economic Committee and a special advisory group, the executive branch developed policy toward problems raised by automation. The report of President Kennedy's Advisory Committee on Labor-Management Policy in 1962 created guidelines for federal policy. Proclaiming automation a necessity and a benefit, the committee proposed concerted government and business action to eliminate "structural unemployment." Congressional advice on automation seconded this approach. Senator Joseph Clark's 1964 report, "Toward Full Employment," praised automation and suggested that retraining and other programs would help

American workers adjust to the new industrial reality. Accepting what was essentially management's position on automation, Washington rejected labor's call for a shorter workweek. Under Kennedy and subsequently under Johnson, the federal government instituted extensive retraining programs.

Kennedy took a strong interest in technological unemployment because of the sharp recession of 1960 and 1961, which focused attention on rising long-term unemployment. Two acts in the first years of his administration established Kennedy's policy of cautious guidance in economic matters. The government, he pledged, would not interfere with the deployment of new technology; it would concentrate on aiding workers already adversely affected by automation. The Area Redevelopment Act, of 1961, for example, committed the government to seek means to prevent older industrial areas from declining. The Manpower Development and Training Act of 1962 bolstered this program. In this comprehensive bill, Congress authorized establishment of the President's "Manpower Report" to investigate and report on the causes of current unemployment and to predict future employment needs. The core of the program established training programs for workers laid off by "automation and technological changes and other types of persistent unemployment." When funded in August 1962, this legislation provided money, administered by the Labor Department and HEW, for scores of retraining programs. Hardcore unemployed heads of households were eligible for admission to programs that lasted up to fifty-two weeks.

As temporary measures, these programs did not end the automation debate. In July 1963, President Kennedy established a commission to examine the broad social and economic effects of automation. Earlier in the year, the American Foundation on Automation and Employment held an all-day conference at the Waldorf-Astoria Hotel in New York, cochaired by industry and labor representatives. Other conferences sponsored by the International Labor Organization, in London and Geneva, underscored the international dimensions of the discussion. Although one staff member of the House Subcommittee on Unemployment and the Impact of Automation proposed a GI bill of rights for the unemployed, the federal government committed itself to less drastic measures to soften the impact of automation. From 1963 to 1965, Congress added retraining provisions to economic legislation, including the Vocational Education Act of 1963 and the Economic

Opportunity Act of 1964. This commitment remained through the 1970s.

No one could deny that technological innovation and automation exposed serious economic problems. But, neither the worst fears nor the most optimistic predictions materialized. The workweek remained at about forty hours. Worker productivity did not rise as Walter Reuther calculated; instead, after 1967, it fell sharply. Automated production did speed changes in the workplace; it undoubtedly pushed jobless rates up, until the federal government had to redefine the meaning of unemployment. But the dream— and the nightmare—of cybernation remained a distant vision in 1980.

☆   ☆   ☆

While labor, management, and government regarded automation as a problem about jobs and profits, much of the popular discussion worried that technological advance increased leisure for workers. How would the working classes spend their spare time once automation shortened the workweek to twenty-five hours?— sociologists and popular magazine articles wondered—although a shorter workweek for most employees was not an immediate possibility.

Apprehension about increased leisure emerged from fears that the work ethic might disappear. Once assumed to be a powerful instinct that generated pride in accomplishment and labor, the work ethic, some observers feared, had been usurped by the desire to consume and spend. Since the beginning of industrialization, Americans had questioned whether repetitious labor tasks would strengthen or weaken an employee's devotion to hard work and individual accomplishment. Automation simply posed this same question more intensively: if work ceased to be the central preoccupation of the population, would consumerism take its place? Even union leaders worried: in 1952, Mark Starr, educational director of the International Ladies Garment Workers Union, declared: "Our problem today is leisure for the mass."

David Riesman, who wrote extensively on the sociology and psychology of the modern industrial world, summarized this popular view of automation as calamitous. Even the *Saturday Evening Post* made this the subject of a story in 1958. The plot of "A Holiday for Howie" followed the hero's reaction to a new four-day week. Unable to fill up his new leisure with anything constructive,

Howie discovered happiness by finding a part-time job to fill the empty space in his week. Exchanging leisure for more work was certainly a stopgap measure, but it probably reflected a dominant public view.

A Gallup poll, in 1957, found little public enthusiasm for a shorter workweek. Another poll taken in the same year reflected the persistence of older ways of thinking about work. Most parents, the survey discovered, felt that children, especially, needed work to occupy their spare time; too much leisure meant delinquency. Suspicion that leisure would demoralize workers and youth was a complicated and sometimes patronizing attitude that reflected vague fears of social disorder, brought on by rapid changes in the workplace and in social life.

On the other hand, prolongation of schooling and the decline in the centrality of work added to the enthusiasm for permissive child-rearing after World War II. Even the U.S. Children's Bureau disseminated pamphlets stressing the "fun morality" in child-rearing, advising parents to allow children to pursue pleasure and amusement rather than duty. Modern parenting seemed more a schooling in interpersonal relationships and consumer skills than a traditional preparation for a life of hard work, savings, and sacrifice. Advertisers underscored this tendency by aiming their efforts increasingly at children and adolescents in the 1950s and 1960s.

If adolescence seemed an ambiguous, possibly dangerous, period of leisure time, retirement, at the other end of the work life, became an even more pronounced problem during this period. With increased longevity during the twentieth century, the average individual's work life increased by almost a decade. In 1900, the normal work expectancy of a laborer was about thirty-two years; in 1950, it rose to almost forty-two years. Nonetheless, an increasing percentage of Americans lived several years beyond retirement. At the same time, the federal government encouraged early retirement through lower eligibility for Social Security payments as one means of controlling unemployment. Inevitably, whatever else elderly Americans suffered—poor health care, inadequate retirement benefits, and small pensions—boredom and inactivity also posed a major threat to the "Golden Years."

For other Americans, leisure time represented opportunity, not just problems. Slightly shorter working hours for men and increased life expectancy changed the average proportion of time spent in and out of work. In 1950, the average man generally spent

Come on - let's have a 'COKE'!

Coca-Cola is real refreshment for everybody—any time of day. Out and about, or at home with the family, it's always the right time and place for 'Coke'. Pure and wholesome, delicious and refreshing, Coca-Cola is unlike any other drink in the world. Enjoy 'Coke' whenever you feel like a 'break'— and return to work (or play) wonderfully refreshed!

Drink
Coca-Cola
TRADE MARK REG.

Call it 'Coke' or Coca-Cola
it's the same delicious drink

Around the world, Coca-Cola came to symbolize the importance of leisure and the achievement of a high standard of living in the United States. *(NYPL Picture Collection)*

63 percent of his years working and 37 percent of his time outside work. In 1975, this changed to 60 percent in work and 40 percent outside. In the same period, due to their rapid entry into the labor force, women spent an increasing proportion of their lives on the job. Such changes in the use of time revolutionized American leisured activities. The "Do-It-Yourself" fad in the 1950s and the rapid expansion of home hobbies reflected increased spare time, as well as wider home ownership and the desire of many Americans to practice the manual skills learned during World War II in the army or defense industries.

American sports activities also evolved rapidly in this period. Participation in and attendance at sporting events changed markedly after the war. Traditional spectator sports like baseball declined, while horseracing and professional football and basketball gained. Technological improvements in television, new suburban stadiums, and rule changes transformed both football and basketball. At the same time, participation sports like bowling, boating, riflery—and toward the end of the period—camping, skiing, bicycling, and jogging attracted millions of new adherents.

The social importance of spectator sports made them a primary target for racial and, later, sexual integration. In 1947, the Brooklyn Dodgers breached baseball color bars by hiring Jackie Robinson as the first black major league player. Sports writers had long agitated for desegregation of national sports, but clubowners refused, until Branch Rickey of the Dodgers broke ranks. Rickey selected Robinson for his experiment because of this player's undeniable talent and his ability to take the jibes and insults of fans, other players, and the press. As Rickey told him, "You can't fight back, boy. That's going to be the hardest part of all. No matter what happens, *you can't fight back*."

In 1950, the first black players entered pro basketball. By 1970, black Americans accounted for 25 percent of all pro baseball players, 32 percent of football, and 55 percent of basketball. Integration of women into spectator sports occurred on a much smaller scale and later. Under guidelines established by HEW, major university systems that received federal funding began to move more funds into athletic programs for women, but progress in this field remained limited.

Because the nation paid so much attention to sports, its heroes increasingly became national celebrities. More than ever, heroes achieved renown for their hard play, not their diligent work or inventiveness. After 1968, the United States acquired in Richard Nixon a president who self-consciously invoked the sanctity of sports language and heroes whenever he encountered a difficult situation; he refused to punt when he was cornered. The old work ideals of competition and achievement still existed; they had simply moved over to the sports arena.

☆   ☆   ☆

The unfaltering expansion of technology and communications convinced many Americans that society had entered a new phase of development shaped by transmitted images and information-access rather than burdensome hard work and self-sacrifice. The identification with sports heroes was just one phase of this larger revolution caused by information technology. Of those who sought to measure this development, the Canadian writer Marshall McLuhan most successfully popularized the theory that modern communications had transformed life. In several books, *The Gutenberg Galaxy* (1962) and *Understanding Media* (1964), he outraged and prodded Americans into considering the effects of the communications revolution. McLuhan argued that no medium of information (print or television, for example) could be value-free. Each deeply altered a society's perception of the world. Print created one world; radio and movies generated another; and television inspired a third. "If the formative power in the media are the media themselves," he wrote, they deserve the full attention of modern intellectuals.

McLuhan's most perceptive speculation focused on television, a medium that, he claimed, had extended the perceptions of its viewers, transforming their psychologies by making the distant world an immediate experience. This "nowness" precipitated a new attitude toward the world for a generation that viewed reality through the mechanical eyes of television. Some of the programming of modern television appeared to validate this idea. From Walter Cronkite's *You Are There* series (1954 to 1957), which placed a TV cameraman and interviewer on the scene of reenacted historic events, like the martyrdom of Joan of Arc and the Boston Tea Party, to the nightly saga of the war in Vietnam during the 1960s, a generation and a society experienced television as if it were a sixth sense, added to their ability to hear, smell, taste, feel, and see the world around them.

Television—the irresistible eye—seemed also to work another

kind of revolution. McLuhan's concept of the "global village" implied an inevitable unity of diverse experiences and a breakdown of the distinctions between private lives and public exposure. Television relentlessly surrounded the viewer with the intimate experiences of others. It beamed visions of luxury into poverty-stricken urban ghettos. It exposed the private lives of those who made news. It reduced politics to a dependent relationship with pollsters and image makers who helped to decide the shape and content of campaigns. And, it selected instant reality from the blur of contemporary history.

☆　　　　　　　　　　☆　　　　　　　　　　☆

As McLuhan suggested, the postwar changes in the economy, in technology, work, and leisure occurred in the context of a revolution in communications and in organization. Larger organizations, performing a multitude of tasks, required new forms and uses of information. In turn, computers, television, and other information technology facilitated the growth of organization and bureaucracy in business and government. This spiral of invention and growth reshaped the United States' economy. Eric Johnston, former president of the American Chamber of Commerce, described the new scale of organization in 1957: "We have entered a period of accelerating bigness in all aspects of American life. We have big business, big labor, big farming and big government." Was this, he wondered, the beginning of an age of "socialized capitalism"? The tendency toward great organized blocks of economic power, described by Johnston, occurred most notably in corporate consolidations. While government expansion and economic regulation increased rapidly after World War II, private organizations also greatly expanded their size and power, as if both were engaged in a bureaucratic arms race.

Large American corporations adopted planning and operations research procedures during and immediately after World War II, although they vigorously opposed federal government planning in the economic field. Spurred by the Ford and Carnegie foundations, management training schools revised their curricula during the 1950s to offer extensive courses in administration. Corporations, as they grew, adopted elaborate internal information-transfer systems.

The increasing size and scale of corporate consolidation, accompanied by mounting bureaucratic complexity, was nothing new; in the late nineteenth century, partly by default and partly by design, primary industrial producers in rail transport, steel, and oil rapidly consolidated. In the resulting corporations, management committees tended to replace pioneering entrepreneurs. To writers of the 1930s, this consolidation and the separation of management from owners of stocks suggested a new form of capitalism in which long-range interests, not short-range profits, had the highest priority.

Following World War II, corporate consolidation and reorganization proliferated with two extremely visible types of mergers. One was the conglomerate; the other was the multinational corporation. Some business organizations combined both types of operation; for example, in its American operations, International Telephone and Telegraph owned a conglomeration of other companies, many of them entirely unrelated to the communications industry. These included Avis Rent-a-Car, Aetna Finance, Continental Baking, the Sheraton Hotel Corporation, Levitt and Sons Construction, the Hartford Fire Insurance Company, and others. An example of the multinational corporation is General Motors, with plants in Germany producing automobiles for sale within the European Common Market.

Corporate consolidation in the postwar period reached a peak in 1968 with 4,462 mergers. By 1968, the 500 largest American corporations (most of them conglomerates and multinationals) accounted for 64 percent of total industrial sales in the United States. Between 1955 and 1971, the economic activity of these same companies increased at a rate about 1 percent faster annually than the total United States gross national product, indicating their growing dominance in the economy. At the same time, the public share of economic activity also increased, so that by 1969, federal, state, and local governments generated about 23 percent of all economic activity. Between them, the largest corporations and the public sector dominated the American economy.

Operations of multinational corporations abroad expanded so rapidly during the 1960s, that by the mid-1970s, the output of United States-owned companies abroad constituted the third largest productive capacity in the world, trailing only United States domestic output and the output of the Soviet Union. During the same time, American investment abroad rose rapidly to $78 billion in 1970, with two-thirds placed in Japan and Western Europe and one-third in the underdeveloped countries. This enormous outflow of capital went primarily to build new plants and productive facilities, which then competed with local European and Japanese firms. Increasingly, this American-owned foreign production returned home in the form of imports that competed with domestic industry in the United States. Some foreign countries, notably France during the early 1960s, vigorously protested this invasion of American capital. By the late 1960s, American trade unions also raised their voices to oppose foreign investment. The AF of L-CIO, for example, estimated that between 1966 and 1971, investments in cheap labor areas had erased 900,000 American jobs.

Corporate consolidation during the 1950s and 1960s was only the most visible phase of the growing managerial sophistication of American business. Inside corporations, increasing size dictated bureaucratization, the division of tasks by function, and the rise of a corporate mentality that often preferred the stability of government regulation to the risks of a free-market economy. As price competition declined, businesses increasingly adopted what some economists called "administered prices." These were set by major corporations that did not lower prices when demand fell. Instead, they increasingly passed their costs—and, sometimes, inefficiencies—on to the consumer.

The new businessman spawned by this system was very much the subject of discussion during the 1950s and 1960s. Economist John Kenneth Galbraith wrote perhaps the most influential works on the new ethic of the "executive suite." Beginning with his *Affluent Society* (1958) and extending through the *New Industrial State* (1961), Galbraith charmed many readers who disagreed, nonetheless, with his conclusions. Designating the new corporate economy a "technostructure," he argued that corporate managers were motivated to seek security for themselves and their corporations, not to maximize profits. According to the economist, the bureaucratic committees that administered prices and planned production paid little heed to the dictates of traditional economic thinking. In the name of stability, they supported immense military production, financed and underwritten by the federal government. For them, economic success depended upon controlled markets, prices, and access to raw materials. And, through advertising, they attempted to shape the market and consumer behavior. Their enormous power and anonymity sheltered them from public scrutiny and control. To Galbraith, they constituted a new ruling class.

While some of Galbraith's conclusions have been resolutely opposed by other economists, his concern for the size, scale, and inaccessibility of American business organization became a public concern by the late 1960s. Some conglomerates and multinational corporations had incomes larger than the budgets of all but the richest industrial nations. By the 1970s, this unchecked potential power became a significant political issue.

To other observers, this scale of success demonstrated a fortuitous turn in the history of capitalism. The postwar transformation of the economy and the prosperity of the 1950s convinced economist Walt Whitman Rostow that the United States had outrun the traditional problems of capitalism, crossing over into a mature industrial society. In this stage of development, possibilities of consumption, not the "imperatives of scarcity," marked the new economy. Sociologist Daniel Bell described this new society from a different angle. He stressed the absence of ideologies and rigid social classes from American politics. However, both men came to the same conclusion: the United States had achieved an abundance, social cohesion, and political equality only imagined by nineteenth-century utopian thinkers and revolutionaries like Karl Marx.

☆   ☆   ☆

American prosperity from 1945 until the mid-1970s constituted a success story unmatched by other industrial societies. An endless bounty of goods flowed out of manufacturing establishments into the homes of Americans, who purchased them with an apparently limitless supply of consumer credit. Led by spending for automobiles, short-term consumer indebtedness multiplied twenty-two times between 1945 and 1970. From a society in 1940, in which farm animals generated more horsepower than airplanes, the United States swept into an era of abundance, power, and productivity, but the social distribution of this plenty remained unequally divided.

While more equitable than in many other societies, including Western industrial countries, the American distribution of income remained unequally divided after World War II.

Percentage of Money Income Received by Each 5th of Families and Individuals*

	1947	1957	1967	1975
lowest 5th	5.1%	5.0%	5.5%	5.4%
second 5th	11.8	12.6	12.4	11.8
middle 5th	16.7	18.1	17.9	17.6
fourth 5th	23.2	23.7	23.9	24.1
highest 5th	43.3	40.5	40.4	41.1
top 5%	17.5	15.8	15.2	15.5

*Figures rounded.
Source: Barry R. Chiswick and June A. O'Neill, Human Resources and Income Distribution (New York: Norton, 1977), p. 6.

Income taxes and federal and state payments for welfare or other forms of financial assistance changed this percentage only slightly in the favor of the lowest 5th, although the goods and services delivered to poorer families often dramatically changed their quality of life. Even after taxes, the distribution of income remained fundamentally lopsided in favor of the wealthiest Americans. Recurrent unemployment and job and wage discrimination forced a disproportionate number of blacks, other minorities, and women into these bottom categories, exacerbating racial and class and sex distinctions. When the focus of politics changed from celebration in the 1950s to confrontation in the 1960s, these problems emerged with a force that demanded immediate attention. The contrasts of wealth and poverty made the possibility of abundance for everyone a compelling political issue.

8 The Limits of Liberal Politics: Part I

If any single word captures the tone of the administrations of John Fitzgerald Kennedy and Lyndon Baines Johnson, it is the ambiguous term, "idealism." Despite remarkable differences of style, intellect, political skill, and manners, Kennedy and Johnson shared the rhetoric of crisis idealism, shaping the events of which they spoke with an almost missionary fervor. While some of this was political rhetoric and not seriously intended, both presidents conceived of their commitments as high moral purposes. They pursued domestic and foreign programs with zeal, promising to cross "New Frontiers" or build "Great Societies." They aroused, but ultimately could not control, a wave of political idealism that flowed into the civil rights movement, into groups opposing the war in Vietnam, and finally, into opposition to liberalism itself. By 1968, at the Democratic convention in Chicago, an older generation of tired and compromised leaders discovered a younger generation demonstrating in the streets for nothing so much as a chance to revitalize and extend the traditions that had nourished them. Instead of being welcomed in, thousands of young demonstrators were confronted by Mayor Daley's police brigades. During the long night of riot that followed, the extraordinary idealism of 1960 died in a ritual of shadow and light played out before millions of Americans, as the demonstrators chanted: "The whole world is watching."

☆   ☆   ☆

For the first time, much of the nation watched the inauguration of a new President on television. This gala event, in early 1961, celebrated the personality and intellectual tastes of the new President. Washington filled temporarily with artists, writers, and performers, who received prominent seats in the reviewing stands. The glittering inaugural ball and the solemn and stylish formal dress made this a memorable pageant of fashion and power, carefully recorded and transmitted through television. The Capitol resounded with Kennedy's promise to make it a cultural center, not just the bureaucratic capital of the nation.

The young President's speech, read in the clear, ringing voice that marked his style, somberly announced a new, crusading foreign policy. Kennedy honed a long campaign against Eisenhower's policies of moderation and conservatism and a repeated call to get America moving again to a single issue that afternoon of January 20, 1961. His administration, he proclaimed, would accept the call to defend "freedom in its hours of maximum danger." This challenge was welcome; the young President pledged the lives of all Americans in the struggle "to assure the survival and the success of liberty. This much we pledge—and more." Yet, standing at his side in the cold winter wind of Washington, Eisenhower, the elderly ex-President must have wondered: Was this not the enthusiasm he had warned against in preparing his farewell address? Where would it lead?

John Kennedy began his race to the White House two giant steps ahead; he inherited great wealth and had a father with power in the Democratic party. Joseph Kennedy, John's father, was the son of an Irish-Catholic political boss in east Boston. Making his way through Harvard and ignoring the snubs of his Protestant classmates, Joe Kennedy showed shrewd financial judgment. Purchasing valuable Florida land after the speculation boom collapsed in the mid-1920s, investing money in Hollywood film productions, and then moving his stockholdings into real estate shortly before the 1929 crash, he became one of America's wealthiest men during the 1930s and an important contributor to the Democratic party. His reward came in an appointment to the Securities and Exchange Commission, created to oversee the stock market in 1934. By 1938, he received appointment as ambassador to Great Britain, although he had to resign in 1940, when his off-the-cuff remarks criticizing Roosevelt's foreign policy found their way into print. Stung by this experience, he became a bitter foe of the liberal wing of the Democratic party.

To some extent John Fitzgerald Kennedy inherited his father's prejudice against liberals. Although he counted on their support in political campaigns, he was not always at ease with them. Kennedy's approach was active, not contemplative; witty, not reflective. The author of two books, *Why England Slept* and *Profiles in*

Courage, he was not an intellectual. He admired action and courage, but became impatient with hesitancy and circumspection. A
voracious reader with excellent recall, the new President recognized accomplishments in the arts and letters, but, in politics, he
determined to surround himself with "pragmatic liberals" like himself.

From the outset, ambition, charm, and especially an intense
commitment to family made Kennedy's career an unusual one.
After Choate Preparatory School for boys, Princeton, and then
Harvard, from which he graduated *cum laude*, Kennedy joined the
navy in 1941. Already he was something of a celebrity: his senior
thesis was published as the bestselling book *Why England Slept*.
Given command of P T boat 109, during an operation in the Solomon Islands, in 1943, his ship was rammed and sunk by a Japanese
destroyer. Although he had hurt his back in the fracas, he pulled
an injured sailor three miles through the dark waters and then got
word out to rescuers. For this act, he received a Purple Heart; he
had proven himself as heroic as his boyhood heroes: Talleyrand,
John C. Calhoun, and Lincoln.

Elected to Congress from Massachusetts in 1946, 1948, and
1950, he entered the Senate in 1952 and was reelected by a landslide in 1958. Unlike Johnson, Kennedy did not ingratiate himself
with the inner circles of House and Senate leadership. In fact, he
earned a reputation for independence, when, for example, he
attacked Truman for not spending enough on defense. Labor leaders suspected the zealous efforts of Kennedy and his brother
Robert to indict Teamster leader Dave Beck and subsequently
Jimmy Hoffa. Although he lacked a power base in Congress and a
distinguished legislative record, Kennedy was a national political
celebrity by the mid-1950s. Attention came partly from his marriage to socially prominent and fashionable Jacqueline Lee Bouvier
in 1953. In part, it came from his brave bout with a back illness
that threatened his life in 1954. In part, too, it came from his
bestselling book *Profiles in Courage*, written while he was re-
cuperating.

The courage Kennedy praised most in his book was the willingness of men like President John Quincy Adams to sacrifice political
position to principle. Yet, his own courage did not run in this
direction; it had more to do with physical risks and military con-
frontations. Given several chances during the early 1950s to condemn Senator McCarthy, Kennedy refused to do so. When the

Senate voted condemnation in 1954, Kennedy was too ill to participate, but even then he refused to take a public stand against the Wisconsin senator, perhaps out of deference to his father's friendship with McCarthy. This reluctance earned him the suspicion and hostility of important Democratic party liberals like Eleanor Roosevelt, who considered opposition to McCarthy to be the litmus test of political credibility.

Almost the vice-presidential nominee in 1956, Kennedy became a presidential contender in the next four years. In 1960, he was a leading candidate. His strategy centered on beating his strongest opponent, Senator Hubert Humphrey, of Minnesota, in preferential primaries when Humphrey might be expected to win. On April 5, in Wisconsin, Kennedy took six of ten districts and then won a large plurality in West Virginia in May. This second victory was decisive, for it defused the issue of Kennedy's Catholic faith. By winning in a rural, Protestant state like West Virginia, he demonstrated to hesitant Democratic party leaders that Americans could elect a Catholic president. With a well-heeled media blitz and personal appearances, Kennedy bumped Humphrey out of the race.

Other contenders played a more cautious game. Lyndon Johnson, relying on his power base in the Senate, hoped that the front-runners would knock each other out, forcing the party to choose him. And, Adlai Stevenson, still supported by a coterie of liberal Democrats, waited in the wings for his third successive nomination. However, the Kennedy machine did not falter, and, with the weight of primary victories, crushed its opponents at the Los Angeles convention. Only Lyndon Johnson salvaged anything: the Vice-Presidential nomination.

Governor Nelson Rockefeller, of New York, and Vice-President Nixon sparred for first place on the Republican ticket. A grandson of John D. Rockefeller, the architect of the Standard Oil monopoly, Nelson inherited fortune and family notoriety. Devoting himself to public service, Rockefeller pushed liberal projects in the 1940s and 1950s in the State Department, and later as head of Eisenhower's committee on administration reorganization. One result of his work was the new department of HEW. On military spending, he advocated expansion, pushing civil defense measures and larger defense budgets. Warning of increased Soviet power, he used a report prepared for him by Professor Henry A. Kissinger (later National Security Adviser and Secretary of State under Nixon and Ford) as the basis of his campaign in 1960. Perhaps his combination of liberal federal programs and large defense budgets better suited him to the Democratic party, but his chief failing in 1960 was an indecisive and fuzzy campaign. This continued to be Rockefeller's role throughout the 1960s: a sometimes almost successful candidate who couldn't quite commit himself. Richard Nixon, on the other hand, was nothing if not committed to the cause of his own political advancement.

Nixon's rise through American politics is like the plot of a Horatio Alger tale of success and gives a vivid accounting of the costs of such success. Furthermore, his background contrasts sharply with both Kennedy's and Rockefeller's. Born into a modest Quaker family in California, Nixon worked his way through Whittier College and then graduated from Duke Law School. After short service in the Office of Price Administration during World War II, he joined the navy. Elected to Congress in 1946 and 1948, he won a Senate seat in 1950 after a bitter campaign against Helen Gahagan Douglas in which he questioned her loyalty. Detested by liberals, Nixon was the youngest and the brightest of the congressmen to exploit the anti-Communist issue. Although serving in the late 1940s on the House Un-American Activities Committee, where he doggedly pursued Alger Hiss, his anti-Communist tactics were more opportunism than ideology. During this same period, he ingratiated himself with the more liberal, Eastern wing of the Republican party, earning the Vice-Presidential nomination in 1952.

In 1960, Nixon's surest power base appeared to be in the Republican conservative wing, but he focused his campaign on his experience and closeness to Eisenhower. The elderly Eisenhower, rumored to be privately hostile and sometimes cruel to his Vice-President, could not shake off the tenacious grip of this ardent public admirer.

The 1960 Presidential campaign was a spectacle of bravado, matching the tough rhetoric of Nixon, trumpeting his ability to deal with the Russians, against the equally stern rhetoric of Kennedy, who criticized a "missile gap" and demanded firm measures to prevent erosion of America's world position. Forced to defend a modest foreign policy and facing a deepening recession, Nixon still might have won, had he asked Eisenhower for active support earlier in the campaign. As it was, Nixon's poor performance in the first of four televised debates with Kennedy crippled his effort.

Election of 1960

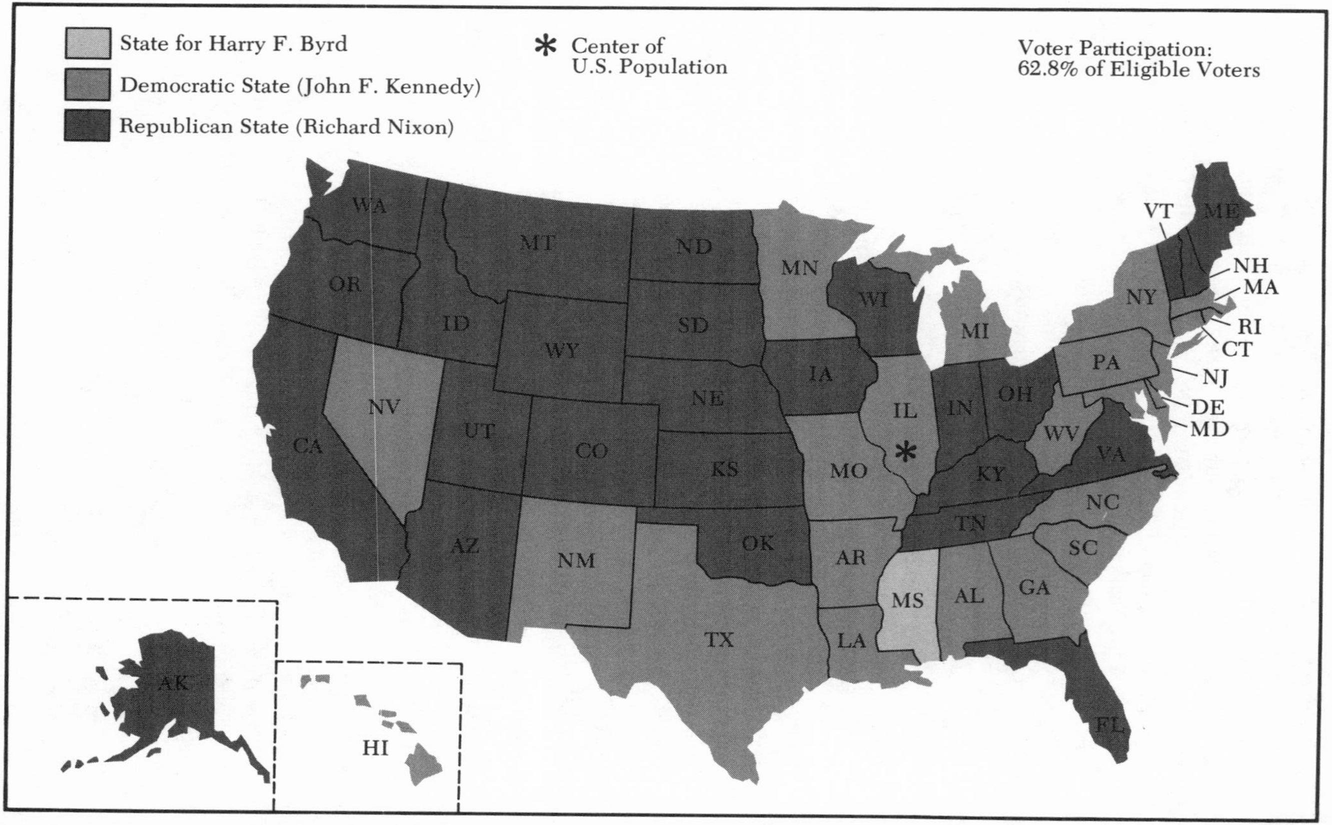
State for Harry F. Byrd
Democratic State (John F. Kennedy)
Republican State (Richard Nixon)
* Center of U.S. Population
Voter Participation: 62.8% of Eligible Voters
WA
OR
CA
NV
ID
MT
WY
UT
AZ
CO
NM
ND
SD
NE
KS
OK
TX
MN
IA
MO
AR
LA
WI
IL
MS
MI
IN
KY
TN
AL
OH
WV
VA
NC
SC
GA
FL
PA
NY
VT
ME
NH
MA
RI
CT
NJ
DE
MD
AK
HI

Kennedy emerged looking and sounding a leader next to Nixon, whose forced gestures revealed nervousness and insecurity, not the experience and maturity that he claimed as his advantage.

Kennedy had other advantages. He could criticize Eisenhower's slow-motion action on civil rights. He would get America moving again; or, as he put it in his Labor Day speech in Cadillac Square, Detroit, he would lead America toward a New Frontier. Voters perceived Kennedy to be a flexible, open-minded, and tough liberal committed to the basic, shared premises of American idealism. Defusing most negative reaction to his Catholicism, Kennedy benefited from a solid vote from Catholics.

Kennedy's assumption of power reaffirmed the basic continuity of Democratic administrations. Familiar faces from the Truman administration returned to government, but Kennedy also appointed a new generation of lawyers, academics, and corporate executives, whom reporter David Halberstam called "the best and the brightest." Several of these advisers, including historian Arthur Schlesinger, Jr., speech writer Theodore Sorensen, and economist John Kenneth Galbraith, already belonged in the Kennedy entourage. Others, such as Robert McNamara, appointed to head the Defense Department, and Dean Rusk, appointed to head the State Department, joined the administration after the election. Some, such as Douglas Dillon, head of Treasury, had been Republicans. The President named labor lawyer Arthur Goldberg as Labor Secretary. Luther Hodges, of North Carolina, went to the Commerce Department. The Attorney General was the President's brother, Robert Kennedy. To his Council of Economic Advisers, Kennedy appointed several outstanding academics, led by Walter Heller. McGeorge Bundy occupied the key post of National Security Adviser. Taken together, this was a group of intelligent and competent advisers, with well-deserved reputations for accomplishment and managerial skills. Embellished by several well-known intellectuals, Kennedy's advisers were dominated by skilled managers like McNamara.

The new President's foreign policy emphasis in his inaugural speech indicated the initial direction of his administration. For him, American determination had to be tested against Communism. Above all, the United States required a more flexible strategy in the Cold War. Eisenhower's massive deterrence policy, Kennedy felt, had been paying too little attention to revolutions in the Third World. Nikita Krushchev's tough speech on January 6, 1961, supporting "wars of liberation," only confirmed Kennedy's belief that American policy should focus on underdeveloped nations.

The new President also felt confident that he understood revolutions in Latin America, Africa, and Asia. Having read the works of important contemporary guerilla warriors, such as Che Guevara, of Cuba, and Mao Tse-tung, of China, he believed that anticolonial revolutions could be guided into the American camp if the United States would bolster liberal middle-class and local reform groups. The romantic appeal of antiguerilla tactics and individual heroism also appealed to the President, who was an unabashed admirer of the dashing secret agent James Bond, hero of Ian Fleming's adventure novels. Failing limited intervention, the United States could send economic aid and military advisers to struggling anti-Communist regimes. Willing to confront the Russians with nuclear warfare, should they alter the status quo in East-West spheres of interest, the President was optimistic about success.

In the three years of his administration, Kennedy had ample opportunity to test his strategy, as twenty-seven countries in Africa and Asia achieved independence. Perhaps the most innovative policy developed toward these new nations was the Peace Corps, announced on March 1, 1961. Directed by Kennedy's brother-in-law, Sargent Shriver, the agency sent hundreds of Americans abroad to help educate and lend expertise to new Third World nations. Although the Peace Corps was never a top priority of policy, its combination of idealism, voluntarism, and technical assistance represented some of the most creative thinking of the Kennedy administration, providing a prototype for subsequent programs initiated under President Johnson.

Unfinished business from the Eisenhower administration, however, became the first public test of Kennedy's approach to revolutions in the underdeveloped world. Eisenhower briefed the President-elect on CIA plans to invade Cuba and overthrow Castro. Kennedy decided to continue preparations; here was a chance to test his theories about counterinsurgency and flexible, limited force. The new President carefully kept American troops, ships, and aircraft out of the operation, but he could not prevent news of the impending invasion from spilling into the press. For those who cared to read about it, the coming action was described in rich detail in *The New York Times* and the *Nation* magazine.

With Kennedy's approval, the invasion of Cuba began on April 17, 1961. It quickly became a disaster. By the time the ragtag

American Peace Corps volunteers often found themselves in situations in which their skills and resources could barely scratch the surface of the poverty and deprivation in the host country. This volunteer (left) in Colombia worked on nutrition and food programs, as well as teaching macramé and drawing to children.   (ACTION, Photo by Jim Pickerell)

army of counterrevolutionaries hit the shore at the Bay of Pigs, conservative elements with little, if any, support inside Cuba dominated it. Castro's efficient and loyal army had no trouble defeating them. The Bay of Pigs debacle suggested the shallowness of CIA understanding of the Cuban revolution; more ominously, the experience displayed a tendency of moderate alternatives to revolution to evolve into right-wing juntas. Furthermore, Kennedy's hasty approval of covert military actions undercut faith in his Alliance for Progress, announced one month earlier. Failure in Cuba did not substantially change Kennedy's belief that elite or middle-class groups would willingly create more democratic societies, as the Alliance aid programs hoped to encourage, or that military force was an effective last resort.

Despite the Cuban setback, Kennedy continued to push for a flexible military force, concentrating his efforts on the creation of a special strike force, called the Green Berets. He also tested the waters of censorship, asking a very suspicious and uncooperative group of publishers to institute self-censorship during "our country's peril . . . which knows no precedent in history." When the publishers refused, Kennedy backed off. The new President had learned one lesson at least: to distrust the CIA. Shortly after the Cuban fiasco, he replaced Allen Dulles with John McCone.

Events in the Third World—the beginning of the liberation struggle against Portugal in Angola in early 1961 and trouble in the former Belgian Congo (called Zaire since 1971), Cuba, and Vietnam—buffeted Kennedy's first days in the White House, but the most perilous storms swirled around relations with the Russians. In June 1961, Kennedy agreed to meet Khrushchev in Vienna. By the time the two leaders confronted each other, both had marked off nonnegotiable positions. The President had pushed for an increased defense budget, announced a grandiose space program to bolster American prestige, pressed Congress for a fallout shelter program, and approved the invasion of Cuba. The Russians had proposed a "troika" (three leaders) to head the United Nations, instead of one person, and they began to push again for a final settlement of the German question.

When the two leaders met on June 3, their encounter resembled the preliminaries to a match between two wary boxers. Each leader spent considerable time sizing up his opposite. There were harsh and enigmatic words, but little agreement when the parley ended a day later. Still, the bluster on both sides might have evaporated, had it not been for Germany. Always a special problem in itself, the shared occupation of Berlin symbolized the failure of East and West to agree on a peace treaty with Germany. American policy since Eisenhower promoted the industrialization and rearmament of West Germany, aiming toward reunification and ultimate integration into the Western alliance. The Russians recognized West Germany, but demanded equal treatment for their client state in East Germany. As the West German economy grew rapidly in the late 1950s, West Berlin was resurrected as a glittering showcase of consumer capitalism. Increasingly, the city siphoned off East German intellectuals, scientists, and engineers, whose defection caused an acute crisis in 1960 and 1961 for the East German government of Walter Ulbricht.

On June 21, 1961, Khrushchev acted to help his East German ally by announcing he would sign a peace treaty with East Germany by the end of the year, turning over control of East Berlin to it and access to West Berlin. This would force the Americans, French, and British to recognize the Ulbricht government and its sovereignty over Berlin. Kennedy's advisers were divided in their suggestions. Dean Acheson favored proclamation of a national emergency. Arthur Schlesinger, Jr., Hubert Humphrey, and others suggested negotiations. Kennedy struck out for a middle ground, but leaned toward some tough response. His decision was announced on June 25, during a solemn national television speech requesting increased defense expenditures and higher draft quotas. He also asked for more civil defense funds. Most importantly, he called up military reserves. It was a slide toward the brink.

Khrushchev's response nineteen days later settled the German problem in a way that angered many Americans. On August 13 and 14, East German workers erected a barbed-wire and concrete wall between East and West Berlin. Thereafter, the flow of refugees slowed to a trickle. In what amounted to a public relations gesture, Kennedy sent 1,500 American troops along the East German autobahn into West Berlin. Short of war, however, he could do nothing to remove the wall. Thereafter, American-Russian relations continued to deteriorate. On August 30, the U.S.S.R. ended its self-imposed nuclear-test ban and exploded the largest weapons ever constructed. On September 12, the United States began underground testing and on March 2, 1962, resumed open-air testing.

Soviet-American hostility peaked during the next summer, this time ninety miles from home. With the approval of the Cubans, the U.S.S.R. began construction of nuclear-missile launching sites in Cuba. Whatever his reasons—pressure from hard-liners in his government, desire to probe American defenses, or eagerness to defend the Castro revolution—Khrushchev probably underestimated the swift and stern character of Kennedy's response. On October 15, 1962, an American U-2 plane positively identified the missile sites, and the President quickly called his advisers to consider American responses. Brushing off Adlai Stevenson's suggestion for broad negotiations with the Russians, aimed at neutralizing Cuba and withdrawing American forces from the naval base at Guantánamo Bay, Kennedy only seriously considered varieties of confrontation. When more hawkish advisers, like Dean Acheson, argued for a surprise air strike against the sites, others, led by Robert Kennedy, counseled caution and a policy more easily justified before international law: a blockade to prevent arming of the missiles. For several days, the advisers debated. Their final consensus reflected sensitivity to international opinion. As Bobby Kennedy put it, referring to the surprise Pearl Harbor attack of 1941: "My brother is not going to be the Tojo of the 1960s."

The President chose a relatively moderate course from among extreme possibilities, but he nonetheless brought the nation to the edge of nuclear war. Preliminary preparations for extensive conflict began: troops massed in Florida, and Press Secretary Pierre Salinger sketched out the functions of an emergency Censorship Advisory Board. On October 22, Kennedy spoke on national television, announcing the discovery of the missile site and the countersteps he had already taken. Ridiculing the Soviet assurances that these were defensive weapons, the President announced a "quarantine" (blockade) of all Cuban ports, insisting that all incoming ships would be searched for weapons.

Kennedy's actions presented the American people with a *fait accompli* and policy steps that could not be debated. At the same time, the President had compelled the Russians to decide for or against war. They could try to steam through the blockade and risk seizure, or they could stop and agree to American hegemony on the high seas. It was a difficult choice, but in this test of wills, the Russians backed off. On October 25, missile-carrying cargo ships of the Russian merchant marine stopped. In the meantime, Khrushchev sent a message to Kennedy promising to withdraw the missiles in exchange for United States guarantees not to invade Cuba. As the President prepared to accept this offer, the Soviet leader suddenly raised his demands, pushing the United States to withdraw its missiles from Turkey. The events of October 27 plunged the administration back into crisis, and Kennedy stepped up plans for military action. At the same time, he wisely decided to ignore Khrushchev's second message, cabling agreement with the first proposal. The Russian leader then accepted Kennedy's guarantees, and the crisis ended. The Russians dismantled their missile sites under the watchful eye of American airplanes. But the world had come dangerously close to nuclear warfare, as two men surrounded by their advisers, sitting in the situation rooms of their capitals, decided on the fate of humanity.

Confrontation seemed to soften the Kennedy-Khrushchev relationship in the months that followed, as both leaders backed down from antagonistic gestures. In December, the Soviet leader suggested a nuclear-test ban treaty. Kennedy's American University speech of June 10, 1963, confirmed a new emphasis upon reaching a peaceful accommodation with the Soviet Union. Although the final agreement, signed on July 25, 1963, excluded underground tests and did nothing to slow the arms race, it did stop the atmospheric discharge of large amounts of radioactive waste. Détente had begun in a small way.

Kennedy's foreign policy helped shape his attitude toward important domestic considerations, such as economic growth and civil rights. He stressed the need to increase America's gross national product in campaign speeches, but he was not clear about why this should be done: to add to defense capabilities or to aid those in the distress of unemployment and poverty. In areas like civil rights he remained cautious, because he did not wish to alienate Southern support for economic and defense programs.

On overall policy, the President gradually accepted the advice of economist Walter Heller and others on the Council of Economic Advisers for his strategy. Heller called these Keynesian tactics the "New Economics," or federal direction of the economy, using fiscal measures. His agenda stressed tax incentives to business for modernization, general tax cuts and reforms, and informal price-and-wage guidelines. Some of these measures might unbalance the federal budget, but Heller persuaded Kennedy that economic growth, stimulated under the program, would more than compensate by bringing in new tax revenues. For success, the program depended upon cooperation from Congress and the business community.

The President's relationship to business, however, was troubled and sometimes acrimonious. Businessmen suspected his liberal rhetoric and promises to use the power of the federal government in the economy. They disliked the activism of his administration, preferring the pleasant drift of Eisenhower's approach. His advisers seemed suspiciously like government planners—indeed, one of them, John Galbraith, was, although Kennedy kept him at arm's length.

Kennedy's initial policy tested the water. In February 1961, he announced plans to begin sailing America out of the economic doldrums. His tack included supplements to unemployment benefits, aid to distressed areas, a higher minimum wage, and more Social Security benefits. All of these measures passed through Congress by September. In other areas, he had less success. Of an investment tax-credit plan, tax reform to provide withholding on stock dividends and interest payments, and revision of expense-account deductions, only the tax credit survived. This plan for a 7 percent increase in deductions on new business equipment found a wide channel of support in Congress.

Nothing in this program should have angered business, yet Kennedy touched a raw nerve of confidence. In late 1961, the new administration had begun to worry about the wage-price spiral. According to this theory, wages that rose above increases in productivity pulled prices upward, in turn inspiring workers to demand higher compensation. By early 1962, Kennedy had accepted his economic council's advice on price-wage guideposts. He advised unions to seek only those wage hikes warranted by productivity increases, and he asked business to hold down prices. He had clearly signaled that economic growth, and not income redistribution, was the administration's aim.

Since the 1930s, the labor movement had been the largest organized component of the Democratic party, from which it demanded special consideration after elections, but the AF of L-CIO had never been close to Kennedy. Nonetheless, it willingly accepted the President's economic leadership. Interested only in selective intervention, Kennedy decided to set an example of wage-and-price restraint in steel. Beset by several long and expensive strikes since World War II, the industry had shut down for 116 days prior to its last settlement in 1959. Kennedy wanted to avoid this trend.

Meeting secretly on January 23, 1962, with Roger Blough, of the giant firm of U.S. Steel, and with President David McDonald, of the Steel Workers Union, Kennedy and Arthur Goldberg thought they had hammered out a noninflationary agreement. Labor's demands would be so low that the industry could maintain its current prices. In his estimation, the President was half-right. On March 31, the union settled for an embarrassingly slight $.10 per hour wage package plus fringe benefits, well within the economic council guidelines.

When he saw an appointment with Roger Blough on his April 10 schedule, Kennedy was surprised. He became furious when he understood the meaning of the meeting, for Blough had come to announce a $6 per ton price increase in steel. Arthur Goldberg, who had been standing by, came into the President's office. Accusing the steel executive of a "double cross," Goldberg attacked Blough for breaking the understanding of the January conference. After a half-hearted effort to justify himself, Blough departed. Kennedy, visibly shaken, called in his staff to announce the price hike, acidly commenting: "My father always told me that steel men were sons-of-bitches, but I never realized til now how right he was." Understandable as it was, this injudicious remark, when it appeared in the press, confirmed business exasperation with the President. Shortly afterward, New York businessmen began sporting buttons proclaiming, "I'm an S.O.B." The deeper message was clear.

Kennedy's off-the-cuff expletives did not embitter business as much as the substantial action he took the following day. At a press conference, the President used his Cold War rhetoric against the steel industry. "In this serious hour in our nation's history," he warned, when servicemen were dying in Vietnam or leaving their homes to join the reserves, a few arrogant men had defied the national interest. "Some time ago," he concluded, "I asked each American to consider what he would do for his country and I asked the steel companies. In the last twenty-four hours we had their answer." Several actions matched these tough words. The Defense Department promised to shift its purchases of steel to any company that maintained low prices. The Justice Department began to investigate whether simultaneous price rises in other companies indicated an illegal conspiracy. The FBI, meanwhile, sent agents in the middle of the night to rouse a reporter who had suggested that Bethlehem Steel wanted to resist the price rise. In the Congress, an investigation began into the monopoly practices of the industry.

Challenged from all sides, the large steel producers broke ranks. On April 13, 1962, Bethlehem Steel rescinded its price rise, followed quickly by U.S. Steel. The crisis ended with Kennedy, the apparent victor. But the injury to relations between the administration and business remained an open wound, upon which the President thereafter poured the balm of tax credits and special favors. Partly an aftershock, the stock market began a steep plunge in late May. Restoration of confidence and a new policy were in order.

The President moved on three fronts. He sought to restore business confidence, in a series of speeches, one to the Economic Club of New York, in December 1962, which John Galbraith called "the most Republican speech since William McKinley." In this address, Kennedy called for a tax cut and moderate tax reforms to block the most flagrant deduction loopholes. Inspired by Walter Heller, this program went to Congress in January 1963, featuring $13.6 billion in tax relief, most of it for individuals. Although the tax cut was not enacted until early 1964, several months after his death, Kennedy accurately assessed its effects. During the early years of the Johnson administration, production increased rapidly to around 6 percent a year, increasing tax revenues and decreasing the federal budget deficit. But the program also had a more subtle effect. Instead of pushing investment into useful social production for housing, transportation, or education, it emphasized consumer spending as the route to economic health.

Aside from some minor tax reforms and a Manpower and Development Act, passed in 1963, Kennedy's economic programs remained stalled in the conservative committees of Congress; they emerged for approval only later under the leadership of President Johnson. The reluctance of Congress to act on economic proposals typified relations between the legislature and Kennedy and the suspicions of Kennedy in the business community. He proposed, but Congress refused to dispose, and only a small percentage of his programs survived to return to the Oval Office for his signature. Lacking the skill, political clout, favorable political climate, and persistence of Johnson, he suggested programs for medical care for the elderly, aid to education, an Urban Affairs Department, and most importantly, a civil rights bill, but could not shepherd them through the legislative corridors of Congress.

In civil rights, Kennedy showed initial promise, as well as quickness to compromise. He attempted to avoid a treacherous and difficult route through Congress, while concentrating on legal desegregation initiatives pushed through the Justice Department. Although he appointed more black ambassadors and middle-level officials than any previous President, Kennedy ceded to compromise with Southern Democrats and named men unsympathetic to black equality to federal judgeships, in such states as Georgia and Mississippi. His caution on civil rights legislation gave way gradually, as the movement for its achievement deepened. Increasingly, the President began to side with these forces, but with a commitment tempered by his need for Southern votes on other issues. For example, only after Congress rejected his proposal for a housing and urban development Cabinet post (to be headed by Robert Weaver, a black city planner) in January 1962, did he finally fulfill a campaign pledge to eliminate by executive order, by "the stroke of a pen," segregation in federally financed public-housing projects.

During this period, Attorney General Robert Kennedy increasingly turned his attention to prosecuting school-integration cases and worked quietly to desegregate such transportation facilities as airline waiting rooms in the South. The administration also integrated the Army reserves and the National Guard, while it pushed desegregation of facilities surrounding United States military camps. But, not until February 28, 1963, did the President propose sweeping civil rights legislation.

By then, Kennedy could not ignore, and chose not to ignore, increasing demands from civil rights advocates all over the country. The force of events and the logic of his own beliefs compelled him to take action. Confrontation over the admission of black student James Meredith to the University of Mississippi required intervention. After the federal courts ordered "Ole Miss" to admit Meredith in the fall of 1962, a hostile mob of white segregationists rebuffed the new student. When state police refused to protect his rights, rioting broke out, eventually leaving two persons dead. Kennedy then federalized the Mississippi National Guard, and under the watchful eye of troops and marshall, Meredith enrolled.

The drama of Birmingham, Alabama, in the spring of 1963 more than matched this sample of resistance. The Southern Christian Leadership Conference, headed by Martin Luther King, Jr., began a nonviolent protest movement to crack segregation in the city's commercial life. Met by strong oppositon from state and local officials—especially "Bull" Connor, of the Birmingham Police Department—the city's black residents began marches and demonstrations. The police countered with arrests, beatings, and police dogs. Behind the scenes, Kennedy worked to arrange a truce. Deploying Cabinet members and advisers to contact their friends in the Southern business community, the President achieved something of a triumph with an agreement, reached on May 10, to integrate rest rooms, lunch counters, fitting rooms, and drinking fountains. Business promised changes in hiring practices, with a biracial committee established to oversee the pact. When state and local officials tried to renege on the agreement, Kennedy dispatched 3,000 troops to the outskirts of the city. Organized resistance crumbled.

Still, the movement continued to push beyond the President. On June 19, 1963, Kennedy proposed new civil rights legislation to strengthen voting rights and school desegregation. Despite a rousing speech on June 11 in favor of civil rights, he refused to endorse or attend the August 28 March on Washington, led by King and other black leaders. This celebration of black rights brought labor leaders, church officials, and thousands of black and white citizens together in the high point of the religiously oriented, nonviolent crusade against segregation. Martin Luther King's speech and sermon, "I Have a Dream," thrilled the enormous crowd by reaching into the very heart of America's moral and religious traditions. In some sense, it was the fulfillment of those traditions. King's biblical cadences intensified his incantation: "I have a dream." "I have a dream that one day every valley shall be exalted, every hill and mountain shall be made low, the rough places will be made plains, and the crooked places will be made straight, and the glory of the Lord shall be revealed, and all flesh shall see it together . . ." Kennedy held back from joining this vision of Judgment Day, partly because this movement challenged his leadership and partly because he still did not see racial inequality as a moral equivalent of the Cold War.

However, during the last three months of his life, Kennedy increasingly paid attention to questions of social reform. He supported the much amended and strengthened civil rights bill pending before Congress. But, even as tension over the issue built, the administration could not convince Congress to act. Three days before his death, Kennedy instructed Walter Heller to block out legislation for a war on poverty. Pressure to move decisively in this direction had been building in his administration, and Kennedy recognized that poverty had become an important issue. Outside academic consultants and advisers close to the President began informal discussions on a comprehensive attack on persistent joblessness and depressed economic areas in 1962.

A different, more ambiguous legacy of the Kennedy administration, was Vietnam. On this decisive issue, Kennedy's reputation seems to stand or fall, yet history cannot judge because of incomplete and contradictory evidence. From the beginning of his term in office, Kennedy personally involved himself in Vietnam, with an increasing commitment to winning the civil war in that nation. But, all the while, his skepticism grew. At the moment of his assassination, he was fast approaching a crossroads; either he increased American participation in the war or gradually disengaged United States forces.

Many of Kennedy's closest advisers, like Robert McNamara and General Maxwell Taylor, agreed with his faith in the special forces and quiet military intervention in the Third World. Rather than Cuba, with which Kennedy showed some signs of desiring an accommodation, Vietnam became the essential test case of this faith. Upon advice from Taylor and National Security Adviser Walt W. Rostow, after their mission to Vietnam in October 1961, Kennedy agreed to increase the number of military and political advisers, but he resisted requests for combat troops. At the same time, he increased pressure on Prime Minister Ngo Dinh Diem to institute social reforms. But Diem realized—if Kennedy did not—an inherent flaw in the policy. He knew that the United States would support him so long as he maintained a semblance of order.

By 1962, Kennedy's policy of material and political support was in full swing; the South Vietnamese Army, supported by American air power, in the form of helicopters and fighters, introduced napalm, defoliants, and a strategic hamlet program designed to isolate the Viet Cong revolutionaries from sympathetic peasants. Optimistic battle reports flowed in, but still the fighting increased, and Kennedy increasingly doubted the figures. By late 1962, Diem's situation grew bleak. When Buddhists rioted against his government in May 1963, Kennedy signaled to his South Vietnam ambassador that he would support the replacement of Diem. When the coup came in early November, the President was shocked at its violence: Diem was assassinated by rival generals.

"Sent to all posts, 11/22/63." This photograph of Vice President Lyndon Johnson (left) and President John Kennedy was one of several similar photographs sent to American information posts throughout the world on the day of Kennedy's assassination in order to stress the continuity of government.   (National Archives)

How Kennedy would have dealt with the political coup that followed is unknown. The young American President himself was struck down by an assassin's bullet three weeks later, on November 22, in Dallas. Some evidence indicates that Kennedy was reconsidering Vietnam. He had clearly come to distrust the optimistic reports emanating from the battlefield. His speech at American University on June 10, 1963, indicated a new hesitancy and skepticism about the Cold War. Yet the President had been convinced by his own enthusiasm for counterinsurgency to commit almost 20,000 personnel to Vietnam. Furthermore, it is doubtful that the President had even begun to consider how the United States could terminate its intervention: how to do this in an upcoming election year, when right-wing Republicans could be expected to cry sellout to the Communists.

Many of the programs to uproot poverty and end segregation, to reverse the desperate decay of cities, had their initial hearing in this administration, but they were still in an embryonic state in 1963. Unfinished and still unformed, the Kennedy administration was short on legislative accomplishment but far-reaching in its impact on American society. Reality became indistinguishable from the myths that assuaged the collective guilt and shock most Americans felt at the President's assassination. The young President's style and humor, his wife's cultural activities, gave many Americans the impression of great movement and energy. Kennedy was hated by segregationists and revered by many black Americans, but neither reputation was entirely deserved. In economics, the President touched off the same heat lightning. Even his foreign policies were shifting and changing at the moment of his death. Yet, the effect he had was enormous. His energy helped unleash the idealistic forces that created the splendor, but also the failure, of Lyndon Johnson.

9 The Limits of Liberal Politics: Part II

In the terrible moments of November 22, 1963, after the assassination of John Kennedy in Dallas, on the airplane flying back to Washington, and in the days that followed, Lyndon Johnson skillfully managed a transition of leadership while the nation mourned its young President. Johnson quickly took over the duties of office while the nation fixed its attention upon the pageantry of burial. The new President first persuaded the Cabinet, press corps, and White House staff to remain in office. He offered Jacqueline Kennedy any assistance she might need. And, to quiet speculation, he appointed a special commission, headed by Chief Justice of the Supreme Court, Earl Warren, to investigate Kennedy's assassination and the murder of the suspected assassin, Lee Harvey Oswald, by Jack Ruby. Its task was to lay to rest fears of a political conspiracy. Johnson also decided in these early moments to turn the unfinished legislation of John Kennedy into a monument for the slain leader and a justification of his own administration. He promised to complete the program of domestic legislation and civil rights pending before Congress. Five days after the assassination, he called for action on the civil rights bill as a tribute to Kennedy.

This masterful and quiet assumption of command demonstrated Johnson's immense political skill and his position as a Washington insider. The path to this position of power and influence began in the unlikely place of Stonewall, Texas, on August 27, 1908. Johnson's childhood was a happy one, but tension between his parents took its toll. His mother, Rebekah, relished her "superior advantage," as she put it, and saw in her son "the deep purposefulness and true nobility that had shone in her own father's steady brown eyes." Lyndon's father, on the other hand, had few pretensions to culture or superiority; he was a tough, hard-drinking man with a small-time political career. Perhaps biographer Doris

Kearns is right in ascribing Lyndon's lifelong insecurity and desire to be loved to a struggle between his parents for his affection. But Johnson's personality also reflected contradictions of the Southwest frontier—a place where culture stuck like a thin veneer over a vast terrain of frank brutality and struggle. Johnson grew up only partly his mother's boy. Deeply dependent upon her, he nonetheless nourished an abiding suspicion of the intellectual accomplishments she desired for him.

Lyndon Johnson, when he assumed the presidency in 1963, was a large, unhandsome man, with a slushy drawl. A person with uncommon magnetism and political skill, he had a swollen, but tender ego. Vulgar in private to the point of aggressive crudeness, he became the model of propriety and common-sense morality in public. He could be remarkably generous to those close to him or shockingly brutal. As White House adviser Eric Goldman reported, staff members sometimes left his office white with anger and embarrassment. It amused Johnson to invite the sedate members of his Cabinet or the press corps to swim nude in the White House pool. He often conducted business in the men's room. And White House reporters were always abuzz with his latest homey invective: for example, he declared an opponent so stupid he couldn't "pour piss from a boot with the instructions written on the heel."

Yet, Johnson was a masterful congressional manipulator. Schooled in the politics of the Senate's inner circle, he played the strengths and weaknesses of his fellow senators. More influential than Kennedy or Humphrey or Kefauver, he became the Senate majority leader in January 1955. Not known as a liberal, despite his reverence for F.D.R. and the New Deal, Johnson had been placed on the 1960 presidential ticket to provide geographic weight. The strategy worked well, as Johnson loyally canvassed the South and Southwest for votes. But the results were not satisfactory to him; deprived of his leadership role in the Senate, Johnson agonized over the inactivity and loss of power associated with the vice-presidency. Although Kennedy included him in important decisions, Johnson knew well that some of the President's advisers disliked him, that some mocked his speech behind his back. In return, Johnson disapproved of the late parties, the style and glitter that surrounded the administration.

The chance to be President gave him an opportunity to test himself against the already mythic heroism and accomplishments of Kennedy. In this pursuit, he turned Kennedy's failures into his own triumphs, while Kennedy's hesitations became the new President's passionate goals. On neither score, however, could he disentangle himself from the shadow of his predecessor. Yet, from the beginning, the new President bent his office to his own priorities. It surprised no one when Theodore Sorensen resigned as special counsel to the President in January 1964, less than two months after the assassination. One by one, Kennedy's entourage moved out of office, until only a few of his former advisers remained.

Johnson's first address to Congress as President came on November 27, five days after he assumed office. Stressing the theme, "Let us continue," he pledged enactment of the "ideals" of the Kennedy administration: action on civil rights, taxes, medical care, education, and jobs. He also underscored the need for firmness in Vietnam, warning "those who seek to impose upon us or our allies the yoke of tyranny." Johnson's thrust, however, was to promise success where his predecessor had failed.

If faintly critical, this tone went unnoticed, and Johnson earned praise for eloquently picking up the mantle of power. And, he made good his promises. Reform legislation flowed steadily in 1964, as the President skillfully rolled over legislative roadblocks. By the summer, Congress enacted three large and important programs: a major tax cut bill that reduced the withholding rate from 18 percent to 14 percent and lowered corporate and individual taxes by $11.5 billion; the Civil Rights Act, signed on July 2; and the Equal Opportunity Act, of August, establishing the Office of Economic Opportunity to coordinate the President's "war on poverty." Johnson had guided the passage of reform legislation on a scale matched only by Franklin Roosevelt's first administration during the 1930s.

Johnson's most spectacular victory came in civil rights. Portraying Kennedy's death as a martyrdom and subtly playing upon the desire of Americans to exonerate their society through some formal act of generosity, he called in political favors and applied strong pressure. Johnson succeeded because he worked both aisles of Congress, acquiring crucial Republican support from Republican Charles Halleck, of Indiana, in the House and Everett Dirksen, of Illinois, the minority leader in the Senate. Bypassing Southern opponents, his forces closed off a filibuster and then enacted the most powerful civil rights legislation since the 1860s. The act, essentially the same as introduced in 1963, although sharpened by amendment, created an Equal Employment Opportunity Commission, increased the power of the Civil Rights Commission, strengthened federal capacity to push the desegregation of schools, outlawed segregation in public facilities, and strengthened voting rights through strict regulation of literacy tests. If the act did not achieve integration at one stroke, it did nonetheless knock down most of the visible barriers to equal opportunity.

On taxes, Johnson again proved his mastery of the sideline run. By promising budgetary restraint and lowering projected federal expenses below the plus $100 billion mark for 1964, Johnson effectively neutralized potential opposition to a tax cut from Virginia's Senator Harry Byrd, chairman of the Senate Finance Committee. The effect of the bill matched the anticipations of Johnson and his advisers. It helped increase economic growth and consequently increased federal tax revenues, so that until 1967, the budget deficit was slight: $5.9 billion in 1964, $1.6 billion in 1965, and $3.8 billion in 1966. Unemployment shrank from 5.7 percent to 3.8 percent in 1966, and the inflation rate remained low.

The war on poverty, first suggested by Kennedy, but developed by Johnson, became his most ambitious and original program. Suggested in his State of the Union speech on January 3, 1964, the program began before it had firm legal standing. The President appointed Sargent Shriver, of the Peace Corps, to direct the effort when it became law. In a special message to Congress on March 16, accompanying the proposal for an Economic Opportunity Act, Johnson defined his plans. The major purpose of the legislation would be to centralize scattered and uncoordinated federal anti-poverty activities into one new executive branch office, the Office of Economic Opportunity (OEO). Various titles of the act offered a wide assortment of training programs and support services. The act would set up a job training corps for young people between the ages of sixteen and twenty-one. It encouraged formation of community action groups to assist local agencies in the distribution of comprehensive social services to the poor. It provided grants to farmers to purchase agricultural materials and offered incentive loans to businesses willing to hire the hardcore unemployed. As well as a variety of educational benefits, it offered job training for heads of households currently on public assistance. Finally, the Equal Opportunities Act created VISTA, a domestic peace-corps volunteer service for work in poverty areas. Associated programs, such as Head Start (1965) and Upward Bound (1966), were later

In the late 1960s and early 1970s, many universities became increasingly involved in the affairs of their surrounding communities. Students like this one at the University of Nebraska at Omaha often received academic credit for working as volunteers in the community. (ACTION)

attached to the general program. As *Time* magazine put it in 1964, the OEO reflected the uniquely American belief that "evangelism, money and organization can lick just about anything."

Using a ceiling of $3,000 per year income for a family of four in 1964 as a definition of destitution, this ambitious program proposed to eliminate poverty in America in time for the bicentennial celebration of 1976. Its stress on education, self-help, and equal opportunity represented a culmination of the optimistic, social engineering hopes of modern reformers. Viewed dispassionately, however, it set unrealistic goals. As the authors of the various programs understood, ending poverty was a complex and long-term proposition. While parts of the OEO touched these complexities, for example, by promoting community action and the organization of the poor, other aspects were too limited to have much effect. As conceived and legislated, the OEO never attempted to alter the income shares of rich and poor through taxation, although such a drastic route was probably the only way to eliminate poverty quickly. Nonetheless, presidential rhetoric and media attention to programs implied that the OEO meant to soak the rich and the middle classes. Thus, much of the controversy surrounding the programs came from public misunderstanding of their scope and purposes.

Despite the genuine successes of some OEO programs, difficulties in job corps centers and controversial activities of community action groups brought on increasing opposition. In 1966, leading Republicans effectively attacked the program. By 1968, it was clearly in trouble; President Johnson's attention by then focused almost entirely upon the war in Vietnam. The deterioration of the total approach to poverty began when pieces of the OEO were lopped off and programs, such as Head Start, were transferred to the Department of Health, Education, and Welfare in early 1969.

As the war in Vietnam began to suck funds out of the federal budget, programs like the OEO became domestic casualties. Johnson could not keep his promise of guns and butter. But, beyond funding and administrative problems, thinking about poverty was seriously limited. Being poor in America was not just bad luck or the accident of birth; it had fundamental structural and cultural causes, compounded by race and class divisions, that the war on poverty could not eliminate. Yet the President's grandiose rhetoric seemed to indicate his commitment to radical change. This created bewilderment among those supposed to be the recipients of change and angry opposition from thousands of taxpayers convinced that their hard-earned dollars were budgeted for a social revolution.

Early in 1965, however, President Johnson remained exhilarated with his legislative victories and his enormous electoral triumph over Republican Barry Goldwater in the fall presidential election. Now a President in his own right, Johnson pushed another wave of legislative programs through Congress, including Medicare, establishing compulsory hospital insurance for the elderly and voluntary medical insurance. Along with this program, Congress passed Medicaid for those below the age of sixty-five unable to pay for medical services. Other legislative victories included a new Civil Rights Voting Act (August 1965), which eliminated literacy tests, as well as other restrictive practices designed to keep blacks away from the polls. In August, Johnson fulfilled another Kennedy promise by securing a law to create the Department of Housing and Urban Development, authorized to subsidize the rents of low-income families. More legislation followed: federal aid to higher education, the Urban Mass Transportation Act of 1966, a Demonstration Cities Bill, the Clean Water Restoration Act, the Highway Beautification Act, and others. This remarkable burst of lawmaking, touching everything from the arts to education, from air pollution to poverty, testified to Johnson's power and versatility. Johnson's programs epitomized the notion that social reform could be achieved by technical adjustments to the economy. Based upon his own experience during the 1930s, his genuine commitment to ending poverty and racism, and his own immense self-confidence and belief in the effectiveness of federal government programs, he orchestrated a national attack on a myriad of serious social problems. But, like Johnson's thinking about his office, his programs lacked coherence and sustained support. Once created, an innovative program required careful funding, caretaking, and coordination. The "Great Society," as Johnson named his collective efforts, required executive talents and attention beyond his capacity. In this way, the social reform of the mid-1960s increased social tensions by promising more than it could deliver.

Poor and black Americans gave Johnson an early and sharp indication that his programs raised frustrations as well as hopes. The programs that gushed through the federal pipeline probably intensified black demands. As much as Johnson sympathized with the poor or adopted the rhetorical goals of the early civil rights movement, he could not contain the revolution of rising expectations, whose fires he stoked. Beginning in the summer of 1964, American cities began to explode one after another, as if tied to the same short fuse. These riots intensified each year, through the summer of 1968, making the Johnson years among the most violent and unsettled of this century.

Urban riots, destruction of property, and intractable demands of black civil rights organizations in the North distressed and confused many Americans. Gallup polls from 1963 onward reflected this anguish. Americans consistently included civil rights agitation with the most serious and worrisome problems—crime and lawlessness, the war in Vietnam, high prices and unemployment. Public opinion also indicated that Kennedy and Johnson moved further and quicker on civil rights than most Americans wanted. Indeed, white resentment over integration crested in 1964 and 1968 in the presidential candidacy of Governor George Wallace, of Alabama. Wallace not only articulated anti-integrationist sentiment, but he also attacked federal interference in state and local affairs.

The polarity in American society that President Johnson tried to reduce with legislation and encouraging words revealed itself in the report of the National Advisory Commission on Civil Disorders, headed by Governor Otto Kerner, of Illinois. Appointed in late July 1967, after severe urban rioting across the nation left sixty-three dead, hundreds injured, and thousands arrested, Kerner and his board of labor leaders, law-enforcement officers, businessmen, and prominent blacks considered evidence and reported in 1968. Warning against the possible degeneration of American society into two distinct and warring civilizations, one white and the other black, the Kerner report confirmed what many sociologists and political leaders already felt about official investigations. They repeated shopworn advice and warned about possibilities that already existed. Although the Kerner Commission argued that "white racism" lay behind the riots, opinion polls taken in 1968 discovered that only about one-third of Americans agreed with this conclusion.

Confusion about integration degenerated into bitter resentment and backlash by the end of Johnson's administration, but the President continued to propose more civil rights legislation. After the summer riots of 1967, the President angrily warned lawbreakers that they would be punished: "Violence must be stopped, quickly, finally, and permanently." Yet, his solution remained political: a legislative "attack—mounted at every level—upon the conditions that breed despair and violence."

Liberal legislation and more programs constituted Johnson's panacea for racial turmoil but they represented an end, not a further evolution of broad attacks upon inequality. In the last year of his administration, he successfully sought a new civil rights act, signed on April 11, 1968, barring discrimination in most American housing. Yet this last act was consummated in tragedy. On April 4, Martin Luther King, Jr. was assassinated by a sniper in Memphis, Tennessee. King's death touched off riots in over 120 American cities. In this angry reflex, urban disorder resulted in more deaths and arrests. This time, however, the riots seemed to have a lasting, splintering effect. After 1968, civil rights legislation stalled, and the black movement sputtered.

Urban riots, assassinations, rising crime statistics, and mounting antiwar protests on college campuses etched a picture of America in violent colors. After the murder of Senator Robert Kennedy on June 5, 1968 by a Jordanian immigrant, Sirhan Bishara Sirhan, President Johnson appointed another national commission, instructed to explore the causes of violence in America. Headed by Milton Eisenhower and including clergymen and legislators, the commission was charged to discover what caused Americans to "inflict such suffering on ourselves." Reporting a year-and-a-half later, the commission summarized the conclusions of its various task forces. Many of its proposals sensibly aimed at solving underlying social problems—even questioning large defense expenditures and calling for reordered social priorities. Anything of the sort, however, fell on deaf ears. In 1969 and 1970, concern for violence had evolved into a national obsession with law and order. Congress increasingly became hostile to anything resembling a change in priorities. As early in 1967, for example, the House refused to consider a $40 million rat extermination program for urban ghettos, even after, much to its embarrassment, Washington newspapers revealed the substantial sums spent on rat control in the Capitol building itself.

☆ ☆ ☆

If anyone, President Johnson inadvertently reordered priorities in his own administration by focusing attention on the war in Vietnam. Over and above his enviable legislative victories, the war loomed larger and larger, until it almost entirely blocked his vision. Johnson's initial decisions about Vietnam established the character of American escalation: increased force applied to a deteriorating situation. Not privy to his predecessor's growing frustration with the war, the new President had to make the decisions that would have eventually revealed the scope of Kennedy's reservations. In late 1963 and early 1964, Johnson tried to maintain quiet on the Vietnam front, in order to consolidate his administration and gather dependable advisers around him. This came to mean shifting men who had enthusiasm for a tough line on Vietnam into prominent positions on the White House staff. A serious complication emerged outside the administration. Preparing for the Republican party convention in 1964, enthusiasts for Barry Goldwater built a powerful, conservative movement. Should Johnson demonstrate weakness on Vietnam, he might be ambushed in the presidential election. By downplaying the war, however, he could present himself as a moderate.

The President's own views, as he revealed them, defined Vietnam through a scrim of 1930s analogies. He repeatedly invoked the "Munich" analogy, based upon belief that British and French appeasement of Hitler had brought on World War II. This he combined with Eisenhower's "domino theory," a simplistic view of containment that pictured Communism as a single force emanating from the Kremlin, and able, with increasing momentum, to topple one strategic nation after another. Behind both analogies lay a deep suspicion that Western capitalism lacked force and resolve to prevent the spread of Communism.

The other half of Johnson's view derived from a positive vision of the 1930s. He hoped to offer the Vietnamese—if they accepted American intervention—a Southeast Asian version of the New Deal. "I want to leave the footprints of America in Vietnam," he said in 1966. "I want them to say when the Americans come, this is what they leave—schools, not long cigars. We're going to turn the Mekong [River] into a Tennessee Valley." A Mekong River Redevelopment Commission would prepare a massive system of dams, power plants, and water projects to rebuild the country once the war ended.

Inside the administration, Johnson listened carefully to the leading hawks among his advisers. As he told reporters early in his tenure, "I have found the myth of McNamara to be true." The myth he referred to was the belief in McNamara's absolute administrative competence.

Early in 1964, Johnson made several moves up the ladder of escalation. In January, he approved plans to step up covert harassment of North Vietnam. He began more and more to depend upon men in the defense and foreign relations bureaucracy who had convinced themselves that increased bombing would cut off the Viet Cong from supplies and strengthen the generals now controlling Saigon. This interpretation rested upon two questionable assumptions: that the Viet Cong rebels actually depended upon the North and that bombing would not touch off increased infiltration of arms and armies from the North. The President also shifted leadership inside the American command in South Vietnam, replacing General Paul D. Harkins with General William C. Westmoreland. In this new position, Westmoreland pushed his strategy of open and increased American combat.

These decisions were either hidden or downplayed, but they set the stage for a public event during the summer that provided Johnson with authorization to wage war. On July 30, 1964, South Vietnam P T boats attacked bases in the Bay of Tonkin area of North Vietnam. Almost simultaneously, an American destroyer, the *Maddox*, steamed into the area on a mission to disrupt North Vietnamese communications. On August 2, North Vietnamese P T boats attacked the *Maddox*, probably interpreting its presence as cover for the South Vietnam attack. The *Maddox* returned fire and sank one of the attack ships. Receiving news of the attack, Johnson ordered the *Maddox* to remain in the area, while he sent another ship, the *C. Turner Joy*, into the bay. On August 3, both destroyers reported that they had been attacked. Johnson and his advisers then decided to use this skirmish as a pretext to retaliate, sending bombers into North Vietnam to destroy naval targets. That evening, the President summoned Congressional leaders to inform them of the incident—minus any background details about the activities of the American or South Vietnamese navies. He requested their support of his bombing raids, and he suggested that Congress specifically confirm his power to protect American interests in South Vietnam. Despite spirited opposition by Senators Wayne Morse, of Oregon, and Ernest Gruening, of Alaska, the resulting Bay of Tonkin Resolution, sponsored by Foreign Relations Committee chairman William Fulbright, of Arkansas, sailed through the Senate on August 7. Johnson had a mandate to pursue full-fledged war in North and South Vietnam.

In addition to providing legal justification for policy, the Bay of Tonkin incident perfectly fit the pattern of American escalation: an incident provoked by North Vietnam, the Viet Cong, or the United States itself became justification for increasing firepower or troop levels. And, as American forces became stronger and more active, the Viet Cong also mobilized, while North Vietnam began to infiltrate troops and material into the South in large quantities. In turn, this buildup on both sides weakened the South Vietnamese government, requiring further American intervention. Thus, pretext became cause in a never-ending upward spiral of men, arms, and destruction.

For most of 1964, after the Tonkin Resolution, Johnson played down America's Vietnam role. As anticipated, the Republicans nominated Arizona conservative Barry Goldwater for president. Also, true to predictions, Goldwater proved unwilling and unable to distance himself from the right-wing John Birch Society, which had canvassed for his nomination. Goldwater rewarded these followers with a widely quoted line in his acceptance speech: "Let me remind you," he said, "that moderation in the pursuit of justice is no virtue, and I would remind you that extremism in the defense of liberty is no vice." The Democrats didn't need to sling charges in his direction; Goldwater had declared himself an "extremist." Even the Republican National Committee seemed fated to smear its own candidate. When it adopted the slogan, "In your heart you know he's right," it inspired a rhapsody of parodies on other parts of the body: "In your guts you know he's nuts," for example. In case the American public missed the point, the Democrats exhibited a television commercial showing a small girl plucking the petals from a daisy, followed by a picture of an atomic blast, followed by words urging voters to support Johnson. The implications of this political montage couldn't be clearer: a vote for Goldwater meant a vote for war.

Nothing the Republicans could do would have changed the election, for Johnson's legislative successes, his sensitive, self-assured role as executor of John Kennedy's political legacy made him an unbeatable candidate. The mood of the country was polarized, but still largely liberal. By choosing Hubert Humphrey as his running mate, he confirmed active aid of the Democratic party's liberal and labor wing. The results disclosed one of the great landslide victories of American electoral history: Johnson gathered 61 percent of the vote and Goldwater only 38.5 percent. Whatever the American public thought were the issues of the campaign, however, a vote for Johnson was not a repudiation of war.

With a landslide victory behind him and a vigorous Democratic majority in both houses of Congress, the President moved ahead quickly on his legislative program. At the same time, he walked straight into a bog of war. For the next four years, escalation continued, and the effects of war returned home in a rising tide of inflation, protest, and uncertainty. At first reluctant to commit American troops to a ground war in continental Asia, Johnson also refused to consider withdrawal without face-saving concessions from the North Vietnamese. Daily, he became more preoccupied with selecting bombing sites or reading reports on "body counts"— enemy casualties that were puffed up by American commanders in Saigon. Increasingly too, Johnson cut himself off from his great strength in the political wisdom of Congress. He defined hesitation and dissent as weakness and honest press coverage as hostile bias. The President had changed his own personal priorities, sacrificing good political sense to the prosecution of a victoryless war.

Never friendly to intellectuals, Johnson became the object of scorn and satire. His reaction was angry yet cautious. Early in his administration, he invited historian Eric Goldman to act as liaison with the academy. Goldman convinced him to sponsor a White House Festival of the Arts in June 1965. Johnson liked the idea. It had a Kennedy ring to it, and it would establish the President as a patron of the arts. But Johnson was shocked and infuriated when poet Robert Lowell, one of the invited guests, published a letter stating his refusal to attend. Other intellectuals followed suit, explaining that their principled opposition to the war in Vietnam made it impossible for them to come.

Those who opposed the President were reacting to a series of escalations undertaken over the winter. Convinced by his advisers, among whom only Hubert Humphrey—temporarily—and George Ball—openly—dissented, Johnson agreed to more troops and more bombing. In February 1965, after a Viet Cong attack at the American base in Pleiku, the President ordered retaliation raids against Northern targets and authorized regular bombing sorties one week later. In the spring, he agreed to Westmoreland's call for offensive American action, dubbed "search and destroy" tactics, in the oblique parlance of the war. By the summer, the United States had

General William C. Westmoreland (center right) thanks entertainer Bob Hope for his many years of service to American troops in the field. Vietnam, December 24, 1965. (U.S. Army Photograph, Photo by Sp4 Ralph Boatwright)

over 30,000 troops in South Vietnam and over 185,000 by the end of the year. When Johnson claimed that nothing had changed and that conditions were improving, the reverse was true.

Johnson's embattled foreign policy in Vietnam pushed him into hasty action elsewhere. In the Dominican Republic, during the years that followed the overthrow of Rafael Trujillo in 1961, that country passed through instability and political turmoil. In April 1965, open conflict erupted between forces supporting reformer Juan Bosch and those backing more conservative army officers. As the conflict grew, the American ambassador hastily wired Washington that American lives were in danger: "The time has come to land the Marines." The President agreed and ordered in American forces, not just to prevent attacks on American nationals, but to prevent Bosch from steering the small republic on a leftward course. Eventually 22,000 Americans landed, and their presence enabled a government acceptable to Washington to assume power. Foreign aid, private investment, and stability eventually returned.

In his State of the Union message in January 1966, Johnson began a long review of foreign affairs with a strange sentence: "Tonight," he solemnized, "the cup of peril is full in Vietnam." It was indeed, but the President himself had already drunk deeply from its bitter brew. Promising not to rob resources from social programs to pay for the Asian war, he was, in fact, preparing to do so. He grossly underestimated the costs of Vietnam at around $5.8 billion a year, and he advocated no new taxes. Putting the most favorable appraisal on the face of conflict, he declared: "The enemy is no longer close to victory."

Nothing in the remainder of the year warranted this optimism. Convinced by Westmoreland and Defense Department experts, the President committed 385,000 American troops to the conflict by the end of the year. Expenditures for stepped-up air strikes and naval maneuvers added to the cost of this expeditionary force. At home, military expenditures distorted the federal budget; with no new revenues, the government escalated deficits and borrowing. Inside the administration, Johnson faced increasing uneasiness. National Security Adviser McGeorge Bundy quit to take a position heading the Ford Foundation. Johnson replaced him with Walt Whitman Rostow, an enthusiast for the war. In the fall, critic George Ball quietly left his position in the State Department. Feeling it useless to issue a blast at Vietnam policy, Ball reluctantly admitted his ineffectiveness in the administration. The most

Vietnam, 1966

General Lewis Hershey, head of the Selective Service System, indicates his own birthday and position on the draft eligibility chart. The lottery system of determining draft eligibility by birthdate, while continuing the policy of student deferments, made conscription controversial during the war in Vietnam.   (Courtesy, Ted Green)

important doubter was Robert McNamara. After a trip to Saigon in October, where he repeatedly questioned bogus body-count figures and unwarranted optimism, the Secretary of Defense returned, shaken, although not yet a convinced opponent of the war. He did, however, order a careful historical study of American policy in Vietnam and assigned Daniel Ellsberg to the task. Taking his own doubts to his research, Ellsberg uncovered a secret history of intervention and deceit revealed in classified documents. So disturbed was he, that he later defied all rules of security and passed his report to *The New York Times* for publication in 1971. The result was the *Pentagon Papers*. McNamara himself gave way to serious questioning in 1967; on learning this, the President abruptly moved him out of Defense and into a job as head of the World Bank. But even his replacement, long-time Democratic party stalwart Clark Clifford, appointed in early 1968, worked on the inside to prevent further escalation of the war.

Defections from his administration, mounting criticism in Congress, the loss of forty-seven House and three Senate seats in the 1966 elections, at first did nothing to deflect Johnson from his course; they only isolated him further. The master politician succumbed to the ideologue, and Johnson turned his large talents to the single purpose of winning the war. During 1967, escalation continued, with about 100,000 more American troops pouring into the beleaguered country. From the North, Communist units continued to infiltrate south, despite the fury of American air strikes. As draft calls mounted at home, critics took stronger and stronger stands, compelled, they felt, by the crumbling social and political consensus. An important sign of the times appeared when Martin Luther King, Jr., joined opponents of the war, stating that the United States had become "the greatest purveyor of violence in the world today." In King's mind, the administration had sacrificed the struggles of black Americans to a war in Asia.

Nonetheless, Johnson persisted. Orchestrating bombing pauses, often followed by more devastating raids, the President offered negotiations to the North Vietnamese in December 1966, February 1967, December 1967, and finally, again in March 1968. The North Vietnamese, led by Ho Chi Minh, however, rebuffed his offers. They refused to accept a permanent, separate, anti-Communist enclave in South Vietnam, allied to the United States. On this point, they were adamant.

In early 1968, the United States had stationed over 500,000

Two Viet Cong suspects captured in Hobo Woods during Operation "Crimp." (U.S. *Army Photograph, Photo by Sgt. Bernie Mangiboyat)*

Soldier-artists and Army photographers sometimes recorded their shock and dismay at the war in Vietnam in their work.

Left—"*Death in the Delta*," by Col. Robert Riggs, Vietnam, 1963. (*U.S. Army Photograph, Army Art Collection*)

Right—"*The Parentless Ones*," by Col. Robert Riggs, Vietnam, 1963. (*U.S. Army Photograph, Army Art Collection*)

troops in Vietnam. Inflation and budget deficits mounted so rapidly that Johnson acceded to demands of his economic advisers and pushed for a tax surcharge. In effect a 10 percent war tax, the bill remained stuck in Congress for a year, but the message was clear enough: Johnson finally admitted the real cost of war. Early spring brought worse news from the battlefield. During the Tet lunar New Year holiday, a massive Viet Cong offensive destroyed the credibility of Johnson's assurances about the war. Beginning in January and lasting for almost a month, the struggle challenged American forces everywhere. Viet Cong forces besieged the American Embassy in Saigon and took over several urban centers, including the ancient ceremonial city of Hue. Although American and South Vietnamese armies eventually won back the cities, the Viet Cong had delivered a serious blow to American willingness to fight, a lesson replayed nightly in television news broadcasts, which cut deeply into the confidence and sense of purpose many Americans had felt about the war. When General Westmoreland requested more troops in the thousands, the futility of United States strategy was apparent.

For Johnson, the battle presented a shock that demanded attention. Deception, half-truths, and secrecy no longer protected him from critics. On March 12, in the New Hampshire presidential primary, liberal Minnesota Senator Eugene McCarthy shepherded antiwar sentiment into a large vote that almost upset the incumbent. With opposition rising in his own party and Congress rumbling, Johnson exercised the political acumen that had escaped him for several years. In late March, he summoned his Senior Advisory Group on Vietnam to Washington. In a moment reminiscent of Truman's first conference on the Cold War, military men and political figures joined Dean Acheson, Arthur Dean, McGeorge Bundy, Douglas Dillon, and John McCloy in informing the President that his policy had lost the support of a great many Americans, including the business establishment. Johnson realized that he could not continue. As a candidate for reelection, he would tear open the Democratic party. On March 31, he announced his withdrawal from the race. It was perhaps the saddest moment, but still a brave one, in his political life.

The withdrawal was even more bitter, because he abandoned the field to Robert Kennedy. While Kennedy waited until the shock of New Hampshire to announce his own candidacy, he immediately captured support in primaries and from powers in the

Democratic party. Once a zealot in pursuit of labor union racketeers, Kennedy had gradually adopted a position of strong support for integration and opposition to the war. He was, by 1968, the liberal and humanitarian alter ego of his brother, and he was a favorite of many party leaders.

Johnson's step, however, settled nothing. Bitter months followed with violent urban riots and the final confrontation at Chicago between the police of Mayor Daley and protesters supporting the candidacy of Eugene McCarthy. As convention delegates moved inexorably to nominate Hubert Humphrey, the nation watched a pitched battle between police and protesters.

The political exit of Lyndon Johnson in a hail of controversy obscured significant foreign policy events of his last years: the containment of the June 1967 conflict in the Middle East, when Israel defeated Egypt, Jordan, and Syria; the Nuclear Nonproliferation Treaty with the Soviet Union in 1967; and the successful return of the crew of the spy ship *Pueblo*, seized in early 1968 while on mission near North Korea. All of these events were buried in an avalanche of bad news from Vietnam.

After eight years, the words spoken by John Kennedy at his inauguration became eerily true. In 1968, the world had entered a dangerous and terrible period, when civilization seemed threatened. But the rhetoric of idealism evoked on that cold morning in 1961 and reaffirmed every year since, had soured into clots of opposition and bitterness. By 1968, the political system was impoverished and exhausted, and Americans prepared to select a new President by default.

10 The Awakening: Beyond Liberalism

One of the most successful science fiction movies of the 1950s, *The Invasion of the Body Snatchers* (1956), pitted moral bravery against conformity. In this disturbing tale of mind-controlling invaders from outer space, the whole population of a town is gradually replaced by blank-staring replicas of human beings. This destruction of the soul entirely deprives each citizen of privacy. With no resistance and no conscience, each individual acts out the prearranged plans of conquest. Mindlessly happy, the transformed person becomes a willing participant in the film's horrifying version of mass society. Only one man escapes, fleeing up onto a freeway buzzing with fast-moving cars. Vainly trying to stop someone, to wake the nation to a threat it should have anticipated he cries, "They're here already!" Perhaps the "they" is Communism, or the manipulators of mass culture, but whatever the inspiration, the fear takes the shape of conformity: unfeeling, unemotional inaction. In this film, inability to act or focus moral attention on duty is a typical community failing. Only the solitary individual perceives the threat.

The conformity depicted in this film expressed itself during the 1950s as an ideology of compromise. Yet, the 1950s were also a time of enormous social ferment. Much of this ferment began as a reaction to the low-key politics of the Eisenhower administration and the limited appeal of contemporary liberalism. Around a variety of issues, a number of new movements organized to challenge the status quo in religion, politics, and culture. Some of these favored right-wing causes; some favored more radical causes; some focused primarily on cultural or religious issues. But all of them shared a sense of the inadequacy of American politics—the prevailing liberal theories of the day—to solve the larger problems of society. All of them shared a yearning for a moral, ethical, even religious awakening. By the late 1960s, these movements had become the most important phenomena in American culture.

The wave of idealism that swept American society in the 1960s had its origins in the feeling that conformity masked moral and political inertia. Despite appearances, America in the early 1950s was still reacting to the profound disturbances and aftershocks of World War II. The unfinished business of war, the ideological challenge from Third World revolutions and Communism, and the unresolved domestic inequities required resolution. Beset by these demands, many Americans began a reevaluation of their institutions in a fashion that invoked some of the oldest political and religious traditions of the nation. This movement, beginning in the 1950s, had all the confusion and contradictory facets of earlier awakenings, as in the 1830s and 1840s, when a similar extraordinary mix of women's rights, radical democratic ideas, communitarian experiments, concern for black Americans, and conservative evangelical religion burst into the mainstream of American politics. During the 1950s and 1960s, these same causes reappeared in a new guise. Once again, millions of Americans reaffirmed an old and traditional faith that society could not be guided by politics alone. Whatever the bias of their politics—left or right—they occupied the edges of the same culture that envisioned America as the beacon of hope and rectitude for the world—the single grand exception.

One of the leading students of such reform periods, Arthur M. Schlesinger, Jr., wrote *The Vital Center* in 1950. This justly renowned tract examined the nature and resilience of American society. To Schlesinger, the political philosophy of liberalism (embodied in the New Deal interventionist state) constituted the "vital center" of American society. Providing a lighted path between the darkness of left and right philosophies, liberalism, he wrote, could solve most domestic social problems and face the ideological challenges of the Cold War. Schlesinger recognized that liberalism occupied the center of American politics in the 1950s—even the Republicans accepted its basic premises. He also realized that liberalism seriously needed an infusion of vitality and energy.

Understanding this, Schlesinger hoped to ground a new, lean, and combative liberal philosophy in religious insights. Borrowing some of the theological premises of Reinhold Niebuhr, he adopted a tough-minded, even pessimistic stance toward achieving a just society. He also affirmed Niebuhr's suggestion that the balance attained in welfare capitalism by the competing claims of labor unions and capital would ultimately benefit all of society. Aware of individual sin and social evil, modern society should proceed cautiously toward the goals of justice. To Schlesinger, Niebuhr's neo-orthodox Protestantism affirmed vital liberalism; it sustained a belief in American ideals at "a high pitch of vibration."

Many Americans in the 1950s and 1960s agreed with Schlesinger that liberalism occupied the center of domestic political philosophy, but they disagreed that it had either the political vitality or moral breadth to solve the immense social problems of the day. In its ascendancy in 1950, liberalism was besieged from all sides by 1968. Schlesinger's firmest assumption became the era's most persistent doubt: was liberalism vital?

A search for the vital center of American civilization preoccupied a multitude of authors in the late 1940s and early 1950s. Reevaluations of democratic society streamed from the pens of American historians, sociologists, philosophers, and political scientists. This purpose even inspired a new academic discipline, American studies, dedicated to defining the distinct features of American civilization. Begun in earnest during World War II, at institutions such as Princeton and Vassar, the study spread rapidly after the war to several large state institutions. By 1949, it had a journal, *The American Quarterly*, and by 1951, a professional association. Probably the most famous work in this field was Henry Nash Smith's *Virgin Land*, published in 1950. This book explored the nature and uses of agrarian myths in the United States and, by implication, suggested some of the reasons for the distinctiveness of American culture.

Not only political liberals and academics sought to define an essential Americanism during these years. The same goal energized Senator Joseph McCarthy and his anti-Communist movement. McCarthyism and liberalism shared the premise that essential American traditions should be revered and foreign ideas rejected. Yet, in the hands of the Wisconsin senator, the notion of orthodoxy became the inspiration for inquisition. He turned his tactics of bluster, intimidation, and innuendo against a Democratic party establishment that surely did not merit the accusation of being soft on Communism. He transformed "un-Americanism" into a partisan issue. Gathering support on the state and local level, in the press, and in the Catholic hierarchy, McCarthy linked anti-

Communism to suspicion of Easterners, ethnic and racial minorities, and political radicals, in a mixture that threatened to create a "know-nothing" coalition of broad proportions.

McCarthyism also precipitated a crisis in liberal philosophy by challenging its claim as the vital defender of tradition. The question of rights of free speech for American Communist party members and sympathizers seriously split the liberal community. Firings of left-wing professors and the intellectual justification for intolerance of opinion divided liberal organizations like the American Civil Liberties Union. Verbal warfare between intellectuals reached a fevered pitch, as journals, such as the *Nation*, rushed to defend the rights of Communists, while others, like the *New Leader* denied them. The most sophisticated justification for denying rights to Communists probably came from philosopher Sidney Hook's book, *Heresy Yes, Conspiracy No*, published in 1953. Despite his intelligence and care, the book lent intellectual stature to the elusive and impossible attempt to define true Americanism.

What some defended as vital orthodoxy, critics of American culture and society denounced as conformity. In February 1951, *Fortune* magazine published a scathing attack on the new impulse to conform. Contemporary Americans, wrote the editors, had lost touch with society. No one, they complained, could explain the meaning of American principles. Other social critics shared *Fortune*'s puzzlement about conformity. Beginning in 1951 and 1952, marked at mid-point by Alan Valentine's *Age of Conformity* (1954), and rising to a peak in 1956 and 1957, scores of books and popular magazine articles deplored the blandness of American society, the insipid quality of opinion, and the decline of intellectual curiosity. When the *Reader's Digest* discovered the problem in December 1958 and published "The Danger of Being Too Well Adjusted," the discussion of conformity reached barbershops, doctors' waiting rooms, and millions of homes.

Yet few observers could agree about the causes of conformity. Opinion ranged from David Riesman's picture of the *Lonely Crowd* and philosopher Hannah Arendt's perceptive remarks about mass society to religious assaults on conformist Christianity, corporate second thoughts about large enterprise and government regulation, and popular fears about the impact of television. There was no real accord on defining the conformity syndrome, just a vague set of symptoms without a prescription for cure. To critics, conformity symbolized a lack of motion in society, the effects of McCarthyism, and the soporific effects of Eisenhower's low-keyed presidency.

To theologian Will Herberg, conformity had transformed even competing religions into a vague "civic religion." As he understood it, civic religion was a shared Jewish, Protestant, and Catholic theology that "validates culture and society, without in any sense bringing them under judgment." Looking at the 1950s, Herberg noted that major American religious sects had gradually grown together; all of them accepted tolerance and pluralism; all of them claimed religious belief as a fundamental part of citizenship; all of them believed that religion validated the American way of life. As Dwight Eisenhower put it: "Our government makes no sense unless it is founded in a deeply felt religious faith—and I don't care what it is." Or, in the words of the popular song "I Believe," released in 1952: for the flowers that grow and candles that glow, for prayers that are heard, for leaves, for sky, for babies' cries. In other words, faith was nondoctrinal—simply belief in belief. Perhaps most typical of nondenominational uplift was Norman Vincent Peale's *The Power of Positive Thinking*, published in 1952. Culminating almost two decades of work in religious broadcasting and publishing, Peale's book combined elements of modern psychology, self-help religion, and traditional Protestantism into a prescription for happiness and success.

Statistics measuring religiosity moved upward during the 1950s. Church membership rose from 57 percent to 64 percent of the population. Bible sales increased suddenly and dramatically from 1949 to 1953. Church attendance remained high throughout the decade. In 1954, 96 percent of persons interviewed in a Gallup poll declared their belief in God. In 1964, 63 percent claimed they prayed frequently; only 6 percent admitted they never prayed. As late as 1968, America topped Greece, the European nation with the highest recorded extent of belief: in God, the existence of afterlife, and the reality of hell. New church construction approached $1 billion in 1958, over twice the funds devoted to construction of public hospitals and a little less than one-third devoted to public school construction. In 1953, a religious fiction book, *The Robe*, made the best-seller list for the first time since 1943, while, in that same year, five of six nonfiction best-sellers had a religious theme.

Despite this placid surface of tolerance and conformity, conservative and evangelical sects grew rapidly, indicating dissatisfaction with the religious status quo. Lutherans, Baptists, Catholics, Latter-Day Saints, and the Church of Christ gained members much more rapidly than liberal, suburbanized congregations. Thus, while the liberal National Council of Churches worked out a revised standard and updated version of the Bible, moved toward eliminating differences between faiths, and took liberal stands on social issues, many conservative congregations rejected this aspect of civic religion, searching for faith in more traditional experiences of revivalism.

Revivalism during the 1950s drew upon the particular strength and talent of two great evangelistic preachers: Baptist Billy Graham and Catholic Monsignor Fulton J. Sheen. Both men combined a conservative political orientation, fundamentalism, and media appeal that made them as much cultural celebrities as religious leaders. Both skillfully used television to bring vitalized religion into millions of American living rooms.

Fulton Sheen's weekly television series, *Life Is Worth Living*, began in 1951 and extended through 1957. A leading television personality of the day, Sheen often outdrew Milton Berle's comedy show at the same hour. Sheen was an experienced radio showman, as well as a television star, and he credited both media with spiritual attributes, calling them "beautiful examples of the inspired wisdom of the ages." Projecting a relaxed and friendly image, he examined moral and political problems, spicing his serious remarks with poetry, jokes about Milton Berle, and amusing asides about his role as a TV priest.

Born in the small town of El Paso, Illinois, and educated in St. Paul, Minnesota, Catholic University in Washington, D.C., and in Europe, Sheen was known for his firm anti-Communism. No doubt this reputation helped account for the most famous conversions he precipitated: Clare Booth Luce, the playwright, and Louis Budenz and Elizabeth Bentley, two renowned anti-Communist witnesses for the House Committee on Un-American Activities. Dismayed by the progress of Communism worldwide, Sheen doubly felt America's need for spiritual revival. He explained the drift of American culture as a movement into "spiritual vacuum." In his first television show, he asked a question that troubled many other observers in the 1950s: "Is life worth living, or is it dull and monotonous?" To Sheen, the answer was emphatically, yes! life had a purpose. He repeated this message through his nondoctrinal religiosity, his comforting moralisms, and his patriotism.

Another brilliant master of religious drama, and even more widely known than Bishop Sheen, was revivalist Billy Graham. Born in 1918 into a strict Scotch Presbyterian family, Graham experienced a deep religious conversion at the age of sixteen. Relinquishing thoughts of becoming a professional baseball player, he dedicated himself to spreading the news of his awakening. After Wheaton College in Illinois, he worked on a weekly radio religious broadcast, *Songs in the Night*. His growing reputation then led to an invitation to join Youth for Christ. By 1944, he achieved his first success as a revivalist preacher in Chicago. By 1948, Graham had put together a large organization for the production of revivalist meetings. In 1949, he completed a three-week crusade in Los Angeles, with song leader Cliff Barrows and soloist George Beverly Shea, converting thousands of men and women and attracting the attention of William Randolph Hearst. Spotlighted by Hearst's national newspaper chain, Graham became a celebrity by 1950, planning international crusades and meeting with important world leaders. Measured in numbers, Graham's success was remarkable. By 1955, his national headquarters in Minnesota had 125 employees and a budget of $2 million annually. His radio show, *The Hour of Decision*, beamed into 1,000 stations with 20 million regular listeners.

At the beginning of his career, regular Protestant churches often refused to welcome Graham, but as his success increased, so did his acceptance. Relying primarily upon public conversion, he preached a message of anti-Communism, antimaterialism, and faith in the capacity of conversion to overcome moral perils, like divorce and juvenile delinquency. He rejected reliance upon progress, political institutions, and social reform.

Graham's sermons reflected a keen awareness of contemporary social issues and the format of his radio and television shows incorporated the cultural tastes of his audiences. His homey language suggested companionship and intimacy. For example, in his *Talks to Teenagers*, he depicted Christ as a sort of baseball star: "Christ is the Hero and Idol of my heart."

Attuned to some issues, Graham often remained silent on social questions like integration. Touting "rugged individualism," he criticized powerful labor leaders, strikes, and "socialistic" legislation. Consequently, he was a welcome guest at the Republican White House during the 1950s and a frequent golf partner of Vice-President Nixon. By the late 1960s, he had become something of a Protestant confessor to Nixon, who recounted that Graham, during long walks on the beach in 1968, had helped him decide to make a race for the presidency. Graham's social and cultural conservatism did not, however, become completely partisan. His first priority was souls, not votes. Deeply disturbed by the smug, complacent attitude of the 1950s, he sought to restoke the fires of revivalism.

☆   ☆   ☆

To the avowed right wing, the problem of complacency and conformity resulted from twenty years of Democratic liberalism, as well as religious lassitude. The ascendancy of William F. Buckley—witty, sarcastic pundit on the right—quickened right-wing thought in the 1950s. Buckley's new magazine, *The National Review*, begun in 1955, lent coherence and direction to conservative criticism of liberals. His first book, *God and Man at Yale*, appeared in 1951, a youthful but interesting attack on his alma mater. Offended by the liberal economics and social reformism espoused by his professors, Buckley lectured his readers on the merits of academic reorganization. He proposed to reconstruct Yale as the mirror of business corporation. In his model, the alumni, who financed the school occupied the position of owners of the corporation; students were its consumers. This left the professor in the anomolous position of employee, hired to create a product— that is, to teach the ideals defined by the alumni. In Buckley's estimation, these ideals ought to be private enterprise, individualism, and religion. Existing academic freedom, which allowed professors to teach their own ideals, subverted this purpose. Therefore, teachers should be required to subscribe to established notions or should be invited to leave to find another university that espoused their principles.

This sacrifice of free speech to the free marketplace reappeared as the basis of a second book, published in 1954. In this tract, *McCarthy and His Enemies*, Buckley once again proclaimed his intolerance of ideas that he felt were generally despised. Defending McCarthy, Buckley could not agree that American Communists had the right to civil liberties.

Like many conservative intellectuals of the day, Buckley devoted his efforts primarily to right-wing journalism, not serious political organizing. Nonetheless, important right-wing political action groups flourished in the 1950s and 1960s, and toward the middle of the 1960s, they made serious inroads into the Republican party. Several of these organizations relied heavily upon radio broadcasting, such as the Twentieth-Century Reformation Hour, of Reverend Carl McIntire, and the Christian Crusade, of Reverend Billy James Hargis. Some, like the White Citizens councils, stood strongest in the South, appearing principally to oppose integration. Others, like the Minute Men, a secret paramilitary group much discussed in the press in 1966, were organized to prevent a leftist takeover believed brewing in Washington. Although these groups issued similar political jeremiads, denouncing moral degeneration and conjuring images of a Communist-liberal conspiracy in government, they rarely cooperated with each other. Well financed by conservative benefactors, most remained obscure, regionally contained, or peripheral to American politics.

The John Birch Society proved an exception to this general rule of political impotence. The Birch Society successfully defined a national program and established outposts in every section of the country. At its height in the mid-1960s, it comprised perhaps 4,000 semisecret chapters and almost 100,000 members. Beyond this, its influence extended into police forces, school boards, state and national legislatures, and into the Republican party. More than any other group, it represented a broadly based, right-wing rejection of liberalism. To Robert Welch, its founder, the liberal vital center had betrayed American principles, and he organized a political movement to destroy it.

For men like Robert Welch, the early 1950s seemed an age of the Apocalypse. Eisenhower's defeat of Taft in 1952 and the demise of McCarthy in 1954 shattered their confidence in the Republican party. The party, they felt, had succumbed to the enticements of government planning and high taxes. Rejuvenation could only come from the outside. Thus, Eisenhower's modern Republicanism played the role of catalyst in the creation of the John Birch Society. Its attacks on the President came from Welch's belief that Eisenhower had sold out individualism and militant Christianity for a hollow crown of political office.

Welch's career up to the official founding of the Birch Society in 1958 prefigured his later controversial activities. Raised as a fundamentalist Baptist, Welch was something of a child prodigy, enrolling at the University of North Carolina at the age of twelve.

After graduation, he went to Harvard Law School. After a confrontation with Harvard Professor Felix Frankfurter (later a Supreme Court justice), he quit law school in 1921 for a career in candy-making. Success in this field eluded him until the mid-1930s, but by the early 1940s, Welch was a wealthy and widely known business executive. Named "Candy Man of the Year" in 1947, he served two terms as chairman of the National Association of Manufacturers' Advisory Committee. In 1950, he ran unsuccessfully for the Republican nomination as Massachusetts' lieutenant governor.

During World War II, Welch began his public crusade against collectivism and political democracy. His electoral defeat in 1950 derailed his strategy, but Eisenhower's 1952 landslide confirmed a new direction in his thinking. When he discovered the controversial career and death of the missionary John Birch (after whom he named his political organization), he knew what he wanted to do; he now had a cause.

John Birch had been a Baptist missionary in Asia during World War II and worked closely with American forces operating in China. When the war ended and the Chinese civil war flared up, Birch was caught in a skirmish and killed by Communist troops on August 25, 1945. The U.S. War Department reported the death. After closely examining the facts, Welch concluded that Washington had hushed up the incident for its own dark purposes. To explain why this was so, Welch plunged into a sea of conspiracies, emerging with a theory that Communists and their handpicked stooge, Harry Truman, dominated Washington. To Welch, the "mysterious" death of John Birch revealed the tragic infiltration of America by Communist agents. They had entered, camouflaged by a bankrupt liberal tradition that stretched back into nineteenth-century English philosophy. Only militant Christianity, joined to anticollectivism, he wrote, could save America and generate a "spiritual resistance."

To spread the word, Welch began his periodical, *One Man's Opinion*, in 1956, changing the title to *American Opinion* in February 1958. That shift marked the formal beginning of the John Birch Society, organized during a marathon meeting at the home of an Indianapolis friend. By 1960, the secret organization had spread nationwide, undertaking an "Impeach Earl Warren" campaign because of the Chief Justice's role in civil rights and First Amendment decisions. In 1960, the society also initiated a campaign to control local PTAs and, in 1963, enjoined its members to organize support for local police forces. Strongest in California, Arizona, and suburban areas of the industrial East, the society received bad press and publicity and was often subjected to hostile investigation.

Nevertheless, in 1964, the Birch Society's influence in the Republican party was so strong that presidential candidate Barry Goldwater would not repudiate its support. In 1965, after the disastrous results of the November election, leading conservatives in the party denounced Welch. In October of the same year, William Buckley attacked Welch in the pages of the *National Review*. Public disapproval of Welch and his organization rose to a crescendo in 1966, after leading society members made remarks interpreted to be anti-Semitic. Thereafter, Welch's conspiratorial interpretation of politics, once convincing to thousands of Americans, became confused and hesitant, and the movement began to crumble. But it left a legacy that resurfaced in American politics a decade later.

Attacks on liberalism by conservatives generated considerable energy and attention in the 1950s, but their wrath struck especially at the Supreme Court. Under Chief Justice Earl Warren, appointed in 1953, the Court transformed the procedures of democracy and redefined citizenship in ways that neither Congress nor the President dared to undertake. Of all the institutions of government, the Court was the most vital in transforming American society—and the most controversial. Accused of legislating where it should only have adjudicated, the Chief Justice and the majority that voted with him stepped actively into the major social issues of the day. It is no accident that by the early 1960s, Earl Warren had become the leading enemy of conservatives.

Nothing in Earl Warren's early career suggested this aggressive judicial liberalism. Born in 1891, the son of an upwardly mobile railroad worker, he attended the University of California. Attorney General and then Governor of California, he was a large, fair-haired, stolid, but kindly-appearing man. Not known for liberal ideas, on the Court he became the leader of one of the most activist phases in the institution's history.

The Warren Court's notoriety rested on decisions in four areas: civil rights and school integration, legislative reapportionment, criminal justice procedures, and protection and extension of the rights of free speech. In *Brown* v. *Board of Education* (1954), the

Justice Earl Warren.   *(Historical Pictures Service, Chicago, Illinois)*

Court rejected the legal and moral justification of segregation. According to Warren, the 1962 decision, *Baker* v. *Carr* was the most important in his tenure. Affirming the doctrine "one-man, one-vote," the Court redefined the nature of legislative representation. In *Miranda* v. *Arizona* (1966), the Court closely defined the rights of arrested persons and circumscribed the power of police. In the category of free speech, the Warren Court generally struck down obscenity laws, banned Bible reading in public schools, and extended legal rights of political dissidents.

☆ ☆ ☆

The most important challenge to the vitality of the American political center came from the civil rights movement. Although the movement allied itself to liberalism frequently during the 1950s and 1960s and black voters most often cast their ballots for Democratic candidates, the relationship remained a coalition rather than an agreement on principles. The demands of black Americans for social justice constantly pushed against the confines of liberal politics. Liberals supported many of these demands, but not all of them, and with differing degrees of fervor and urgency. The result was an uneasy truce between principle and party.

The roots of the civil rights movement lay deep in twentieth-century struggles for equality: in the legal activism of the NAACP, in the skillful pressure on F.D.R. exerted by A. Philip Randolph for job equality during World War II, in the growing numbers of black voters in northern cities, in the political commitments of the Democratic party, and in the emerging sophistication of black leaders. Influenced by anticolonial revolutions in the Third World, touched by the same forces awakening many white Americans, black leaders also drew from a deep well of Christian consciousness. The moral and political vitality of this movement came also from the strange position of American blacks: once the objects of scorn, in the 1950s and 1960s, they became the subjects of conscience.

If the civil rights movement of the 1950s had a pivotal point, it was the desegregation decision of the Supreme Court in 1954. The civil rights movement, however, had to assume the initiative in enforcing the rights of black citizens, because Congress and the executive branch procrastinated. The Court ordered desegregation, but black Americans had to seize their rights through confrontation with local, state, and even national officials.

At the same time as it demanded enforcement of existing laws, the civil rights movement pushed ahead of the political center with demonstrations, passive resistance, and even violence to achieve more than simple integration. Living at the edge of politics, the civil rights movement courted liberals and often won their support. At the same time, its own priorities sometimes alienated this support. Ultimately, this precarious existence split the black movement into competing groups, reflecting the deeper divisions, aims, and generations that constituted the black community itself.

Undoubtedly, the central figure of the civil rights movement was Martin Luther King, Jr. Born in January 1929, King grew up in a family deeply anchored in the traditions of Southern fundamentalism. A handsome, bright youngster, who fancied himself something of a ladies' man, King attended Atlanta's Morehouse College. Switching from medicine to sociology and finally to the ministry in his senior year, he graduated in June 1948. Next, he went to Crozer Theological Seminary, in Pennsylvania. There, he discovered the religious and philosophical writings that influenced the remainder of his life: theologians Reinhold Niebuhr and Walter Rauschenbusch and the Indian pacifist Mahatma Gandhi. In fundamental ways, these thinkers contradicted each other, but King, choosing portions of each, created a tough-minded passive resistance strategy that became the mark of the early civil rights struggle. Finishing his studies with a Ph.D. in philosophy at Boston University, he married a young civil rights activist, Coretta Scott, in 1953 and took up the pastorate at Dexter Avenue Baptist Church in Montgomery, Alabama, the following year.

Commanding complex philosophic concepts, but drawing out a rich skein of imagery from slave songs and Biblical stories, King became a widely known preacher in a city where such a position connoted power in the black community. Events quickly proved this point. On December 1, 1955, Rosa Parks entered a Montgomery city bus but refused to move to the rear seats set aside for blacks. Following her arrest, Montgomery black citizens began a protest boycott of the bus system. Community leaders brought King into the leadership of the movement, and he quickly assumed an important role. Emerging as the prime mover of this protracted struggle, King gained international attention and praise for his nonviolent tactics. Already strong in his belief that pacifist means could topple the empire of Jim Crow, he was doubly receptive to the influence of pacifists Bayard Rustin and A. J. Muste, of

Martin Luther King, Jr. (UPI)

the Fellowship of Reconciliation, who visited him in Montgomery during the struggle.

After a hard-fought agreement with Montgomery's white business leaders desegregating the city, King received invitations to visit Ghana in 1956 and India in 1959. With other black ministers in 1958, he organized the Southern Christian Leadership Conference (SCLC), the organization that served as an umbrella for his civil rights activities until his death in 1968.

In the first years of the Kennedy administration, the civil rights movement greatly enlarged its demands. Southern segregation flourished, despite the desegregation decision and the Civil Rights Act of 1957. Waiting rooms, transportation facilities, rest rooms, fitting rooms, drinking fountains, hotels, schools, restaurants, clubs, universities, political organizations, voting regulations, and jobs were divided by the accident of birth and skin color. King's group, now joined by the Student Nonviolent Coordinating Committee (SNCC) and the Congress for Racial Equality, demanded a redress of the segregationist imbalance.

Very quickly, King and other leaders discovered that Kennedy's campaign promises of 1960 had to be extracted, painfully, from the new administration. Certainly friendlier to the cause of civil rights than Eisenhower had been, Kennedy avoided new legislation. During 1961 and 1962, civil rights leaders sought the President's moral support. After the integration marches and freedom rides in Albany, Georgia, and Birmingham, Alabama, dragged out into violent and brutal police attacks on pacifist demonstrators, the President intervened. Even in August 1963, however, Kennedy could not be persuaded to address the March on Washington organized by King and other black leaders. With broad support from white religious figures, liberals, and labor leaders (George Meany of the AF of L-CIO, however, was conspicuously absent), the march was the high point of King's career. His great address, coming at the end of the day, was an unforgettable and moving sermon on the political rights and duties of the nation. For his efforts, he received the Nobel Peace Prize in 1964.

Growing criticism of King inside the black movement tarnished the glory and accomplishment of such moments. Faulted for conservatism and an overbearing attitude, he was sometimes referred to as "De Lawd" by some of the younger SNCC members. Yet, in 1964, King had begun to push harder for economic demands. As the black movement spread northwest and began to soak up the bitter and violent frustrations of big-city ghettos, King found himself the chief spokesman for a movement that divided deeply over demands, needs, and traditions. Regardless of public appearances, President Johnson distrusted King, and in 1964, FBI chief J. Edgar Hoover, who had long counted King a subversive, blurted out that the black leader was the "most notorious liar in the country."

These troubles mounted in the last years of King's life. The black movement split along generational and tactical lines. King's criticism of the war in Vietnam cut him off from influence over the administration after 1966. More importantly, the urban riots, beginning in 1964, demonstrated that civil rights agitation could not satisfy many black Americans. An end to second-class citizenship demanded a deep revision of priorities that even the most liberal politicans scarcely considered, and never discussed, in public. Himself a victim of the bitter backlash against civil rights in 1968, King had long since ceased to preside over a movement that knew what it wanted or where it was headed. It had accomplished much under his leadership, but the next steps were for others to take.

King's tragic assassination in 1968 left the civil rights movement in disarray and America's large cities smoldering with fires of revenge. It removed the most vital politcal figure of the era. But splits in the movement had long been apparent. Some of these represented old divisions, extending back to the controversy over the Marcus Garvey movement during World War I. Extolling the virtues of blackness—in culture and physical appearance—Garvey devoted considerable organizing skills to the project of a reverse migration to Africa. When his venture failed in the early 1920s, he left millions of black Americans, touched by his promises of a new future, without leadership. But the idea of a separate black nation did not disappear.

Revived again briefly during the 1930s, black separatism grew rapidly in the late 1950s and early 1960s. Inspired by Malcolm X, one of the leaders of Elijah Muhammad's Nation of Islam, thousands of followers joined the movement. In the guise of Islam, this philosophy of self-regeneration and self-help appealed particularly to lower-class, urban blacks who rejected integration because it offered no solution to their problems of grinding poverty, violence, crime, drug addiction, and alcoholism. An entirely black, separatist nation—inside America—seemed to offer hope for the future, and Malcolm X, who had been a drug addict and a convict himself, painted these dreams in a moving fashion.

Partly because of political differences and partly because he threatened the hold of other leaders in the movement, Malcolm X was expelled from the Nation of Islam in 1963. During the next year, he traveled widely in Africa and on speaking tours to college campuses. Early in 1965, he established the Organization of Afro-American Unity, designed to promote a united front of black organizations. Although still committed to black separatism, in the last months of his life, Malcolm X had begun to speak more generously about working with white radical groups or other black civil rights organizations. Before anything could come of this, however, he was struck down by assassins in February 1965.

The Student Nonviolent Coordinating Committee, begun as a pacifist organization, absorbed some of the black nationalist ideas articulated by Malcolm X. Under the leadership of Stokely Carmichael, who popularized the slogan "Black Power" as a rallying cry in 1966, SNCC expelled its white membership. Moving from an integrationist organization with religious orientation, SNCC evolved into a group devoted to community organization and independent political action. Members linked American struggles to Third World revolutions against European colonial powers. As the Vietnam War intensified, groups such as SNCC tried to establish ties with Third World revolutionaries.

From this position, it was a small step toward the founding of the Black Panther Party, in 1966, by Huey P. Newton and Bobby Seale. Proposing self-defense against attacks by white police or vigilante groups, the Panthers rejected Islam and the African heritage in favor of revolutionary nationalism. Opposed to cultural exclusiveness and favoring revolutionary socialism, the Panthers, by 1969, expressed willingness to ally themselves (if hesitantly and temporarily) to white radical groups. Never a large movement, the Panthers suffered serious decline after hostile press coverage, police infiltration and confrontation, and meager results from their political alliances.

The variegation of the black movement—Southern, Northern, Christian, Islamic, integrationist, separatist, cultural nationalist, and cultural integrationist—reflected the diverse aspirations of the very complex black experience in modern America. But all of these movements, in one way or another, challenged the integrity of American culture. They provided energy and example to other protest movements. More importantly, however, they burst through the liberal political center to challenge its very premises.

One federal official, J. Edgar Hoover, chief of the FBI, believed it his special calling to oppose the activities of these groups. As head of a national police force, Hoover only minimally acted to enforce civil rights and instead devoted a good measure of his bureau's energies toward collecting dossiers on Martin Luther King, Jr., and other black leaders and political radicals. Hoover, the self-appointed guardian of American liberties and morals (his high school yearbook referred to him as a "gentleman of dauntless courage and stainless honor") lived and died for the federal bureaucracy.

Living alone with his mother until her death, he never married, devoting himself entirely to what Chief Justice of the Supreme Court Warren Burger called "the American dream of patriotism." For Hoover, this dream depended upon a mastery of public relations and the survival skills of a longtime bureaucrat. Whether they wished to or not, American presidents, from Roosevelt on, dared not replace him. Issuing periodic denunciations of Communism, crime, and moral decay, Hoover represented a strong force at the heart of government, opposing civil rights and anti-Vietnam War activists until his death in 1972.

  ☆   ☆   ☆

To many Americans, forces clamoring for change represented a chance to revitalize culture, to move beyond the limitations of political compromise. What Hoover denounced as lurid conspiracy, they saw as fulfilling old promises. For them, black self-consciousness and civil rights activism promised a regeneration that would carry the nation beyond liberalism.

The Beat writers of the 1950s were one such group that drew upon the energy of the turbulent black urban community. They nourished their poetry and prose with sympathy for America's underclasses: the poor, exploited, and down-and-out. There was precedent for this identification. In the poetry and prose of the twentieth-century American writers, the immigrant, the working man or woman, the tenant farmer, have appeared as symbols for humanity, as sparks of energy and authentic experience in a muddle of middle-class culture. The Beat poets and writers saw black culture as the same symbolic force. Cohering around several New

York writers, especially William Burroughs, Jack Kerouac, and Allen Ginsberg, this literary movement celebrated jazz, drugs, and the street life of urban ghettos. Its uniform of a T-shirt and Levi's proclaimed its authenticity. Its characteristic style, typified in the novels of Kerouac, sought spontaneity that resembled jazz improvisation in prose. Poet Allen Ginsberg used the black experience as a symbol for his own generation. As he wrote in his famous poem, "Howl," published in 1956:

> I saw the best minds of my generation
>   starving hysterical naked
> dragging themselves through the negro streets
>   at dawn looking for an angry fix,
> angel headed hipsters burning for the ancient
>   heavenly connection

The public first noticed the Beat writers, in 1952, in an article written for *The New York Times Magazine*. By 1957, when *Life* magazine and other journals featured photo essays on Kerouac and his friends, the movement became something of a fad. Literary critics greeted the publication of "Howl" and Kerouac's novel *On the Road* (1957) with derisive reviews, but the books sold widely. In fact, the movement suffered transformation into popular culture in the guise of the "beatnik" movement, a term coined from "Sputnik" and expressing what one journalist described as its unearthly, far-out qualities. By the late 1950s and 1960s, scores of low-budget films and TV dramas featured beatnik characters—usually violent, unkempt petty criminals or dope addicts.

More authentic versions colored the acting of Marlon Brando and, especially, James Dean and Sal Mineo, whose search for authenticity projected beyond the particular roles they played. Unlike other Hollywood stars, with lives punctuated by publicity stunts and marriages arranged in studio casting, these new stars seemed to be outsiders, much like the roles in their films.

Unlike public caricatures of them, the Beats attempted serious literary innovation. Building upon traditional American poets like Walt Whitman and heavily influenced by a variety of Eastern religions and modern psychologists like Wilhelm Reich, they celebrated the immediate impulse, the instanteous life experience. Like so many other groups in the early 1950s, their celebrations had strong religious overtones. When called to define his movement, Kerouac proclaimed: "The Beat Generation is basically a religious generation. Beat means beatitude, not beat up. You *feel* this. You feel it in a beat, in jazz—real cool jazz or a good gutty rock number." Mixing drugs, music, and Eastern religion; celebrating outsiders and the affinity for the black experience; aiming at self-liberation, the Beats laid the foundation for the counterculture of the late 1960s. They directly influenced the songs of Bob Dylan, the Rolling Stones, and lent their name to the most famous group of that later era, the Beatles. Kerouac's reference to a generation of writers contained an important clue to the appeal of the Beat movement for the 1960s. What society interpreted as vulgarity in music, delinquency in young people, or mindless spontaneity during the 1950s was transformed by a very complex process into counterculture, radicalism, and liberation in the 1960s.

☆   ☆   ☆

The search for authenticity and vitality that infected literature in the late 1950s and early 1960s also disturbed American theology. Two transformations in American Protestantism, and to a lesser extent in Catholicism, coalesced to translate generational politics into religious experience. The first of these was the "God is Dead" movement of the early 1960s; the second was the situation ethics developed to justify the new, looser morality of the decade.

Taking the slogan, "God is dead," from the proclamation of German philosopher Friedrich Nietzsche, several Protestant theologians argued that the God worshipped by early Christians had disappeared from modern worship; in their words, Christianity had become a social religion, with churches acting as businesses to accumulate wealth, buildings, and prestige. For William Hamilton, one of the leading figures of the movement, revived Christianity should affect "life-styles" and change behavior. The center of Christianity, he wrote, was Christology, or the consent of God to suffer as humans suffered. God was dead because modern society denied the essence of human experience, its sin and suffering.

A second important idea to challenge theology in the early 1960s was the new morality. In part inspired by Pope John XXIII's example—his efforts to update church doctrine and strike a middle position in the Cold War—and by the writings of Protestant theologians, the new morality rejected tradition and authority in favor of individual conscience. As John Fletcher wrote in his book *Situation Ethics*, in 1966, the commandments of conscience far outweighed legalistic biblical injunctions: "Always do the most loving thing in every situation," he advised.

This advice fit the changing behavior of the day. Franker public discussion of sex, relaxation of media and film censorship, the widespread adoption of contraceptives, indicated different attitudes toward human relationships. In 1961, the National Council of Churches affirmed the right of women to employ a wide variety of birth-control measures, including oral contraceptive pills and intrauterine devices. Despite the injunction of the Catholic Church, even a majority of Catholic women used contraceptives by 1965. By 1970, 65 percent of white women and 60 percent of black women regularly employed contraceptives (primarily the pill or the IUD).

By emphasizing personal and authentic religion outside institutions and traditions, the new religious morality joined hands with forces in the churches that focused on the war in Vietnam. The intense commitment of many nuns, priests, and ministers to ending the war drew some of them out of organized churches and into radical groups. The conservatism of the Catholic hierarchy in some cities, plus Pope Paul's encyclical *Humanae Vitae* in 1968, reaffirming the Church's absolute opposition to birth-control devices, raised a storm of protests. When the National Association for Pastoral Renewal lobbied to change the celibacy rules of the Church, the papacy refused to bend. To many Catholics and Protestants alike, the path to authentic religion led out of the churches and into a more political, private, and self-satisfying experience. Daniel and Philip Berrigan made the most famous odyssey away from the traditions of the Church and toward a self-authenticating experience. They moved from the traditional priesthood to join the New Left in protesting the war in Vietnam, ending finally in Danbury Federal Prison—for destroying Selective Service records on May 17, 1968, at Catonsville, Maryland. Deeply influenced by the worker-priest tradition in European Catholicism and by experience in organizing the American poor, the Berrigans confronted ecclesiastical authority and state power as they demonstrated for civil rights and protested against the war in Vietnam. In 1964, they organized the Catholic Peace Fellowship, opposing escalation of the conflict. Working inside the Church, the Berrigans helped focus opposition to the war for the next three years. Their step into direct action in 1968 flowed naturally from their beliefs, or as Daniel said, it was something "I believe Christian and Gandhian ethics demand." To exist apart from the struggle would betray its meaning.

The Berrigans expressed in religious terms something very close to the intense idealism and political fastidiousness that distinguished the New Left. This complicated political movement also originated as a protest against the politics of compromise and the ideology of the liberal center. It drew sustenance from the black movement, from the quickening of cultural and religious dissent, and from the vast changes inherent in the demographic shift of the early 1960s. This demographic change separated the 1950s and 1960s and their dominant attitudes like a fault line. During the 1950s, the population gravity of the country edged toward the thirty-five- to forty-year-old age group, reflecting the high birth rate immediately after World War I. By the early 1960s, however, the center shifted down abruptly to the seventeen-year-old age group, because of the post–World War II baby boom. As the population became younger, attitudes of large numbers of Americans, then reaching maturity, began to prevail. Born into a wholly different world of relative peace and prosperity, largely suburban or urban in origin, and attending universities in large numbers, this group felt little in common with its elders. Authenticity was in some sense, then, a function of generational conflict.

As so many other movements of the day, the New Left proclaimed the insufficiency of politics alone to transform critical domestic and international problems. During the 1960s, the New Left became a student movement housed primarily in the largest and most prestigious American universities. Here, middle-class students, predominantly studying liberal arts subjects, joined organizations like Students for a Democratic Society (SDS) and demonstrated for civil rights and against the war in Vietnam. By the late 1960s, these demonstrations intensified into an assault on the university structure itself, and the ideology of the movement deepened into a call for revolutionary socialism.

Students first roused themselves to political protest in the late 1950s. They joined the Student Peace Union, founded in 1959, at the University of Chicago, and participated in scattered campus demonstrations against compulsory ROTC training, the activities of the House Committee on Un-American Activities, and the loyalty-oath provisions of the National Defense Education Act. Other roots of dissatisfaction were nourished by the growing counterculture of the late 1950s, whose heroes—like James Dean and Jack Kerouac—conveyed the alienation, anger, and desire for authen-

Street theater, such as this performance in front of the Selective Service headquarters in Washington, became a part of every major protest march against the war in Vietnam. Television and the media in general tended to focus on these dramatizations. (Courtesy, Ted Green)

ticity that many young people felt, growing up in the suburbs, conscious of the conformity of their environment.

Another trail to the New Left passed through older radical movements. During the 1930s and early 1940s, many Americans had joined or sympathized with the Communist or Socialist parties or one of the smaller left splinter groups, and many more were enthusiastic partisans of the experimental liberalism of the New Deal. Their children were now of college age, and this younger generation had an ambiguous attitude toward their parents; intrigued by the left-wing politics of the previous era, they also judged their parents as backsliders and compromisers.

Intellectually, many sources fertilized the new radical movement, but none so copiously in the late 1950s as the works of sociologist C. Wright Mills and historian William Appleman Williams. Mills, a professor at Columbia University, in a series of widely noted writings, blasted the social science professions for their lack of theory and their reliance upon the cold tools of mathematics and precise measurement to analyze large, complex problems of the social order. He persistently asked: Who ruled America and how? The answer he gave rejected the pluralist hypothesis of 1950s liberalism. The supposed competing forces of government, labor, and business, he wrote in 1956, in *The Power Elite*, actually constituted a small group of powerful and wealthy leaders, sharing the same ideology and determination to rule. Their vision of the world amounted to "crack-pot" realism—the logical policies that flowed from false and misleading assumptions. As someone who sought to explain "the moral uneasiness of our time," Mills had begun a serious reevaluation of Marxist writings toward the end of his life. Although premature death, in 1962, cut short any further movement in this direction, his intellectual life marked off an exemplary path to many of the young radicals who read his works.

William A. Williams, of the University of Wisconsin, even more deeply sounded the moral and idealist frustration of the new radicals. In his *Tragedy of American Diplomacy* (1959), the historian explored a paradox that he and later radicals of the 1960s found between the noble aspirations of American principles and the sordid reality of interventions and compromises dictated by the Cold War. His theory of American foreign policy contrasted moral possibilities with the tragedy of reality in a way that helped shape later criticism of the war in Vietnam. Two grand ideals, humanitarian impulses and the desire to spread self-determination, were every-where undercut by the demands of an economy that overproduced and underconsumed. Thus, the inequalities of American society projected outward onto the world the guise of imperialism. For-eign adventurism, to Williams, signaled weakness, not strength.

In the context of these intellectual stirrings, students reacted to the Cuban Revolution of 1959, the election of John Kennedy, and the increased vigor of the civil rights movement. Aroused and yet distressed by Kennedy's idealism, the New Left, when it formed, did so by rejecting its liberal parentage. In 1962, when Tom Hayden, editor of the student newspaper at the University of Michigan, formulated a position paper for a new organization to be called the Students for a Democratic Society, he evoked a mood of betrayed puzzlement. The "Port Huron Statement" he helped to write reflected the moral dilemma that Williams had depicted. American young people were "uncomfortable" in their inherited world. Shocked out of complacency by black activism and the pos-sibilities of nuclear terror, they had begun to ask why society was unjust and overarmed. Dismissing liberals as apologists for the status quo, Hayden, echoing Mills' words, denounced the ruling elites who had created such a system. He exhorted students to restore a democratic society in America.

The initial phase of student activism in the early 1960s disrupted and then paralyzed the University of California at Berkeley. With-in a few miles of San Francisco, the campus occupied a cardinal point in the nexus of political radicalism and counterculture de-veloping in the Bay area during the period. In part, the Free Speech Movement sprang from the highest standards and liberal-ity of the campus. University President Clark Kerr, a noted sociologist with expertise in labor relations, had helped establish the national preeminence of the university. In 1959, he broadened his liberal reputation by securing an end to preemployment loyalty oaths, previously required of all professors. But Kerr's ambitions for the university raised serious questions about the uses of knowl-edge. Speaking shortly before the crisis of 1964, he defined his efforts to transform Berkeley into a knowledge factory. The aim of the university, he claimed, should be to enhance national purpose. Knowledge created by professors should contribute to national economic growth, and professors should lend their services to in-dustry and government. As elite institutions with democratic trap-pings, "cities of the intellect," universities had become "the port of entry" into the professions. Stepchildren of "middle-class plural-ism," these institutions established permanent links to the burgeoning knowledge industry.

Kerr's optimism was well founded. In the flush, post-Sputnik era, federal grants to university departments in the sciences, social sciences, and medicine flowed lavishly. Total expenditures for higher education during the 1960s in the United States rose from $6.7 billion to $24.7 billion, multiplying over 3.5 times. Scientists and engineers employed by universities increased from 30,000 to about 80,000. And, enrollments in public universities jumped from about 2 million to over 5 million in 1970.

Much of the funding granted to universities in the 1960s was earmarked for defense industry or defense policy research. Smaller amounts went for much more controversial purposes. Secret funds given to Michigan State helped provide South Vietnam with tech-nical and political assistance. Other government money, laundered through bogus foundations, financed the National Student Associa-tion, founded in the late 1940s. Policymakers aided student

Federal Funding for Universities from Federal Government for Research and Development

Date	Directly to Universities ($ millions)	To Federally Funded Centers Run by Universities ($ millions)
1954	160	141
1956	213	194
1958	254	293
1960	405	360
1962	613	470
1964	916	629
1966	1,262	630
1968	1,572	719
1970	1,648	737

Source: Historical Statistics of the United States, *Bicentennial Edition, Vol. II, p. 965.*

organizations because they wanted an anti-Communist group to speak for American students.

Trouble at Berkeley began in the fall of 1964. During the summer, a number of students had participated in the Mississippi Freedom Project to register black voters. It had been a brutal experience—3 persons killed, 35 shootings, 1,000 arrests, 30 houses burned, and only 1,200 black voters registered—and they returned to campus frustrated and angry. When students picketed in an area of the university traditionally designated for soapbox speeches and political recruitment, administrators changed the rules. No one could solicit funds or members on Bancroft Way. As students returned to fall classes, they openly defied the ruling; the university then called in the police. Tempers flared, administrators stiffened regulations, and students organized. Led by philosophy student Mario Savio, their Free Speech Movement attracted thousands of members and eventually forced the university to rescind its limitations on advocacy.

Once formed, part of this movement edged off into the counterculture, beginning a campaign to use salacious words in public. This "Dirty Speech Movement" reflected the apolitical interests of the cultural revolution springing up in San Francisco. The remainder of the movement, however, turned its attention to the stepped-up war in Vietnam. It was joined by a chorus of protests from major colleges and universities throughout the country.

Although students warred against university administrators at Berkeley, the new radical left generally felt comfortable in its academic environment at first. During the spring of 1965, this affirmation increased with the "teach-ins" held at Michigan, the University of Wisconsin, and scores of other colleges, culminating in a national teach-in held in Washington in June. Under this format, university professors addressed students and each other, declaring their opposition to the war and their serious quarrels with American society. Publicity given to this organized doubt did much to activate student radicals, although it had no immediate effect on Johnson's policy of escalation. Furthermore, it convinced many students that American universities were enclaves of liberalism and intelligence in a world of strife and misinformation.

Civil rights activism conscripted many of the new radical students, but the real war became Vietnam. After 1965, many of them began to join SDS chapters, to read Marxist literature— particularly the neo-Marxist writings of philosopher Herbert Marcuse—to subscribe to and edit underground newspapers—like *New Left Notes* and *Radical America*—and to join demonstrations against the war—such as the large campus protests in the fall of 1965. As the news of American actions in Vietnam filtered back into the United States, the nightly TV news in dormitory lounges all over the country became the pretext for intense and personal debate. Borrowing language from the black movement and the cultural underground and ideas from radical theoretical writings— haunted by conspiracy theories that hovered over the indecisive and contradictory Warren Committee Report of the Kennedy assassination—the New Left created a culture of student radical- ism that dominated many American campuses through the early 1970s.

This new tone of intellectual dissent on campus was matched by a curious dependence upon the war for the generation of styles and behavior. As has sometimes been the case with popular move- ments, protesters adopted the styles and even the dress of their opponents. In the middle 1960s, students increasingly began to wear cast-off military clothing in mockery of the real army. Many were attracted to the guerrilla warfare doctrines outlined by Mao Tse-tung and Cuban revolutionary Che Guevara. Most important- ly, some students accepted violence as a legitimate form of politi- cal protest. Thus, the protest movement at home came to be a caricature of the war abroad.

By 1967, SDS had become a large organization whose greatest problems reflected its successes. Attractiveness to students and loose membership requirements brought it over 100,000 members by 1968. But this made it a haven for political recruiters from estab- lished leftist sects. The most important of these, Progressive Labor, following an Americanized version of Maoism, made key inroads into the organization in 1968. Success also frustrated SDS. Able to organize large numbers for demonstrations in the spring mobilization of 1967, when three or four hundred thousand people demonstrated against the war, the movement could not stop the war. Moreover, the university appeared less a haven than before, as radical journalists uncovered secret defense projects on cam- puses and watched administrators protect recruiters for defense contractors, like Dow Chemical (principal manufacturer of napalm), visiting campuses in search of future employees. Kerr's multiversity, it appeared, existed everywhere.

Pent-up anger and frustration engulfed Columbia University in

1968. Two issues were at stake: the university's plan to construct a gymnasium in an adjacent park, thus taking land away from one of Harlem's few green spaces, and the deep involvement of the school in defense-related research. Borrowing civil rights tactics, the demonstrators occupied several buildings, to be removed finally forcibly by New York City police. Similar takeovers of university buildings occurred at other major universities.

Even this tactic was only a temporary stage in the evolving movement. By the late 1960s, students had resorted to firebombings and "trashing" of university buildings or businesses in university towns. Thus, the conflagration that burned the black ghettos in the late 1960s spread into middle-class university sanctuaries. In some ways, the flash point was the same: deep moral outrage, which politics could not contain. In the process, students had sullied their own sanctuaries. Whatever legitimate grievances they had and however much they speeded up much needed academic reforms, students failed ultimately to enlist the universities in their cause, and they became isolated from this potential constituency. In doing so, they lost the moral leadership of the antiwar movement. They raised the cost of pursuing the war, but made its termination into a political issue of ending civil turmoil at home.

At this turning point, the movement halted as if to reexamine the many roots that had entwined in its creation. In the moment of its greatest success, the New Left split into a variety of groups. Some members merely dropped out. Others wandered into religious sects. A few became confirmed revolutionaries, such as the Weathermen of 1969. Women, particularly those who had consciously submerged their own agenda of demands for transforming America, split off into the separate and growing women's movement. Some simply outgrew the movement or accepted America's scaled-down physical presence in Vietnam after 1969. But, perhaps the strongest lure was the counterculture, a vast and variegated life-style revolution that affected millions of Americans in the late 1960s and early 1970s.

☆   ☆   ☆

The counterculture, avowed its leading advocates, represented a revolutionary force for change, encompassing, but moving beyond the New Left. Hailing Beat culture, the drug life of Haight-Ashbury in San Francisco, and the musical genius of late 1960s

This engraving and photograph illustrate the common use of images of pollution and waste to symbolize the destructive aspects of American civilization during the 1960s and early 1970s.

"Aftermath," by Donald Sexauer. Vietnam, 1971.   (U.S. Army Photograph, Army Art Collection)

Smoke rises from Redding, California, city dump, December 13, 1965.
(Environmental Protection Agency)

rock and roll, counterculturists also borrowed extensively from old and respectable American protest traditions. They advocated health foods, rural living, communal family styles, spiritual perfectionism, and the interchangeability of sexual roles that typified some of the most famous experimental and religious communities of the 1830s and 1840s revival. Joined to a vaguely leftist orientation, the counterculture promised a powerful amalgam in reversing the contemporary evolution of American culture. Hostile to technological culture, bureaucracy, careers, and middle-class lifestyles, the counterculture was, ironically, as much the child of television and the electronic media as it was the child of rural innocence, Eastern mysticism, drugs, or the generation gap.

The admixture of these themes formed the foundation for Charles Reich's enormously successful *The Greening of America*, published in 1970. Going back to the roots of dissatisfaction with vital center politics, the Yale law professor portrayed established American culture as the enemy of the human spirit. Responsible for the war in Vietnam, it had pressed logic, reason, and science to the point of madness. In opposition, a growing revolutionary culture had emerged, devised by a young generation raised in the permissive environment of the postwar years. The young militants of the new consciousness, he claimed, would inherit the earth; America would change dramatically when it accepted their nonviolent, loving culture. The trumpet blast of the new consciousness would crumble the walls of the corporate state.

Aggressively apolitical, Reich reflected a flame that burned brightly, but extinguished itself in the 1970s. The counterculture burned for a moment with the incandescence of a religious awakening. Reich heightened its intensity by articulating its moral premises. His work reveals the degree to which the new consciousness was an old moralism smoldering deeply in American tradition. The "greening" of the nation that he predicted did not occur. The structure of society and the economy did not shift. Instead, American culture absorbed the counterculture like an estranged but familiar child. Rather than the announcement of something new, Reich's book delivered a postscript to the rhetoric of idealism that had pervaded the 1960s. American culture in the next decade changed enormously, making pursuit of new lifestyles, individual freedom, and social experimentation far more acceptable than ever before. But the sum of these changes did not constitute the political revolution that Reich had predicted.

In 1979, Hollywood provided another postscript to the period by remaking *The Invasion of the Body Snatchers*. The new version made several significant changes in the original plot. The location was readily identifiable: San Francisco, formerly the center of the counterculture. Unlike the original, the end was hopeless; no one could hope to escape transformation into an automaton. Struggle became useless in this confrontation with the invaders of the self. Thus, the film appeared to emphasize the end of a period. Protest and the counterculture had come full circle, ending where they began in the trancelike state of conformity. Light from the great western city on the hill once more passed behind an obscuring cloud.

Epilogue
Diminishing Returns

Early in the morning of June 6, 1968, after the California primary returns had been counted, Robert F. Kennedy, surrounded by admirers, began to make his way back from a victory celebration at his campaign headquarters. Suddenly, shots rang out, and part of the crowd rushed to subdue Sirhan Sirhan, a young Jordanian immigrant with a revolver, struggling to escape. Others pressed around in horror to gape at the fallen body of the senator. A short time later, Kennedy was dead. Guilt and grief swept the nation. Newspapers throughout the world puzzled once again at the American penchant for violence. In Washington, the mayor urged the police to take precautions against possible riots, and the National Guard was alerted. The Pentagon quietly notified the Army Riot Agency to prepare for possible trouble. However, there was no violence, only sorrow. After ceremonies at St. Patrick's Cathedral in New York, a special train carried Kennedy's body to Washington past what seemed to be an almost unbroken wall of mourners lining the tracks. From Union Station, his casket was carried to Arlington Cemetery for burial close to his brother John Kennedy. Thousands of miles away on the same day, in London, Scotland Yard captured James Earl Ray, the killer of Martin Luther King, Jr.

The fateful events of 1968 did not, by themselves, bring a close to the period that had begun in the midst of World War II. Although less rapidly and obviously, other forces—political, economic, and social—were also at work changing those key elements that had characterized the postwar world, placing earlier events in relief. In effect, the United States had begun to play a different and more restricted role in the world, while the enormous resiliency and economic buoyancy of the previous two decades had begun to diminish at home. In this different sort of atmosphere, many of the same problems and potentialities that had preoccupied Americans in the immediate past reappeared. But the issues and movements changed. American politics, economic potential, and family, cultural, and social life all appeared in a new light, and in a world of somewhat lessened expectations.

In the fateful period of assassination and confrontation of the late 1960s, Americans cast ballots for a new president, exercising their quadrennial vote of confidence in reason, order, and continuity. The presidential election of 1968, however, included neither the incumbent President nor Robert Kennedy, the one Democrat who might have won. Into this vacuum rushed Richard Nixon, representing a minority party, but appealing to a silent majority, the "forgotten man." Pursuing a "Southern strategy" to woo voters away from third-party candidate Governor George Wallace, of Alabama, Nixon gained the enthusiasm of the Republican right wing, as well as the center of the party. He established the beginnings of a conservative coalition that grew throughout the 1970s and rivaled the New Deal coalition of F.D.R. in importance. With a ticket that promised peace with honor in Vietnam, law and order, and economic progress, Nixon correctly judged that the American electorate would turn to conservatism in a time of confusion and crisis.

The forgotten voter that Nixon deftly courted became the hero of the most important television comedy of the 1970s, *All in the Family*. To the traditional struggle between the sexes, Norman Lear, the originator of the series, added a second dimension of contemporary social problems. The husband, Archie, remained an unreconstructed male chauvinist, with values fixed in the culture of the 1950s. As the theme song proclaimed: those were "the days" when hair was short and skirts long, and men were men and girls were girls. What had gone wrong? His wife, Edith, good-natured, naive, and generous, instinctively sided with contemporary trends in race relations, women's liberation, and political liberalism. In each episode, Archie vented his prejudice, but Edith won the argument. One by one, the weekly show exposed social problems by means of the family. Employing an explicitness and frank examination of social prejudices, the program, nonetheless, never really progressed; characters remained frozen in their positions, reflecting a larger sort of social inertia of the 1970s, caught between deep-seated social conservatism and tolerant acceptance of new social practice.

If social problems could all be located in the family, the family itself became the object of persistent media scrutiny and interest.

Election of 1968

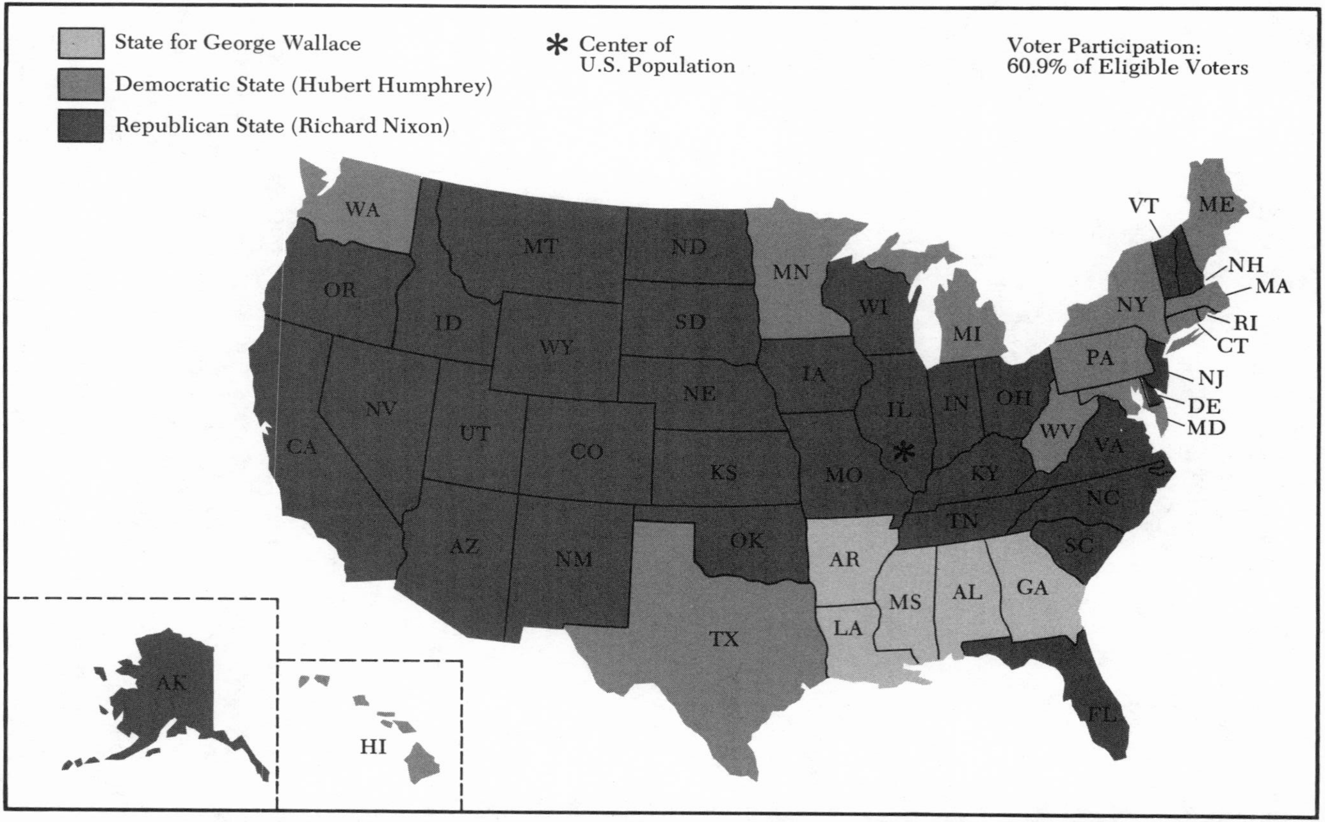
State for George Wallace
Democratic State (Hubert Humphrey)
Republican State (Richard Nixon)
* Center of U.S. Population
Voter Participation: 60.9% of Eligible Voters
WA
OR
CA
ID
NV
MT
WY
UT
AZ
CO
NM
ND
SD
NE
KS
OK
TX
MN
IA
MO
AR
LA
WI
IL
MI
IN
OH
KY
TN
MS
AL
GA
FL
SC
NC
VA
WV
PA
NY
VT
ME
NH
MA
RI
CT
NJ
DE
MD
AK
HI

The increasing popularity of midday television soap operas (there were fifteen regular daytime serials in 1978–1979) and the appearance of evening spin-offs, like *The Jeffersons* (a black middle-class family) and *Dallas*, suggest the degree to which Americans accepted public intrusion across the boundaries of privacy and intimacy. The distinction between public and private, between social interest and political cause, dissolved before the relentless, inquisitive eye of the television camera. Although they all had a powerful economic and political component, many of the social problems of the 1970s were often discussed only in their cultural dimensions. These questions of economics, politics, and ideology were subordinated to problems of life-styles. The personal and the cultural replaced the political.

As the central focus of social concerns, the family in the 1970s had a kaleidoscopic image—each shift in statistics suggested new patterns of social behavior and new problems. Demographically, the American population during the 1970s resumed its rapid aging. The baby boom matured in that decade (aged thirteen to twenty-five in 1970, the cohort was twenty-three to thirty-five years old in 1980). Behind it followed a much smaller generation of children, suggesting that in the future, with increasing life expectancy, fewer and fewer workers would have to support more and more retired Americans. Also, there was a slight but noticeable change in the American family structure. After 1957, the birth rate fell rapidly, in part because of increased use of birth-control measures and abortion. In the mid-1960s, the divorce rate shot upward until contemporary rates approached 50 percent of existing marriages. In addition, the marriage rate declined. Eligible persons who could marry increasingly refrained from doing so.

Economically, the family came more and more to depend upon two incomes. While this helped to equalize national family income, it also heightened the precarious existence of many single-parent families. During the 1970s, the black family continued to reflect, in exaggerated form, the contours of general demographic change. Female heads of households in black families increased by about 65 percent from 1970 to 1978, indicating the continued decline of the traditional nuclear family. Generally limited to one income, these families fell behind in the competition with an increasingly large two-income family segment of the population. While two-spouse black families made income gains, the rising

Old age has become a social problem of increasing importance in the United States since World War II. Many older persons, lacking the support of family or sufficient pensions and sometimes in ill health, spend their waning years in nursing homes or institutions set aside for the care of the elderly. Many others who are not institutionalized feel removed from the mainstream of society. (*Department of Housing and Urban Development*)

proportion of single-head families dragged the overall figures for black income down.

Despite programs like Head Start and a variety of civil rights actions and training programs, wages and incomes of black Americans continued to lag behind those of whites. The earnings of black women provided a single exception to this rule: college-educated black women earned slightly more than their white female counterparts. In general, unemployment of black workers remained disproportionately high. And, despite rising public expenditures for welfare, which went from $146 billion in 1970 to $331 billion in 1976, poverty did not disappear. In no way did welfare or similar programs of aid to the poor constitute a redistribution of income shares. Americans remained committed to equality of opportunity—not equality of income—and disparities inevitably remained strong.

The statistical profile of the black family and income structures suggest diminished political opportunities in the 1970s. Although black elected officials continued to increase during the decade, the nation's commitment to ending poverty languished in the hands of the Republican administration of Nixon and Ford and failed to revive under the weak ministrations of Jimmy Carter after 1976. The bicentennial deadline to end poverty passed unnoticed; poverty programs received less attention. For the masses of black people, the achievements of the civil rights era had not translated into a relative rise in income and status. Most Americans continued earnestly to speak about full racial equality, but were unable to accept structural solutions necessary to realize this goal.

Many of the dramatic statistical changes in the American family hinged upon increased female participation in the labor force, especially married women. From 1970 to 1978, 9.2 million women entered the labor force, while only 6.5 million men joined. The large gain shrank the difference in participation in paid labor between men and women, although only 43 percent of women held full-time jobs compared to 65 percent of men. Nonetheless, the added income of wives dramatically reshaped the pattern of family finances.

Although most noticed in the 1970s, women's participation in the labor force had grown steadily since World War II. What made it seem unusual was the growing awareness by women that neither the traditional homemaker role they had outgrown nor the second-class, low-paid worker's identity many had assumed suited their aspirations. The conflict between opportunities and frustrations—intensified by the crusade for civil rights, in which many of its early political leaders acquired a strategy and political experience—provided enormous energy for the women's movement.

The origins of the modern women's movement lie in a rich heritage of advocacy and in the fundamental changes in the economic, social, and political status of women since World War II. The prime mover of status was work. Growth of female participation in the labor force from 1947 to 1977 was phenomenal, rising from 28.1 percent to 41 percent. Within this broad trend, the portion of married women grew especially rapidly. Women's income, relative to men, increased until about 1970, but then stuck at a level about 60 percent of the median income of men. Another force operating strongly to alter women's status and increase the possibilities of joining the labor force was the rapid, almost universal adoption of birth-control measures and availability, after the 1973 Supreme Court decisions *Roe* v. *Wade* and *Doe* v. *Bolton* of legal, relatively cheap abortions. During the 1972–1974 period, the legal abortion rate was 213 per 1,000 live births for white women and 329 per 1,000 for black women.

As it always had been, the battleground for women's liberation encompassed the family and the workplace. In both arenas, women struggled against prevailing social attitudes that denied their equality on the grounds of biological inferiority. The special privileges of the feminine mystique came to be defined as the bondage of second-class citizenship. Thus, the women's movement argued for biological equality and an end to special treatment that it viewed as a delicate prison. Women challenged the social customs, manners, and even language that reflected a male-oriented social order, for example, the use of the male personal pronoun "he" to denote all of humanity and the use of the distinctive "Miss" or "Mrs." to indicate marital status. Inside the family, many women demanded shared responsibilities in money management and child-rearing, as well as in sexual practices.

Women began to organize after the early 1960s. In part, inspiration came from the Presidential Commission on the Status of Women, appointed in 1961 by John Kennedy. Although it recommended a relatively conservative program in 1963, it did publicize some of the serious inequalities facing American women. The 1963 publication of Betty Friedan's *Feminine Mystique* also had enormous impact, especially on middle-class women. Friedan and

Legal Abortions: Number and Rate per 1,000 Women 15–44
Years Old, 1973–1976

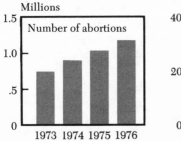

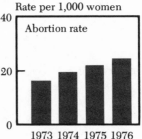

Source: Statistical Abstract of the United States *(1978), p. 57.*

others were delighted when Congress passed the 1963 Equal Pay Act and the 1964 Civil Rights Act, whose Title VII outlawed sex discrimination in jobs. The Equal Employment Opportunity Commission (EEOC) was established to enforce this principle. However, enforcement remained slow and uneven, and in order to increase pressure, the National Organization of Women (NOW) organized in the spring of 1966. Although the group suffered several splits, it continued to grow, concentrating its efforts on the passage of the Equal Rights Amendment, after Congress approved the amendment on March 22, 1972, and sent it to the individual states for ratification.

More radical groups of feminists emerged from the New Left. Often relegated to menial positions—secretarial work, cooking, or baby-sitting—while boyfriends or husbands manned the barricades, radical women demanded that issues of their liberation be raised in their own organizations, as well as in the surrounding society. This was not easily accomplished. Intense acrimony and charges of "splitting the movement" met these demands. As a result, women organized several groups, for example, the Radical Women of New York (1967) and Radical Feminists (1969). These groups demanded fundamental changes in American capitalism rather than legal advances. But they were willing to cooperate with other women on common issues.

As the women's movement spread, it touched all sectors of the American female population, each of which had its special grievances: white working women, middle-class housewives, black women, Chicanas, high-school and grade-school girls, and others. Perhaps the high point of influence in politics came at the 1972

Democratic nominating convention that chose Senator George McGovern for its candidate. Women delegates and their supporters came close to achieving two impressive goals: passage of a plank supporting the right to abortion and nomination of a woman, Frances "Sissy" Farenthold, of Texas, for vice-president.

Years of assault on unequal laws and treatment brought the whole movement both success and notoriety. Misleading publicity and occasional distortion sometimes misconstrued the goals of feminists, picturing them as aggressive, frustrated females, or worse, as sexless automatons. Each step forward met with intense opposition, which ultimately solidified around two issues: the anti-ERA movement and the right-to-life groups opposing abortion. Phyllis Schlafly, veteran conservative writer and the head of Stop ERA, was the spokesperson for the first cause. The right-to-life movement, backed by the Catholic Church, which resolutely opposed abortion, gathered broad support from other social and religious groups. In general, conservatives hoped to prop up the fast-disappearing paternalistic nuclear family.

As the women's movement advanced through the 1970s, it gained significantly, because of the growing body of literature in women's history, sociology, and psychology, because of increased opportunities, and because of heightened self-consciousness. It helped reshape American thinking about social equality and the family. Beyond this great influence, however, it did not always project a conception for a new social order. It helped shatter an old consciousness without really finding a new one to replace it.

The question of lesbian rights inevitably accompanied the movement for women's equality. Organization of gay women's caucuses or separate groups forced the larger, established women's groups to face and defend the exercise of sexual preference. Although reluctant at first, even NOW, in 1971, passed a resolution affirming the rights of lesbians.

A more widely discussed movement for gay men's rights had an even greater impact on American culture and society during the 1970s. Demands for equality of treatment, fair housing practices, and even political recognition were only part of what gay men wanted. They sought open recognition of their life-style as an acceptable alternative to heterosexual family culture. That they achieved even moderate success was a symbol of the remarkable benign neglect of traditional standards that marked American culture in the 1970s.

Questions of alternative kinds of consciousness, not politics, also characterized the impact of the counterculture in the 1970s. Its early coherence around hallucinatory drugs, alternative life-styles, and political radicalism dispersed into the public celebration of self-liberation (what critic Tom Wolfe called the "me generation"), narrow evangelical religious sects, and looser, more tolerant, social attitudes.

Before the decline of its momentum, the counterculture experienced one last surge, in the founding and short reign of the Woodstock Nation. This three-day rock concert took place in mid-August 1969, on a 600-acre farm near Bethel, New York. Organized as the Woodstock Music and Art Fair, the enormous rock concert—the "Aquarian Exposition"—attracted 400,000 young people. Drawn by ads in underground papers and by word of mouth, they came in caravans of cars and vans or by hitchhiking, to hear some of the country's best rock artists: among them, Janis Joplin, Jimi Hendrix, and the Jefferson Airplane. Braving mud and rain, they created a city of sharing and surviving (for three days, the second largest city in New York State), which seemed to contrast sharply with the war-torn society around them. As *Time* magazine enthused: this was the "phenomenon of innocence"—a triumph of the pleasure principle over the work ethic.

Journals that celebrated a new ethic, however, were too quick to praise. The counterculture reflected a violently different tendency at a concert in Altamont, California, four months later. At this free performance, given by the Rolling Stones, the underside of the cultural revolution emerged. Everything about the event was wrong—the tension, the bad drug-trips, and the behavior of the Hell's Angels motorcycle gang, hired to protect the Stones. Together with Woodstock, this concert demonstrated that the most potent force of the counterculture was not its new ethic or revolutionary behavior, but its commercial potential. With the sullen end of expectations, the counterculture disintegrated into smaller groups, responding to the general social compulsion to stress the divisions in society rather than its cohesions. Or it flowed back into the 1970s mainstream interest in health foods, consumer crusades, and personal liberation.

Much of the impulse to draw narrow boundaries around the self—to proclaim self-interest first and foremost—came from a general sense during the 1970s of diminishing economic prospects. Not since the 1930s did so many Americans believe that economic problems were insoluble. The limitless possibilities of the postwar years had been terminated by inflation, stagnation, and pollution. Optimism, real advance, and legislative aggressiveness characterized the 1960s, despite the Vietnam War. The costs of the war were not understood until the 1970s. But even this bitterly paid debt did not absorb enough funds to sap the spirit of reform. Financing the military establishment did not necessarily mean that funds for social reform projects would disappear. In fact, during the 1950s and 1960s, military expenditures consumed proportionately far more of the federal budget than they did in the 1970s.

The source of the problem came from severe strains pulling the American economy in several directions. Together these reshaped the aggregate American economy in new ways. Individuals still made fortunes, families improved their lot, but confidence in solutions to large economic problems associated with pollution, energy, inflation, and income distribution collapsed.

Perhaps the most disheartening recognition of the perils of growth grew out of the activism of Ralph Nader. Educated at Princeton and Harvard, Nader published a disturbing attack on the American automobile industry in 1965, called *Unsafe at Any Speed: The Designed-in Dangers of the American Automobile*. He singled out General Motor's Corvair for special criticism. Rather than admit design faults, or improve its model, GM sent investigators to try to discredit Nader. The effort backfired, and the young consumer advocate won a lawsuit against the giant corporation in 1970. In 1969, he founded "Nader's Raiders" to investigate air pollution, antitrust problems, federal regulatory agencies, and consumer complaints. Persistent, dogmatic, and tenacious, Nader took the promise of American capitalism to deliver the best goods at the cheapest price literally. In cases where it did not so deliver, he rushed to the media to report its failures.

Nader's radical consumerism made many Americans conscious of the costs of waste, greed, and pollution, but beyond the drama of exposing danger, corruption, and planned obsolescence, more significant economic changes diminished the relative power of the American economy in the world. In part, the economy lost its competitive drive because of a downturn after 1966 in American worker productivity increases. Thereafter, the United States lagged behind every European nation, except Britain, in output increases. Rapid rises in fuel costs made competition with more efficient economies in Germany and Japan a serious problem. For example, from 1950 to 1970, the United States share of world steel production fell from 46.6 percent to 20.1 percent. Also, a massive export of capital and technology bolstered economies competitive to the United States. By the end of the decade, even the automobile industry, the barometer of the economy, was in deep distress, with Chrysler facing bankruptcy and Ford sustaining huge losses, as Japanese and European cars outsold many domestic models.

In effect, this decline in competitiveness reflected a postwar shift (accelerated during the 1970s) from investment and employment in such primary industries as automobiles and steel to other sectors, particularly fast-food industries, health-care services, and business services such as data processing. During the 1970s, these industries tended to be labor intensive; they did not pay as well as older industrial establishments; and they hired more than their share of the new female workers entering the labor force. The result was a new kind of consumer economy that did not so much produce mechanical conveniences as provide services that were once a part of the home (fast food and much health care) or a normal part of internal business operations.

The serious recession of 1974 and 1975 highlighted growing problems, exacerbated by the hidden costs of the Vietnam War and the shrinking United States economic power in the world. During the downturn, unemployment rose sharply to over 8.5 percent, although it touched the working population differentially. Industrial output tumbled downward also, sinking about 2 percent for each year of the recession. However, prices during these years rose very rapidly, indicating that the traditional impact of economic decline no longer cooled inflation. The most obvious explanation was the price of petroleum products, which doubled from 1973 to 1975, after the formation of the oil producers' cartel (OPEC) in 1971. This struck the United States especially hard, because after 1968, the nation was no longer self-sufficient in oil production. By 1974, it imported 36 percent of its petroleum. But other factors also played their role, including the cumbersome hand of government bureaucracy and regulations and the administered prices of industry.

The reputation of regulatory bodies created after World War II (or before) declined precipitately in the 1970s. These federal agencies often lacked real power, competence, or desire to control the vast units of economic power that appeared particularly after 1960 and especially in the corporate consolidation boom of 1968. Important enough to harass large institutions, these agencies did not fulfill their mandate to control American and multinational corporations, thereby discrediting the whole idea of control. The federal government, with its tangle of bureaucratic rules, seemed no more approachable or responsive than the General Motors Corporation. This was one more weight sinking the confidence of Americans in the ability of government to solve problems.

The economic decline of 1973–1974 signaled a world-wide phenomenon of shifting economic power that seriously affected the United States. The year 1974 yoked an intenational energy crisis to world-wide food shortages. These strains brought to a head several years of intense debate about the desirability or even the possibility of economic growth. Two important books of the time, *Limits of Growth* and *Mankind at the Turning Point*, both produced by the economic and ecological experts belonging to the International Club of Rome, warned that unlimited growth was probably impossible. Population, resource depletion, and pollution, they argued, meant that optimism about the future, especially for the United States, would have to be revised.

The recovery of the world economy, in general, and of the United States, in particular, from recession by 1976, was caused less by any positive action than by a general recovery fueled by traditional increases in consumer demand. Nor did economists and politicians emerge much the wiser from this chastening experience. They advanced no serious plans to prevent such a future recurrence of stagflation. Public discussion of economic problems remained at the same low level, blaming government deficits for the very complicated and difficult problems of recession and inflation.

As the relative economic preponderance of the United States declined in the 1970s, so did maneuverability and freedom in foreign policy. The United States, living in a smaller and less expansive world, was hedged by interdependencies and compromises. The gradual end of the Vietnam War, in 1972 and 1973, brought to light the diminished international position of the United States. Establishment of a new policy of détente with the Russians (the first Strategic Arms Limitation Treaty—SALT I—was signed in 1972) and friendship with the Chinese Communists recognized a multipolar world, not the bilateral world of the early Cold War

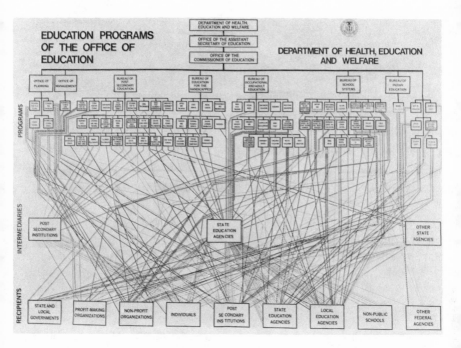

Office of Education programs charted by the Department of Health, Education, and Welfare in the late 1970s. The lines of accountability pictured here illustrate the complexity of the modern federal bureaucracy. (*Department of Health, Education, and Welfare*)

years. The repercussions of this change of policy did not prevent competition with the Soviet Union or even increased hostility in 1980, but the context was one in which policymakers recognized the severe limitations of American power. When Iranian students took United States Embassy employees hostage in 1979, demanding the transportation of the deposed Shah back to Iran, policy was paralyzed. The United States could not act for fear of disrupting oil supplies from other Arab nations. The Russian seizure of Afghanistan shortly afterward brought angry words but little significant action. Here, too, room to maneuver had obviously narrowed.

The uncertainty of the economy and the foreign posture of the United States magnified the political crisis that began in 1968 with Robert Kennedy's assassination and crested in the Watergate scandal. In the key years of the first Nixon administration, Americans poured out their frustrations over the war in Vietnam and the political assassinations of the Kennedys and Martin Luther King, Jr. The terrible uncertainty shrouding these murders gave intrigue, plot, and conspiracy new meaning in the American political vocabulary.

Nixon transformed this mood into policy. While the President changed the scale of war in Southeast Asia and limited its consequences for American soldiers, he continued the struggle for four more years. Domestically, he moved to revoke the 1960s mandate to extend civil rights. He proposed a more limited role for the Supreme Court and pushed law-and-order measures in Congress. Employing Vice-President Spiro Agnew, he sparked an attack on the liberal lawyers, bankers, politicians, and journalists who constituted the Eastern establishment of the Democratic party. He also struggled—frequently in vain—to make the federal bureaucracy amenable to his programs. Reflecting a growing consensus among sociologists and educators that government action had had only minimal effects on serious problems, like poverty and public assistance, Nixon attempted new approaches to welfare and public assistance.

In the beginning of his first administration, he proposed a much simplified Family Assistance plan that would have substituted direct, cash payments to dependent families, replacing the tangle of Great Society programs. Opposed by liberals who probably misunderstood its purposes and by conservatives, the plan failed, but it did reveal Nixon to be a President who understood the complexities of such issues as welfare and, what is more, a President committed to continue the spirit of some of his liberal predecessors. On other issues, particularly those of executive power, Nixon again revealed himself to be an astute student of government. Recognizing the unwieldiness of the executive branch and congressional limitations on his power, he attempted to reorganize and streamline the bureaucracy he commanded. By impounding funds (refusing to spend appropriated money), eliminating programs he opposed, and using the pocket veto, which allowed bills to lapse, he fought to establish more flexibility in the presidency.

On most of these issues, however, Nixon ultimately lost, and resorted instead to belligerent verbal thrusts at his political opponents. Whatever his more complex purposes, he nonetheless came to echo the rhetoric of Americans angered by reform. The result was an administration whose basic premise denied the power of government to solve problems.

Nixon's apparent hostility to social reform projects, particularly those aiding poor or black Americans, matched his aggressive dislike of political dissent. This erupted in well-publicized appeals to patriotism, as well as clandestine FBI operations against political dissidents. The President could push his attacks, because of public fear of radicals and a growing national concern over crime and drug usage. Partly a backlash from the 1968 urban riots, support for tough new crime legislation came from Americans worried about issues of law and order. Police forces were beefed up all over the country with large new expenditures.

While the Republican administration struck out at real and fancied opponents and exploited public fears of violence, crime, drugs, and radicalism, it worried most about disintegration from within the political establishment: leaks of damaging information, like the *Pentagon Papers*, the open hostility and contempt of major newspapers, and the possibility that opposition Democrats might find a winning issue in 1972. Not content with normal fund-raising or intelligence operations against opponents, the Nixon administration sent undercover agents to collect campaign money and spy on political enemies. Campaign "dirty tricks" terminated in the Watergate affair, when operatives hired by the Nixon reelection campaign broke into Democratic party headquarters on June 17, 1972, only to be surprised by District of Columbia police. A small and relatively unimportant event by itself, Watergate grew like Topsy and finally overwhelmed the administration. By refusing to budge or admit any wrongdoing, Nixon forced the press and then Congress to turn over every stone leading to the front entrance of his administration. The investigation fatally exposed the underside of ambition, intolerance, and arrogance upon which Nixon had come to rely.

Perhaps the most important feature of Watergate was the relentless television and newspaper coverage that excavated the ground from under the presidency. Television cameras mercilessly recorded Nixon's physical and moral disintegration. Inside the White House office, the President carefully recorded conversations that linked him to the break-in and subsequent cover-up. When these were discovered and printed, the President's most private thoughts became public. Thus, a media event undercut the symbolic power and mystery of the presidency. Politics had become a protracted soap opera.

The long crisis of Watergate ended finally when the President reluctantly relinquished his office on August 9, 1974, to Vice-President Gerald Ford, of Michigan, who had replaced Spiro Agnew after Agnew had resigned on October 10, 1973, because of an income tax and kickback scandal. Although the falling dominoes of political scandal ended with Gerald Ford's caretaker presidency, the effects of Watergate continued. Hypocrisy and cupidity at the top of government, coupled with revelations about the clandestine activities of the CIA and the FBI, rendered all government officials suspect and led to new legal limitations of agency activities. These scandals fueled American resentment against government in general. Thus, a time when the public might have debated the intricate problems of the economy and the demands of adjusting to a smaller world was diverted to preoccupation with conspiracies. Watergate speeded up the transition to a new form of American politics, dependent upon media credibility and advertising techniques. It symbolized the decline of older forms of coalitions, compromises, and party loyalty. Political crisis, moreover, obscured the substantial gains in foreign policy accomplished by Nixon and his chief adviser, Henry Kissinger: the SALT I treaty on nuclear weapons, several real movements toward détente with the Russians, and the restoration of ties with the leaders of Communist China—even the end of the war in Vietnam, despite its terribly high toll in lives and property. Those who succeeded him neither acknowledged nor followed Nixon's lead.

☆   ☆   ☆

The Boston Marathon. Marathons such as the one held annually in Boston attracted thousands of people who took up running as a physical fitness program in the 1970s. (Environmental Protection Agency)

Living in this society of somewhat more sober possibilities and recurrent political crisis had a variety of effects on Americans. Perhaps the Bicentennial best illustrates these. This celebration of 200 years of nationhood was marked more by spectacle than by serious rethinking of ideals and possibilities. Its best moment came when the stately armada of great sailing ships floated into New York Harbor in July 1976.

Perhaps this diversion from rethinking national purposes was inevitable; great patriotic feelings are seldom raised by distant anniversaries. But beyond this reason, the celebration of the Bicentennial hinted at an underlying reevaluation in American citizenship. Individual identification with shared social goals and national symbols had declined. The great bonanza of postwar America seemed to be over. The factors that diminished the economic, political, and social expansion of American society also rendered the celebration of history a respite from present problems. If anything, it made the Bicentennial a moment that underscored the puzzlement many Americans felt about the direction of society during the 1970s.

The inevitable collapse of political optimism and the hesitancy that gripped both major political parties in the late 1970s reflected the diminished economic world of that decade, its political scandals, and its rapidly shifting social customs. Even more importantly, perhaps, the collapse of meaningful distinctions between public and private lives made the most intimate individual problems the basis of important political movements. Questions of sexual practice, birth control, abortion, religion, ethnicity, and family roles thrust themselves into the political arena. This politicization of personal identity dissolved not just privacy; it also changed political dialogue. Single-issue groups of voters and powerful lobbyists diverted majoritarian politics into questions of life-style. The decline of both major political parties, plus receding voter participation in elections, underscored a loss of faith in the political process. The reluctance of groups to compromise, to see beyond immediate, individual goals to larger social commitments, to form coalitions and programs, testified to the increasing ineffectiveness of political parties as moderators of geographic, racial, class, and religious conflicts in American society. For all its decisiveness, even the election of 1980 revealed a continuing erosion of voter turnout and a growing geographic polarity in American political life. As the population center of the United States crossed the Mississippi for

Election of 1980

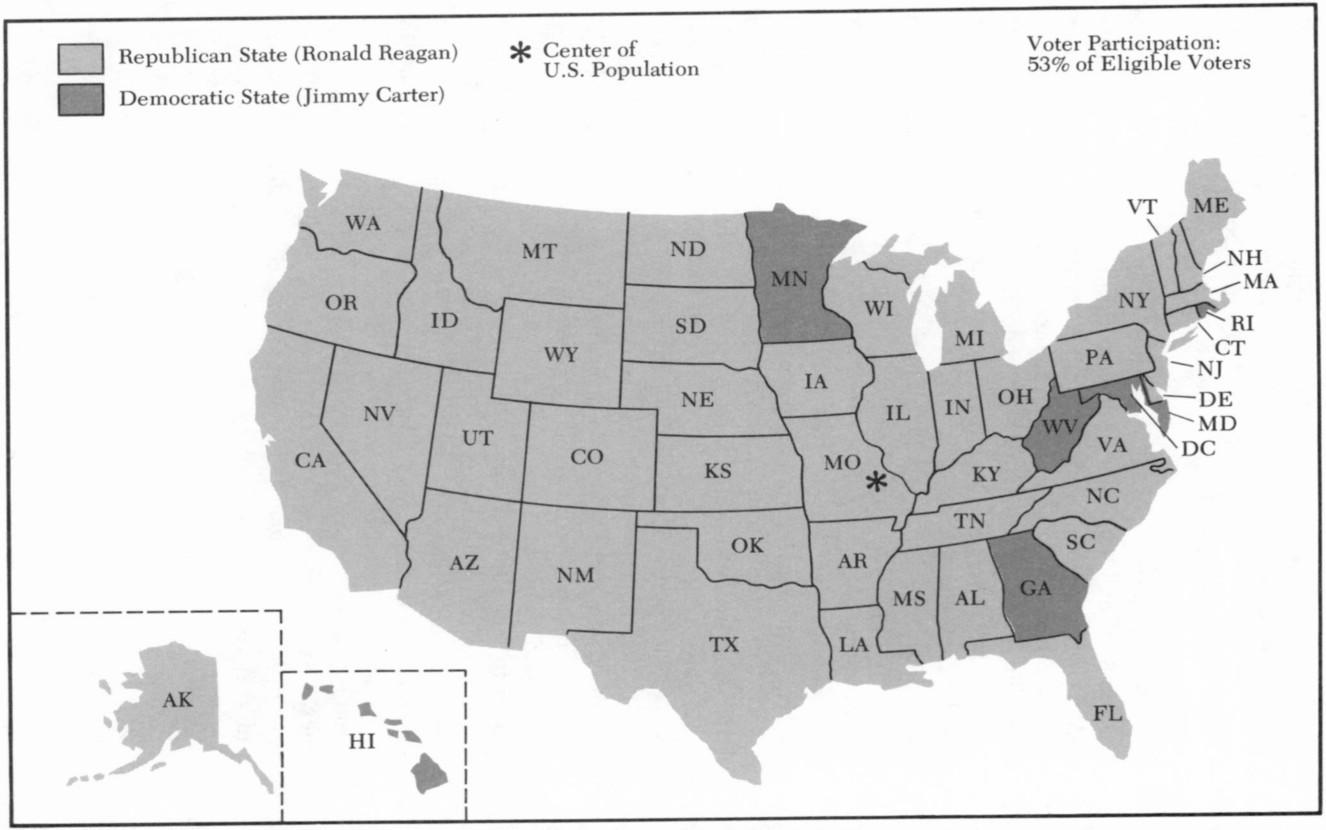
Republican State (Ronald Reagan)
Democratic State (Jimmy Carter)
* Center of U.S. Population
Voter Participation: 53% of Eligible Voters
WA
OR
CA
ID
NV
MT
WY
UT
AZ
CO
NM
ND
SD
NE
KS
OK
TX
MN
IA
MO
AR
LA
WI
IL
MI
IN
OH
KY
TN
MS
AL
GA
FL
SC
NC
VA
WV
PA
NY
VT
ME
NH
MA
RI
CT
NJ
DE
MD
DC
AK
HI

the first time in history, the Western states exercised far greater power in the election than they had ever done. The census reapportionment of 1980, which shifted a number of electoral votes from the North and East to the South and West, confirmed this trend.

The splintering of American self-consciousness into a variety of competing and sometimes antagonistic groups had contradictory effects. On the one hand, the militant assertion of minority-group consciousness led to an unprecedented degree of social toleration. On the other hand, new groups made efforts to redirect power in American society. Evangelical religions, antibusing groups, pro- and anti-abortion groups, gay rights and anti–gay rights activists, pro- and anti-ERA advocates, antinuclear demonstrators, ethnic pride groups, the Gray Panthers, black activists—all contended with essential social values. They tried to redefine national self-consciousness in the way that groups generally do—in their own interest and sometimes with extravagant intolerance.

This struggle over essential values of the family and the shape of the social order indicated a deep need to reorder American social priorities to fit the realities of a world that no longer resembled 1945. The period that began in the exhilarating, but precarious, hopes of military victory ended in complication and the confusion of goals. Along the way, Americans had created a remarkably different culture, one in which openness and experimentation coexisted and competed with tradition. Government had been called upon to legislate and enforce new rights, to regulate and balance as never before. In doing so, it had undertaken responsibilities it scarcely comprehended; it chose to go down a dimly lighted and rough path with no map. For some, this new direction and the tensions it aroused between groups in American society, between traditional culture and the new social ethic, between old ideas and new, were too great a price to pay for progress. For others, however, the struggle between problems and potential was only another version of the challenge that Americans had always risen to answer.

Suggested Reading

The historical contours of the period following World War II have begun to emerge with some clarity in recent years. Two major divisions now seem apparent: from 1945 to about 1968 and from 1968 onward. Because the events referred to in this book are so recent, some of the historical questions have not yet been sharply defined. However, a surprisingly large amount of fine work has already been done, much of which suggests that the period from 1945 to 1968 represents an extraordinarily prosperous and progressive time and possibly even an exception to much previous American history.

One explanation for the economic stability after the war is suggested in Otis Graham's *Toward a Planned Society* (1976), which discusses the increasing tendency of the American government to undertake central economic planning. Gunnar Myrdal's *An American Dilemma: The Negro Problem and Modern Democracy* (1944) indicates the seriousness of the problem of race relations that society was called upon to confront after the war. Keith Olson's *The G.I. Bill: Veterans and the Colleges* (1974) is a good study of the role of this important legislation in revolutionizing higher education in America. Changes in the American family have been discussed by a number of authors. A good, short account is Barry Farber's *Family and Kinship in Modern Society* (1973). Richard A. Easterlin offers an interesting perspective on the sudden increase in the birth rate after the war in his *American Baby Boom in Historical Perspective* (1962). The revolution in American medicine that followed the war is ably sketched in James Bordley and A. McGehee Harvey's *Two Centuries of American Medicine: 1776–1976* (1976). A fascinating study of changes in public attitudes is George H. Gallup's *The Gallup Poll: Public Opinion, 1935–1971* (1972). Some of the difficult concepts and arrangements in postwar economics are clarified in Alfred E. Eckes, Jr.'s *A Search for Solvency: Bretton Woods and the International Monetary System, 1941–1971* (1975). A fine account of the Roosevelt presidency during the war is James MacGregor Burns's *Roosevelt: The Soldier of Freedom* (1970).

The Cold War has been the subject of much debate. Historians have argued over the degree of responsibility that the Soviet Union and the United States should share for initiating and perpetuating this hostile confrontation. John Lewis Gaddis's *The United States and the Origins of the Cold War, 1941–1947* (1972) is a fine, comprehensive account. Stephen E. Ambrose, in *Rise to Globalism: American Foreign Policy Since 1938* (1971), argues that since the late 1930s, the United States has increasingly taken an interventionist position in world affairs. Lloyd C. Gardner's *Architects of Illusion: Men and Ideas in American Foreign Policy 1941–1949* (1970) is a critical essay on the ideology of policy makers.

The complicated policies surrounding the creation and use of the atomic bomb—and the effects of these policies—are admirably documented in a fine book by Martin J. Sherwin, *A World Destroyed: The Atomic Bomb and the Grand Alliance* (1975). A very useful source is Hans L. Trefousse's *The Cold War: A Book of Documents* (1965). An interesting popular account of the Cold War may be found in Carl Solberg's *Riding High: America in the Cold War* (1973). Adam B. Ulam, in *Expansion and Coexistence: Soviet Foreign Policy, 1917–73* (1974), provides a comprehensive account of Soviet intentions during this period.

The memoir literature of foreign-policy figures is particularly interesting and literate. Two of the outstanding works are Dean Acheson's *Present at the Creation: My Years in the State Department* (1969) and George F. Kennan's *Memoirs: 1925–1950* (1967). Also interesting is *Private Papers of Senator Vandenberg*, by Arthur H. Vandenberg, Jr. (1952). A controversial book describing the darker side of diplomacy is Allen Weinstein's *Perjury!: The Hiss-Chambers Conflict* (1978). Weinstein makes a case for the guilt of Alger Hiss, accused of passing secret documents to the Russians in the late 1930s.

Assessment of the Truman presidency has already undergone at least one revision. Viewed unfavorably by many of his contemporaries, Truman has been given high marks by later historians. A good place to begin reading is with Truman's own *Memoirs* (1955). This work is full of interesting anecdotes and gives a sample of the president's feisty style. Alonzo L. Hamby in *Beyond the New Deal: Harry S Truman and American Liberalism* (1973), judiciously assesses the President's relationship to liberalism. Bert Cochran's *Harry Truman and the Crisis Presidency* (1973) is a very readable, iconoclastic account. Special issues surrounding the Truman administration have been covered by Arthur F. McClure, *The Truman Administration and the Problems of Postwar Labor, 1945–1948* (1969). John Snetsinger, in *Truman, the Jewish Vote and the Creation of Israel* (1974), delineates the president's ambiguous policy toward that new nation. Richard S. Kirkendall's *Harry S Truman, Korea, and the Imperial Presidency* (1975), is a good discussion of Truman's policies. William Berman, in *The Politics of Civil Rights in the Truman Administration* (1970), traces the administration's activities in this field. Richard Lowitt provides a balanced account of the *Truman-MacArthur Controversy* (1967). Truman's record on civil liberties has been challenged by two writers: David Caute, in *The Great Fear: The Anti-Communist Purge Under Truman and Eisenhower* (1978), and Anthan F. Theoharis, in *Seeds of Repression: Harry Truman and the Origins of McCarthyism* (1971).

Changes in urban and suburban life were widely studied in the postwar period. Several contemporary books offer a great deal of insight into the suburban culture of the 1950s. The most important is David Riesman's *The Lonely Crowd: A Study of the Changing American Character* (1950). William H. Whyte, Jr.'s, *The Organization Man* (1956) is a fascinating study of suburban culture and Whyte's revulsion by it. J. D. Salinger's *The Catcher in the Rye* (1951), a very controversial novel, captures the tone of much of the youth revolt that began in the 1950s. Herbert Gans, in *The Levittowners: Ways of Life and Politics in a New Suburban Community* (1967) argues that the new suburban culture did *not* display the vapid conformity described in much of the literature of the era. Two other books explore this question: Richard L. Rapson's collection *Individualism and Conformity in the American Character* (1967) and Scott Donaldson's *The Suburban Myth* (1969). Vance Packard's *The Hidden Persuaders* (1957) is a fascinating, contemporary document that identifies advertising as the basic element in the conformist culture of the 1950s.

A good study of how segregation in housing helped create separate spheres of urban and suburban culture is Charles Abrams, *Forbidden Neighbors: A Study of Prejudice in Housing* (1955). A very interesting and acerbic biography by Robert A. Caro, *The Power Broker: Robert Moses and the Fall of New York* (1974), details the impact of highways and the highway lobby on America's first city. Ralph Ellison's *Shadow and Act* (1964) is a superb collection of essays on black issues in America during this period. There are a great many discussions of the impact of black music on the mainstream of American popular culture. Among the best and most readable is Carl Belz's *The Story of Rock* (1969).

In recent years the reputation of Dwight Eisenhower has improved. Historians now judge him to be an enlightened conservative. The best general account of his presidency is Charles C. Alexander's *Holding the Line: The Eisenhower Era, 1952–61* (1975). Robert H. Ferrell's edition of *The Eisenhower Diaries* (1981) sheds important new light on this complex man. These should be read in conjunction with Eisenhower's memoirs, *The White House Years* (1963–1965). A good collection of documents is Robert L. Branyan and Lawrence H. Larsen's *The Eisenhower Administration: A Documentary History* (1971). An interesting popular biography is Steve Neal's *The Eisenhowers' Reluctant Dynasty* (1978). One of the most controversial issues of the Eisenhower administration, the desegregation decision, is handled exhaustively by Richard Kluger, *Simple Justice* (1975). James R. Killian, Jr., discusses the important issue of science in these years in his memoir, *Sputnik, Scientists, and Eisenhower* (1976).

Two particularly interesting biographies add to the literature of this era. They are James T. Patterson's *Mr. Republican: A Biography of Robert A. Taft* (1972) and John Bartlow Martin's two-volume *The Life of Adlai E. Stevenson* (1977). Earl Warren's *The Memoirs of Earl Warren* (1977) provides useful information about and insights into this Supreme Court justice who did much to alter America's social conscience.

Issues of power, productivity, and communications were a vast subject in postwar writing. An early account of automation is John Diebold's *Automation: The Advent of the Automatic Factory* (1952). Howard Boone Jacobson and Joseph S. Soucek discuss the automation controversy in their work *Automation and Society* (1959). Ralph Parkman's *The Cybernetic Society* (1972) is an interesting update of the issue. Discussions of the increasing concentration in the American economy are numerous. Among the more interesting books on this subject are Richard J. Barber's *The American Corporation; Its Power, Its Money, Its Politics* (1970) and Neil H. Jacoby, *Corporate Power and Social Responsibility: A Blueprint for the Future* (1973). As in all of his books, John Kenneth Galbraith, in *The New Industrial State* (1971), is witty and provocative.

Two books in particular offer contrasting views of the potential impact of nuclear warfare on American society. The first, Herman Kahn's *On Thermonuclear War* (1960), argues the feasibility of survival after such a catastrophe. In the second, Arthur I. Waskow and Stanley L. Newman, *American in Hiding* (1962), the authors discuss what they view as the deplorable effects of large-scale civil defense projects. Marshall McLuhan, in his *Understanding Media: The Extensions of Man* (1964), suggests that modern communications, not nuclear power, have most radically transformed modern society.

The Kennedy-Johnson years have been the subject of much disagreement. Historians have disputed the impact of Kennedy's presidency in particular. Some, such as Arthur M. Schlesinger, Jr., in *A Thousand Days: John F. Kennedy in the White House* (1965), contend that the young president must be placed in the pantheon of America's great leaders. Two of Kennedy's advisers share something of this view: Pierre Salinger, in *With Kennedy* (1966), and Theodore C. Sorensen, in *Kennedy* (1965). Other writers are less enthusiastic. Henry Fairlie, *The Kennedy Promise: The Politics of Expectation* (1973), is an interesting account. David Halberstam's *The Best and the Brightest* (1969) is an exhaustive and revealing discussion of the foreign policy that led to defeat in Vietnam. Jim F. Heath, in *Decade of Disillusionment: The Kennedy-Johnson Years* (1975), and Bruce Miroff, *Pragmatic Illusions: The Presidential Politics of John F. Kennedy* (1976), deflate the claims of Kennedy's supporters.

Some of the special issues of the Kennedy administration are well covered in Hobart Rowen's discussion of economics, *The Free Enterprisers: Kennedy, Johnson and the Business Establishment* (1964), and Carl M. Brauer's *John F. Kennedy and the Second Reconstruction* (1977), in which the author documents the president's civil rights activities.

Some of Kennedy's own writings make interesting reading—for example, *Profiles in Courage* (1961). It is difficult to understand Kennedy without some insight into his family. A readable biography of his father is David Koskoff's *Joseph P. Kennedy: A Life and Times* (1974). Arthur M. Schlesinger, Jr., provides a very favorable account of the president's brother in *Robert Kennedy and His Times* (1978). James MacGregor Burns has written an important biography of Edward Kennedy: *Edward Kennedy and the Camelot Legacy* (1976).

Aside from the general works listed above that touch on the Johnson administration, other books specifically assess the Johnson years. The most readable and interesting is Doris Kearns's psychological study and biography, *Lyndon Johnson and the American Dream* (1976). Eric Goldman, resident White House intellectual, has an interesting account, *The Tragedy of Lyndon Johnson* (1969). Frank Cormier, a reporter, provides fascinating details of Washington in *LBJ: The Way He Was* (1977). The origins and implementation of Johnson's most important domestic legislation are discussed in a government publication, Stephen Goodell and Bennet Schiff's, *The Office of Economic Opportunity During the Administration of President Lyndon B. Johnson, 1963–1969* (1973).

Social and political movements of the 1950s and 1960s have preoccupied many observers. A good beginning point is Arthur M. Schlesinger, Jr.'s, *Vital Center: The Politics of Freedom* (1949). William F. Buckley's *God and Man at Yale: The Superstitions of "Academic Freedom"* (1951) is a good conservative response to liberal ideas about the nature of modern thought. The function of religion in America is brilliantly described by Will Herberg in *Protestant—Catholic—Jew: An Essay in American Religious Sociology* (1960). A special issue of *Daedalus* magazine (Winter 1967) contains a broad discussion of the role of religion in American society. Roderick P. Hart, in *The Political Pulpit* (1977), delineates the movement of evangelical religion into the political arena.

The major advance in social relations during the 1950s and 1960s came in the recognition of the rights of black Americans. The central figure in this cause was Martin Luther King, Jr. Probably the best biography of this leader is David Lewis's *King: A Critical Biography* (1970). A very favorable essay on the Student Nonviolent Coordinating Committee is Howard Zinn's *SNCC: The New Abolitionists* (1965). Good source material and articles may be found in a work edited by August Meier and Elliot Rudwick, *Black Protest in the Sixties* (1970). Black self-consciousness helped to strengthen other varieties of self-consciousness in this period. An interesting discussion is contained in Arnold Dashefsky's edited work, *Ethnic Identity in Society* (1976).

Radical student politics had a major impact on American society during the 1960s. Assessment of the principal organization of the New Left—Students for a Democratic Society (SDS)—differs. A sympathetic account is contained in Kirkpatrick Sale's *SDS* (1973). Irwin Unger, in *The Movement: A History of the American New Left, 1959–72* (1974), is more critical. A good sample of New Left ideas can be found in Abbie Hoffman's *The Conspiracy* (1969), which discusses the trial of several leftist leaders for their activities at the 1968 Democratic National Convention in Chicago.

American culture also changed profoundly during the 1960s. An interesting account of one of the earliest rebels is Dennis McNally's *Desolate Angel: Jack Kerouac, the Beat Generation, and America* (1979). Morris Dickstein, *Gates of Eden: American Culture in the Sixties* (1977), is an excellent essay on the connections between radical movements and American culture during this era.

Most of the history of the 1970s is, as yet, unwritten. There are, however, a number of important books on the women's movement. Any study should begin with Betty Friedan's landmark, *The Feminine Mystique* (1963). William H. Chafe's *Women and Equality: Changing Patterns in American Culture* (1977) is a good short history that concentrates on the recent period. Anne Koedt, Ellen Levine, and Anita Rapone, in a volume entitled *Radical Feminism* (1973), provide a sampling of radical feminist writings. The National Commission on the Observance of International Woman's Year Report, *To Form a More Perfect Union* (1976), indicates a high degree of government support for women's rights. Another important issue of the 1970s—the older population—is well covered in William Graebner's *A History of Retirement: The Meaning and Function of an American Institution, 1885–1978* (1980). Herman P. Miller's *Rich Man, Poor Man* (1971) contains an important discussion of income distribution in the United States.

Richard Nixon has been the subject of endless controversy since the beginning of his career. His own *Six Crises* (1962) and his *Memoirs* (1978) are important and illuminating. Garry Wills's *Nixon Agonistes: The Crisis of the Self-Made Man* (1970) is an irreverent but delightful book. Carl Bernstein and Bob Woodward's *All the President's Men* (1974) is the best work on Watergate, by the two reporters who unearthed much of the incriminating evidence.

Index

About the Author

JAMES GILBERT received his B.A. from Carleton College and his M.A. and Ph.D. from the University of Wisconsin. He has taught at Teachers College, Columbia University, the Centre for Social History at Warwick University, Coventry, England, and at the University of Maryland. In 1978, he was chosen Distinguished Scholar-Teacher at Maryland. In 1968 he published *Writers and Partisans*. His other books include *Designing the Industrial State* (1972) and *Work Without Salvation* (1978). In 1977 his "Wars of the Worlds" was named the best article of the year by the Popular Culture Association. He has been a Fellow of the Woodrow Wilson Foundation and the National Endowment for the Humanities.

A Note on the Type

The text of this book was set in the film version of Caledonia, originally designed by W. A. Dwiggins. It belongs to the family of printing types called "modern faces" by printers—a term used to mark the change in style of type letters that occurred about 1800. Caledonia is reliably readable even in small sizes and borders on the general design of Scotch Modern, but it is more freely drawn.

Book design by Sara Eisenman.
Typeset by Eastern Graphics.
Printed and bound by the Vail-Ballou Press, Inc.

Date Due

Ascension, had as central a place as belief in the Cross and was distinct from it.[1] In the Hellenistic kerugma the moment of exaltation cannot then have been the moment of death; the latter could only be accepted if Phil. ii. 6–11 by itself was regarded as defining the kerugma, an argument which we cannot allow.

When we turn to the Gnostic Saviour myth it is at least open to doubt if this has affected primitive Christianity to the extent which Schreiber assumes. 'The myth of the Urmensch-Redeemer has been adequately examined by others, and the view that such a myth, if it ever existed, exercised a formative influence on the early Church is now generally rejected.'[2] Only if we find overwhelming evidence within the Gospel itself of influence from the myth may we assume that Mark has shaped his Christology and soteriology in its light. Some of the evidence which Schreiber produces for this is most slender. The derivation of the pre-existence of the Son from the Parable of the Vineyard (xii. 1–12) may serve as an example; such pre-existence was of course an essential item in the myth. According to Schreiber[3] the Son of the parable is sent by the Father, and this can only be a sending from heaven in view of the general usage of ἀποστέλλειν. But (a) The servants are also sent; the same verb is used. Must pre-existence then be assumed for the prophets? (b) The sending of both servants and Son is an essential item in the story of the parable; it could not be told without this element; but the emphasis does not lie on this detail of the narrative; it is wrong therefore to over-emphasise it unless Mark gives us the hint to do so, and this he does not do. Schreiber further argues that as the Redeemer of the myth associates the saved with himself, so in Mark there is a community associated with the Saviour.[4] Undoubtedly there is a community associated with the Saviour in Mark, but many great men have left behind them a community of disciples dedicated to carry on their work; that does not imply they were influenced by the

---

[1] Bultmann, *Theologie des Neuen Testaments*, pp. 80–2.

[2] Wilson, *The Gnostic Problem*, p. 220; for substantiation of this judgement see pp. 218 ff. and the references given in the notes. Cf. G. Quispel, 'The Jung Codex and its Significance', in *The Jung Codex* (ed. F. L. Cross), pp. 76–8; C. Colpe, *Die religionsgeschichtliche Schule* (Göttingen, 1961), p. 191.

[3] Pp. 166 f.   [4] Pp. 167–70.

myth. Moreover the distinctive traits that we find in the Gnostic saved community are lacking in Mark; in the myth the association of the saved with the Saviour is described in fundamentally non-personal terms; they are drawn to him because they have souls that respond as sparks of the divine; they are worn by him as a garment.[1] In Mark the relationship of the community to its Lord remains couched in purely personal terms, in terms of following and obedience. The terms of Pauline theology, 'the Body of Christ', 'in Christ', etc., which with somewhat more justification have been viewed by some scholars as reflecting the myth, are wholly absent in Mark. Lastly when Schreiber argues that Mark portrays Jesus as successful in exorcism and miracle and in the routing of those come to dispute with him and that this shows the influence of the θεῖος ἀνήρ idea,[2] we may rejoin that many ancient biographers, and some modern also, glorify their heroes in the same way and are not therefore necessarily suspected of being under the influence of the myth. Schreiber does not reckon with the possibility that Jesus may in fact have exorcised demons, healed the sick and out-argued his opponents! Mark would not thus seem to adhere to the myth as closely as Schreiber suggests, and when he does adhere he is only following the general tendency of all writers, and therefore ideas similar to some of those adhering to the myth need not be traced to the myth.

In a sense, however, these are minor points; our major concern is with Schreiber's view that the Cross is Christ's exaltation; though, if we have shown that the influence of the myth on Mark cannot be stated as dogmatically as he assumes, we have removed a possible reason why we should support Schreiber in the peculiar position he has adopted in regard to the death of Christ. Schreiber's main arguments lie in his understanding of the crucifixion scene as told by Mark and in his playing down of the significance of the Resurrection for Mark, to which he adds certain confirmatory evidence from earlier parts of the Gospel.

When we turn to Schreiber's view of Mark's account of the crucifixion scene (xv. 20–41) we are at a great disadvantage since his work on this has not been published. But reading

---

[1] Cf. Best, *One Body in Christ*, pp. 85–7, 224 f.
[2] Pp. 158, 163, 173.

between the lines we may suppose that he has drawn attention to certain 'cosmic' elements in the account which suggest a cosmic victory, for example the great cry, the rending of the Temple veil, the darkness. These appear in the apocalyptic source which he separates out in the account. We have already discussed these in detail and have seen that they can be interpreted satisfactorily without reference to Christ's Ascension. They fit the pattern of a death which is both a judgement on the sin of men and a deliverance for them from sin.[1]

A further point at which it might be argued that a cosmic dimension should be seen in the Passion would lie in the linking of it to I Cor. ii. 8. If the high priests and those who crucified Jesus are taken as representatives of the demonic powers, then their failure in that he rose from the dead may be an indication of his victory over them. It was a common belief of the time[2] that behind governing authorities were 'supernatural powers' (cf. Rom. xiii. 1–7) and that the actions of the two were closely related. Amongst the Jews the nations were regarded as under the control of folk-angels. There is, however, no trace of such a view in Mark. The priests and leaders of the Jews whom Mark largely holds to be responsible for the death of Christ hardly occupy the same role as the civil authorities of the nations. Moreover if Mark viewed them as demonically inspired in their behaviour we should expect that as in many of the other demonic incidents they would have displayed supernatural knowledge of the true nature of Jesus, and Jesus' self-testimony of xiv. 62 would have been unnecessary. In I Cor. ii. 8 there is obviously a different theory of demonic knowledge from Mark's. The supernatural authorities behind civil rulers were not necessarily regarded as evil; if Mark accepted the common position in this matter then xii. 13–17 would probably imply that he regarded rulers and their 'angels' at least as neutral. When Mark tells the story of the Passion he seems however to treat the high priests, etc., as individuals, as men, and not as front-pieces for spiritual powers.

[1] Pp. 97 ff. above.
[2] This has been clearly demonstrated by C. D. Morrison, *The Powers that Be* (London, 1960), though he himself would not connect the Lordship of Christ over them with his Cross but would rather see it as a fact of creation; cf. Morrison, *ibid.* pp. 116 ff.

We must now examine how Mark deals with the Resurrection. It must be admitted with Schreiber that, if xvi. 8 is the conclusion of the Gospel, then Mark contains no account of any Resurrection appearances. But this is not necessarily evidence for the belief that Mark makes the moment of death the moment of exaltation. It is equally evidence for the equation of the exaltation and the Resurrection. There are good grounds for holding that in the primitive kerugma Ascension and Resurrection were not clearly distinguished; the risen Jesus is the exalted Jesus. This is probably found reflected in Phil. ii. 6–11, where the death might be the moment of exaltation but need not necessarily be taken so. We may also allow to Schreiber that the Christ of the Transfiguration is the exalted Christ, but this is no proof that the exaltation took place on the Cross.[1] If the exaltation and the death are identified then no place is left for the Resurrection as a distinct event; such a place may remain however even if the Resurrection and the exaltation are identified. Mark moreover does appear to give the Resurrection a distinct place. It is always μετὰ τρεῖς ἡμέρας (viii. 31; ix. 31; x. 34).[2] The distinctness of the Resurrection as an event is also implied in the empty tomb; the crucified Christ is left there; by the third day he is risen; the Resurrection is thus subsequent to the burial and the death (xvi. 6). These passages may have come to Mark in the tradition, but surely he must have accepted what he received when it was set down so clearly; he could easily have modified the predictions of the Passion and Resurrection by the omission of μετὰ τρεῖς ἡμέρας and so have created the possibility that the exaltation might be contemporaneous with the death.[3] Lacking convincing evidence that Mark desired such a modification of the primitive kerugma we must reject the idea that the moment of death was the moment of exaltation, and therefore we cannot use this theory

[1] Though admittedly there is no easy explanation, Schreiber's interpretation of the six days (ix. 2) is too fanciful (pp. 161 f.); for other suggestions cf. Mauser, pp. 111 f.; C. E. Carlston, 'Transfiguration and Resurrection', *J.B.L.* LXXX (1961), 233–40.

[2] The three days of xiv. 58; xv. 29 are almost certainly also implicit references to the Resurrection of Jesus; viii. 2 may be also.

[3] If the addition of the reference to the Resurrection in the Passion predictions was made by the early Church, it would have been all the easier for Mark to omit it.

covenant and to the pouring out of blood in the saying attached
to the cup are interpretative additions to the original words of
Jesus, but they will have been in the text before Mark received
it. If of course they were Markan additions then they would
emphasise strongly the view that Mark was putting out on his
own a doctrine of the death of Jesus which connected it to the
sin of men rather than the defeat of the Devil. We, however,
assume that Mark did not add them; but in using them in
the account he presumably agreed with their interpretation of
the death of Jesus. It is important for the understanding of the
Markan account that we realise that it was a Paschal meal at
which the Eucharist was instituted (xiv. 12, 14, etc.). Mark
may or may not have known of the alternative tradition which
made Jesus die at the time of the slaughtering of the Passover
lamb and thereby made the Last Supper take place prior to the
Passover, but he clearly excludes it by his careful description of
the preparation for the meal. The account is also firmly held
within the Passion story; there may be allusions to the Eucharist
in the feeding accounts, but the institution is tied to the night
before the death of Jesus, and accordingly must be interpreted
in the light of that death.

The saying about the bread is left without interpretative
addition and whatever meaning we give to it must be read out
of the total context, or out of the meaning of σῶμα itself, or out
of its parallelism with the saying about the cup. It is almost
certainly erroneous to derive the meaning of the bread logion
from the fact of its fraction, that is, that as the bread is broken,
so Christ's body is broken in death. The breaking of bread
was a normal part of the action of asking a blessing on a meal,[1]
and the actual words, 'This is my body', are connected in the
account to the distribution and eating of the bread and not to
its breaking.[2] Equally the saying about the cup is not to be
connected to its pouring out but to the participation in it; the
saying actually follows the participation. If the bread logion is
taken by itself, and we shall see that this is more probable, then
σῶμα probably has the meaning of 'self'—the body is the outward expression of the self and cannot be detached from the

---

[1] Cf. C. F. D. Moule, *Worship in the New Testament*, p. 19; A. J. B.
Higgins, *The Lord's Supper in the New Testament*, pp. 51 f.
[2] Cf. Jeremias, *The Eucharistic Words of Jesus*, p. 142.

self.[1] To eat the bread which is Christ himself is then to participate in Christ, and the saying will be interpreted along the lines of I Cor. x. 16 f.[2] Naturally the Christ in whom the Christian participates is the crucified Christ, but this of itself does not tell us anything about the meaning of the death of Christ. For an interpretation of this we must turn to the saying associated with the cup.

When we now consider this we are forced, as in the case of x. 45, to accept the argument that there is not sufficient evidence to show formative influence from the Servant concept.[3] It is possible to link the usage of covenant with the Servant concept through Isa. xlii. 6; xlix. 8,[4] but the theme of the covenant is so general in the Old Testament that it is impossible to tie it down to these two texts, especially since it is here connected to the shedding of blood, of which there is no mention in the Servant passages; moreover in the Isaianic passages the Servant is himself the covenant. It is much more natural then to see in the cup-logion when it speaks of the covenant a reference to Exod. xxiv. 8 or Zech. ix. 11 under the influence of Jer. xxxi. 31 ff.; or to circumcision. The use of πολλοί is again as in x. 45 too widespread a Semitic idiom to ensure a connection to Isa. liii. 11, 12; and ἐκχύννειν has no place in the Servant imagery. The most difficult phrase in the saying is τὸ αἷμά μου τῆς διαθήκης. As it stands this would normally refer in Judaism to the blood of circumcision.[5] This hardly seems possible in the present context. Blood and the institution of a covenant are also associated in Exod. xxiv. 8; if this connection is accepted, then Jesus would be understood as instituting a new covenant, διαθήκη, carrying within itself the concept 'new',[6] and this saying would be brought into line with the

[1] Cf. Pedersen, *Israel*, I–II, p. 171, cf. pp. 171–81; Best, *One Body in Christ*, pp. 215 ff.

[2] Cf. F.-J. Leenhardt in Cullmann and Leenhardt, *Essays on the Lord's Supper*, pp. 41–3.

[3] The majority of commentators appear to accept the influence of the Servant concept. It is rejected by Hooker, *Jesus and the Servant*, pp. 80–3, and doubted by Behm, *T.W.N.T.* II, 136.

[4] Fuller, *The Mission and Achievement of Jesus*, pp. 72–5.

[5] Jeremias, *The Eucharistic Words of Jesus*, p. 134.

[6] In the Qumran writings there are many references to the 'covenant'; normally 'the new covenant' is intended though the adjective 'new' is

similar Pauline cup-logion. If the connection is made to Zech. ix. 11 then it is unlikely that we deal here with the institution of the covenant; rather we are concerned with its maintenance through the daily sacrifice.[1] The association with Exod. xxiv. 8 appears preferable. The presence of this phrase about the covenant renders difficult any attempt to create a parallelism between the cup and bread sayings and to interpret them together. Most of those who take them as closely associated, for example Jeremias,[2] draw their conclusions from the form of the sayings which they regard as primitive and prior to the Markan. Thus we cannot argue that Mark would have taken the two sayings together as referring to a sacrificed animal in the moment of its death when flesh and blood are separated.[3] It is interesting that Mark places the saying about the cup after it has been drunk, and not at the moment of distribution, as in the case of the bread. This would again indicate that he did not see the two as closely associated in meaning; the bread refers to the fellowship of believers with Christ and the cup to the sacrifice of Christ for them. Within the early Christian Church the two ideas were inevitably linked together—Christ in us and Christ for us. The reference to the death of Jesus is present in the pouring out of the blood; ἐκχυννόμενον may probably be taken as having a future meaning and as passive, God being the subject;[4] this underlines the frequent idea of the Gospel that the death of Jesus is divinely determined. It is a death ὑπὲρ πολλῶν, that is, as we have seen, for all. Jesus does not die for himself; he does not die merely as a martyr, he dies for men. Moreover we are forced to see here a sacrificial significance; as the old covenant was instituted through the death of an animal, so the new is instituted through the death of the Son of God for the benefit of men. The fact that men drink the wine and do not merely watch it poured out suggests that the blessings of the death are for them to participate in.

added only on four occasions, and the cognate verb is used only four times (cf. Kuhn, *Konkordanz*). Equally the concept of the 'covenant' was widespread in early Christianity and need not always have required the addition of 'new' to imply that the 'new covenant' was intended.

[1] So most commentators.
[2] *The Eucharistic Words of Jesus*, pp. 139 ff.
[3] So Jeremias, *op. cit.* pp. 143 ff.   [4] So Jeremias, *op. cit.* pp. 122 f.

At this point we must diverge from our study of individual texts to inquire whether Mark makes use of the Servant Christology, and if so in what way. We have dismissed a direct relationship to the Servant in x. 45 and xiv. 24; the literary links are not sufficiently clear. Yet we do move in a realm of ideas which is not far distant from that of Isa. liii: the death of Jesus is for men and benefits them. Moreover the Servant Christology cannot be eliminated from the early Church.[1] How far has Mark come under its influence? The presence of this conception has been seen in a series of texts in Mark beginning with the divine voice at baptism.[2] At no point can it be said that identification with the Servant of Deutero-Isaiah is certain, and indeed in many of the suggested passages the identification has been disputed. Typical in this respect is i. 11 (cf. ix. 7). It is generally accepted that the Markan report of the words of the heavenly voice represents the tradition more faithfully than the western form of the Lukan text (iii. 22). In the Markan text the identification with the Servant supposes the existence of an Old Testament translation of Isa. xlii. 1 in which ὁ ἀγαπητός replaced the ἐκλεκτός of the LXX; Matt. xii. 18–21 implies this possibility. Yet many commentators are convinced that 'sonship' rather than 'servanthood' is the predominating theme in Mark i. 11.[3] There are three possibilities. (a) In the logion as it reached Mark there was no reference to servant-hood; Mark then introduced the reference. If so, he did it very poorly. This possibility is most unlikely.[4] (b) The logion is in the form in which it reached Mark and he has preserved it unchanged.

[1] We believe that Jeremias in Zimmerli and Jeremias, *The Servant of God*, pp. 79 ff. (= *T.W.N.T.* v, 698 ff.), has made out a much better case for its presence in the very early tradition used in Acts and by Paul than Miss Hooker (*Jesus and the Servant*) allows. For further criticism of Jeremias, etc., cf. Iersel, '*Der Sohn*' in den synoptischen Jesusworten, pp. 20–3, 52–65.

[2] Miss Hooker (*Jesus and the Servant, passim*) has gathered together the various passages in which a Servant Christology is suspected, and we use this as the basis of our discussion. She gives full references both to those who have upheld and those who have disputed the reference to the Servant in these passages.

[3] E.g. Taylor, *ad loc.*; Fuller, *The Mission and Achievement of Jesus*, pp. 87 f. Moreover the use of ἀγαπητός can be explained in terms of Gen. xxii. 1–18; cf. below, pp. 169 ff.

[4] Cf. Hahn, *Christologische Hoheitstitel*, pp. 338, 340, who considers that an original עַבְדִּי was replaced by ὁ υἱός μου in i. 11; ix. 7.

In that case we must again say that, since the reference to the Servant in the saying is not certain, Mark has not made it clearer and therefore cannot be said to have thought the conception important at this point. (c) Mark has modified the logion as he received it in order to emphasise the conception of sonship, and thereby has pushed servanthood into the background.[1] A decision between (b) and (c) is hardly possible on the evidence at our disposal. We can certainly say that Mark does not stress servanthood here, but rather shows his interest is in Jesus as Son of God.

The remainder of the material in Mark in which the Servant influence is suspected may be divided into two classes— material which he received in the tradition and passed on more or less unchanged, and material which he himself created or, receiving it, considerably modified.

Let us take first the former category: (a) i. 9, 10, the descent of the Spirit on Jesus at baptism: Mark has certainly not introduced this and he has done nothing to ensure an obvious connection with the Servant. In the reference to the opening of the heavens Luke and Matthew modify Mark's use of σχίζειν to ἀνοίγειν which is found at Isa. lxiii. 19. (b) i. 11; ix. 7, the voice at Baptism and Transfiguration; we have already discussed this. (c) x. 45, see above (pp. 140ff.). (d) xiv. 18, 21, the use of παραδίδωμι. The fact of the betrayal must have come to Mark in the tradition and this is the natural word to describe it (cf. Isa. liii. 6, 12).[2] (e) xiv. 24, see above (pp. 144ff.). (f) xiv. 65; xv. 16–20, the mocking of Jesus. Mark will hardly have introduced this event into the account; the references to the Servant are not sufficiently certain. (g) xv. 27, the crucifixion between two thieves: as the Markan gloss shows this was early interpreted as a reference to Isa. liii. 12. Mark is unlikely to have invented the detail about the thieves; if it was created by the early Church it would imply that it viewed Jesus as the Servant, but the point is not made clear in Mark; if it is an historical event then it can hardly be closely linked to the

[1] Maurer, 'Knecht Gottes und Sohn Gottes im Passionsbericht des Markusevangeliums', indicates that the Servant Christology lay in the material prior to Mark and gradually received less emphasis.

[2] Iersel, '*Der Sohn' in den synoptischen Jesusworten*, pp. 57 f., argues that it is a general word by no means restricted to the Servant imagery.

Isaianic passage. To sum up, we may say that some of the material which Mark received may have contained the idea of Jesus as the Servant, but in the places we have discussed he has done nothing to sharpen the conception.

But what of the second category, the material he has modified or created? (*a*) i. 1–3, the use of εὐαγγέλιον and the Old Testament quotations. Whether we retain the quotation from Mal. iii. 1 as an original part of the Gospel or not, the use of Isa. xl. 3 is certainly Markan. The combination of this and εὐαγγέλιον shows Mark's indebtedness to Deutero-Isaiah at this point. But it is difficult to trace a precise reference to the Servant; Deutero-Isaiah is concerned with a great deal more than the Servant alone. If Mark intended us to see such a connection he has not done much to ensure we do. He has made clear that the salvation of which Deutero-Isaiah spoke is present in Jesus Christ. (*b*) iii. 27. We take this verse here because it may have been partly formed by Mark under the influence of his view of the Temptation. Isa. xlix. 24 f. probably lies behind it; but in Isa. xlix. 24 f. it is God, and not the Servant, who spoils his enemies. (*c*) viii. 31; ix. 12; ix. 31; x. 33 f., the passages in which Jesus predicts his death. These may have been modified by Mark; but if so it has not been to bring them into line with Isa. liii, but to make them closer predictions of the actual Passion. Many details and words from Isa. liii could easily have been incorporated; the fact that this has not been done suggests that the Servant theology does not dominate them. (*d*) xiii. 27, 31, in the Little Apocalypse, cannot be excluded from Markan editorship, but they do not make a clear connection to the Servant. (*e*) xiv. 21, the statement that Jesus goes to his death 'as it is written about him'. The predetermination of the death of Jesus is a Markan theme. But what Scripture has he in mind here?[1] It is natural to think of Isa. liii and difficult to think of any other suitable passage.[2] But though the divine predetermination of the death of Jesus is strongly emphasised by Mark, it would seem probable that Mark would not have left the reference to Scripture so vague if

---

[1] Possibly Gen. xxii. 1–18; cf. below, pp. 169 ff.

[2] On the predictions, and the use of παραδίδωμι in them, cf. H. E. Tödt, *Der Menschensohn in der synoptischen Überlieferung* (1959), pp. 142 f., 144–50, 155 f.

the reference was due to him; rather he has received it in the tradition (the use of the term 'Son of Man' is traditional rather than Markan), and left it vague because he himself did not know the precise reference. This passage should then be classified rather with the material that Mark has transmitted than with that which he has modified. (*f*) xiv. 61; xv. 5, the silence of Jesus. This has been traced to Isa. liii. 7. This may be its origin, but in Mark the silence of Jesus appears to play a definite role independent of a hidden reference to the Servant; in each case it is strongly contrasted with an immediately preceding or following statement of Jesus himself about his own position. Isa. liii. 7 would demand a total silence. The silence in Mark is dramatically rather than biblically determined.

To sum up, we may say that Mark has transmitted some material in which the concept of the Servant may be present, but that he has not modified material to introduce the conception or to clarify it where it already appeared only dimly. Moreover if Mark has set out Jesus as the strong Son of God— victor in every circumstance, clothed with authority from heaven, in control of his own destiny—this clashes with the conception of the Servant who meekly suffers (cf. Isa. xlii. 2, 3). 'The very terms (meekness and gentleness) are unknown to Mark. But they are typical of the Servant.'[1] The conception has consequently not been absorbed into a dominant place in the Christology of Mark. Certainly there are explicit Old Testament references within the Passion narrative, but a glance at the margin of a Nestle text will show that these are to the Psalms rather than to Isaiah. We must thus conclude that Mark does not emphasise Jesus as the Isaianic Servant.[2]

Before we return to the discussion of the passages in which the activity of Jesus is set out we will look for a brief moment at those Old Testament passages which are found in Mark's Passion narrative. With the exception of Zech. xiii. 7, which we discuss later,[3] they are all taken from the Psalms. There is a sense in which their quotation may be regarded as 'superficial'. They are not deeply wrought into the traditional material but have been imposed on it to show its correspondence with the

[1] Bacon, *The Gospel of Mark*, p. 223.
[2] *Ibid.* pp. 227 f.　　　　　[3] Below, pp. 157 f.

Old Testament.[1] (The quotation of Ps. xxii. 2 would appear to lie more deeply in the tradition.) We cannot be sure that they were added by Mark, but, since they lie on the surface and are more than allusions, he must have been aware of them and consciously accepted their use. The other evangelists added many more similar quotations and modified those used by Mark. All are intended to show that what happened to Jesus was in accordance with the Old Testament, and a part of the divine necessity. Thus the quotation of Ps. xli. 10 at xiv. 18 demonstrates that the part played by Judas was within the purpose of God. Most interesting is the use of Ps. xxii. Whether the word of Jesus from the Cross (Ps. xxii. 2 = xv. 34) is genuine or not we must hold it to have been in the tradition from a very early stage. This drew attention to the Psalm from which the other verses were quoted as confirmatory of events in the Passion (Ps. xxii. 8 = Mark xv. 29; Ps. xxii. 19 = Mark xv. 24). This is a Psalm in which the sufferings of the righteous Psalmist are described. So also are Pss. xli, xlii, xliii, lxix from which quotations are drawn (Ps. xli. 10 = Mark xiv. 18; Ps. xlii. 6, 12; xliii. 5 = Mark xiv. 34; Ps. lxix. 22 = Mark xv. 36). Nothing is said in these Psalms suggestive of any interpretation of the meaning of the Passion as redemptive, but it is worthy of note that each of them concludes in such a way as to suggest that God has delivered the Psalmist from his trials, just as God delivered Jesus in the Resurrection (cf. Ps. xxii. 23 ff.; xli. 12 ff.; xlii. 6b, 12b; xliii. 5b; lxix. 31 ff.).[2]

Returning now to those passages in which Jesus testifies to the purpose of his own ministry we examine Mark x. 38 f. In it two images are combined, Baptism and the drinking of a cup. Matthew omits the former, which is undoubtedly the more difficult; Luke has the saying about Baptism in another form, drawn from his special material, and he does not record the saying about the cup. The metaphors refer in the first instance to the whole mission of Jesus; we note the present tenses

---

[1] Cf. Lindars, pp. 90 f. On Mark's use of the Psalms in the Passion narrative cf. A. Rose, 'L'influence des psaumes sur les annonces et les récits de la Passion et de la Résurrection dans les Évangiles', *Le Psautier* (ed. R. de Langhe), pp. 297–356.

[2] Lindars, pp. 89 ff., 106 f.; cf. Iersel, '*Der Sohn*' *in den synoptischen Jesusworten*, pp. 55–7.

πίνω, βαπτίζομαι; but for Mark the whole mission of Jesus is summed up in his death, and these images occur in a passage which has explicit reference to that death (*v.* 45). We are not then incorrect in taking the principal reference in the sayings as we find them in Mark as being to the Passion of Jesus.

The saying about the cup has occasioned less divergence among commentators than that about the Baptism. Paralleled in xiv. 36, it would appear to be solidly based on Old Testament imagery. Thus viewed it is neither a metaphor for destiny or fate in general, nor for suffering and death in particular. It denotes the judgement of God (Jer. xxv. 15–38; xlix. 12; li. 7; Ezek. xxiii. 31–4; Isa. li. 17, 22, etc.).[1] That God reaches out the cup of wrath to men (Ezek. xxiii. 31; Hab. ii. 16; Jer. xxv. 15, 17) accords with Mark's view that the Passion of Jesus is determined by God. At xiv. 36 Jesus shrinks from taking this cup; this can hardly mean only that he feared physical death but implies something more terrible; he is himself the object of the wrath of God. This interpretation accords with the cry of dereliction (xv. 34).

The meaning of the image of Baptism is by no means so easily determined. It is extremely unlikely that the saying should be taken in the later sense of martyrdom as a Baptism of blood; evidence for this is lacking earlier than Irenaeus.[2] The real question is, Does the word contain an explicit reference to Baptism or is it used purely metaphorically of overwhelming floods bringing disaster? Cullmann,[3] contending for the first alternative, argues that Jesus himself, unlike John, did not baptise men, but in his death underwent a general baptism on their behalf, and it is to this that reference is made in x. 38 f. Here we would then find the origin of the Pauline connection of baptism into the death of Christ.[4] On the other hand, Delling has argued cogently that 'baptism' did not have its

---

[1] Cf. Goppelt, *T.W.N.T.* vi, 149 ff.; G. Delling, 'βάπτισμα βαπτισθῆναι', *N.T.* ii (1957), 92–115. In Rabbinic Judaism the image may denote 'destiny, fate', but that the Old Testament understanding of it continued through to the New Testament period is testified by its use in such passages as 1QpH xi. 10–15; Ps. Sol. viii. 14.

[2] Cf. Oepke, *T.W.N.T.* i, 536, n. 44; J. H. Bernard, 'A Study of St Mark x. 38, 39', *J.T.S.* xxviii (1927), 262–70.

[3] *Baptism in the New Testament*, pp. 19 f.

[4] Flemington, *The New Testament Doctrine of Baptism*, pp. 31 ff.; cf. Fuller, *The Mission and Achievement of Jesus*, pp. 59 ff.

fixed theological sense in the time of Jesus but attained this after his death.[1] Therefore the saying contained originally the idea of disaster in water; this disaster did not necessarily imply the death of the one on whom it fell, but was rather symbolic of his judgement (Ps. lxix. 2, 3, 15, 16; Ps. xlii. 8; cxxiv. 3–5; xviii. 17, 18; xxxii. 6; Job xxii. 11).[2] Delling further argued that in the parallel passage in Luke (xii. 49 f.) the baptismal metaphor is associated with that of judgement by fire (i.e. the same theme of judgement), and that similarly his interpretation accords with the parallel of the 'cup' in Mark x. 38 f. However, even if we allow that originally the usage of the baptismal image by Jesus was a reference to the judgement he was about to suffer in death, it is unlikely that by the time Mark wrote, when Baptism was most definitely a technical word in the Christian vocabulary, the word could carry no reference to Baptism. Already the connection of the Baptism of the believer with the death of Christ was widespread; note that Paul in writing to the Romans regards it as something known to them, although he himself had not previously been instructing them about it (Rom. vi. 3).[3] The conception of judgement will have remained attached to the saying, but there will have been added to it the idea that the death of Jesus was a Baptism: as Mark's Gospel begins with a Baptism, that by John, so it ends with another, that of the crucifixion,[4] and if we take seriously the present tenses in *v.* 38 then it is also a Baptism which continued throughout his ministry. Closely related to the Baptism of Jesus is that of his disciples, James and John; their Baptism is yet to take place, that is, future in terms of the Baptism of Jesus. James and John must surely be taken here as typical believers; for Mark all believers must pass through this future Baptism and drink this future cup.[5] Mark is not interested in the historical fate of two disciples, but in the way all disciples should live.

We must examine how the disciples are brought into this

---

[1] *N.T.* II (1957), 92–115.

[2] *Ibid.* p. 97. Cf. Lagrange, *ad loc.*; Moulton–Milligan, Stählin, *T.W.N.T.* v, 437 f. Although βαπτίζειν was not usually used in the LXX translation its use is found in Aq. (Job ix. 31; Ps. lxix. (lxviii). 3); Al. (Ps. ix. 16).

[3] Fuller, *The Mission and Achievement of Jesus*, p. 60.

[4] Cf. Wellhausen, *ad loc.*

[5] The evidence for the martyrdom of John the Apostle is not satisfying.

saying. On the surface it might appear that they are to suffer exactly the same fate as Jesus, and that therefore their fate would achieve the same result as his. This cannot be the meaning of Mark. He sets out the person and ministry of Jesus as unique. Throughout the Gospel strong contrasts are drawn between the faithfulness of Jesus and the unfaithfulness of the disciples (e.g. ix. 14–29; xiv. 32–42); between his sight and their blindness (e.g. viii. 14–21; viii. 31–3); between his humility and their self-importance (e.g. ix. 33–7; x. 32–45). The testimony of the divine voice at his Baptism and Transfiguration strongly reinforces this uniqueness. Furthermore, as we have seen, his death is given a special significance (x. 45; xiv. 24), even though others are commanded to take up their cross and follow him (viii. 34). In the very passage we are discussing (x. 35–45) we must note that, while x. 45 is linked to x. 44 through the idea of service, it goes much beyond it; both Jesus and disciples serve, but only Jesus gives his life a ransom for many. It would therefore be wholly wrong to imagine that Mark saw in the statement about the Baptism which the disciples would have to undergo any suggestion that their deaths would be comparable to the death of Jesus. If the original reference in the baptismal statement of x. 38 was to the overwhelming tragedy which would engulf like flood-water, then probably this was taken in the early Church to refer in the case of the disciples to the persecution and death that lay ahead for believers. These sufferings, necessarily entailed in a faithful following of Jesus, were not just in imitation of his, but to some extent part of the Messianic woes which had to be fulfilled before the Messiah would come, or, in Christian terms, before he would return (cf. Col. i. 24; I Pet. iv. 13).[1] But if as Mark uses the saying we cannot restrict the reference to overwhelming floods in the case of Jesus, neither can we in the case of the disciples. It must therefore in their case also carry a reference to Baptism. This can only be their own Baptism. The Baptism of the believer according to the Pauline pattern, which was also that of the Primitive Church,[2] is not simply a re-enactment of the dying of Jesus; in Baptism the believer is carried back to the

---

[1] So Delling, *N.T.* II (1957), 92–115; Schniewind, etc. On the Messianic woes cf. Schlier, *T.W.N.T.* III, 144 ff.; Strack–Billerbeck, IV, 977–86.

[2] Cullmann, *Baptism in the New Testament*, p. 15.

very death of Jesus and participates in it.[1] But the death of Jesus was the principal incident of his ministry and therefore of the Baptism which he himself underwent. In this sense the believer is carried back to the Baptism with which Jesus was baptised and is baptised with the same Baptism and therefore committed to take up his cross and follow after Jesus. The once-for-all death with Jesus is followed by a daily dying.[2] In this way we approach a position similar to that of Dr J. A. T. Robinson, who speaks of the Baptism of Jesus as all-inclusive.[3] All men participate in his Baptism, which is of course more than the literal Baptism of Jordan, but includes also his ministry and Passion. Thus again we come back to the position that the ministry and death of Jesus are on behalf of men. Within the Primitive Church, in so far as the New Testament bears witness, Baptism is in no way connected to the conquest of Satan but is related to forgiveness of sin.

Before we turn to examine the saying about the cup in relation to discipleship we must look at the second occasion on which Jesus refers to his own drinking of the cup, xiv. 36. Here it refers quite obviously to his death, something which lying in the just immediate future he prays he may escape. He shrinks from it, ἤρξατο ἐκθαμβεῖσθαι καὶ ἀδημονεῖν. This cannot be a shrinking only from physical pain and death; his own followers, as Mark knew, faced death for his sake more courageously than that. The cup must be given its full significance: it is the cup of the wrath of God. God can take the cup from him, so God must be the one who gives it; this is fully in line with the Old Testament references to the cup as given by God to men to drink. But why should he be the object of the wrath of God and what will his drinking of the cup achieve for men? This is certainly not made clear on the surface. We must remember that the cup is mentioned a third time in Mark, xiv. 24—and it is remarkable that Jesus talks about bread and cup and not bread and wine which are the natural equivalents. The cup carries here again a reference to his death in that it is ὑπὲρ πολλῶν. The cup of wrath will then also be drunk ὑπὲρ πολλῶν. But may we link x. 38 and xiv. 36 with xiv. 24? Are

---

[1] Cf. Best, *One Body in Christ*, pp. 44 ff.   [2] *Ibid.* pp. 49 f.
[3] *Twelve New Testament Studies*, 'The One Baptism', pp. 158–75 = *S.J.Th.* VI (1953), 257–74.

not the cups entirely different? Here we must remember that in the Old Testament there is a cup of salvation (Ps. cxvi. 13, cf. xxiii. 5) as well as a cup of wrath,[1] there is the peculiar usage of ποτήριον instead of οἶνος in Mark xiv. 24 and there is the association of the cup of salvation in Ps. cxvi with the death of God's saints, an association which is made all the closer because the LXX omits *v.* 14 of the Psalm. We are thus entitled to see in the cup of wrath which Jesus drinks a cup which is partaken for others. Now quite obviously Mark no more means to imply by the reference to James and John in x. 38 f. that they will share in the drinking of the cup of wrath (at xiv. 36 Jesus stands starkly alone in relation to the cup), which is also the cup of salvation 'for many', than that they must undergo the same Baptism for all as Jesus endured. May we not conclude that as in x. 38 f. the application of Baptism to the disciples means their own Baptism, so the cup which they drink is the cup of the Eucharist?[2] It is the cup which renews their participation in the death of Christ and their obligation to take up their own crosses and follow after him.

Expressing a somewhat similar thought to the drinking of the cup of judgement is the picture of the striking of the shepherd (xiv. 27). This is derived from Zech. xiii. 7 b. Mark follows the A text of the LXX rather than the B; the A is itself closer to the Hebrew. The B text speaks of shepherds in the plural from whom the ἄνδρα πολίτην μου (*v.* 7a) must necessarily be distinct. The A text, as the Hebrew, permits the identification of this person with the shepherd himself. There is thus one person who is smitten. In Zech. xiii. 7 God speaks to his sword to smite; in Mark xiv. 27 the first person singular is used: it is presumably God himself who smites,[3] for it would be difficult to believe that Mark saw Jesus as striking his shepherd Peter, which the first singular of *v.* 28 might lead us to suppose.[4] The

---

[1] The cup of Ps. cxvi. 13 as a cup of thanksgiving may be related to the 'cup of blessing' of I Cor. x. 16; cf. H.-J. Kraus on Ps. cxvi.

[2] Cf. Lohmeyer, *ad loc.*

[3] xiv. 27 b, 28 appear to break the flow of the narrative from *v.* 27a to *v.* 29 and are probably a Markan insertion, cf. pp. 90, 173 ff.; this would make them all the more important for the determination of his view of the death of Jesus. Mark would appear to have an especial fondness for Zech. ix–xiv; cf. Smith, 'No Time for Figs', pp. 321 f.

[4] Cf. Lindars, pp. 127–32.

one who is struck by God is described in the LXX (A text) as ποιμήν μου καὶ ἀνὴρ πολίτης μου (v. 7a).[1] The shepherd is then probably one who is acceptable to God. But the whole theme of the passage in Zechariah is judgement and salvation.[2] Judgement is meted out on this shepherd and on the flock, two-thirds of which perish, but one-third of which are saved as a remnant. In Mark, however, the shepherd bears the whole judgement meted out by God, just as he had to drink the cup of God's judgement. Thus Mark sets forth Jesus as smitten by God in God's judgement over his people Israel. But just as the passage in Zechariah is not without its message of salvation as well as judgement—one-third of the people are saved—so here the quotation from Zechariah is followed by the promise that Jesus goes ahead of the community into Galilee; whatever this may mean, it means at least the recreation of the community, the remnant saved because the Shepherd has been struck by God. Thus again the Cross means judgement borne by Jesus for men. And if, as is probable,[3] xiv. 27b, 28 is a Markan editorial insertion, then this represents the Markan view of the death of Jesus; it is a view which we have found to be echoed in the meaning of the cry of dereliction (xv. 34), in the Baptism endured for men (x. 38) and in the cup drunk on their behalf (x. 38; xiv. 36). We may observe that we have suspected Markan editorial work also in xiv. 36, where there would appear to be the combination of two accounts of the incident at Gethsemane.[4] In this view of the death Mark is not then merely reflecting the ideas of the material he had received but is positively putting his own interpretation on the death of Jesus by introducing, or creating, material in which a particular view was expressed.

It is possible that a similar line of thought is to be detected in the Temptation story, that is, that in the wilderness Jesus

---

[1] M.T. reads גֶּבֶר עֲמִיתִי: an unusual phrase meaning someone standing near.

[2] Cf. C. F. Evans, 'I will go before you into Galilee', J.T.S. v (1954), 3–18. He also argues, 'The sequence of events in the Marcan account of the last week in Jerusalem—triumphal entry, cleansing of the temple, cursing of the fig tree, the saying about "this mountain", the blood of the covenant, the prophecy of the smiting of the shepherd and of the scattering of the flock, all preceded by the discourse on the last things—reflects a similar presence, if not combination, of ideas in Zechariah' (p. 8).

[3] Cf. p. 157, n. 3.   [4] Cf. pp. 92 ff.

bore the judgement of God. This would be so if Jesus' expulsion by the Spirit to the desert was conceived as similar to that of the scapegoat bearing the sins of the people and driven out to Azazel (Lev. xvi. 7–10, 20–2).[1] Azazel was regarded in Judaism as an evil spiritual being[2] and therefore Mark might have taken him to be Satan. We cannot accept this suggestion because its assumptions have not been proved, namely, that for Mark Jesus was the scapegoat and Azazel the supreme evil being.

[1] Mauser, p. 98, n. 2.
[2] Langton, *Essentials of Demonology*, pp. 43 f., 108, 130–2.

CHAPTER VII

THE TITLES OF JESUS[1]

JUST as place-names and personal names become liable to alteration, subtraction and addition in the handing on of the tradition in the primitive community, so it is reasonable to assume that the titles used of Jesus might also have been changed. If the same person is known by a number of titles it is *a priori* probable that the title used in a particular speech or account could be varied, provided the particular title is not relevant to the content of what is being said. Preachers, speaking from memory, constantly misquote texts through the substitution of one title of Jesus for another. Young people repeating answers to catechism questions frequently make the same mistake. Paul had a number of variants for the phrase 'in Christ', for example 'in the Lord', and there does not appear to have been much alteration in the total meaning of the phrase when he varied the title.[2] Different schools of theological thought have favourite titles for Jesus; for example, the liberal school popularised the title 'Master', and this because it represented a strong strain in their thinking about Jesus. It may thus be that an author's choice of titles for Jesus may reveal something of his theology. We therefore examine the titles used by Mark to see what we can learn from them about his theology in relation to the mission of Jesus.

If we consider the manner in which Luke and Matthew have varied the titles used by Mark of Jesus, it will be seen that they cannot have regarded Mark's choice as sacrosanct. On certain occasions they were not free to make changes unless they were prepared to alter drastically the content of the passage; for example, to eliminate the use of 'son' in the words of the Divine Voice at the Baptism and the Transfiguration and replace by another of the titles, say King, would have completely altered the fact that the Divine Voice by its particular choice of title

[1] V. Taylor, *The Names of Jesus*, is valuable for its accumulation of material. Cf. also Hahn, *Christologische Hoheitstitel*.
[2] Cf. Best, *One Body in Christ*, pp. 30–2.

on those occasions set up a relationship between God and Jesus, whereas the other title 'King' would have set up a relationship between him and men. Neither Matthew nor Luke is keen on Mark's title 'King of the Jews (Israel)' used in the Passion narrative (xv. 2, 9, 12, 18, 26, 32), so they succeed in altering or omitting it; Luke does so by completely rewriting some of the passages where it occurs, or by using another source; both can change it to 'Christ' (Matt. xxvii. 17, 22; Luke xxiii. 35). Luke eliminates the term 'Son of God (of the Blessed)' from Mark xiv. 61 and xv. 39. Matthew adds references to Jesus as Son of God at xiv. 33; xxvii. 40 (cf. xxvii. 43). Luke adds a reference to Jesus as King of the Jews at xxiii. 37 where Mark has no title and Matthew has independently added 'Son of God'. On a number of occasions when Mark has 'teacher' Matthew has changed this to κύριος (viii. 25; xvii. 4, 15; xx. 31–3),[1] and where Mark has either no address or the personal pronoun he has introduced it (Matt. viii. 2; xvi. 22; xxvi. 22); Luke has also brought in this title at v. 12; xviii. 41; xxii. 61. To Peter's confession that Jesus was the Christ (Mark viii. 29) Matthew adds 'the son of the living God' (xvi. 16). At Mark xv. 32 where Mark uses the double title 'Christ' and 'King' Matthew omits the title 'Christ' but retains 'King'. On a number of occasions Matthew adds the title 'Christ' (xvi. 20, 21; xxiv. 5; xxvi. 68). Matthew replaces the title 'Son of Man' at Mark viii. 31 with the personal pronoun (cf. Mark viii. 38 with Matt. x. 33 and Luke xii. 9). Matthew introduces this same title at xvi. 13 (cf. xvi. 28). These variations may have been made either because Matthew or Luke thought the choice of title was a matter of indifference, or because they had favourite titles they wished to use, or because the change expressed more adequately their thought at that particular point. It is unnecessary for us to enter a discussion of their reasons for change. The fact that they did change renders it *a priori* probable that Mark will have altered the titles in the material as it came to him. We have no adequate means of checking if he did so, but because change was a possibility it is natural to assume that the titles which he wrote in his manuscript meant something to him. If he retained them from the

[1] For Matthew's use of κύριος cf. Bornkamm in Bornkamm, Barth and Held, *Tradition and Interpretation in Matthew*, pp. 41–3.

tradition it was not out of mere respect for it but because they expressed what he wished to say; if he varied them it was because the variation expressed his meaning more fully.

SON OF MAN[1]

This most enigmatic of titles is varied very little by Matthew and Luke in their adoption of the passages in which it occurs in Mark. This would suggest a particular reverence for it. It was continued because its use lay deep in the tradition; this view is reinforced by the fact that it is to be found in all the strata of the tradition, Mark, Q, Special Matthew and Special Luke; most scholars therefore assume that its usage goes back to Jesus himself. We do not need to argue whether this is so or not, nor do we need to argue whether when Jesus used it he intended himself or someone other, or whether he regarded the Son of Man as a corporate being; for Mark the Son of Man is Jesus.[2]

It is generally recognised that the Son of Man title is used in the Gospels in three different ways: in relationship to (a) the incarnate activity of Christ, (b) his sufferings, (c) his appearance in glory. All these three usages appear in Mark. Our only question is whether Mark, having received one type of saying, may have applied the title to other types; for example, if the eschatological type of saying came to Mark in the tradition did he derive the title from that type and then take it and apply it to sayings about suffering? We have seen that x. 45, a saying of type (b), probably came to Mark in the tradition.[3] It also seems reasonable to assume that at least one of the three Passion predictions came as traditional material to Mark; he may have manufactured the others on the basis of one but would

[1] A valuable summary of views on the Son of Man and full references to recent literature will be found in A. J. B. Higgins, 'Son of Man', in *New Testament Essays* (ed. Higgins), pp. 119–35. To this we may add E. Schweizer, 'Der Menschensohn', *Z.N.T.W.* L (1959), 185–210, 'The Son of Man Again', *N.T.S.* IX (1963), 256–61; Hahn, *Christologische Hoheitstitel*, pp. 13 ff.; M. Black, 'The Son of Man Problem in Recent Research and Debate', *Bull. J. Rylands Lib.* XLV (1963), 305–18; Tödt, *Der Menschensohn in der synoptischen Überlieferung*. Most of the discussion of the title is taken up with the way in which Jesus himself used the phrase and does not relate directly to Mark's usage.

[2] Above, pp. 121 ff.   [3] See pp. 140 f. above.

hardly have invented *ab initio* the idea of prediction. viii. 31 has a typically Markan editorial introduction,[1] but the remainder of the verse is not particularly Markan. Furthermore, sayings of type (*b*) are found, possibly independently, in Special Luke (xxii. 22; xxiv. 7). The two sayings of type (*a*) which occur in Mark (ii. 10, 28) may originally have been sayings in which 'Son of Man' was not a title but meant 'man'; it is possible that Mark may have sharpened them to apply only to Jesus, but it seems more probable that they came to him already with this application. On the face of it it seems much more likely that possessing sayings of type (*b*) Mark should have added sayings of type (*c*), for here he would have biblical material (Daniel vii. 13) to guide him; but this is such an obvious addition that it would almost certainly have taken place in the tradition earlier than Mark and not be due to him; xiv. 62 is too closely interwoven into its incident for it to have been added by him. We may therefore conclude that in the material as Mark received it the title occurred, certainly in forms (*b*) and (*c*), and probably also in form (*a*). If Mark moulded one or more of the Passion predictions on the model of one that he had received which itself used the title Son of Man, then the use of the same title in the others can hardly be termed editorial in the full sense. But it is not certain that Mark did form any of the Passion predictions. We cannot then speak of Mark's use of the title Son of Man as editorial. He received it in the tradition and preserved it. He may have preserved it either because it had meaning for him or because its meaning had been lost and it had become almost magical in its use; not knowing its meaning he would not know to what other title he might change it.

The majority of sayings in Mark about the suffering and death of Jesus are cast in terms of the Son of Man. There are certainly some that are not, but in most of these the metaphor which is used forbids reference to the Son of Man; for example, the reference to the death of Jesus at ii. 19 f. is so expressed in terms of marriage that it would be unthinkable to change 'bridegroom' to 'Son of Man', cf. xii. 6–8, 10 f.; xiv. 27. To say at xiv. 8 that the woman had anointed the body of the Son of Man would be clumsy. xiv. 24 and x. 38 are cast in terms of

[1] See pp. 79 f.

the first person and this almost seems a necessity of their context. The suffering sayings are not connected with any of the other major titles, for example Son of God. Certain of the Son of Man sayings are concerned with the divine necessity (viii. 31) which may be explained as pre-ordained in Scripture (ix. 12; xiv. 21). It is natural to include within the Scriptural reference the term 'Son of Man'. A suffering Son of Man is found in Scripture in at least two places: Dan. vii. 13, 21, 25, 27 and Ps. lxxx. 18.[1] In each case there is a period of suffering followed by restoration at God's hand, which would correspond to the Resurrection. And since Mark (xiv. 62; xiii. 26) does connect Jesus to the Son of Man of Dan. vii. 13 these may well be the passages he had in mind. We may note the use of παραδίδωμι in both Mark xiv. 21 and Dan. vii. 25 (LXX). Whether this is the ultimate origin of the use of the term Son of Man in the suffering sayings is another matter altogether. The fact that Mark preserves the term Son of Man in reference to one whom he can also describe as yet to come in clouds with power and glory (xiii. 26; xiv. 62) brings out the paradox of the nature of the one who suffers. From the beginning of this Gospel Mark has made it clear to us that it is the Gospel of the Son of God whom men killed. The double use of the term Son of Man to describe both suffering and glory underlines this. It achieves the same effect as Mark's insertion of the Little Apocalypse directly before the Passion.

Mark first introduces us to the Son of Man as one who forgives sins (ii. 10) and immediately afterwards he sets him out as superior to the law which defines what sin is (ii. 28).[2] So also the final references to the Son of Man coming in glory carry similar implications in that they set him out with judicial functions; the High Priest who has judged him will himself be judged, and the elect, the faithful, will be gathered from all parts. The Son of Man is thus set in a definite relationship to sin: he as Lord of the Sabbath can define the Law and therefore

[1] Cf. W. D. Davies, *Paul and Rabbinic Judaism*, p. 280, n. 1; C. H. Dodd, *According to the Scriptures*, p. 117, n. 2.

[2] It is perhaps incorrect in the case of Mark to speak of ii. 10 and ii. 28 as sayings of the incarnate Christ, i.e. of type (*a*). In them Mark sees the exalted Lord as speaking through the incarnate Christ with authority in relation to sin and the Law.

define what sin is; he can forgive it and he can judge men in respect of it. It is only natural then that the suffering sayings should bear the same positive relationship to sin; this comes to the surface explicitly at x. 45, where as we have seen the death of the Son of Man is for the sin of men. As Son of Man, a title which Mark receives in the tradition and retains, Jesus is set out as the one who deals with sin either through forgiveness or punishment; he is not set in relationship to the cosmic powers.

THE CHRIST

This title does not appear to have great significance for Mark, despite the fact that it forms the substance of Peter's confession at Caesarea Philippi. A brief review of the evidence will confirm this conclusion. In the very instance of Peter's confession, Jesus when he speaks of himself varies the title to that of Son of Man (viii. 31). Likewise at xiv. 61 when the High Priest asks Jesus if he is the Christ, the Son of the Blessed, Jesus while admitting this makes a positive statement in terms of the Son of Man (xiv. 62).[1] The same is apparently also true of xiii. 21, where the presence of false Christs is contrasted with the coming of the true Son of Man (xiii. 26). At xv. 32 the title is used by the enemies of Jesus who mock him on the Cross and its use is in no sense a confession of faith. At xii. 35, which has been regarded both as a defence of the Davidic descent of the Messiah and as an attack upon it, 'Christ' is the natural title to use. The usage at ix. 41 is not textually certain; it implies the existence of a community centred on Christ. All these instances would appear to have come to Mark in the tradition.[2] The one usage of Christ which is certainly Markan is found in i. 1; it is significant that it is not here a title but a personal name.[3] Matthew and Luke use the title more frequently than Mark, Luke adding it to Markan material at iv. 41 and Matthew at xvi. 20 (in *v.* 21 it is not a title); xxiv. 5; xxvi. 68; xxvii. 17, 22.

[1] If we do not accept the reading ἐγώ εἰμι at xiv. 62 then Jesus does not necessarily agree even with the High Priest's use of the title 'Christ'.

[2] The reading ὅτι Χριστοῦ ἐστε, ix. 41, even if part of the genuine text of Mark, can certainly not be traced back beyond the early Church to Jesus himself.

[3] We have not considered i. 34 where the appearance of 'Christ' in some texts is very probably due to assimilation to Luke iv. 41.

Mark leaves the title, so far as we know, in the material as it comes to him; he does not deny that Jesus is the Christ, nor does he stress it. In itself the title tells us nothing about the achievement of Jesus; it may even suggest a false conception of the central figure of Mark's Gospel.

THE KING OF THE JEWS[1]

This title is used five times by Mark in one chapter (xv. 2, 9, 12, 18, 26), always on the lips of Gentile enemies of Jesus; once we have 'King of Israel', spoken by the Jews in mockery at the Cross. Both Matthew and Luke freely change it; Luke adds it on one occasion (xxiii. 37). Apart from the Johannine writings it is scarcely used elsewhere in the New Testament. It may be that in the early Church it was partly equivalent to κύριος, denoting the Lordship of Christ over the Church;[2] but if so, nothing of this appears in Mark's usage. It is a variant of the Messianic title (cf. Matt. xxvii. 17, 22 and Luke xxiii. 35 with Mark xv. 9, 12, 32), and the fact that Jesus is crucified as the Jewish king emphasises the guilt of the Jews. It fails to disclose anything more of the Markan conception of the achievement of Jesus.

SON OF DAVID

This is closely related to the Messianic title. It occurs four times in Mark (x. 47, 48; xii. 35, 37). It would appear to have come to Mark in the tradition of the two incidents in which it appears. It adds nothing to our knowledge of the Markan soteriology.

LORD

This title is rarely used by Mark of Jesus;[3] Matthew and Luke insert it frequently and its use was widespread in early Christianity. When Mark uses the word we have to determine whether he refers it to Jesus, and, if so, whether he intends it in the full sense which it attained in the early Church, or whether it is only used as a title of respect like Rabbi. The one certain place where

---

[1] Cf. above, pp. 95 f.

[2] Cf. Cullmann, *The Christology of the New Testament*, pp. 220 ff.

[3] If, as Schreiber maintains, Mark reflects the Hellenistic kerugma we should expect the title to be prominent.

it is used of Jesus in its full sense by Mark is xii. 36, 37; here the reference is eschatological: at some future point the enemies of Jesus are to be under his feet. At v. 19 the original reference was probably to God; the healed demoniac is told to go and preach what God had done to him; but the fact that in v. 20 he is said to tell what Jesus had done (ποιεῖν is used in both cases) makes it likely that Mark and his readers would have understood that 'the Lord' was Jesus: here then Jesus as Lord is seen in his present saving activity; he is Lord over the demonic world. The use of the vocative κύριε by the Syro-Phoenician woman (vii. 28) may well be original; she intended it as a title of honour without any special significance; it would be the equivalent of 'teacher' as used by Jews of Jesus; again it may have been taken in a fuller sense by Mark and his readers, but if so this passage throws little light on what it meant for them. At xi. 3 the natural meaning is to take it of Jesus;[1] as a designation of Jesus, at whose disposal are all things, it would be here an appropriate title. As Jesus is Lord of all that has been created, so he is also Lord of the Law (ii. 28). The title thus expresses the Lordship of Jesus over all things and therefore his saving power in this present age and the eschatological fulfilment of his Lordship in the age to come.

SON OF GOD

It is generally recognised that this is the most important of the titles of Jesus in Mark—yet it is used sparingly and, with the possible exception of i. 1, there is no point at which we can be certain Mark introduced this title into the material; it is possible that on various occasions (for example xv. 39) Mark altered some other title to it, but we cannot prove this. Like the other titles it lays emphasis on the being of Jesus rather than on his activity. An initial problem concerns the reading in i. 1; there are good grounds for accepting υἱοῦ θεοῦ as original,[2] but we cannot be certain; whether we accept it or not, its actual usage here has no light to shed on its meaning.

---

[1] Taylor, *ad loc.*, takes it for the unidentified actual owner of the colt; again this may have been the original meaning, but it hardly retains it in the Markan context.

[2] Cranfield makes a strong defence.

It is pre-eminently the title of confession. If the reading is correct at i. 1 then Mark confesses Jesus as Son of God at the very beginning. But even if this reading is not allowed then at i. 11 God himself confesses Jesus as his Son. The Gospel is not a mystery story in which the identity of the main character has to be guessed; from the outset it is made clear who this is—the Son of God. This divine confession is repeated at the Transfiguration (ix. 7); if at the Baptism it is made to Jesus alone, on the second occasion it is made to the inner ring of disciples; but in the Gospel it is made on each occasion to all its readers. Between these two divine testimonies there lie the two demonic (iii. 11; v. 7). Thus the opposite sides of the spiritual world, as we might say, agree in their witness. It is also his own testimony to himself at the solemn moment of his trial before the High Priest. Finally it is the confession of the centurion after his death. Whether the centurion used the title in a Hellenistic way as denoting someone with exceptional powers or not, Mark clearly understands it as a unique designation of Jesus. Thus the Gospel beginning with the divine testimony to the sonship of Jesus ends with the same human testimony; Jesus is the Son of God, and he is this, not despite, but because of his death. Closely allied to the conception of confession is that of obedience. The demons who confess him are subject to him; at iii. 11 the demons have already fallen down before him when they acknowledge his sonship; at v. 7, as *v.* 8 shows, he has already demanded their obedience; *v.* 8 may indeed be an editorial comment of Mark justifying *vv.* 6, 7.[1] When in the Transfiguration the divine voice has described Jesus as Son it goes on at once to tell the disciples to 'hear' him; 'hear' must be given its full sense of 'obedience'; the only true hearing known to the Bible is obedient hearing. In so far as the title 'Son of God' implies obedience it is used somewhat similarly to κύριος in other parts of the New Testament.

But how is the title used in relationship to the activities of Jesus? It is as Son of God that he overcomes the demons. Just as he had been proclaimed Son of God at the Baptism and then went into the wilderness and defeated Satan,[2] so as Son he

---

[1] So Taylor, *ad loc.*

[2] In the Q account of the Temptations Jesus is expressly tempted as Son of God.

deprives Satan's minions of their power. As Son of God he has
a certain status and evil must be subject to one of that status.
And yet though possessing that status he dies. In the Parable
of the Vineyard (xii. 1–9) it is because he is the Son that he is
put to death. And it is in his dying that he is recognised as Son
by the centurion.[1] Perhaps also the nearness of the Transfiguration, in which he is announced as Son, to the first prophecy of
the Cross is meant also to indicate the role of suffering in the
destiny of the Son of God.[2] In xiv. 36 Jesus in the Garden
of Gethsemane and face to face with death calls on God as
his Father; elsewhere he speaks little in this Gospel of God
as Father, either as his own Father (viii. 38; xiii. 32) or as the
Father of the disciples (xi. 25). The invocation of God as Father
is emphasised moreover in xiv. 36 by the double use of the
address, ἀββὰ ὁ πατήρ. Thus the title of Son is linked closely to
the death of Jesus. This is unexpected since in the early Church
it would appear to have been linked rather to his Resurrection;
cf. Rom. i. 4; I Thess. i. 10; Acts xiii. 33.[3] This latter connection
is of course found in Mark in the use of the title in the Transfiguration. It is the natural connection, made through Ps. ii. 7;
the relationship of sonship to death is by no means so obvious.

What is there in 'sonship' which relates it to the death of
Jesus? It may be that in i. 11 we should associate the 'Servant'
conception with that of 'sonship' and hence arrive at a 'dying'
sonship; we have already given reasons for supposing that the
'Servant' Christology did not occupy a large place in the
Markan theology.[4] It cannot then have profoundly modified
the sonship theme. Moreover this would only connect sonship
to death indirectly, whereas the evidence seems to require a
more direct link.

Another approach is possible. We may link ἀγαπητός in
i. 11 and ix. 7 with Isaac. As Isaac was almost a sacrifice so
Jesus is a sacrifice. ἀγαπητός is used in Gen. xxii. 2, 12, 16
of Isaac. C. H. Turner has demonstrated that the probable

---

[1] In Matthew (xxvii. 54) Jesus is recognised as Son of God by the
centurion because of the accompanying miracles.

[2] In viii. 38 the Son of Man and the Son of God are identified by means
of the reference to the Father.

[3] Cf. Iersel, 'Der Sohn' in den synoptischen Jesusworten, pp. 174 f.

[4] Cf. pp. 148 ff.

meaning of the word is 'only' rather than 'beloved'.[1] He supplies evidence to show that it was taken in this way in pre- and post-biblical literature. He also points out that in taking it with this meaning both Irenaeus (*Adv. Haer.* IV, 5, 4) and Athanasius (*Oratio* IV *contra Arianos*, 24) relate it to the story of Isaac. Further confirmation that the Abraham–Isaac imagery might be seen in the baptismal account (i. 9–11) is given by Test. Levi xviii. 6, 7.

The heavens shall be opened,
And from the temple of glory shall come upon him sanctification,
With the Father's voice as from Abraham to Isaac.
And the glory of the Most High shall be uttered over him,
And the spirit of understanding and sanctification shall rest upon
    him in the water.[2]

Charles brackets the last three words as a Christian editorial addition. If the remainder is pre-Christian then it shows that the Isaac imagery was already attached to the figure of the new priest whom God would raise up and whom Christians would naturally identify with Christ; the addition of the words 'in the water' shows that in fact the early Christians did make this identification of Jesus with Isaac. If, however, the whole passage should be taken as a Christian construction then again we see that Christ was seen as the new Isaac at an early period.[3] We can also see evidence within the New Testament that Jesus was taken as the new Isaac.[4] It is found in Heb. xi. 17–19 where the sparing of Isaac at the last moment is a type of the Resurrection.[5] The same idea is also probably present in Rom.

---

[1] *J.T.S.* XXVII (1926), 113–29; XXVIII (1927), 152; A. Souter, 'ΑΓΑΠΗΤΟΣ', *J.T.S.* XXVIII (1927), 59 f.

[2] Translation as in Charles, *Apocrypha and Pseudepigrapha*, II. Cf. M. Black, 'The Messiah in the Testament of Levi xviii', *E.T.* LX (1949), 321 f.; LXI (1950), 157 f.; and J. R. Porter, *E.T.* LXI (1949), 90 f.

[3] Cf. Richardson, *An Introduction to the Theology of the New Testament*, pp. 180, 228.

[4] From Barnabas vii. 3 onwards Isaac becomes a type of Christ in Patristic literature; cf. J. Daniélou, 'La typologie d'Isaac dans le christianisme primitif', *Biblica*, XXVIII (1947), 363–93; *Sacramentum Futuri* (Paris, 1950), pp. 97 ff. Cf. A. M. Smith, 'The Iconography of the Sacrifice of Isaac in Early Christian Art', *Amer. J. Archaeology*, XXVI (1922), 159–69.

[5] Even in Judaism it could be taken as a symbol of Resurrection; e.g. Pirqe de Rabbi Eliezer 31 (16b), quoted in Strack–Billerbeck, III, 746. Cf. E. R. Goodenough, *Jewish Symbols in the Greco-Roman Period*, IV, 172–94.

iv. 24;[1] Jesus was not spared as Isaac was but he did, like Isaac, come back from the dead. At Rom. viii. 32 Paul will have had Isaac in mind;[2] knowing that ἀγαπητός means 'only' he uses in its place ἴδιος; he repeats φείδεσθαι from Gen. xxii. 12; God did not spare his Son as Abraham was permitted to spare his. We may also suspect its presence in Acts iii. 25 f.; the quotation here of Gen. xxii. 18, which was closely related in the Targumic tradition to the redemptive sacrifice of Isaac (the *Akedah* or binding of Isaac), seems to imply the equation of Jesus with the seed of Abraham.[3] The *Akedah* may again be the background to the very difficult reference to the lamb in John i. 29; Jesus is Isaac, the lamb, by whom the sins of men are taken away.[4]

Knowledge of the *Akedah* must have been widespread in Judaism of the first century: Josephus, *Ant.* I, 225–36 (especially 227, 232); IV Macc. xiii. 12; xvi. 20; Ps.-Philo, *Liber Antiquitatum Biblicarum*, XVIII, 8; XXXII, 2–4; XL, 2; it is also found in the various Targums, in particular the *Fragmentary* and *Neofiti*.[5] In these passages Isaac appears as the willing victim who requests that he be bound for the sacrifice.[6] In Rabbinic teaching the sacrifice of Isaac, though no blood was shed, came to be accepted as the one perfect sacrifice by which the sins of the people of Israel were forgiven.[7]

In short, the Binding of Isaac was thought to have played a unique role in the whole economy of the salvation of Israel, and to have a permanent redemptive effect on behalf of its people. The merits of his sacrifice were experienced by the Chosen People in the past, invoked in the present, and hoped for at the end of time.[8]

[1] Cf. Barrett, *Romans, ad loc.* He considers that the Isaac imagery is also present at Rom. viii. 32. Cf. H. J. Schoeps, *Aus frühchristlicher Zeit*, pp. 229–38, and *Paul*, pp. 141–9; G. Vermes, *Scripture and Tradition in Judaism*, p. 220.

[2] Turner, *J.T.S.* XXVII (1926), 119 f.

[3] Vermes, *Scripture and Tradition in Judaism*, pp. 221 f.

[4] *Ibid.* pp. 224 f. Cf. Richardson, *An Introduction to the Theology of the New Testament*, p. 228.

[5] All the relevant passages are quoted in Vermes, *Scripture and Tradition in Judaism*, pp. 194 ff.; cf. Schoeps, *Aus frühchristlicher Zeit*; Moore, I, 536 ff., 549. C. K. Barrett, *From First Adam to Last*, pp. 26–30, is more sceptical about the prevalence of the developed Jewish ideas on Isaac in the New Testament period.   [6] Cf. Sifrè Deut. § 32 on Deut. vi. 5.

[7] Vermes, *Scripture and Tradition in Judaism*, pp. 204–8.

[8] *Ibid.* p. 208.

The Rabbis also taught that Jerusalem was Mount Moriah[1] and that the sacrifices offered in the Temple had their foundation in the once-for-all sacrifice of Isaac.[2]

According to ancient Jewish theology, the atoning efficacy of the *Tamid* offering, of all the sacrifices in which a lamb was immolated, and perhaps, basically, of all expiatory sacrifice irrespective of the nature of the victim, depended upon the virtue of the Akedah, the self-offering of that Lamb whom God had recognised as the perfect victim of the perfect burnt offering.[3]

Whereas later tradition associated the *Akedah* with the New Year Festival, Vermes has shown that it was earlier related to the Passover.[4] It may also be that Jewish tradition in the first century A.D., or earlier, had already connected the *Akedah* with the Suffering Servant,[5] though the evidence for this is not so certain. It may also be noted that in IV Macc. (xiii. 12; xvi. 20) Isaac is the sacrificed Martyr; elsewhere in this book we find allusion to the blood of the martyrs (vi. 27 ff.; xvii. 22; xviii. 4). Either the connection of Isaac with the Suffering Servant or with the idea of the meritorious blood of the martyrs may have inspired the doctrine of his atoning sacrifice; or it may have emerged from the general Jewish doctrine of the merits of the Fathers.

Returning now to the death of Jesus, we may view him in Mark's picture as an only (i. 11; ix. 7) and an obedient (xiv. 32 ff.) son who goes willingly to his death like Isaac, and whose death is a sacrifice for the sins of men. If this interpretation is accepted, sonship is fulfilled in willing sacrifice, which is for others, and sonship is recognised in the moment of death (cf. xv. 39). Thus taking Jesus to be the new Isaac we find that

[1] In II Chron. iii. 1 Mount Moriah is the temple hill; in Gen. xxii. 14 the same idea is suggested by the reference to the 'Mount of the Lord' (cf. Isa. ii. 3; xxx. 29; Ps. xxiv. 3); it is made more explicit in T. Onk. and in Gen. R. lvi. 10 on Gen. xxii. 14. Cf. Schoeps, *Aus frühchristlischer Zeit*; Vermes, *Scripture and Tradition in Judaism*, pp. 208 f.

[2] Vermes, *Scripture and Tradition in Judaism*, pp. 209–11. The *Akedah* is depicted on the right of the Torah Shrine panel in the synagogue of Dura-Europos, thus showing redemptive significance, cf. C. H. Kraeling, *The Synagogue* (Part 1 of *The Excavations at Dura-Europos Final Report*, VIII), pp. 54–62 and plate XVI.

[3] *Ibid.* p. 211.   [4] *Ibid.* pp. 214–18.

[5] *Ibid.* pp. 202 f.

the theme of sonship is linked to the sacrifice of the Cross, with the underlying conception, as in Judaism, of a sacrifice for others (cf. Rom. viii. 32). (See Addendum on p. 177).

TEACHER

Unlike the preceding titles this is not one which describes the status of Jesus but one which rather contains within itself a designation of his activity. Mark uses διδάσκαλος twelve times[1] and Rabbi, an equivalent, three times.[2] Matthew and Luke often vary the usage. In almost every case the words appear in the vocative case as parts of the material which will have come to Mark in the tradition. We have already seen that in his editorial seams Mark has set out Jesus as 'teacher'.[3] His retention of the word in the material, whereas Matthew and Luke vary it, is in accordance with this trait in his own presentation of Jesus.

SHEPHERD

In two places Mark depicts Jesus as the shepherd (vi. 34; xiv. 27). The former of these two we have seen to be an editorial insertion of Mark in which he showed the shepherd Jesus feeding his people with the Word.[4] xiv. 26–31 is probably also a Markan construction.[5] In particular it would appear that *v.* 28 here interrupts the flow of thought from *v.* 27 *a* to *v.* 29; cast in the first person its grammatical subject is Jesus, but its actual subject must be God.[6] Probably therefore it and *v.* 27 *b* were inserted at this point by Mark. It is future in form and therefore preparatory for xvi. 7, but this does not explain the reason for its insertion precisely at this point. Rather it may be regarded as explanatory of *v.* 27: the shepherd is killed; the sheep are scattered; the shepherd rises again and gathers together his scattered flock in Galilee. προάγειν has two possible meanings; it can either refer to going on ahead in time or going on ahead in space, that is leading. C. F. Evans[7] has argued that the

---

[1] iv. 38; v. 35; ix. 17, 38; x. 17, 20, 35; xii. 14, 19, 32; xiii. 1; xiv. 14.
[2] ix. 5; xi. 21; xiv. 45.
[3] Pp. 71 f.   [4] Pp. 76 f.   [5] Pp. 92, 157 f.
[6] Cf. Lohmeyer, *ad loc.*; Marxsen, pp. 47 f.; Lindars, p. 129.
[7] 'I will go before you into Galilee.'

latter is the more usual meaning of the word. As we have seen it fits the conception of the shepherd leading his flock; moreover it corresponds to x. 32: Jesus leads his people in suffering and in salvation. But does not xvi. 7, which is parallel to xiv. 28, conflict with this interpretation? Jesus according to xvi. 7 is already in Galilee where he awaits his disciples to show himself to them in the Resurrection.[1] This assumes that Galilee is used here as an actual place, but as we shall shortly see Galilee is a theological term in Mark and denotes the place where the Gospel is preached; therefore it does not denote a place where the disciples will find Jesus but an activity to which Jesus leads them. In 'Galilee' the flock is reconstituted, and this is the work of the Shepherd who has willingly been smitten (cf. Zech. xiii. 9*b*).

Before we leave this we must examine the view that the reconstitution of the flock does not take place until the Parousia. Lohmeyer, followed by Marxsen, has maintained that xiv. 28 and xvi. 7[2] refer to the Parousia as about to happen in Galilee. Lohmeyer alleged that ὄψεσθε must refer to the Parousia rather than the Resurrection for which the technical term is ὤφθη.[3] Furthermore, Galilee was the land of eschatological fulfilment; Jerusalem according to the other Gospels the place of Resurrection appearances. Thus xvi. 7, and consequently xiv. 28, refer to the Parousia. Marxsen elaborates this thesis by his stress on the theological meaning of Galilee for Mark. Galilee is introduced at appropriate places into the Gospel narrative by Mark because it is geographically important to his readers who expect the conclusion of all things to come shortly in that land.[4] That Mark does not use Galilee in a simple geographical sense has been recognised since Lightfoot's fundamental work.[5] We may observe that Galilee is mostly

[1] As Evans, *ibid.*, points out the idea of Resurrection appearances in Galilee arises out of this verse; the natural place for their occurrence was Jerusalem, where Luke places them. If Galilee is taken as a theological term, then this divergence of statement in regard to their locality is removed.

[2] Neither xiv. 28 nor xvi. 7 can be a gloss but either, probably both, were insertions made by Mark into existing material.

[3] *Ad* xvi. 7; cf. Lohmeyer, *Galiläa und Jerusalem*, pp. 10 ff.

[4] Marxsen, pp. 33–77.

[5] Cf. p. 92, n. 2.

mentioned in verses which are Markan, either summaries
(i. 14, 39; iii. 7?) or seams (i. 16, 28; iii. 7?; vii. 31; ix. 30).[1]
Mark's Gospel divides into two sections: the first recounts the
activity of Jesus in Galilee and Gentile environs, the second his
Passion in Jerusalem. 'Galilee is the sphere of revelation,
Jerusalem the scene only of rejection.'[2] Despite this rigid
division of the Gospel in regard to locality there are indications
within the material received from the tradition and incorporated
in Mark that Jesus had been in Jerusalem before his final entry
and was known there (xi. 2 f.; xiv. 3; xiv. 13–16; xiv. 49;
xv. 43).[3] If then Mark used Galilee editorially why did he
introduce it and what did he intend to teach us by his introduction of it? We see at once how often it is connected with the
proclamation of the Gospel by Jesus (i. 14, 39; iii. 7); it is the
place of the call of disciples (i. 16), of the spread of reports
about him (i. 28) and of the instruction of disciples about his
coming Passion (ix. 30). The Gospel is not written as an
historical outline of the life of Jesus but to instruct its readers in
their Christian faith and duties; they have to proclaim the
Gospel, which is Jesus; we have seen that his proclamation is
meant to be typical of theirs (e.g. i. 14 f., which is expressed in
the theology of the early Church). The readers of Mark's
Gospel are thus in the stage of 'Galilee'—that is, that of the
preaching of the Gospel.[4]

So far we can go, but Marxsen takes this a stage further,
arguing that Galilee is also the place of the completion of the

[1] Apart from these instances Galilee is used at i. 9, where it is in a Markan
passage describing the origin of Jesus, but this must have been a fixed fact
of the tradition; vi. 21, Herod's feast, does not describe the activity of Jesus;
xv. 41, referring to the days of Jesus' activity in Galilee; xiv. 28 and xvi. 7,
with which we are at present concerned.

[2] Lightfoot, *Locality*, p. 125.

[3] Cf. Schmidt, pp. 301–3.

[4] It is probably also the stage of preaching to the Gentiles; Galilee is
Galilee of the Gentiles; cf. Evans, 'I will go before you into Galilee', p. 13;
Karnetzki, 'Die Galiläische Redaktion im Markusevangelium', pp. 249 ff.;
G. H. Boobyer, 'Galilee and Galileans in St Mark's Gospel', *Bull. J.
Rylands Lib.* xxxv (1952/3), 334–48. Boobyer would appear to go too far in
practically restricting the preaching of the Gospel to Gentiles alone; Jesus'
disciples were Jews; so were most of those who were healed. Mark provides
justification for the Gentile mission, but this does not mean he would have
excluded Jews.

Gospel: here it began with the preaching of Jesus and here it ends with his Parousia. We cannot follow him at this point. If, as he himself shows, Galilee is a theological term and denotes the place of preaching it cannot then revert in xiv. 28 and xvi. 7 to the status of a geographical term. Apart from these two texts, and they are the texts in dispute, there is not sufficient evidence that Galilee is connected with the Parousia. Further it is exceedingly doubtful if we read Mark aright when we argue that he expects an imminent Parousia. Mark incorporates the growth parables in ch. iv and must be surely credited with realising their import, namely, that there is a period of growth before the Kingdom comes, and that that period of growth is still in progress.[1] An uncertainty about the time of the coming of the Parousia is seen in xiii. 32–7; xiii. 10 would suggest a certain measure of delay. xvi. 7 is in the present tense and, if addressed not only to the women at the tomb but also to the Church of Mark's day, this requires a present and continuous fulfilment. Unless then there is some definite reason for regarding xvi. 7 as referring to the Parousia it is easier to refer it to the Resurrection/Exaltation and to a present fulfilment. Lohmeyer considered he had found such a reason in the use of ὄψεσθε. It must be granted that ὤφθη is the normal word used in describing Resurrection appearances. However we do find ὁρᾶν used of them in Matt. xxviii. 10, 17; John xx. 18, 25, 29; I Cor. ix. 1. Mark refers so little to the Resurrection that it is impossible to say which term he would have used for seeing the risen and exalted Jesus. We find therefore no difficulty in taking the natural meaning of xiv. 28 and xvi. 7 which makes them refer to the Resurrection.[2] The early Church is now in Galilee, but there, as a Shepherd, it has its Lord with it and can see him as it carries on the work of proclamation to which he has called

---

[1] Cf. Karnetzki, 'Die Galilaische Redaktion im Markusevangelium', pp. 249–51. He also criticises Marxsen, holding that Bussmann's B redaction emerged from a Hellenistic Jewish community situated in Gentile territory, *ibid.* pp. 241 ff.

[2] Cf. W. G. Kummel, *Promise and Fulfilment*, pp. 77–9; Taylor, *ad loc.*; Marxsen, pp. 53 f. There would appear to be no reason for insisting on a risen Christ as distinct from an exalted Christ; the Resurrection and the Exaltation were probably not conceived as distinct events by Mark (see above, pp. 132 f.). The Christ who leads his Church in Galilee, and therefore in all its mission, is the exalted Christ.

it, and for which he has gathered together its scattered members, and to which he leads it.[1] Here is the Markan equivalent of the 'Great Commission' of Matt. xxviii. 16–20.[2]

ADDENDUM

R. le Déaut, *La Nuit Pascale* (*Analecta biblica*, 22), only came into my hands after this chapter was finished and had gone to the Press. Chapter III of his book covers much the same ground as Vermes, *Scripture and Tradition in Judaism*, with whom he agrees at almost all points. Le Déaut stresses more especially the Paschal association of the *Akedah*. Although in Mark's chronology Jesus was not killed at the same time as the Passover Lamb, yet his death has certainly Paschal associations (xiv. 24). In any case Isaac's death was associated with the Paschal night rather than the time of the slaughter of the Paschal Lamb in the afternoon. It may be that the darkness of which Mark speaks (xv. 33) is meant to correspond to that of the Paschal night.

[1] Cf. G. Hebert, 'The Resurrection Narrative in St Mark's Gospel', *S.J.Th.* xv (1962), 66–73. The same thought of the recreation of the community through the Resurrection is probably present in xiv. 58 and xv. 29; cf. p. 99.

[2] Cf. Evans, 'I will go before you into Galilee'.

CHAPTER VIII

THE CHRISTIAN COMMUNITY

WE are not concerned here to discover the nature of the fellowship of the disciples with Jesus in Galilee, but to determine the kind of community which Mark envisages as arising from the preaching of the Gospel he records.

The place of the apostles in the Gospel might appear somewhat ambiguous: are they to be regarded as typical believers of the new community? As typical of its leaders? Or as the foundation on which the new community is built? Mark uses the word 'apostle' of the Twelve only once (vi. 30), though he does use the cognate verb of their activity on two occasions (iii. 14; vi. 7); on each of these two occasions it was the natural word to use. We cannot then say that Mark stresses the position of the Twelve as apostles. In Luke and Matthew they occupy a much more official position.[1] Mark cannot but have known the discussion about the authority of the apostles as evidenced in the Pauline letters, yet he lays no emphasis on that authority. The only reference to their leadership in the Christian community is negative: in x. 42–4 they are instructed in the nature of true rule over others as service. The activities to which the Twelve are called are those of any Christian (iii. 14, 15; vi. 7); the mission charge of vi. 8–11 is in quite general terms and cannot be restricted to the Twelve alone. ix. 38–40 would seem to contradict deliberately any attempt to reserve special functions to them alone; the work of any man who casts out demons in the name of Jesus must be accepted. We may then conclude that in Mark's eyes the Twelve are typical believers rather than officials of the Church.

We have no need to examine all that Mark envisages about the community called into being by the Gospel but only what sheds light on our central problem: what did Jesus accomplish by his ministry? If we view this primarily as the defeat of Satan, then we should expect to meet a community living in the light of that victory; if we view this primarily as the redemption

[1] Cf. Matt. xix. 28 and Luke's frequent use of the term 'apostle'. Cf. C. H. Turner, *J.T.S.* xxvi (1925), 232 f.

of men from sin, then we shall expect to meet a community whose members enjoy the forgiveness of sin and overcome its power in their own lives.

Much of what we should say has already been considered in detail and therefore need only be mentioned. If Christ by his death ransoms the many, then we must assume that the community has been ransomed (x. 45); if the community is called into existence by the preaching of the word, and that word is the forgiveness of sin (ii. 2, 5),[1] then we may assume that the sins of the community are forgiven. Thus those statements which we examined in chapter VI about the activity of Jesus in relation to men must be considered as fulfilled, at least in part, in the members of the community. We have already seen that in those statements the main emphasis lay on Jesus as bearing the judgement and wrath of God and on his ability to save from sin; the community must then be one which has been saved from sin and is no longer under God's judgement. We do not need then to recapitulate the passages discussed there and the conclusions drawn therefrom.

The community has been called into existence by Christ (i. 17, 20; ii. 14; x. 21); its members are the elect, those who have been chosen (xiii. 20, 22, 27). This called community is also the 'calling' community: those who have responded to the call become themselves those who issue it as fishers of men (i. 17). The community is thus extending itself, widening the circle of those who enjoy the privileges and duties which belong to membership. The aim of members of the community is to bring others into the position in which they themselves are. And this means bringing in Gentiles as well as Jews;[2] in the summary statement of iii. 7 f. the crowds come to Jesus from Gentile as well as Jewish areas. In vii. 24–viii. 26 Mark depicts Jesus on a journey which takes him into Gentile territory. In particular we note that the Syro-Phoenician woman was a Gentile (vii. 24–30) and Jesus healed her daughter.[3] It would

---

[1] Cf. pp. 69 ff.

[2] We are not concerned to argue whether Jesus himself envisaged a Gentile mission (cf. J. Jeremias, *Jesus' Promise to the Nations*), but only what Mark had in mind.

[3] Ἑλληνίς means a 'pagan' or 'Gentile' and not a Greek speaker; cf. Turner, *J.T.S.* XXVI (1925), 150. To a Greek it might more properly

appear that the second feeding (viii. 1–9) was a feeding of Gentiles;[1] the Gadarene demoniac may well have been a Gentile. At xii. 9 the 'others' to whom the vineyard is given at least include the Gentiles.[2] These indications are reinforced if we accept the suggestion that Galilee signifies for Mark the Gentile mission.[3] But if then membership of the community does not depend on birth or race, on what does it depend?

The answer is surely faith. J. M. Robinson has shown that the fundamental attitude of the disciple is not numinous awe but faith.[4] Indeed the member of the community may be defined simply as 'the believer' (ix. 42). The fundamental call of Jesus (i. 15) is to repentance and belief; we have seen that this is formulated in the theological terms of Mark's own time and is addressed to his contemporaries.[5] Faith is also the continuing attitude of the disciple; by faith he is saved from evil of one kind and another: this appears in the healing miracles of Jairus' daughter (v. 36), of the woman with the issue of blood (v. 34), of the man with the epileptic son (ix. 19, 23, 24), and of blind Bartimaeus (x. 52), and in the deliverance from the storm at sea (iv. 40). While in the last incident we are to see a parallel to the delivery from demonic powers, the healing miracles represent delivery from sin.[6] Faith is explicitly connected with the forgiveness of sin in ii. 5, where the man carried by four others is forgiven his sin because of their faith. Through their faith the disciples are able to carry out the tasks laid on them by the Gospel: lack of faith prevented them healing the epileptic boy (ix. 19); faith enables them to remove mountains (xi. 22–4). Mark does not make clear towards whom or what this faith is directed. At xi. 22 it is connected with God; in other places it seems related to the healing and saving activity of Jesus; even though at times it appears to be expressed

designate the opposite to 'barbarian'; cf. e.g. M. Hadas, *Hellenistic Culture* (New York and London, 1959), pp. 11 f.; but this would hardly be the meaning to a Jew or a Christian, cf. Rom. i. 16.

[1] G. H. Boobyer, 'The Miracles of the Loaves and the Gentiles in St Mark's Gospel', *S.J.Th.* VI (1953), 77–87, holds that in both feedings the crowds were composed of Gentiles.

[2] Cf. p. 86.   [3] Cf. pp. 174 ff.

[4] Pp. 68–78. Cf. J. C. Fenton, 'Paul and Mark', *Studies in the Gospels* (ed. Nineham), pp. 107 ff.

[5] Cf. pp. 64 ff.   [6] Cf. pp. 106 ff.

absolutely (x. 52; v. 34), as if faith itself saved, this faith can never be dissociated from the active presence of Jesus. Thus the disciple is someone who has been saved through faith both from demonic evil arising outside himself and from sin arising within his own nature, saved through the power of God active in Jesus Christ.

Closely linked to the conception of faith is that of understanding. The disciples are given an understanding of the Kingdom of God through the parables (iv. 11 f.); this, as we have seen in our discussion of the Kingdom of God in Mark,[1] is an insight into the coming of the Kingdom, which is still future for Mark. Likewise in the Little Apocalypse (ch. xiii) they are given some understanding of the consummation of all things. Those outside cannot understand many of the matters in which Jesus instructs the disciples (iv. 11, 34; vii. 17; x. 10). Some things the disciples themselves fail to understand, for example the two feedings (vi. 52; viii. 17), and are reproved for their failure. In these feeding accounts we see Jesus as supplying the needs of men with spiritual food and with spiritual understanding; the disciples must understand that in the Eucharist Jesus is continually ministering to their requirements, and that his ministry is connected with his death (xiv. 24). But the major points at which the disciples fail to understand are in relation to the nature of Jesus himself and to the divine necessity of his death (viii. 32 f.; ix. 32). The Christian reader of the Gospel is in no doubt about these things. From the very beginning Mark makes clear who Jesus is by the testimony of God, the demons and the centurion, and Jesus himself continually proclaims the necessity of his death and its meaning. At no place is there emphasised an understanding of the demonic world or of its defeat by Jesus. The very fact that the understanding of the disciple is stressed and that there is no suggestion that the demons prevent understanding shows how little Mark is concerned to show the member of the Christian community over against the demonic world.

Closely related also to faith, but on the other side from understanding, as if to preserve against intellectualism, is the conception of 'following'. It is the duty of the disciple to come after Jesus (i. 17, 20; ii. 14), to take his cross like Jesus (viii. 34)

[1] Cf. pp. 64 ff.

and to serve like Jesus (x. 42–5). But any idea that this is only imitation of Jesus is removed by the central place that is given to Jesus' own death.[1]

The community lives in tension in the world. This is shown first in the interpretation of the Parable of the Sower (iv. 14–20). The community is a mixed bag containing those who bear good fruit and those who promise for a while but then fail. Three different reasons are given why failure may come—and these reasons represent some of the tensions under which the community lived. There is first the Devil who comes and takes away the word that has been sown (iv. 15); it is not specified how the Devil does this. Secondly the tension comes from those who persecute the Church (iv. 17); there is no reason to see the Devil as behind this persecution and thus as troubling the Church in another way;[2] we have seen that evil affects men quite independently of the Devil.[3] There is no reason to suppose that in vv. 17, 19 Mark is explaining v. 15; these are three different ways of failure, not one followed by two interpretations of it. Indeed the failure of those mentioned in v. 17 would appear to be due to a fault within themselves—οὐκ ἔχουσιν ῥίζαν ἐν ἑαυτοῖς;[4] tribulation plays on this inner weakness and works their downfall. The third cause of failure is a combination of worry, wealth and lust (iv. 19); wealth similarly caused tension in the case of the rich man who asked Jesus about eternal life (x. 17–31). The three causes of failure given in this parable are not the only tensions which exist, but they summarise them and indicate that the Devil is only one cause of tension alongside others.

If we are correct in interpreting the two stories about storm at sea as indicating the lot of the community, a ship in the storm of life,[5] then here again we find the tension in which the community lives. In the earlier of these two stories (iv. 35–41) the storm is addressed like a demon, indicating that tension does

---

[1] Cf. pp. 154 f.   [2] So Robinson, p. 77.
[3] Cf. chap. II.

[4] So Swete; Lagrange; Wohlenberg. It is interesting to observe that we have to go back to commentators of a generation or two ago for comments on the interpretation of the parable. Modern commentators having decided that it is an early Church creation have apparently written it out of Scripture and see no need to deal with it in detail.

[5] Cf. pp. 105 f.

come from demonic forces; probably this interpretation should be applied also to the second storm (vi. 45–51). It is interesting that in neither of these stories can we see clearly where the Devil applies his pressure to the Church; this is left open as in iv. 15. The source of tension is made quite clear however in the case of the weakness of the disciples at the time of the arrest of Jesus; the context is that of possible persecution, but the weakness lies in 'the flesh', that is, in the disciples themselves.[1] The combination of outward attack by hostile men and inner weakness is strikingly similar to what we have just seen in the second group in the interpretation of the Parable of the Sower (iv. 17). The tension arising from the opposition of men appears again in the Little Apocalypse. Authorities persecute and the Christian is to take care how he bears witness in the moment of such persecution (xiii. 9–13). Tension may come from the mere fact that war exists (xiii. 7). The tension becomes professedly future from the standpoint of Mark's readers in the reference to τὸ βδέλυγμα τῆς ἐρημώσεως (xiii. 14). If we assume that Mark wrote prior to A.D. 70 the reference is probably to Anti-Christ; Luke, writing later, makes the reference purely historical. The historical is not necessarily excluded in Mark; the μετὰ τὴν θλῖψιν ἐκείνην (xiii. 24) suggests that the sacrilege of v. 14 takes place within the time sequence, but II Thess. ii. 3–10 combined with the masculine ἑστηκότα supports the idea of Anti-Christ. The two conceptions may well be combined in that the appearance of Anti-Christ may be a historical event. With the reference to Anti-Christ we pass from trials inflicted by men on the Church to those arising from the demonic world. Thus this future tension is demonic, but not wholly so; for in xiii. 21 f. the saints are deceived by false preachers. This is true also of an earlier stage in the eschatological events, where (xiii. 5 f.) false preachers are again said to lead astray members of the community. Lastly the tension is seen more remotely in the call to disciples to take up their crosses and follow after Jesus; in so far as the opposition to Jesus at the time of the Passion was human rather than demonic so the tension will come to the community from human rather than demonic agents.

To sum up, the tension under which the community lived arose from a number of different sources of which the demonic

---

[1] Cf. p. 30.

was one. It is not the underlying source from which the others derive their power but one source alongside the others. Thus while it is true 'that the struggle between the Spirit and Satan continues in the history of the Church'[1] this is only part of the truth. The opposition does not come from Satan alone but also from the persecution of men, from the enticements of the world, and from the inner weakness of the members of the community.

At this juncture we must return to a point which we raised in our first chapter:[2] If Satan has been already bound how is it that the early Christians were very much aware of his power? In particular, how is it that Mark can refer to Satan as assailing members of the community (iv. 15)? We have already seen that in the Apocalyptic literature the binding of Satan is often temporary.[3] In the majority of cases Satan is restrained thereby until his final judgement and condemnation (I Enoch x. 4–6; x. 11 f.; xviii. 12–xix. 2; Jub. v. 10). But in Jub. xlviii. 15 f. Mastema is said to be bound for five days until Israel is able to make its escape from Egypt, and is then set free again to assail it; in Rev. xx. 2 f. Satan is bound for a thousand years and then set free for a short period to make a final assault on the Church (xx. 7 f.). It may be that Mark regarded Satan as bound during the time of Jesus on earth, the time of the new Exodus, and then as again set free to attack the community.

It may, however, be that Mark is inconsistent at this point. It is only at iv. 15 that there is a direct reference to the assault of Satan on the early Church. Elsewhere the Church is seen in conflict with demons, Satan's underlings, not Satan himself (iii. 15; vi. 7; ix. 29; iv. 35–41; vi. 45–51). The material which Mark received will have included the interpretation of the Parable of the Sower and Mark may have incorporated it without realising that his main line of argument in relationship to Satan was not in harmony with this allusion to him. We may note that while for Mark there is a final cataclysm (ch. xiii) there is no account in it of the defeat of Satan.[4]

There is a third possibility. Mark does not always use 'Satan' of a personal devil, but sometimes in a corporate manner of the community of unclean spirits. This is his usage in iii. 23–6,

---

[1] Robinson, p. 63.   [2] P. 15.   [3] Cf. pp. 12 f.

[4] τὸ βδέλυγμα τῆς ἐρημώσεως (xiii. 14) may be an historical figure, and even if not, it is not necessary to equate him with Satan.

where Satan is imagined as divided against himself and the unclean spirits which are cast out are described as Satan. Yet in iii. 27 the personal aspect reappears. It may then be that in iv. 15 Mark has in mind this corporate aspect of Satan, and we may observe that in the part of the parable corresponding to iv. 15 it is 'birds' (plural) who take away the seed (iv. 4). Just as after the defeat of Satan in the Temptation there still remain demons whom Christians have the power to exorcise, so there remain demons, corporately described as Satan, who are able to afflict them in the moral sphere.

This is all part of a more general question which arises, whether we place Christ's victory over Satan and the powers of evil at the Temptation or at the Cross and Resurrection. iv. 15 does not really apply to the time of Jesus between the Temptation and the Cross but to the time of the early Church; it was presumably composed after the death of Jesus.[1] If we suppose that Christ won his victory over the Devil in the Cross and Resurrection how can Satan still be regarded as assailing members of the community? By moving the victory to that period we do not remove the problem. Robinson writes,

The history which Mark selects to record is presented in its unity as the eschatological action of God, prepared by John the Baptist, inaugurated at the baptism and temptation, carried on through the struggles with various forms of evil, until in his death Jesus has experienced the ultimate of historical involvement and of diabolic antagonism. In the resurrection the force of evil is conclusively broken and the power of God's reign is established in history.[2]

But if the force of evil, which Robinson would hold to be Satan in Mark's Gospel, is conclusively broken how can it still afflict man either morally (iv. 15) or through possession, and require to be exorcised?

This problem might be evaded if we were to hold that the victory of Christ in the Cross and Resurrection or in the Temptation were purely a personal victory, for example that in the Resurrection he escaped the clutches of the Devil and was enabled to live on. This would hardly seem a possible solution, for the whole New Testament lays too much stress on the

[1] Cf. Jeremias, *The Parables of Jesus*, pp. 61 ff.
[2] P. 53; cf. p. 51.

Resurrection as a triumph for mankind as well as for Christ; it would mean that the Resurrection of Christ was no longer 'for us' but only a display of the might of God. We cannot then escape the question in this way.

It is easy to see that the problem is not one that occurs in the exegesis of Mark alone. It arises in every writing which speaks both of a conclusive victory over Satan and also sees man as still under assault by evil spiritual forces. On the one hand, evil powers are viewed as still able to operate against man, I Cor. v. 5; II Cor. ii. 11; Gal. iv. 9; II Thess. ii. 3–10; Eph. vi. 10 ff.; I Pet. v. 8 f.; I John iv. 3; v. 19; Rev. xii. 12. On the other hand they are regarded as already vanquished, Rom. viii. 38 f.; Col. ii. 15; Eph. i. 20 ff.; I Pet. iii. 22; John xii. 31 f.; xvi. 11, 33; I John iii. 8.[1] We note that often the same writers contain both ideas. If the spiritual powers are defeated, how can they still be regarded as rampant? The apparent inconsistency that we have found in Mark[2] would thus seem to be written into the texture of the whole New Testament, but to pursue this problem further would take us far beyond our present purpose. Mark has been caught in a difficulty which exists for the whole New Testament and which exists whether we put the defeat of Satan in the Temptation or in the Passion, and we cannot claim that he has wholly resolved it.

Returning to the tensions under which we have seen the Christian lives and which come from the spiritual forces of evil,

[1] Col. i. 20 stands apart in that it speaks of the reconciliation of the spiritual powers to God. I am unable to accept the argument of C. D. Morrison, *The Powers that Be*, pp. 116 ff., that the Lordship of Christ over the powers belongs to the sphere of creation rather than of redemption, and that the Cross made the Church to be the place in which that Lordship is effective. The texts we have quoted do seem to imply that in the event of Jesus Christ something happened to the powers themselves, and not merely that the Lordship was given to believers over them. Christ's own relationship to the powers would appear to be different now that he has returned to Heaven and sits at God's right hand from what it was prior to his incarnation. Paul and some of the other New Testament writers would place the moment of this victory in the Cross–Resurrection–Ascension event. Mark (and perhaps John xii. 31 f.) places it in the Temptation. Even if the thesis of Morrison was to be accepted we would have to argue that for Mark the moment in which the Lordship of Christ over the powers became effective for his followers was the Temptation rather than the Cross.

[2] Cf. Mark xii. 36 and pp. 87 f. above.

the persecution of men, the enticements of the world, and the inner weakness of members of the community, we must go on briefly to indicate the forces which sustain the Christian in this tension. (*a*) The community has been baptised with the Holy Spirit (i. 8), and he is present to support it in moments of strain (xiii. 11; xiv. 38). We may note that the Holy Spirit is not set over against Satan or any spiritual force of evil in these references. (*b*) There is Jesus' own presence; he delivers his followers from the storms (iv. 35–41; vi. 45–51); when men are shepherd-less he feeds them (vi. 34, 35–44; viii. 1–9; xiv. 22–5). His disciples are chosen to be 'with him' (iii. 14); he regards them as his brothers and sisters, with all this implies in the way of help within the family (iii. 33–5). (*c*) Man needs the grace of God to enter the Kingdom (x. 26 f.), and doubtless this is supplied. Likewise through prayer he is enabled to heal (ix. 29). (*d*) In the losses he has sustained through entry into the Christian community he is upborne by the fellowship that he finds within its membership (x. 29, 30).

Jesus has given the community a task in and to the world. Given representatively to the apostles, it is, in fact, laid on the whole Church. It is found first in i. 16–20, where Peter and Andrew, called by Jesus, are to fish for men. When the Twelve are appointed they are sent to preach and to have authority to exorcise demons (iii. 14 f.). At the moment when they are sent out two by two Jesus is only said to have given them authority over unclean spirits (vi. 7), but once they are on the mission their activities are described as preaching repentance, exorcising demons and healing the sick by anointing (vi. 12 f.). When they return to Jesus they tell him what they have done and taught (vi. 30). Of these passages i. 16–20 came to Mark in the traditional material; vi. 7, 12 f., 30 are his creations;[1] it is difficult to determine whether iii. 15 came in the tradition or not. We can thus conclude that Mark sees the activity of the community as threefold: to preach repentance, to exorcise demons and to heal the sick.

The phrase ἵνα ἀποστέλλη ... ἔχειν ἐξουσίαν ἐκβάλλειν τὰ δαιμόνια (iii. 15) is very awkward.[2] We find it modified by DW to ἔδωκεν αὐτοῖς ἐξουσίαν. At vi. 7 Mark uses the much

---

[1] We find an accumulation of Markan terms; cf. Taylor, *ad loc.*

[2] Cf. Lagrange; Wohlenberg.

simpler phrase ἐδίδου αὐτοῖς ἐξουσίαν, whence DW probably derived their correction of iii. 15. It may be that the original tradition as received by Mark read ἵνα ἀποστέλλῃ αὐτοὺς κηρύσσειν καὶ ἐκβάλλειν τὰ δαιμόνια; Mark, however, did not wish to say that they were sent to cast out demons (cf. vi. 7), but rather wished to stress the element of authority which came from Jesus' original victory over Satan; he could not say, 'they were sent to give authority', so he inserted the awkward ἔχειν. If this explanation is not correct and Mark is held to have composed the sentence (it surely could not have come to him in the tradition in this form!), then he has done his best to avoid saying that the disciples were sent to exorcise and has rather emphasised their authority. This, of course, is what we find in vi. 7. We must then conclude that Mark does not envisage the community as sent to exorcise. This is important. It agrees with the way in which Mark depicts the activity of Jesus. With one exception he never describes Jesus as going to a conflict with demons or with Satan. Where he encounters demon-possessed men, he heals them; he is not depicted as going to search for them. He speaks of himself as sent to preach (i. 38), but never as sent to exorcise. The one exception to this is the Temptation. Here, driven out by the Spirit, he seeks Satan and defeats him; thereafter he exercises the victory he won in the desert whenever he encounters demons, but he does not go to seek them. Similarly the community is sent to preach the Gospel and given authority over demons; it is not sent to exorcise, but where demons are encountered it may exercise the authority Jesus has won and given to it. Thus the community is not sent out to a conflict with Satan; it is sent out to preach repentance—to deal with the sin of men. In passing we may note that a similar attitude exists in Jesus in relation to sickness. In every story of healing except one Mark shows the sick or their friends as coming to Jesus and appealing to him to heal; in his summary statements he shows the sick being brought to Jesus in crowds and then he heals them; at i. 35 Jesus even seeks to avoid the crowds of sick. There is no occasion on which Jesus calls the sick to come to him to be healed, nor is he depicted as going to look out the sick. The sole exception is iii. 1–5; here Jesus does pick out the man with the withered hand; but this pericope is told, not to demonstrate the healing

power of Jesus, but for the sake of the final pronouncement of
Jesus on the Sabbath; thus the form-critics do not classify it
among the miracle stories but among the pronouncement
stories. If Jesus does not go to heal the sick, likewise in Mark he
does not send the disciples to this task. Their primary task is to
preach, they are to fish for men; if they encounter evil as sickness or demon-possession they have authority to deal with it.
Their task is not to defeat Satan nor wage a continual war with
him, but to call sinners to repentance, to proclaim the death of
Jesus, with which the whole of Mark's Gospel is taken up, and
to show its meaning as the fulfilment of the judgement of God
and as a ransom for men, to show his blood as poured out for
them. This reflects the primary concern of the Markan Gospel,
a concern with the redemption of men from sin rather than
with the cosmic defeat of Satan, and the greater achievement
of Jesus is the former, not the latter.

CHAPTER IX

CONCLUSION

FOR Mark the Devil is defeated so far as the life of Jesus is concerned at the Temptation; in this conclusive contest Satan is bound and Jesus is thereafter able to reduce to obedience evil-spiritual powers, the demons which possess men and evil-cosmic forces met in sea storms. This encounter with the Devil in the Temptation is the decisive meeting of the forces of light and darkness, of order and chaos, of good and evil; this struggle which lay behind so much of the Old Testament and of the religion of the Near East of the period has now had its issue. But all the evil in the world is not seen by Mark as due to the Devil. In particular sin may arise from the tempting power of the Devil, but also from the seductive power of wealth, from the fear of persecution, from the enticements of other men and women, and from a man's own inner weakness in that he is flesh and not Spirit. Undoubtedly later Christian thought regarded the Devil as responsible for all temptation, but we are no more correct in reading such a view back into Mark than we are in reading it back into the Old Testament. How then is this other sin in men dealt with?

In the first place Mark views Jesus as the authoritative teacher who brings men to an understanding of the truth. This truth is known in the Church but is veiled from the eyes of those outside. Yet Jesus is not just a Gnostic revealer who gives insight to the initiated. The main purpose of his teaching is to bring his followers to an understanding of his own Cross, not only as redemptive, but also as a way of life for themselves; they must take up their crosses as he did and serve as he served. Thus it is not that he only enlightens their minds but that he calls for them to go on the way of discipleship, which is the way of love and service. In teaching he is, however, meeting the evil of ignorance and leading men away from it.

But ignorance and sin are not the same, and if in Mark the teaching of Jesus is ultimately directed towards the Cross he teaches not only about its necessity but also about its meaning.

The Cross is judgement; this is seen in the rending of the veil and the darkness that came over the world at the time. The judgement is borne by Jesus, in that he drinks the cup of God's wrath, is the shepherd smitten, and is the one who is over-whelmed by the floods of baptism for men. His blood is shed for others as his life is given for them. And all this is not to turn from men the wrath of Satan nor to conquer him, but to bring them into the new community which is formed out of the Cross and Resurrection from those who are saved, enjoy the forgiveness of their sin and themselves go to seek others as fishers of men.

What Mark thereby preaches is not the kerugma of Phil. ii. 5–11; it lies nearer that of I Cor. xv. 3, 4. Yet the kerugma of Phil. ii. 5–11 is fulfilled in intention because the Devil and the evil-spiritual powers were overcome—in the Temptation but not in the Cross and Resurrection. The fact of the appearances of Jesus is not stressed; instead he is felt throughout the Gospel as the risen and exalted Lord who is still speaking to his disciples and who leads them in 'Galilee' on the mission of preaching himself. Unlike I Cor. xv. 3, 4 the empty tomb is brought into the picture; this is necessary since if the risen Lord is to be seen in the stories of the Gospel then he must be recognised as having left the realm of death. No stories of resurrection appearances are told since to have recounted them would have marred the conception of risen Lord in the whole of the Gospel.

BIBLIOGRAPHY

Achtemeier, P. J. 'Person and Deed. Jesus and the Storm-Tossed Sea', *Interpretation*, XVI (1962), 169–76.

Albertz, M. *Die synoptischen Streitgespräche* (Berlin, 1921).

Bacon, B. W. *The Gospel of Mark: Its Composition and Date* (New Haven, 1925).

Barrett, C. K. *The Epistle to the Romans* (London, 1957).

—— 'The Background of Mark x. 45', in *New Testament Essays*, ed. A. J. B. Higgins, pp. 1–18 (Manchester, 1959).

——*From First Adam to Last* (London, 1962).

Bartsch, H. W. 'Historische Erwägungen zur Leidensgeschichte', *Evangelische Theologie*, XXII (1962), 449–59.

Bauer, W. 'The Colt of Palm Sunday', *J.B.L.* LXXII (1953), 220–9.

Bauernfeind, O. *Die Worte der Dämonen im Markusevangelium* (Stuttgart, 1927).

Behm, J. διαθήκη, *T.W.N.T.* II, 127–37.

Bernard, J. H. 'A Study of St Mark x. 38, 39', *J.T.S.* XXVIII (1927), 262–70.

Best, E. 'Mark ii. 1–12', *Biblical Theology*, III (1953), 41–6.

—— *One Body in Christ* (London, 1955).

—— 'Spirit-Baptism', *N.T.* IV (1961), 236–43.

Beyer, H. W. διακονέω, κτλ., *T.W.N.T.* II, 81–93.

Billerbeck, P. *See* Strack, H. L.

Black, M. 'The Messiah in the Testament of Levi xviii', *E.T.* LX (1949), 321f.; LXI (1950), 157f.

—— *An Aramaic Approach to the Gospels and Acts*, 2nd edn. (Oxford, 1954).

—— 'The Son of Man Problem in Recent Research and Debate', *Bull. J. Rylands Lib.* XLV (1963), 305–18.

Blinzler, J. *Der Prozess Jesu²* (Regensburg, 1955).

Boobyer, G. H. 'The Eucharistic Interpretation of the Miracle of the Loaves in St Mark's Gospel', *J.T.S.* III (1952), 161–71.

—— 'Galilee and Galileans in St Mark's Gospel', *Bull. J. Rylands Lib.* XXXV (1952/3), 334–48.

—— 'The Miracles of the Loaves and the Gentiles in St Mark's Gospel', *S.J.Th.* VI (1953), 77–87.

—— 'The Redaction of Mark iv. 1–34', *N.T.S.* VIII (1961), 59–70.

Bornkamm, G. in Bornkamm, G., Barth, G. and Held, H. J. *Tradition and Interpretation in Matthew* (London, 1963).

Bousset, W. *Die Religion des Judentums im späthellenistischen Zeitalter³*, ed. H. Gressmann (Tübingen, 1926).

Branscomb, B. H. *The Gospel of Mark* (Moffatt Commentaries; London, 1937).

Büchsel, F. *Der Geist Gottes im Neuen Testament* (Gütersloh, 1926).

—— γενεά, κτλ. *T.W.N.T.* i, 660–3.

—— λύτρον, *T.W.N.T.* iv, 341–51.

Bultmann, R. *Theologie des Neuen Testaments* (Tübingen, 1953).

——*The History of the Synoptic Tradition*, Eng. trans. J. Marsh (Oxford, 1963).

Bundy, W. E. *Jesus and the First Three Gospels* (Cambridge, Mass., 1955).

Burkill, T. A. 'St Mark's Philosophy of the Passion', *N.T.* ii (1958), 245–71.

—— 'Anti-Semitism in St Mark's Gospel', *N.T.* iii (1959), 34–53.

—— 'Strain on the Secret: An Examination of Mark xi. 1–xiii. 37', *Z.N.T.W.* li (1960), 31–46.

—— *Mysterious Revelation* (Ithaca, New York, 1963).

Bussmann, W. *Synoptische Studien*, i–iii (Halle, 1925–31).

Caird, G. B. *Principalities and Powers* (Oxford, 1956).

Carlston, C. E. 'Transfiguration and Resurrection', *J.B.L.* lxxx (1961), 233–40.

Charles, R. H. (ed.). *The Apocrypha and Pseudepigrapha of the Old Testament*, 2 vols. (Oxford, 1913).

—— *Revelation* (*I.C.C.*), 2 vols. (London, 1920).

Citron, B. 'The Multitude in the Synoptic Gospels', *S.J.Th.* vii (1954), 408–18.

Colpe, C. *Die religionsgeschichtliche Schule* (Göttingen, 1961).

Conzelmann, H. *The Theology of Saint Luke*, Eng. trans. G. Buswell (London, 1960).

Cranfield, C. E. B. *St Mark* (Cambridge, 1959).

Cross, F. L. (ed.). *The Jung Codex* (London, 1955).

Cross, F. M. *The Ancient Library of Qumran* (London, 1958).

Cullmann, O. *Baptism in the New Testament*, Eng. trans. J. K. S. Reid (London, 1950).

—— *Peter: Disciple, Apostle, Martyr*, Eng. trans. F. V. Filson (London, 1953).

—— *The Christology of the New Testament*, Eng. trans. S. C. Guthrie, Jr., and C. A. M. Hall (London, 1959).

Dalman, G. *Jesus-Jeshua*, Eng. trans. P. P. Levertoff (London, 1929).

Daniélou, J. 'La typologie d'Isaac dans le christianisme primitif', *Biblica*, xxviii (1947), 363–93.

—— *Sacramentum Futuri* (Paris, 1950).

Daube, D. 'Four Types of Question', *J.T.S.* ii (1951), 45–8.

Daube, D. *The New Testament and Rabbinic Judaism* (London, 1956).

Davey, F. N. *See* Hoskyns, E.

Davies, W. D. *Paul and Rabbinic Judaism* (London, 1948).

—— 'Paul and the Dead Sea Scrolls: Flesh and Spirit', in *The Scrolls and the New Testament*, ed. K. Stendahl (London, 1958).

Déaut, R. le. *La Nuit Pascale* (*Analecta Biblica*, 22; Rome, 1963).

Dehn, G. *Der Gottessohn*[6] (Hamburg, 1953).

Delling, G. βάπτισμα βαπτισθῆναι, *N.T.* II (1957), 92–115.

Dibelius, M. *From Tradition to Gospel*, Eng. trans. B. E. Woolf (London, 1934).

Dodd, C. H. *The Parables of the Kingdom* (London, 1943).

—— *According to the Scriptures* (London, 1952).

—— 'The Framework of the Gospel Narratives', in *New Testament Studies*, pp. 1–11 (Manchester, 1953).

—— 'The Appearances of the Risen Christ: An Essay in Form-Criticism of the Gospels', in *Studies in the Gospels*, ed. D. E. Nineham (Oxford, 1955).

Doudna, J. C. *The Greek of the Gospel of Mark* (J.B.L. Monograph Series, XII; Philadelphia, 1961).

Dunkerley, R. 'Was Barabbas also called Jesus?', *E.T.* LXXIV (1963), 126f.

Ebeling, H. J. *Das Messiasgeheimnis und die Botschaft des Marcus-Evangelisten* (Berlin, 1939).

Eichrodt, W. *Theologie des Alten Testaments*, II/III, 4th edn. (Stuttgart and Göttingen, 1961).

Emerton, J. A. 'Some New Testament Notes', *J.T.S.* XI (1960), 334f.

—— 'τὸ αἷμά μου τῆς διαθήκης: The evidence of the Syrian versions', *J.T.S.* XIII (1962), 111–17.

Evans, C. F. 'I will go before you into Galilee', *J.T.S.* V (1954), 3–18.

Farrar, A. M. *A Study in Mark* (Westminster, 1951).

Feine, P. *Theologie des Neuen Testaments*, 8th edn. (Berlin, 1953).

Fenton, J. C. 'Paul and Mark', *Studies in the Gospels*, ed. D. E. Nineham (Oxford, 1955).

Feuillet, A. 'Les perspectives propres à chaque évangéliste dans les récits de la transfiguration', *Biblica*, XXXIX (1958), 281–301.

Fichtner, J. *Weisheit Salomos* (*Handbuch zum Alten Testament*, Zweite Reihe, 6; Tübingen, 1938).

Flemington, W. F. *The New Testament Doctrine of Baptism* (London, 1948).

Foerster, W. Βεεζεβούλ, *T.W.N.T.* I, 605f.

—— δαίμων, κτλ., *T.W.N.T.* II, 1–21.

Foerster, W. διαβάλλω, διάβολος, *T.W.N.T.* II, 69–80.
—— σατανᾶς, *T.W.N.T.* VII, 151–64.
Fuller, R. H. *The Mission and Achievement of Jesus* (London, 1954).
Geyer, J. *The Wisdom of Solomon* (London, 1963).
Goodenough, E. R. *Jewish Symbols in the Graeco-Roman Period*, IV (New York, 1954).
Goppelt, L. ποτήριον, *T.W.N.T.* VI, 148–59.
Grant, F. C. *The Earliest Gospel* (New York and Nashville, 1943).
—— 'The Gospel according to St Mark' (*Interpreters' Bible*, VII; New York and Nashville, 1951).
Gregg, J. A. F. *The Wisdom of Solomon* (Cambridge, 1922).
Grundmann, W. ἄγγελος, κτλ. *T.W.N.T.* I, 72–5.
—— ἰσχύω, κτλ. *T.W.N.T.* III, 400–5.
Guy, H. A. *The Origin of the Gospel of Mark* (London, 1954).
Hadas, M. *Hellenistic Culture* (New York and London, 1959).
Hahn, F. *Christologische Hoheitstitel* (Göttingen, 1963).
Hauck, F. *Das Evangelium des Markus* (Theologischer Handkommentar zum N.T.; Leipzig, 1931).
—— καθαρός, κτλ. *T.W.N.T.* III, 416–21, 427–34.
Hebert, G. *The Christ of Faith and the Jesus of History* (London, 1962).
—— 'The Resurrection Narrative in St Mark's Gospel', *S.J.Th.* XV (1962), 66–73.
Higgins, A. J. B. *The Lord's Supper in the New Testament* (London, 1952).
—— 'Son of Man', in *New Testament Essays*, ed. A. J. B. Higgins (Manchester, 1959).
Holmes, S. 'Wisdom of Solomon', in *The Apocrypha and Pseudepigrapha of the Old Testament*, vol. I, ed. R. H. Charles (Oxford, 1913).
Hooker, M. D. *Jesus and the Servant* (London, 1959).
Hoskyns, E. and Davey, F. N. *The Riddle of the New Testament*, London, 1947.
—— *The Fourth Gospel*, 2nd edn. (London, 1947).
Hunter, A. M. *Paul and his Predecessors*, 2nd edn. (London, 1961).
Iersel, B. M. F. van. '*Der Sohn' in den synoptischen Jesusworten* (*Supplements to N.T.* vol. III; Leiden, 1961).
Jeremias, J. 'The Gentile World in the Thought of Jesus', *Bull. S.N.T.S.* III (1952), 21f.
—— *The Parables of Jesus*, Eng. trans. S. H. Hooke (London, 1954).
—— *The Eucharistic Words of Jesus*, Eng. trans. A. Ehrhardt (Oxford, 1955).
—— *Jesus' Promise to the Nations*, Eng. trans. S. H. Hooke (London, 1958).

Jeremias, J. Ἀδάμ, *T.W.N.T.* i, 141–3.

—— ποιμήν, κτλ. *T.W.N.T.* vi, 484–501.

—— πολλοί, *T.W.N.T.* vi, 536–45.

—— 'Nachwort zum Artikel von H.-G. Leder', *Z.N.T.W.* LIV (1963), 278f.

Jeremias, J. and Zimmerli, W. *The Servant of God*, Eng. trans. H. Knight *et al.* (London, 1957), = παῖς θεοῦ, *T.W.N.T.* v, 653–713.

Johnson, S. E. *The Gospel According to St Mark* (London, 1960).

Kähler, M. *Der sogenannte historische Jesus und der geschichtliche, biblische Christus* (Leipzig, 1896). New edition (Munich, 1956).

Kallas, J. *The Significance of the Synoptic Miracles* (London, 1961).

Karnetzki, M. 'Die Galiläischeed Raktion im Markusevangelium', *Z.N.T.W.* LII (1961), 238–72.

Kittel, G. ἄγγελος, κτλ. *T.W.N.T.* i, pp. 79–87.

Klostermann, E. *Das Markusevangelium*[2] (Tübingen, 1926).

Knox, W. L. *The Sources of the Synoptic Gospels*, vol. i (Cambridge, 1953).

Kraeling, C. H. *The Synagogue* (Part i of *The Excavations at Dura-Europos Final Report*, VIII; New Haven and London, 1956).

Kraus, H.-J. *Psalmen*, 2 vols. (*Biblischer Kommentar: Altes Testament*, xv) (Neukirchen, 1960).

Kuby, A. 'Zur Konzeption des Markus-Evangeliums', *Z.N.T.W.* XLIX (1958), 52–64.

Kuhn, H. W. 'Das Reittier Jesu in der Einzugsgeschichte des Markusevangeliums', *Z.N.T.W.* L (1959), 82–91.

Kuhn, K. G. 'New Light on Temptation, Sin and Flesh in the New Testament', in *The Scrolls and the New Testament*, ed. K. Stendahl (London, 1958).

—— *Konkordanz zu den Qumrantexten* (Göttingen, 1960).

Kümmel, W. G. *Promise and Fulfilment*, Eng. trans. by Dorothea M. Barton (London, 1957).

Lagrange, M.-J. *Évangile selon Saint Marc* (Paris, 1947).

Langton, E. *Essentials of Demonology* (London, 1949).

Leder, H.-G. 'Sündenfallerzählung und Versuchungsgeschichte; zur Interpretation von Mc i. 12f.', *Z.N.T.W.* LIV (1963), 188–216.

Leenhardt, F.-J. (with O. Cullmann). *Essays on the Lord's Supper*, Eng. trans. J. G. Davies (London, 1958).

Leivestad, R. *Christ the Conqueror* (London, 1954).

Lightfoot, R. H. *History and Interpretation in the Gospels* (London, 1935).

—— *Locality and Doctrine in the Gospels* (London, 1938).

Lightfoot, R. H *The Gospel Message of Mark* (Oxford, 1950).

Lindars, B. *New Testament Apologetic* (London, 1961).

Ling, T. *The Significance of Satan* (London, 1961).

Lohmeyer, E. *Galiläa und Jerusalem* (Göttingen, 1936).

—— *Das Evangelium des Markus*[11] (Göttingen, 1951).

Loisy, A. *L'Évangile selon Marc* (Paris, 1912).

Manson, T. W. *The Teaching of Jesus*, 2nd edn. (Cambridge, 1943).

—— 'Realised Eschatology and the Messianic Secret', in *Studies in the Gospels*, ed. D. E. Nineham (Oxford, 1955).

Mansoor, M. *The Thanksgiving Hymns* (Leiden, 1961).

Marxsen, W. *Der Evangelist Markus*[2] (Göttingen, 1959).

Maurer, C. 'Knecht Gottes und Sohn Gottes im Passionsbericht des Markusevangeliums', *Z.T.K.* L (1953), 1–38.

Mauser, U. W. *Christ in the Wilderness* (Studies in Biblical Theology, 39; London, 1963).

Mead, R. T. 'The Healing of the Paralytic—A Unit', *J.B.L.* LXXX (1961), 348–54.

Menzies, A. *The Earliest Gospel* (London, 1901).

Meyer, R. καθαρός, κτλ. *T.W.N.T.* III, 421–7.

—— σάρξ, κτλ. *T.W.N.T.* VII, 109–18.

Michel, O. 'Eine Philologische Frage zur Einzugsgeschichte', *N.T.S.* VI (1959), 81 f.

Milik, J. T. *Ten Years of Discovery in the Wilderness of Judaea*, Eng. trans. J. Strugnell (London, 1959).

Moore, G. F. *Judaism*, 3 vols. (Cambridge, Mass., 1927–30).

Morris, L. *The Apostolic Preaching of the Cross* (London, 1955).

Morrison, C. D. *The Powers that Be* (London, 1960).

Moule, C. F. D. *Worship in the New Testament* (London, 1961).

Munck, J. 'I Thess. i. 9–10 and the Missionary Preaching of Paul', *N.T.S.* IX (1963), 95–110.

Neil, W. *Thessalonians* (London, 1950).

Nineham, D. E. 'The Order of Events in St Mark's Gospel—an Examination of Dr Dodd's Hypothesis', in *Studies in the Gospels*, ed. Nineham (Oxford, 1955).

—— *Saint Mark*, The Pelican Gospel Commentaries (London, 1963).

Oepke, A. βάπτω, κτλ. *T.W.N.T.* I, pp. 527–44.

Pedersen, J. *Israel*, I–II (Oxford, 1926).

Ploeg, J. van der. *Le Rouleau de la Guerre* (Leiden, 1959).

Porter, J. R. 'The Messiah in the Testament of Levi xviii', *E.T.* LXI (1949), 90 f.

Proksch, O. ἅγιος, κτλ. *T.W.N.T.* I, 101–16.

Quispel, G. 'The Jung Codex and its Significance', in *The Jung Codex*, ed. F. L. Cross (London, 1955).

Rad, G. von. ἄγγελος, κτλ. *T.W.N.T.* I, 75–9.

—— διαβάλλω, διάβολος, *T.W.N.T.* II, 69–80.

Rashdall, H. *The Idea of the Atonement* (London, 1920).

Rawlinson, A. E. J. *The Gospel According to St Mark*, Westminster Commentaries (London, 1925).

Richardson, A. *The Miracle Stories of the Gospels* (London, 1941).

—— *An Introduction to the Theology of the New Testament* (London, 1948).

Robinson, J. A. *St Paul's Epistle to the Ephesians*, 2nd edn. (London, 1909).

Robinson, J. A. T. *Jesus and His Coming* (London, 1957).

—— *Twelve New Testament Studies* (London, 1962).

Robinson, J. M. *The Problem of History in Mark* (Studies in Biblical Theology, 21; London, 1957).

Ropes, J. H. *The Synoptic Gospels* (Oxford, 1960).

Rose, A. 'L'influence des psaumes sur les annonces et les récits de la Passion et de la Résurrection dans les Évangiles', *Le Psautier* (ed. R. de Langhe), pp. 297–356.

Sawyerr, H. 'The Marcan Framework', *S.J.Th.* XIV (1961), 279–94.

Schechter, S. *Some Aspects of Rabbinic Theology* (London, 1909).

Schlatter, A. *Der Evangelist Matthäus*[3] (Stuttgart, 1948).

Schlier, H. θλίβω, θλῖψις, *T.W.N.T.* III, 139–48.

Schmidt, K. L. *Die Rahmen der Geschichte Jesu* (Berlin, 1919).

—— βασιλεία, *T.W.N.T.* I, 579–92.

Schmidt, K. L. and M. A. παχύνω, κτλ. *T.W.N.T.* V, 1024–32.

Schniewind, J. *Das Evangelium nach Markus*[6] (Göttingen, 1952).

Schoeps, H. J. *Aus frühchristlicher Zeit* (Tübingen, 1950).

—— *Paul*, Eng. trans. H. Knight (London, 1961).

Schreiber, J. 'Die Christologie des Markusevangeliums', *Z.T.K.* LVIII (1961), 154–83.

Schulze, W. A. 'Der Heilige und die wilden Tiere', *Z.N.T.W.* XLVI (1955), 280–3.

Schweizer, E. 'Der Menschensohn', *Z.N.T.W.* L (1959), 185–210.

—— 'Anmerkungen zur Theologie des Markus', in *Neotestamentica et Patristica (Suppl. to N.T.* vol. VI) (Leiden, 1962).

—— 'Two New Testament Creeds Compared', in *Current Issues in New Testament Interpretation*, ed. W. Klassen and G. F. Snyder (London, 1962).

Schweizer, E., Baumgärtel, F. and Sjöberg, F. *Spirit of God*, Eng. trans. A. E. Harvey (London, 1960), =πνεῦμα, κτλ. *T.W.N.T.* VI, 330–453.

Seesemann, H. πεῖρα, κτλ. *T.W.N.T.* vi, 23–37.

Smith, A. M. 'The Iconography of the Sacrifice of Isaac in Early Christian Art', *Amer. J. Archaeology*, xxvi (1922), 159–69.

Smith, C. R. *The Bible Doctrine of Sin* (London, 1953).

—— *The Bible Doctrine of Grace* (London, 1956).

Smith, C. W. F. 'No Time for Figs', *J.B.L.* lxxix (1960), 315–27.

Souter, A. ΑΓΑΠΗΤΟΣ, *J.T.S.* xxviii (1927), 59f.

Stählin, G. ὀργή, *T.W.N.T.* v, 419–48.

Strack, H. L. and Billerbeck, P. *Kommentar zum Neuen Testament aus Talmud und Midrasch*, 5 vols. (Munich, 1922–8).

Sundwall, J. *Die Zusammensetzung des Markusevangeliums*, Acta Academiae Aboensis, Humaniora, ix, 2 (Åbo, 1934).

Swete, H. B. *The Gospel According to St Mark* (London, 1908).

Sykes, M. H. 'And do not bring us to the test', *E.T.* lxxiii (1961/2), 189f.

Taylor, V. *Jesus and His Sacrifice* (London, 1943).

—— *The Gospel According to St Mark* (London, 1952).

—— *The Names of Jesus* (London, 1953).

Tennant, F. R. *The Fall and Original Sin* (Cambridge, 1903).

Thiel, R. *Drei Markus-Evangelien* (Berlin, 1938).

Tödt, H. E. *Der Menschensohn in der synoptischen Überlieferung* (Gütersloh, 1959).

Turner, C. H. 'Marcan Usage: Notes, Critical and Exegetical, on the Second Gospel', *J.T.S.* xxv (1924), 377–86; xxvi (1925), 12–20, 145–56, 225–40, 337–46; xxvii (1926), 58–62; xxviii (1927), 9–30, 349–62; xxix (1928), 275–89, 346–61.

—— Ο ΥΙΟΣ ΜΟΥ Ο ΑΓΑΠΗΤΟΣ, *J.T.S.* xxvii (1926), 113–29.

—— 'A Textual Commentary on Mark i', *J.T.S.* xxviii (1927), 145–58.

—— 'Western Readings in the Second Half of St Mark's Gospel', *J.T.S.* xxix (1928), 1–16.

Tyson, J. B. 'The Blindness of the Disciples in Mark', *J.B.L.* lxxx (1961), 261–8.

Vermes, G. *Scripture and Tradition in Judaism* (Leiden, 1961).

Volz, P. *Der Geist Gottes* (Tübingen, 1910).

Weiss, J. *Das Älteste Evangelium* (Göttingen, 1903).

Wellhausen, J. *Das Evangelium Marci* (Berlin, 1903).

Wernberg-Møller, P. *The Manual of Discipline* (Leiden, 1957).

Williams, N. P. *The Ideas of the Fall and of Original Sin* (London, 1929).

Wilson, R. McL. *The Gnostic Problem* (London, 1958).

—— *Studies in the Gospel of Thomas* (London, 1960).

Wilson, R. McL. *The Gospel of Philip* (London, 1962).
Winter, P. *On the Trial of Jesus* (Berlin, 1961).
Wohlenberg, G. *Das Evangelium des Markus* (Leipzig, 1910).
Wrede, W. *Das Messiasgeheimnis in den Evangelien*[2] (Göttingen, 1913).
Yates, J. E. *The Spirit and the Kingdom* (London, 1963).
Zimmerli, W. *See* Jeremias, J.

INDEX OF AUTHORS

INDEX OF SUBJECTS

INDEX OF PASSAGES QUOTED

INDEX OF PASSAGES QUOTED

OTHER ANCIENT WRITINGS

INDEX OF GREEK WORDS